D1824656

Issues in Business Ethics

VOLUME 42

Series Editors

Wim Dubbink, *Department of Philosophy, School of Humanities, Tilburg University, Tilburg, Netherlands*

Mollie Painter-Morland, *Department of Philosophy, De Paul University, Chicago, Illinois, USA*

For further volumes:
http://www.springer.com/series/6077

Martin Calkins

Developing a Virtue-Imbued Casuistry for Business Ethics

 Springer

Martin Calkins
Department of Management and Marketing
University of Massachusetts, Boston
College of Management
Boston
Massachusetts
USA

ISSN 0925-6733
ISBN 978-94-017-8723-9   ISBN 978-94-017-8724-6 (eBook)
DOI 10.1007/978-94-017-8724-6
Springer Dordrecht Heidelberg New York London

Library of Congress Control Number: 2014932678

Printed on acid-free paper

Springer is part of Springer Science+Business Media (www.springer.com)

This is dedicated to Patricia Werhane
A great teacher
A great leader in business ethics
A great colleague
And a great friend

Preface

Developing a Virtue-imbued Casuistry for Business Ethics is the first book to explore the overlap and synergy of casuistry and virtue ethics and to proffer the combination of the two as a useful way to incorporate ethics in business practice.

On one level, it is a book that brings together seemingly disparate methods for the purpose of offsetting some of the shortcomings of each when used in isolation. In this regard, the book details how case-based and virtue ethics approaches compare to other approaches, how various stakeholders can approach a similar problem differently, and how business practices can be enhanced by means of virtue-imbued casuistry.

On another level, *Developing a Virtue-imbued Casuistry for Business Ethics* takes on select business-related social issues—the genetic modification of foods, aging pharmaceuticals, disease eradication, and risk management—to show how virtue-imbued casuistry can be instrumental in business problem solving, strategizing, and risk management.

Throughout, *Developing a Virtue-imbued Casuistry for Business Ethics* recognizes the longstanding objections to casuistry as a method and virtue ethics as a normative approach. It addresses these objections directly and in depth and ultimately determines that the objections are not meritless, but mostly due to failures to understand casuistry and virtue ethics fully and in contrast to other moral approaches.

In addition, the book acknowledges the limits of its own expansiveness, particularly in regard to the issues of risk management. Nevertheless, it tackles these and other complex business issues in a clear and simple manner to encourage the reader to go on to learn more about the topics and the ways ethics might be more effectively advanced there.

In the end, *Developing a Virtue-imbued Casuistry for Business Ethics* maintains that the combination of casuistry and virtue ethics can not only stand its ground against alternative approaches, but that it is more suitable than other moral methods for everyday business contexts and use by the ordinary people charged with actually making moral decisions.

Overview

Let us endeavour, then, to think well; this is the principle of morality.[1]

—Blaise Pascal

Oliver Cromwell (1599–1658)—English military and political leader and one of the most reviled figures in Irish history—allegedly once quipped: "He who stops being better stops being good."[2]

Although regicidal and tyrannical, Cromwell nevertheless made the important observation that when we cease to practice habits of moral excellence we begin to atrophy as moral beings. Our moral fiber begins to weaken just as an athlete's prowess deteriorates when he or she stops exercising. We become not just frozen in the state we were in when we stopped striving, but we decay and become worse off as people.

Cromwell's observation is not so important in itself as it is as a caution against moral entropy and its ensuing atrophy. His is a challenge to figure out how not to just stem moral deterioration, but to discern how to advance in moral excellence and become better people.

Developing a Virtue-imbued Casuistry for Business Ethics attempts to address these challenges in its own way, by explaining how ordinary people can make better ethical judgments in the context of business by means of a case-based approach imbued with virtue ethics.

The book is divided into four main parts. The first three parts describe the terms and history of each portion of the approach and how casuistry and virtue ethics compare with other methods. Throughout, these sections show how the two methods overlap and create a synergy in combination that compensates for the shortcomings of each when used in isolation.

The fourth part applies the combination of casuistry and virtue ethics to select business issues. Here we see how the approach can help break stalemates by defusing ideological polarization and how it can caution against attractive but ultimately harmful exclusively mathematics-based strategies. This section also shows how the

---

[1] (Pascal 1958, p. 347).

[2] Oliver Cromwell supported the regicide and the overthrow of the Stuart monarchy and as 1st Lord Protector of the Commonwealth of England, Scotland and Ireland, massacred Catholics who stood in the way of his invasion of Ireland. For more, see (Gaunt 2004).

method can be integrated deeply and effectively as a viable element of model driven scenario-based risk management processes to thereby help managers better assess their companies' risk exposure.

In the end, *Developing a Virtue-imbued Casuistry for Business Ethics* charts new ground in moral theory and business practice. It reinvigorates interest in casuistry for business, applies virtue ethics to business in new ways, brings casuistry and virtue ethics together for the first time, and then applies the combination to specific business problems. In these ways, this book explains and models the proposed approach while simultaneously challenging business managers to account for moral norms in their day-to-day operations.

Acknowledgements

This book has been over fifteen years in the making and would not have been possible without the aid and support of a number of people. I would like to express my thanks to those who helped make this book possible.

First and foremost, I would like to thank and dedicate this book to Patricia Werhane. Her willingness to read numerous early drafts of the text and provide insightful criticisms and good advice about its philosophical and business ethics content were invaluable. Moreover, her encouragement pushed me to complete and publish a book that otherwise would be languishing on a computer. Thank you for everything, Pat.

I also want to extend my gratitude to James Keenan for introducing me years ago to virtue ethics and casuistry and to John Arras for his insights into the nature of moral reasoning and casuistry's history in biomedical ethics. My thanks, too, to R. Edward Freeman for pushing me early on to pursue what he called the "interesting questions" associated with virtue ethics and casuistry.

I am grateful, too, for the careful research assistance of Svetlana Shatalova, Kristina Martin, David Thibeault, and Eric Pinsoneault, each of whom helped direct, hone, and improve this text in identifiable and appreciable ways. I am thankful as well for Tara Radin's assistance in sharpening the style and format of an early version of the text, to Russell Powell for tips on certain aspects of Islam, to Mark Sioma for insights and advice about risk management, and to Kate Archard for final copy editing assistance.

Not least, I would like to thank the College of Management and Marketing and Management Department of the University of Massachusetts Boston for backing me with the time and resources to accomplish this work and Neil Olivier, and Wim Dubbink, and Mollie Painter-Morland of Springer Science+Business Media for agreeing to publish this book.

Finally, I would like to express my gratitude to my late grandmother, Rose McManus Calkins, for modeling prudence in meaningful ways as I grew up; my late father, James Calkins, for exemplifying moral courage in the context of a lifetime of entrepreneurial business; and my sister, Therese Calkins Frenson, for illustrating how ethics in business is not just an academic exercise but something nuanced and full of practical challenges.

To all of these wonderful people—I extend my deep thanks.

Contents

Part IV   Using Virtue-Imbued Casuistry in Business Practice

List of Tables

Part I
Building a Casuistry for Business

Chapter 1
Features and History

Writing intellectual history is like trying to nail jelly to the wall.
—attributed to William Hesseltine

Virtue-imbued casuistry is a form of casuistry that derives from the recognition of a pervasive lack of understanding of how average people use cases and examples in making moral judgments in business. It also stems from the realization that every moral decision depends upon virtuous people who are both well intentioned and disposed to seek their own and others' betterment.

Although posited as a new approach here, virtue-imbued casuistry's two key components—casuistry and virtue ethics—are anything but new[1]. Both have long and somewhat checkered histories, having flourished for a while and then fallen into disrepute or disuse before being revived. What is new, aside from the revival, is the combining of the two processes in a way that minimizes the shortcomings of each in isolation to create a synergy that makes the process helpful in moral problem solving in business contexts.

Beginning with the following section, we will see how casuistry and virtue ethics work separately and together.

We begin with casuistry.

Characteristics of Case-Based Reasoning

Casuistry (meaning "concerned with cases") is a method of moral discernment that uses analogical reasoning and settled cases to derive moral judgments. An old process rooted in religious practices, casuistry fell into disrepute but was revived with Albert Jonsen and Stephen Toulmin's *The Abuse of Casuistry* where it was described as follows:

> (Casuistry is) the analysis of moral issues, using procedures of reasoning based on paradigms and analogies, leading to the formulation of expert opinions about the existence and stringency of particular moral obligations, framed in terms of rules or maxims that are general but not universal or invariable, since they hold good with certainty only in the typical conditions of the agent and circumstances of action. (Jonsen and Toulmin 1988, p. 257)

---

[1] The perspective here is western. Although meaningful narratives and notions of virtue exist elsewhere, identifiable casuistries and theories of virtue are mostly western.

M. Calkins, *Developing a Virtue-Imbued Casuistry for Business Ethics,* Issues in Business Ethics 42, DOI 10.1007/978-94-017-8724-6_1, © Springer Netherlands 2014

Table 1.1 Casuistry's Characteristics

Case Usage: the chief tools of deliberation are settled (resolved) truth-bearing cases (real-life situations) that are amalgams of narratives and ethics

Paradigm Cases: deliberations turn to quintessential cases having intrinsic and extrinsic certitude

Inductive Reasoning by Analogy: deliberations draw parallels between past and present situations

Maxims: deliberations invoke pithy sayings that embody a particular truth and act as shortcuts in discourse

Complexity: deliberations retain their situational messiness

Probability: deliberations de-emphasize the absolute certainty of judgments in favor of their high probability

Cumulative Arguments: judgments emerge from a "bottom up" process of multiple arguments

Practicality: resolutions can be applied

Resolution: judgments are expected to be acted upon

Ordinary Constituency: deliberations do not depend upon experts

Casuistry is a "bottom up" inductive process that uses previously resolved (settled) truth-bearing cases to derive judgments. Its overarching goal is to determine the best course of action in the present by referring to judgments of right action in similar circumstances in the past.

As an approach to moral problem solving, casuistry is different from "top down" deductive applied principles approaches. In casuistry, principles are embedded and contextualized in particular circumstances. They are not drawn out for inspection, but used within the settings in which they are found. As a result, principles are of less importance than they are in other methods of moral reasoning.

Casuistry has a number of identifiable characteristics per Table 1.1.

First, casuistry features the use of truth-bearing cases that are simply events or happenings in which there is a "confluence of persons and actions in a time and a place" (Jonsen 1995, p. 241). Cases are not just stories, but whole, complex, and deliberative narrative instruments that are rich in detail, practical, concrete rather than abstract, and formed by the congealing or growing together of many different circumstances (Jonsen 1995, p. 241).

Casuistry's cases contain within them the details of circumstances as well as the ethical criteria used in making moral judgments. They are therefore not simply illustrations or examples of principles applied to situations, but comprehensive independent accounts of situations wherein a variety of moral precepts have been applied. They are self-sufficient truth-bearing narratives that nuance, support, or rebut proposed ethical alternatives so as to ascertain a judgment consonant with right actions taken in similar circumstances in the past. In short, the cases used in casuistry are amalgams of narratives and ethics that are used without reference to outside sources, including principles, when making moral judgments.

Second, casuistry features a *taxonomy* (order) of cases that proceeds from more certain to less certain. In casuistry, not all cases have the same moral standing. Some more clearly evidence right or wrong than others. Those cases that are clearly normative or unambiguous are called *paradigm cases* and occupy the extreme positions in a hierarchy of cases while less clearly normative cases, so called *marginal cases* are placed deeper within the taxonomy.

Paradigm cases are quintessential cases that convey intrinsic and extrinsic certitude. They recount unambiguous incidents of good and evil and reveal "the most manifest breaches of the general principle, taken in its most obvious meaning" (Jonsen and Toulmin 1988, p. 252). This notion of a paradigm is consistent with Thomas Kuhn's description of paradigms as "model problems and solutions to a community of practitioners" (Kuhn 1970, p. viii). In the context of morality, paradigm cases are useful to moral deliberation because they demonstrate the most obviously and unarguably wrong or right course of action that should be taken.

Marginal cases, on the other hand, are less clearly normative than paradigm cases and are therefore placed relative to the paradigm cases according to their ability to convey moral certitude. Marginal cases are useful in the casuistic process because they provide necessary exceptional information to aid the analogically deliberative process.

Paradigm and marginal cases are arranged in a distinct order or taxonomy, with cases arranged from greater to lesser certainty. The taxonomy therefore appears as a diamond-shaped ◊ hierarchy, with paradigm cases at the top and bottom and a wide set of marginal cases in the middle.

It should be noted here that casuistry's cases reflect both right *and* wrongdoing. Paradigmatic cases are not just best case examples, but clear incidents of right and wrong and so can be cautionary as well as inspirational.

Third, casuistry features the comparison of a new situation (the current moral problem) to previously settled truth-bearing cases of the past by means of an inductive process of analogy.

In this process, similarities and differences between the present set of circumstances and previously settled cases are sought out. Typically because the present and past circumstances do not dovetail, other incidents of the past where judgments have been satisfactorily rendered must be located. A number of settled cases are brought forward to inform the deliberation until a satisfactory judgment can be rendered.

As part of this process, an appeal is made first to the clearest incident of right and wrong, that is, the paradigm case. Then, more ambiguous cases are brought to bear and deliberation moves away from the paradigm by the introduction of "various combinations of circumstances and motives that (make) the offense in question less apparent" (Jonsen and Toulmin 1988, p. 86, 252). In this way, as Donald Klinefelter summarizes,

> (The casuist) works outward from the paradigm by analogy to more or less problematic instances…. As the analogy weakens, the debate concerning the morality of the proposed action intensifies, and we must move to a more careful description of the particulars of the case. (Klinefelter 1990, p. 19)

Fourth, casuistry is characterized by the use of maxims. While paradigm cases reflect one or more unquestioned principles, they are understood more easily through maxims or general truths expressed in sententious form.

Not unlike the rhetorical device of enthymemes, maxims presume and leave unstated at least one of the propositions of an argument. Rooted in intuition and a common-sense view of the world, maxims are pithy sayings or aphorisms of a proverbial nature that appeal to common knowledge in a formulaic manner.[2]

Advocates of principles have long favored the use of maxims in moral decision-making, distilling their complex moral rules to short useful phrases. Immanuel Kant, for one, strove to establish an overarching maxim with his Categorical Imperative when he states, "Act only on that maxim whereby thou canst at the same time will that it should become a universal law" (Kant 1990).

Business people likewise invoke maxims often. "A penny saved is a penny earned" and "waste not, want not" are two examples of business-related maxims that convey the benefits of frugality. "Nothing ventured, nothing gained" and "no risk, no reward," in contrast, convey the advantages of risk-taking.

In practice, maxims are invoked when there is a fit between a saying and a particular circumstance. Usually, the fit helps direct subsequent action appropriately, but at times the pithiness of the maxim omits important aspects of the situation that can lead to a bad judgment. Even so, the compact nature and easy access of maxims are useful in informing the judgment process and advancing moral arguments in powerful ways.

Fifth, casuistry is noted for its ability to account for the complications posed by circumstances. Circumstances, the "who, what, when, where, why, how and by what means" of a situation, "stand around the center of the case" (Jonsen 1991, p. 298; Jonsen and Toulmin 1988, pp. 253–254). They provide the rich details that go into cases and, as Richard Miller notes, impinge upon our moral reasoning in ways that enable us to respond appropriately (Miller 1996, pp. 22–24).

Casuistry maintains the unrefined complexity of circumstances throughout the judgment process. It includes complications in its cases and refuses to excise the abstract elements of circumstances for isolated review. In this way, casuistry remains tied to the concrete reality at hand and does not fly off to the world of ideas. Its judgments are therefore more inclined to be practically relevant and useful.

Sixth, casuistry is noted for its de-emphasis of epistemic certainty. It accomplishes this by concentrating less on the theoretical aspects of moral issues and more on their concrete features.

Rather than striving for epistemic certitude, casuistry attempts to reach defensible and practically wise judgments that can be applied effectively within real-life circumstances. It does not eschew abstractions or eliminate intrinsically convincing general rules or principles, but it does not overly involve itself in satisfying the intricate nuances of abstract principles. As Klinefelter notes,

> (This shift) deflect(s) the charge of moral *hubris* that is so frequently leveled against applied ethicists by skeptical philosophers, while at the same time it avoids the radical relativism and cynicism frequently associated with so-called "market solutions" to... practical problems. (Klinefelter 1990, p. 20)

---

[2] Maxims are "the kinds of phrases typically invoked by ordinary people when arguing a moral issue: "Don't kick a man when he is down" or "One good turn deserves another." These maxims are seldom further proved; their relevance is seldom explicitly demonstrated; yet they play an important role in the development of a moral argument" (Jonsen and Toulmin 1988, p. 253).

Casuistry's concentration on practical rather than epistemologically pure judgments allows it to be more effective in moral deliberations than other approaches. For instance, Jonsen and Toulmin point out with the example of their 1974 meeting with the National Commission for the Protection of Human Subjects of Biomedical and Behavioral Research how the concentration on practical conclusions helped commission members agree upon practical recommendations even though they did not necessarily agree on the reasons or principles underlying recommendations.[3] By focusing on practical conclusions, the Commission members were able to get around the insurmountable problems associated with epistemological foundationalism. While members were not absolutely certain that their decisions fulfilled the requirements of a universal principle, they were convinced their conclusions were valid. In casuistic deliberations then, just as in the Commission meeting, epistemic certainty is de-emphasized to ultimately allow the formation of practical judgments about pressing moral matters.

Seventh, casuistry makes judgments by means of cumulative arguments so as to persuade users of the correctness of a particular course of action. In casuistry the justification of an opinion rests on relatively short arguments derived from a number of seemingly disparate sources. These arguments are piled upon each other in a way that convinces (persuades) users of the overall merit of a course of action (Jonsen and Toulmin 1988, pp. 255–256).

Casuistic argumentation follows an inductive, almost rhetorical, sort of logic. Each point is stacked upon the previous one until a multifaceted, interrelated, and complex argument is made. In this way the argument is built up from small and varied sources not unlike a *pousse-café*. In the end, just as with the powerful layered drink, the argument delivers a punch more powerful than any single of its ingredients and thereby convinces its users of the validity of one course of action over another rather than proving it to them in a deductive and analytically pure manner.

Eigth and finally, casuistry strives to resolve actual moral problems rather than academic puzzles. Casuistry's goal is not to establish "formal proofs of a kind that

---

[3] (Jonsen and Toulmin 1988, pp. 16–19). Albert Jonsen and Stephen Toulmin describe the debate within the 1974 US Congressional National Commission for the Protection of Human Subjects of Biomedical and Behavioral Research as follows:

The eleven commissioners had varied backgrounds and interests. They included men and women; blacks and whites; Catholics, Protestants, Jews, and atheists; medical scientists and behaviorists psychologists; philosophers; lawyers; theologians; and public interest representatives. In all, five commissioners had scientific interests and six did not; and before they started work, few onlookers expected them to have much basis for agreement, either about general moral principles or about the application of these principles to particular problems. On hearing the composition of the commission one respected commentator reportedly said, "Now we shall presumably see matters of eternal principle decided by a six-to-five vote!" All the same, things never worked out that way in practice. At no time in its activities did the commission's opinion divide cleanly along a line between scientists and laypeople; nor did the other differences of background have anything resembling their expected effect on the practical discussions. Quite the contrary: so long as the commissioners stayed on the taxonomic or casuistical level, they usually agreed in their practical conclusions. (Jonsen and Toulmin 1988, p. 17)

can be judged by anyone with an eye for 'necessary connections'" (Jonsen and Toulmin 1988, p. 257). Rather, its goal is to provide "advice about the moral licitness or permissibility of acting in one particular way or another" (Jonsen and Toulmin 1988, p. 256). In this way, casuistry's main objective is to direct people to practical moral judgments that they can act upon.

History of Casuistry

Although sometimes thought to be new, casuistry is an old form of moral reasoning with a checkered past. It pertains mostly to religious ethics (Arras 1990; Bedau 1997; Jonsen and Toulmin 1988; Keenan 1993; S. J. Keenan, James 1996; Keenan 1995, 2010; Keenan S. J. and Shannon 1995; MacIntyre 1990; Macpherson-Smith 1994; Wildes 1993) but has been considered for secular settings as well by (Davis 1997; DeMarco 1991; Hauerwas 1983; Jackall 1987; Johansen 1995; Jonsen, "Casuistry" 1986, 1987, 1993, 1995; Kopelman 1994; Kopfensteiner 1995; Kuczewski 1994; MacIntyre 1990; Macpherson-Smith 1994; Miller 1994, 1996; Wenley 1911).

As Jonsen and Toulmin explain, today's so-called "new casuistry" grew from ancient Greek philosophical ideas, Roman legal practices, and the traditions of rabbinical debate within Judaism (Jonsen and Toulmin 1988, p. 47). Cicero, Jesus, Muslims, Jesuit English Roman Catholics, Anglican and Puritan Protestants, and New England colonists all employed it variously. Because most of these groups influenced Western business ethics in some fashion, a summary of their casuistries is in order.

In general, casuistry can be divided into four types: Greek, Hebrew, Muslim, and Christian casuistries.

Ancient Greek Casuistry

Casuistry did not have a distinctive role in Greece before the age of Stoicism. As R. M. Wenley notes, moral consciousness at the time was incidental rather than normative until polytheism eroded to the level of superstition and a search for another sort of ideal began, around the fifth century BC (Wenley 1911). With time, philosophers' investigations began to turn from the cosmos to human affairs and the notion of ultimate sanctions emerged. With sanctions, a kind of utilitarian normativity that became the Sophists' casuistry of opportunism was established. However, as Joanne Ciulla argues, the Sophists' casuistry was not properly casuistic because it lacked an ethicolegal dimension and did not distinguish between externally imposed moral principles and individual moral character (Ciulla 1994, pp. 171–172). While it created standard procedures and definitions that ordered politics better, it was relativistic and lax (Ciulla 1994, p. 172).

With Plato's *Gorgias* morality started to be illuminated by reason. That which was the most real was thought to be something most knowable. Also with Plato, a self-likening to the divine emerged and man came to think that, "the origin of ideals lies in his own nature."[4] Later, with Aristotle's emphasis on practical wisdom (Greek: *phronēsis*, Western ethics began to focus more on character and narratives. Although I will develop these notions later, it bears mentioning here that Aristotle's emphasis on practical wisdom as a guide in moral decision-making was key to understanding the role of upstanding moral character and the interest in stories in moral discernment going forward.

At this time, the notion of practical wisdom as neither a purely intellectual sort of wisdom (Greek: *sophía*) nor a craft-like skill (Greek: *technê*) began to take hold and the ability to discern well about the natural world grew in importance. So, too, did the idea that good discernment often came about through the use of truth-bearing narratives—the sorts of stories found in Plato's *Republic*, for example. Stories grew in importance and were used in a dialectical fashion in order reach a deeper understanding of the subject at hand. The invocation of stories as part of a process of deriving moral judgments thus became critical to the development of cases and later, casuistry.

After Aristotle bequeathed his writings to Theophrastus, Greek casuistry became more refined, especially in terms of its integration in law. Trevor Saunders provides a good explanation of the dual traditional use of casuistry in ancient Greece (Saunders 1998). In any event, as time progressed, Christian moralists turned to these ancient Greek notions of moral reckoning when developing their own moral treatises. Not surprisingly, their Christian casuistries reflect those of the ancient Greeks.

Hebrew Casuistry

Hebrew casuistry also influenced Western ethics, albeit in a manner different from that of the ancient Greeks. Unlike the ancient Greeks, early Jews used cases to deliberate about interpretations of Judaic Law and in this way developed an identifiable casuistry that explained, particularized, concretized, and gave meaning to their specific religious rules. Two main features characterize Hebrew casuistry: the rabbinic influence within the religion and the use of law in Judaism.[5]

First, Jewish casuistry is the product of the religion's reliance on religious teachers (rabbis) to interpret oral law (Hebrew: *mishnah*). Because post-diaspora Judaism has no official central body or authority figure such as a pope to arbitrate religious tenets, rabbis have had a great deal of authority in directing the practice of the faith through their instruction and guiding influence on the interpretation of scripture. Their interpretations of oral law effectively forged Jewish morality and

---

[4] Wenley explains further: "apart from questions… that seem to us as if they savoured of narrow casuistry (like the position of women, personal purity, slavery), the absence of dislocation between the ideal spirit and the real career, so evident in the Greek ethos… restricts casuistry in the main to those larger vital problems that must accompany further definition of the ideal itself" (Wenley 1911, p. 242).

[5] For more on Jewish law's historical roots, see (Derrett 1974; Falk 1972).

established a trajectory for the religion in practically relevant ways. Moreover, the record of their decisions in case format forms the basis of a distinctly Jewish form of casuistry.

Second, the role of law in Judaism has framed a distinctly identifiable form of Hebrew casuistry. Judaism possesses an oral law (Hebrew: *mishnah*) and legal system in which ethical deliberations are heavily rule-oriented and more legalistic than those of other religious traditions. Even so, religious laws are not applied unquestioningly. Rather, they are interpreted and contextualized through the use of casuistic narratives.

Oral law in Judaism is summarized and retained as a body in what is called the *halakhah*, a corpus of religious law that includes the moral precepts in the Torah and Talmud as well as Jewish moral customs and traditions (Jonsen, "Casuistry" 1986, p. 78; Jonsen and Toulmin 1988, pp. 56–57). From antiquity, rabbis have authoritatively interpreted the *halakhah* for followers of the faith. Their formal interpretations extend back to the time of Moses Maimonides (1135–1204) and can be found in the hair-splitting practice of *pilpul* (or "spicing," a method of studying the Talmud through intense textual analysis) promoted by Jacob Pollak (1460–1541) as well as Moses Mendelssohn (1729–1786) in the eighteenth century reforms that led to the so-called Jewish Enlightenment (Wenley 1911, p. 243).

As Wenley points out, rabbinic interpretation of oral law typically oscillated between the living, ethical ideal, and minute, often clever, sometimes puerile, interpretations of traditional rules (Wenley 1911, pp. 242–243). In other words, oral law was heavily interpreted and interpretations varied widely. As part of this process, Jewish moralists often used a distinct sort of casuistry to nuance, support, or rebut proposed moral judgments. Through the use of cases, they explored the boundaries of religious laws without undermining the laws themselves and in this way, facilitated the law's effectiveness and made it more relevant and applicable to everyday affairs.

Two case-based examples illustrate how this was done.

In the first case, a Jewish woman, fearing for her life, pulls a gun from her purse, shoots, and kills an assailant. The governing precept related to the killing is clear: the Ten Commandments tenet that states, "Thou Shalt Not Kill." She has violated the precept that one should not kill another and is therefore guilty of violating religious law. Because the woman did so for fear for her life, however, the Hebrew moralist could argue that she is not in violation of the religious proviso that moderates general religious norms to accommodate particular situations of endangerment. Her need for self-defense moderates the application of the law, "Thou Shalt Not Kill," such that she is relieved of moral culpability. The narrowly didactic nature of the law is in this way widened and softened to accommodate an exception.

A second case involving war is more complicated than the first, but also illustrates the idea of moderation through case-based reasoning. In this instance, an individual member of the military kills another (others), but not in self-defense and again the precept against killing in the Ten Commandments is abridged. In this case, however, there can be no appeal to self-defense because the killing was willful and offensive. Is the military person culpable or can the law be modified to allow such killing?

Hebrew moralists in this case would not appeal to a single extenuating proviso but would have to draw upon a number of cases related to law to reach a judgment. In other words, they would need to turn to a taxonomy of cases related to *halakhah* and a distinctly Jewish casuistry that focuses "on the obligations to which Jews are subject *as Jews*" (Jonsen and Toulmin 1988, p. 57). The resulting judgment from such case use would determine the individual military member's guilt or innocence. Moreover, the judgment as well as the use of the taxonomy of cases would result in a widening of the narrowly didactic nature of religious law to allow exceptional differences in the present situation.

In the end as both cases illustrate, the use of cases—either singly or together—according to a distinct Jewish casuistry influences the interpretation and application of law in Judaism in practically important and precedent-setting ways. While Jewish casuistry is not used as much as it was in the past, the tradition continues with the work of Brody and others in the realm of bioethics (Brody, 1989).

Muslim Casuistry

Muslim casuistry is also a distinct casuistry that relies heavily on religious law and teachers for interpretation. In Islam, *sharia* (Arabic: *shariya*) is the particular body of religious law that governs the diaspora of Muslim believers called the *umma* (Arabic: *ummah*) or "community" or "nation of Islam." Jurist-scholars called *mufti* interpret it.

Muslim religious law is a comprehensive legal framework that regulates public and private life. It is sourced in both the holy book of Islam (the *Qur'an*) and the religious acts established by the prophet Muhammad (the *Sunnah*). Typically, the *mufti* interpret Islamic law and issue opinions called *fatwa* to guide the faithful in civic and economic affairs as well as private life.[6] Their style of argumentation (called *hiyal*) is similar to Judaism's *pilpul* in that it seeks to avoid direct confrontation with the law to accommodate human frailty (Jonsen, "Casuistry" 1986, p. 78).

Muslim law's expansiveness sometimes leads to problems with application that require interpretation. This need for interpretation is not new, but goes back to the Prophet himself. As Wenley observes, "(A)lthough the Prophet's position as God's representative made any decision of his absolutely valid, local conditions left a wide margin for opportunism and Muhammad was an eclectic in these matters."[7]

---

[6] (Jonsen, "Casuistry" 1986, p. 78). In certain Shi'a Muslim sects, a qualified interpreter called a *mujtahid* made up his own rulings on the permissibility of an Islamic law, but only for himself.

[7] (Wenley 1911, p. 243). Wenley further describes how interpretation of the Prophet came to be regarded as a science, how conflicts of "sayings" came to form the basis of Muslim casuistry, and how opposition arose between those who appealed to tradition and those who desired to systematize the law. Islam, he concludes, has a casuistic code applicable to private affairs and a parallel law of the land, with the former being sacred and prescriptive. This situation is not unlike the mediaeval condition where canon and secular laws provided private and public codes wherein the application of the private code rendered it more casuistic in a moral rather than legal sense

Interpretation of Muslim law benefits from casuistry at times. As Baber Johansen referencing Joseph Schacht points out, "Muslim jurists often engaged in casuistry in an effort to answer practical problems that evolve from (a) process of social differentiation" (Johansen 1995, p. 135). Among a list of its qualities, casuistry provides "graded transitions" that allow moralists to go from the core of one concept to another and elucidate the precise boundaries of the law (Johansen 1995, p. 136; Schacht 1964, p. 205).

Muslim casuistry was helpful in enabling individuals to make their own moral judgments without outside assistance. In fact, until roughly the 12th century such autonomy of thought and independent deduction of Islamic law through rational thinking (Arabic: *ijtihad*) was common. It began to fall apart in the tenth century, however, when obvious errors in individual judgment arose that led powerful figures within the community to exert their authority. The ensuing and lengthy "closing of the gates of *ijtihad*" eventually abolished the practice of independent moralizing and replaced it with "rightful interpreters"—priests and clerics (Arabic: *ulema*) whose status was elevated by their ability to control the religion's direction. From that time forward, Muslim moral theology became the reserve of a select group of individuals.[8]

Casuistry is not used much in Islam today because religious law is now interpreted more narrowly than it was in the past.[9] Greater emphasis is now placed on the letter of the law than its spirit and moral judgments have largely been relegated to the *ulema*. The effect has been an undermining of the confidence of ordinary people to make their own moral judgments, an increase in power for priests and clerics, an expansion of fundamentalism in Muslim cultures, and a diminishment of casuistry in Islamic societies.

Although a resurgence of casuistry consistent with Muslim traditions and laws would seem to be a good way to offset some of these recent negative developments while also facilitating a more comprehensive and meaningful understanding of Muslim ethics, such a resurgence is unlikely today.[10]

Christian Casuistry

Christian casuistry, not unlike other religious-based casuistries, is identified with a particular faith, religious history, and scriptural-based set of norms. It is one that

---

(Wenley 1911, p. 243). For another survey of Muslim casuistic history see, (Jonsen and Toulmin 1988, pp 111–112, 285, 310).

[8] (Abbas 2004). For more, see (Khare 1999).

[9] Although some such as Ceclia Lynch have used casuistry as an interpretive tool to understand aspects of Islam, Muslim casuistry is not used much today. See (Lynch 2005).

[10] Ayaan Hirsi Ali distinguishes spiritual, social, and political Islam in recounting her experiences as a Muslim woman living in various Muslim and secular cultures. The historical account here provides the rationale behind the politicization of Islam that she describes (Hirsi Ali 2013)

emerged from the narrative nature of its holy book but did not become a recogniz-able form of moral reasoning until centuries after the founding of the religion.

Christian casuistry grew out of the auricular confessional practices that began to emerge in the seventh century as priests began to hear private confessions and refer to books listing sins and their appropriate penances. Later, with the Fourth Lateran Council (1215 AD), the practice of annual confessions was systematized and more elaborate and comprehensive summas or formularies began to surface.[11] As James Keenan points out, as these confessional manuals proliferated, a summist or manualist tradition arose—one informed and shaped by Franciscan spirituality, nominalism's existentialism, and preachers skilled in rhetoric (Keenan S. J. and Shannon 1995).

During this era, casuistry was often employed to resolve problems related to the Church's authority over the consciences and social behavior of believers (the internal and external forums). In most cases it was used in moral problem solving whenever ancient Roman law failed to reach decisions (Jonsen and Toulmin 1988, p. 47, 52–53, 101, 113–121).

By 1556–1656 and the so-called era of high casuistry that began with the publi-cation of the Augustinian cleric Martin Azpilcueta's *Handbook for Confessors and Penitents* and ended with Blaise Pascal's (1623–1662) *Provincial Letters*, the use of casuistry flourished and casuists largely abandoned confessional books in favor of taxonomies based on the Ten Commandments or the Seven Deadly Sins (Jonsen and Toulmin 1988, pp. 142–143, 251). The chief promoters of this transition and casuistry itself were Jesuits—members of the male religious order formally known as the Society of Jesus—who were trained in disputation and logic.

As John O'Malley points out, Jesuits formally studied cases of conscience (Latin: *casus conscientiae*) during the high era's earliest years, but did little more than examine available texts and occasionally lectures on them (O'Malley 1993, p. 147). With the passage of time, however, Jesuits expanded their work to include a discussion after case lectures, a practice that as it expanded was regulated by the religious order. Because of its prevalence, every Jesuit confessor was advised to spend an hour a day in the private study of cases and the discernment of cases of conscience came to play a larger role in Jesuit life than its official documents would suggest (O'Malley 1993, p. 147).

The impetus behind case study related to the Jesuits' roles as priests and confes-sors and their obligation to act responsibly as judge and doctor of souls. Practice with cases enabled Jesuit priests to clarify complicated moral issues for penitents and those seeking moral advice (O'Malley 1993, p. 144).

Perhaps most important, the practice of using cases enabled Jesuits to apply general norms better to the new situations that were emerging during a period of great social change. Jonsen and Toulmin point out how the era was marked by increased literacy, the growth of seminaries, the orderly education of the clergy,

---

[11] Jonsen notes that the summas, "not only listed sins and penances but defined sorts of action, distinguished seriousness, presented mitigating circumstances, and stated, in brief fashion, reasons for these positions" (Jonsen, "Casuistry" 1986, p. 79).

expanding urbanization, improved transportation, nation-states formation, New World explorations, the Protestant Reformation, and the Council of Trent (1545–1563 AD) (Jonsen and Toulmin 1988, pp. 142–153). It was also a period of vicious warfare, rising religious militancy, political turmoil, and improved methods of manufacturing and banking. All of these factors challenged authority in new ways and required a reassessment of the common morality associated with property rights, the purpose of money, the definition of usury, and so forth. Through public debates about "great cases" as well as confession, people were better able to resolve some of the incongruities brought forth by these radical social changes (Jonsen and Toulmin 1988, pp. 142–146).

Every contentious issue was not resolved then, however. With the Protestant Reformation, casuistry itself came under attack for undermining the fundamentals of the faith (Jonsen 1993, p. 59). Martin Luther, for one, despised the Roman Catholic summists' casuistry because of its elaboration of the distinctions of sin, emphasis on penance, and close association with a theology of works (Jonsen and Toulmin 1988, p. 157). Even so, Luther developed another sort of casuistry, one mediated by pietism (Wenley 1911, p. 245). Later Reformists expanded on this version, developing other sorts of casuistries and eventually a distinct form of Protestant casuistry emerged.

In Britain, for example, William Perkins, Richard Baxter, Robert Sanderson, Jeremy Taylor, and others developed Calvinistic-Puritan casuistries.[12] While elaborate, these versions tended to be stricter and more penitential than the Lutheran variety and they were not always popular or effective with the faithful (Wenley 1911, p. 245). Often, they were unwieldy. Jeremy Taylor's *Ductor Dubitantium*, for one, was so complex that it was described as "an elephantine, labyrinthine miscellany of rules, cases, Latin and Greek citations and digressions" and "an acute treatise, evincing great intellectual quickness and subjective subtlety, but not notable either for profound thought or for systematic grasp of ethical principles."[13] Even so, it and other forms of British Protestant casuistry were important to the development of Protestantism's self-reliant forms of piety.

Although Protestant casuists rejected the legalistic tenor of earlier Jesuit practices, they did not reject the casuistic method nor did they eschew manuals (Jonsen and Toulmin 1988, p. 161). Instead, they developed their own distinctive manuals to serve the faithful. These were not wholly unlike the earlier Roman Catholic summas in that they, too, cautioned the faithful, instructed believers in the religion, and inspired followers to pray and seek the moral guidance of Scripture. They differed mainly in their assent to official Roman dogma.

---

[12] (Jonsen, "Casuistry" 1986, p. 80; Jonsen and Toulmin 1988, pp. 159–160; Wenley 1911, p. 245). For more on Perkins and Taylor, see (Keenan 1995, pp. 122–124; Miller 1995, p. 132; Wenley 1911, p. 245).

[13] (Miller 1995, p. 132; Wenley 1911, p. 245) Miller's and Wenley's assessments could be applied as well to Jeremy Taylor's 1,650 tome, *Holy Living and Holy Dying*, a 515 page complicated compilation of prayers, rules, and recommendations published prior to *Ductor Dubitantium* (1660). See (Taylor 1831).

The Reformed Churches' casuistry eventually passed into New England when the British colonized North America. There it influenced the atmosphere of newly formed religious-based colleges until the mid-nineteenth century (Wenley 1911, p. 245). Unlike in Europe, however, manuals were not used exclusively by educators, religious ministers, preachers, or other appointed persons. Instead, ordinary people used them. As Richard Brookhiser points out, even secular leaders such as George Washington carried a small book of the "Rules of Civility" that was a compilation of maxims or proverbial sayings based on a system of courtesy composed by late sixteenth century French Jesuits. Washington, for one, considered his little rulebook helpful in "dealing with others, based on attending to their situations and sensibilities" (Brookhiser 1996).

Eventually casuistry fell out of widespread use in America and Europe due to the rise of theological rigorism in the Church, political disdain for Rome, and the movement in Enlightenment philosophy toward the exposition of the principles of conduct.[14] Even so, casuistry did not die out altogether. It was bloodied by bitter controversies, but lived on to reemerge later when needed.

---

[14] For an explanation of the theological, philosophical, and political reasons for casuistry's decline, see (Jonsen 1993). For more on the trend toward use of principles in modern philosophy, see the commentary on William Whewell and Henry Sidgwick in (Jonsen, "Casuistry and Clinical Ethics" 1986, p. 66; Jonsen and Toulmin 1988, p. 163). and (Jonsen 1991, p. 296).

Chapter 2
Casuistry versus Ethical Pluralism with Applied Principles

You always admire what you really don't understand.
—Blaise Pascal

(Blaise Pascal (1623–1662) was a French mathematician, physicist, inventor, writer, and Catholic theologian and philosopher. His Letters Provincials ("The Provincial Letters") targeted the Jesuits, and in particular Antonio Escobar, and denounced casuistry as a form of complex reasoning to justify moral laxity and all sorts of sins. His most influential theological work, referred to posthumously as the Pensées ("Thoughts") was a defense of the Catholic faith and is considered a fine example of French prose)

To this point we have considered casuistry's features and history and saw that it is an inductive method of moral deliberation involving the comparison of new situations to previously settled cases. We have seen, too, how it is reliant upon settled truth-bearing narratives that are easy to use in practical situations and how the process is reflective and supportive of the *status quo* and enduring norms of society, particularly those of religious groups.

In the following, we will compare casuistry to the ethical (or moral) pluralistic and applied principles approaches that dominate ethics today. We will then contrast some of casuistry's features to those of other methods, especially reflective equilibrium.

Conventional Approach: Ethical Pluralism with Embedded Applied Principles

In general, ethics today is dominated by ethical pluralistic approaches having embedded moral principles and an approach that is largely deductive and linearly sequential.

A multi-perspectival approach within applied ethics, ethical pluralism maintains that different (plural) normative criteria should apply to moral deliberations.[1] The

---

[1] For our purposes, ethics is defined as the study of morality and includes three general branches—meta-ethics (the meaning of judgments), normative ethics (moral norms or conventions), and applied ethics (morality applied to real situations).

M. Calkins, *Developing a Virtue-Imbued Casuistry for Business Ethics,* Issues in Business Ethics 42, DOI 10.1007/978-94-017-8724-6_2, © Springer Netherlands 2014

most common form of it today incorporates the principle-based ethics of utilitarianism and deontology as well as some sort of rights-based justice or common good normative perspective and Aristotle's long-enduring character based ethic called virtue ethics.

The applied principles ethical pluralistic approach is popular today because of the appeal of its clear set of moral principles, the binding qualities of its law-like moral rules, and contemporary society's tendency to turn to compliance with norms when there are questions of ethical propriety. Not surprisingly, it has been applied to contemporary business practices with the works of (Velasquez et al. 1983) and (Bowie 1991) as good examples.

As a process, the applied principles ethical pluralistic approach begins by identifying and isolating the moral aspect of an issue and then scrutinizing it according to various moral criteria. Analysis proceeds sequentially, with the issue judged by each moral method in turn. Individual judgments are then compiled, compared, and contrasted and if or when respective judgments are at odds, other ways of resolving them are brought in and applied. In this way, the entire process is linear and proceeds in a step-by-step orderly way from one method to another until a final overall judgment is reached.

Benefits of Applied Principles Approaches

As a moral approach, the applied principles ethical pluralistic approach is beneficial in a number of ways. First, in relying on multiple moral perspectives, it eliminates or diminishes many of the well-established shortcomings of each of its component methods used in isolation. As judgments are reached using the various criteria, overlaps can emerge and be used together to create a synergy that results in a final judgment that can be more powerful than one derived from any single moral perspective. Even when judgments do not converge, the nature of the differences can contribute to an overall judgment that is more informed. In the end then, a final judgment derived through an ethical pluralistic approach is stronger than one derived by means of a single component perspective used in isolation.

Second, the applied principles embedded ethical pluralistic approach's emphasis on rational principles (rules) works to defuse emotion, reduce subjectivity, and strengthen consensus about judgments in positive ways. Because ethical pluralism is comprised of methods that proceed logically from clearly defined norms, judgments seem more defensible and actionable than those produced by other more seemingly subjective approaches. As a result, ethical pluralism's judgments engender greater confidence than alternative approaches.

Third, the applied principles ethical pluralistic approach provides users with an ordered process that reduces uncertainty in ethical problem solving in positive ways. It does this by offering users a sequential, linear-active method of handling problems—one where each aspect of the problem is isolated, compartmentalized, and scrutinized according to the moral perspectives embedded in it. As a logical and ordered process, it increases the efficiency of reaching judgments. More important, however, it enhances confidence among users that all aspects of analysis and judging have been thoroughly covered.

In sum, the applied principles ethical pluralistic approach is helpful in providing a simple, clear, reasonable, defensible, direct, and directive way to make moral judgments. It is accepted widely and produces highly regarded moral judgments. It is not surprising, therefore, that it is popular among ethicists.

Shortcomings of Applied Principles Approaches

Despite these and other positive features, the applied principles ethical pluralistic approach has certain shortcomings.[2] First, it is too abstract, time consuming, and cumbersome for effective use in practical situations. The complexity of extracting and isolating the moral issue from the mundane and the intricacy of analysis that requires the input of moral experts make it unwieldy for use by the non-experts who bear responsibility for making moral judgments in real life settings. Ethical pluralism is so conceptually driven that it is, in short, impractical and ineffectual for everyday use.

Second, the applied principles ethical pluralistic approach renders clear judgments and its rules orientation makes compliance enforceable, but its judgments are either overly narrow or so expansive that they are ineffective in addressing issues beyond the scope of the circumstances that generated moral inquiry.

Not unlike laws or taxes, rule-based approaches wilt when exceptions arise. Rules (laws or taxes) apply either directly to particular circumstances or generally such that exceptions or loopholes can easily be found to sidestep them. Judgments end up being fragile because they are undermined with new bits of data that negate effective rule application. To remain effective then, rules must be constantly monitored, refined, and updated—a laborious catch up process that does little to shore up the certainty of the process among users.

Third, an ethical pluralistic approach featuring applied principles tends to exalt rules at the expense of individual judgment and moral aspiration—two key components of ethics. Principles take on such an exaggerated importance in this method that they govern people's actions and obscure the relevance of people's reflective judgments and moral aspirations. Compliance with norms rather than discerning thought and concern with developing oneself as a moral agent govern people's actions. Rules dictate people rather than vice versa and people become subservient to the instruments they created to serve them. In this way the creation governs the creator and the normal course of morality becomes warped.

Fourth, an ethical pluralistic approach featuring applied principles champions objectivity as an antidote to subjectivism and relativism, yet the norms it relies upon are little more than subjective preferences. The emphasis on an orderly and sequential application of rules, hypercritical attention to detail in analysis, emphasis on rule compliance, and so forth reflect the values of conventional local morality. The

---

[2] For a critique of current approaches, see (Cavanagh et al. 1995).

preferences of the method are subjectively determined and are therefore on par with those produced my means of cultural or social group relativism. In the end then, while they are promoted as being objective, the norms embedded in the method are basically culturally rooted and subjectively determined.

Fifth and extending from the last point, an ethical pluralistic approach featuring applied principles typically results in conflicting judgments as the different normative pathways embedded in it produce judgments at odds with each other.

Because the approach typically relies on deontology, utilitarianism, pragmatism, and so forth, it concentrates sequentially on narrow aspects of morality and then combines the various outcomes. Sometimes doing so results in conflicting judgments, which then forces the decision-maker to resolve discrepancies by means of proportionalism, double-effect, or some other ancillary reasoning criteria. This, too, can prove to be unsatisfactory because the added complexity further clouds judgments and leads to even more subjective appeals—best guesses based on what seems reasonable and practically wise at the time.

In the end, an ethical pluralistic approach featuring applied principles is popular and seems robust, but its appeal and strength wither under inspection. It can lead to confusion, lull the unwary into a false confidence that compliance with rules is sufficient for good moral judgments, dull awareness of a wide range of important moral features not covered by rules, and do little more than valorize conventions that are distilled and framed in palatable rules and abstractions.

Although popular, scrutiny reveals the ethical pluralistic approach featuring applied principles to be no more robust than casuistry.

Chapter 3
Normativity and Analogy in Casuistry

> *It is the weight, not numbers of experiments that is to be regarded.*
> *(Povinelli 2012, p. xvi)*
> —Isaac Newton

Casuistry is sometimes challenged for its lack of normativity and dependence on analogy. In the following, we will examine these two concepts (normativity and analogy) and see how they are used in casuistry and other methods for deriving moral judgments.

Normativity's Different Locations in Moral Reasoning

The ethical pluralistic approach featuring applied principles described above tends to be clearly prescriptive and its proponents sometimes use this feature to fault casuistry for not having the same sort of clear and binding norms. Although appealing at some level, the argument against casuistry misses how principle-based approaches sometimes fail to convey the essence and fullness of normativity in practical settings and how, as a result, they can sometimes not stand up well against casuistry.

To understand how casuistry can be more normative than principles-based approaches, let us consider the meaning of normativity and how it influences moral judgments.

Normativity refers to the moral standards of a society having to do with how things ought to be, what people consider valuable and good or bad, and the actions regarded as right or wrong—in short, society's "shoulds." Because casuistry does not deconstruct situations to isolate moral standards, casuistry is thought to lack moral standards and to be vacuous and lax. This interpretation is false, however, because it misreads how society's moral standards are communicated through casuistry's settled cases.

The common understanding that casuistry lacks normativity is inaccurate because casuistry is, at its core, conventional. It relies on cases that reflect society's consensus about the rightness or wrongness of various particular judgments and, as a method, reflects orthodox morality at work in particular circumstances. In short, casuistry illustrates how conventional moral standards apply within a given society and how that society thinks one ought to act.

Moreover, at a micro level casuistry's taxonomies illustrate the normative weight society places on particular instances of right or wrongdoing. Thus, as a general process and in the particulars of its structure, casuistry has a normativity that is explicit, relevant, and actionable.

Other approaches, especially applied principles varieties, are unable to explicate and apply norms in this manner. Before moral analysis can proceed, principles must first be extracted and then adapted such that commonly held notions of right and wrong are isolated and framed in ways that they become general rules or principles. This makes the resulting principles easier to apply, but at the same time makes morality less nuanced. The streamlining, in other words, eliminates the complexity of the given problem.

In addition, the process of streamlining moral conventions to fit rules is complicated by the fact that to be effective, the rules must be both sufficiently general to be broadly applicable and narrow enough to be identifiable as maxims. More often than not this balance is not reached. Important elements of the moral problem get sidelined or left out altogether and the rules that result are either overly general or so abstract and narrowly defined that they cannot be used in practical problem solving.

In the end, a process where moral elements are extracted, isolated, and framed as maxims then applied to a complex problem is cumbersome, lengthy, inefficient, and fraught with conflict. In comparison, casuistry is simpler and does a better job of communicating moral conventions than popular applied principles approaches because casuistry is easy to use and can convey the nuance and fullness of society's values as well as its understanding of good and bad/right and wrong in practical settings.

Analogy as Reasoning Process Versus Tool for Principle Formation and Validation

Those who consider casuistry to be inferior to applied principles approaches also dismiss it for its use of reasoning by means of analogy. To casuistry's critics, reasoning by analogy is thought to be less rigorous than reasoning from first principles, an overarching *telos*, or some such, because the nature of comparisons is too subjective, unreflective, or conventional.

Again there is some validity to this argument as we will see presently, but it, too, falls short because all moral reasoning rests at some point on analogy. This is because all moral theories must compare favorably to society's moral conventions to remain viable. Thus, the real problem is not that one moral process is analogical and another is not, but that one applies analogy differently and at different times in the process of reaching judgments than another.

Let me explain.

Moral reasoning proceeds either from a top-down or a bottom-up direction. Deductive reasoning (a top-down approach) moves from a general case to a specific instance while inductive reasoning (a bottom-up approach) moves from a specific case or cases to a general rule. Both processes use analogy at times, but do so at different points in their processes and for different purposes.

Bottom-up inductive processes such as casuistry reason by means of analogy using settled cases. In this process, analogizing is broad and comparisons are multifaceted. Cases are compared to the situation at hand, to each other, and then in such a way that they can be placed within a taxonomy. Throughout, appeals are not made to principles. Only at the end of the process do principles emerge and become apparent. In this way the process is bottom-up and inductive, proceeding from cases to the general principles embedded in those cases.

Top-down approaches such as applied principles methods, on the other hand, reason from general principles to specific applications. Here, analogizing occurs at both the earliest stage of the moral process and as a checking mechanism throughout and especially at the end. Moral elements are isolated, extracted, and compared to each other. In this way, analogies are drawn among various abstract elements excised from reality. The purpose of doing so is to forge rules that can be applied generally. As a result (and unlike bottom-up processes), analogizing in this process occurs at the beginning and not at the level of application. Analogy is also used to check coherence of principle with reality.

To explain the process differently, top-down approaches use comparisons or analogies to determine the fit of the principle to observable facts. The principle itself is drawn from one or more features of observable fact and remains viable only insofar as it is validated by means of comparison to observable fact later in the process. In this way, principles are compared at both the front end and the back end of the process—in the principle's formulation and later validation. In the end, the irony is that while critics disparage casuistry for reasoning by analogy, their own revered applied principles approach ultimately rests upon comparisons or analogies.

The top-down principle approach is reflected in the natural sciences, in particular, Newtonian physics. In both domains the goal is to establish general rules that both apply to and reflect the real world.[1]

As Kuhn explains of science, scientific rules or laws come about by means of comparisons of paradigms. Accordingly, models of worldviews that reflect society's conventions (paradigms) are compared with each other with an eye to discovering the relationship of isolable elements. They are then examined, formulated as hypotheses, distributed ("deployed" in Kuhn's parlance) as rules, and remain authoritative until disproven (Kuhn 1970, p. 43). Insofar as the principles derived in this fashion reflect reality, they hold, but if they do not compare favorably with reality, they are discarded. Coherence with reality is therefore key to principle retention.

Richard Posner and Mark Johnson explain the process in the following way:

> The critics of analogical reasoning sometimes act as if analogies were "things," which either resolve or do not resolve contested cases. If they do resolve contested cases, they are not mere analogies but genuine rules; if they do not, they are nothing at all. But analogies should not be seen in this way. Their meaning lies in their use. They are not simply unanalyzed fact patterns. (Sunstein 1993, p. 779)

---

[1] Isaac Newton espoused the notion of a mechanical universe with set physical laws. Certain seventeenth century natural philosophers emulated Newton in their philosophical treatises.

Analogy is not only essential to science, but also important in other venues, including the formation of civil law. As Cass Sunstein explains:

> (Analogies) help people think through contested cases and to generate low-level principles. In this way they (analogies) have a constitutive dimension, for the patterns we see are a product not simply of preexisting reality, but of our cognitive structures and our principles as well. The principles and patterns we develop and describe are in turn brought to bear on, and tested through confrontation with, other cases. (Sunstein 1993, p. 779)

In both bottom-up and top-down reasoning processes then, analogical reasoning has a critical albeit different role. In bottom-up approaches such as casuistry, it provides the ease of use and expediency necessary for timely judgments in concrete situations. Compared to seemingly thorough approaches that apply principles directly to situations, casuistry's analogical reasoning with cases provides those charged with decision-making in time-pressed situations a way to do so with confidence and without having to turn to moral experts to handle complex and cumbersome rules.[2]

Moreover, bottom-up analogical approaches such as casuistry help people to reach agreement on a course of action even as they continue to disagree on the priority of the principles at work in a situation.[3] Not unlike Jonsen and Toulmin's example of the successful use of casuistry in the 1974 National Commission for the Protection of Human Subjects of Biomedical and Behavioral Research, reasoning analogically can help people sidestep ideological principle-based differences so that they can achieve overlapping consensus on particular solutions. In essence, casuistic reasoning by analogy helps people move ahead with a course of action while they continue to disagree on the role of principles in the situation at hand (Jonsen and Toulmin 1988, p. 16).

Third, analogical reasoning in a casuistic bottom-up approach is adaptable and able to handle problems as they emerge and mutate.[4] Because the process does not attempt to force abstract concepts on problems, it facilitates openness to new facts and perspectives by drawing together select bits of information from various sources in a comparative process and then determining fit with the present circumstances. In this way it avoids the tendency to interpret the present in light of preexisting concepts and instead chooses information according to its fit with what is at hand.

If there is an overlap of analogical reasoning in top-down and bottom-up reasoning processes it is the notion of fit. In top-down approaches, analogy is used to determine the fit of principles to reality in general whereas in bottom-up processes analogy determines the fit of cases to particular situations.

Put another way, unless a principle compares favorably (fits) with reality and tests determine fit over time, it is undermined and eventually replaced or rejected.

---

[2] In Sunstein words, "reasoning by analogy may be the best approach available for people of limited time and capacities" (Sunstein 1993, p. 782).

[3] Sunstein concurs, stating, "reasoning by analogy may have the significant advantage of allowing people unable to reach anything like an accord on general principle to agree on particular outcomes" (Sunstein 1993, p. 782).

[4] Sunstein states, "analogical reasoning may be especially desirable in contexts in which we seek moral evolution over time" (Sunstein 1993, p. 782).

Similarly, unless a case fits the situation at hand, it is rejected and replaced with a more suitable case. Comparison or analogy in both determines the fit of either the principle or the case. In both approaches then, analogy serves a similar validating function, differing in terms of where the comparisons are applied.

In the end, top-down and bottom-up reasoning processes rely on analogy at critical junctures but do so differently and for different purposes. While top-down principles-based methods use analogical reasoning to establish, validate, and then apply principles directly to situations, bottom-up casuistic methods use analogy to fit cases to situations and to weigh cases for ordering. In doing so, top-down principles-based methods establish the purity of principles but do not show how one should act in particular circumstances as well as bottom-up casuistic processes. For this reason, casuistry is better suited to applied ethics in particular circumstances than applied principles approaches.

Chapter 4
The Role of Principles in Casuistry

The pure and simple truth is rarely pure and never simple.
—Oscar Wilde

Questions about casuistry's normativity and use of analogy highlight the different emphases given to principles in moral reasoning. Critics of casuistry often argue that casuistry is lax because it rejects moral principles when making judgments. While it is true that casuistry does not appeal directly to principles when making judgments as other approaches do, it also does not always discount them entirely. Casuistry sometimes incorporates principles indirectly by exposing the relevant features of principles, the overlap of principles with each other, and the shortcomings of principles in the cases it uses.

In the following, we will see how casuistry, as Oscar Wilde observes of truth, is not as simple as it seems and how the application of principles in casuistic judgments can be indirect, subtle, and integrated along with the other normative moral criteria.

Principles and the Proper End of Ethics

Casuistry does not attempt to elucidate or appeal to principles directly when making judgments. Although principle proponents pillory it for this failure, casuistry remains grounded in the proper end of ethics because it remains focused throughout its application on reaching moral judgments that are actionable in concrete situations. For this reason and contrary to popular perception, casuistry fulfills the main objective of ethics better than principle based approaches that are more concerned with satisfying the demands of the theories that generate the principles than fulfilling the central objective of ethics.

The observation of principle-based theory's self-absorption is not entirely new. In a critical overview of principlism (a system of ethics based on four specific principles), Richard Davis questions the functional efficacy of principles in real

((Wilde 2005, p. 12). The full quote is: Algernon. The truth is rarely pure and never simple. Modern life would be verytedious if it were either, and modern literature a complete impossibility!).

M. Calkins, *Developing a Virtue-Imbued Casuistry for Business Ethics,* Issues in Business Ethics 42, DOI 10.1007/978-94-017-8724-6_4, © Springer Netherlands 2014

life settings. Focusing on a debate by K. Danner Clouser and Bernard Gert about the different expectations of moral theory held by foundationalists and principlists, Davis concludes that there is a lack of coherence and development of moral theory regarding the extent to which principles may replace other forms of moral theory in practice (Davis 1995, pp. 86–87).

Within clinical ethics, some have questioned the functionality of principles in real-life moral deliberation as well. William Donnelly, for one, considers principles in light of the move to reconnect medical ethics with the thought, feelings, and motivations of the persons directly involved in ethical dilemmas. He finds there a shift that went "from principles to principals" (Donnelly 1994).

Similarly, David Thomasma looks at the various branches of ethics in an attempt to find an appropriate hermeneutic for medicine and finds that the abstract qualities associated with principles are problematic because "(m)oral abstractions frequently are seen by non-philosophers as empty of the normal ingredients of moral concerns people have in their day-to-day life" (Thomasma 1994, p. 99)[1]. In other words, abstract arguments that conjure up principles satisfy ethicists, but have little practical use in themselves compared to other methods.

In these and other commentaries we see the problems associated with applying principle-based speculative ethical theories directly to concrete situations—problems that suggest that other approaches to moral deliberation—ones that do not rely so heavily on the direct application of abstract moral principles but instead remain grounded in the complexity of concrete situations where principles are embedded alongside other moral criteria—might be better suited to practical use than principles-based approaches.

Others go further, eschewing moral principles altogether. Stanley Hauerwas, for one, maintains that narratives (which include cases) rather than principles are better guides in moral decision-making:

> (Casuistry) is not simply the attempt to adjudicate difficult cases of conscience within a system of moral principles, but it is the form that a tradition must use to test its own commitments. For in fact a tradition often does not understand the implications of its basic convictions. Those implications become apparent only through the day-to-day living of a people pledged to embody that narrative within their own lives. There is a sense, therefore, in which we rightly discover that to which we are deeply committed only by having our lives challenged by others. That challenge does not come only from without but rather is entailed by narrative that has captured our lives. (Hauerwas 1983, p. 380)

According to this view, morality is embedded in deeply meaningful narratives rather than in principles and we draw upon these narratives when testing our commitments and judgments about right and wrong. Ethical decision-making therefore rests not on abstract principles, but upon narratives (cases) and the "imaginative testing of our life against the well lived and virtuous lives of others" (Hauerwas 1983, p. 381).

Still others take a different position by holding a place for principles in casuistic decision-making. While many in this group maintain that casuistry needs principles

---

[1] Hermeneutics is the art and science of text interpretation, usually that of Scripture.

(as well as moral theory) on occasion, their acknowledgement raises questions about how exactly moral principles are used in casuistry.[2]

The Place of Principles in Casuistry

The answer to this conundrum seems to be found in casuistry's organizing function and the way casuistry integrates principles indirectly while simultaneously making them understandable and applicable in real situations.

Let us tackle these in turn.

First, casuistry provides an organizing function that is helpful to making principles more relevant in concrete situations. Jonsen explains how this organizing function works in the context of casuistry with the example of Matteo Ricci's "memory palace" (Spence 1984).

Ricci, a sixteenth-century Italian Jesuit missionary and advisor to China's aristocracy, struggled to find ways to make complicated mathematical and engineering concepts memorable to his sponsors. He eventually settled on an ancient Roman mnemonic device with memorized spatial relationships to establish, order, and recollect memorial content. In his model, a person stored images associated with something to be memorized in each of the various rooms and went, in a mental walk, to the rooms to retrieve images as needed. The rooms of the palace were set up (ordered) according to the usefulness, efficiency, and relationships of the images and, in this way, acted as a framing device to aid the recollection of users.

Casuistry functions in much the same way as the memory palace. It, too, is a framing device, but instead of images related to scientific laws or language, casuistry orders cases in terms of their relationships and the moral principles and theories they contain. In so doing it becomes a way of thinking about and organizing the various moral aspects of complex circumstances—a mental map to help people order seemingly disparate parts of a situation according to generally accepted moral principles and theoretical precepts. In this way, as Jonsen explains, "casuistry is no more an alternative to principles than are walls and foundations to the palace" (Jonsen 1995, p. 246). It does not appeal directly to principles or moral theory but incorporates both obliquely and in terms of their relational qualities.

Second, casuistry contextualizes principles for everyday life, using the gist of principles in a way that makes them understandable and relevant in practical settings. Casuistry appears to use principles and theories partially and incompletely, but uses principles in way that is less concerned with maintaining the purity of principle than advancing the purpose of ethics, which is to facilitate defensible and actionable moral judgments.

Casuistry's aim is not to facilitate the internal consistency of principles but to use what is of value in principles along with other moral instruments to come to a better understanding of the moral underpinnings of a particular situation. Casuistry there-

---

[2] Jonsen admits that principles might be used as a sort of last recourse. (Jonsen 1995, p. 246).

fore, as Ciulla observes "implies a kind of deflection or falling away from a law or principle" (Ciulla 1994, p. 172). Yet in doing so, casuistry makes principles more understandable, relevant, and applicable to concrete situations marked by complexity. Put another way, casuistry fleshes out principles so they can be used more effectively in making moral judgments.

Third and finally, casuistry is an open-ended method of moral deliberation that enables moral principles to be discoverable. In the way that Kuhn explains scientific laws are discovered through comparisons of paradigms, casuistry can be viewed as a process that illuminates and refines principles.

As John Arras explains, in casuistry "ethical principles are 'discovered' in the cases themselves, just as common law legal principles are developed in and through judicial decisions on particular legal cases" (Arras 1991, p. 30, 33). In this understanding, casuistry is not a top-down process from general concepts, but a theory-modest form of "articulated art" with principles having an "open texture" (Arras 1991, p. 29, 35; Jonsen, "Casuistry and Clinical Ethics," 1986, p. 71) and "always subject to further revision and articulation in light of new cases" (Arras 1991, p. 35). It is a process that, as Keenan maintains, "leads to the discovery of needed new moral insights, which include, among other expressions, the articulation of new principles" (Keenan 1995, p. 106). Put simply, through casuistry we discover moral principles rather than begin with them.

Whether casuistry eschews moral principles altogether or incorporates them in the manner described above is open to further discussion. What is clear is that there is a great deal of uncertainty about the casuistry-principles relationship and the prominence of principles and cases in each approach.

Chapter 5
Reflective Equilibrium and Casuistry

People are usually more convinced by reasons they discovered
themselves than by those found by others.

—attributed to Blaise Pascal

In its capacity to derive judgments from cumulative arguments, casuistry bears a strong resemblance to reflective equilibrium. In fact, Cass Sunstein goes so far to suggest that casuistic reasoning, "is a kind of crude, incomplete version" of reflective equilibrium (Sunstein 1993, p. 781).

In the following, we will see that casuistry and reflective equilibrium are similar but not identical processes of discovery and how the two have characteristics that enable them to make important distinctive contributions to moral decision-making.

Reflective Equilibrium

To begin, the term reflective equilibrium refers to the balanced state of beliefs derived through a deliberative process of mutual adjustments among general principles and particular judgments. Popularized by the political philosopher John Rawls, it is a coherentist process for justifying moral principles as well as a pragmatic method for achieving consensus in a pluralistic society (Rawls 1971, 1980; van der Burg and van Willigenburg 1998, p. 145). Its salient features can be distilled to those in Table 5.1.

Reflective equilibrium is typically described as narrow or wide. Narrow equilibrium is a balance of moral judgments that are acceptable to a given person/society/cluster of societies at a given time. Wide or broad equilibrium, on the other hand, accounts for the facts and functions of human nature beyond the realm of narrow reflective equilibrium. Let us explore the two.

Narrow Reflective Equilibrium

Narrow or traditional reflective equilibrium is reached by means of a coherentist method of explanation and justification. It begins with a society's considered moral judgments and then, as Kai Nielsen explains, "seeks to forge them into a consistent and

Table 5.1 Reflective Equilibrium's Characteristics

Introspective: examines society's or a cluster of societies' notions of right and wrong as well as the principles and background circumstances that govern moral actions
Reconciling: seeks to justify moral norms governing society or cluster of societies
Judgmental: strives for considered judgments or verdicts in which moral capacities are displayed without distortion
Ongoing and Self-correcting: new evidence stimulates adjustment of judgments
Conventional: articulates society's beliefs, does not challenge moral foundations
Consensus seeking: seeks a state of balance of views
Abstract: disassociated from any specific instance; concerned with beliefs, moral rules, and the verbal articulation of practices
Formative: modifies users' moral sensibilities
Kinds:
1) Narrow: seeks considered moral judgments acceptable to a given person/society/cluster of societies at a given time
2) Wide (broad): accounts for the facts and functions of human nature beyond the realm of narrow reflective equilibrium

coherent whole that squares with the other things that are reasonably believed and generally accepted in the society or cluster of societies in question" (Nielsen 1997, p. 546). Its goal, as Michael DePaul explains, is to construct a moral theory "by first screening one's initial moral judgments in order to eliminate those in which one lacks confidence, those formed on the basis of inadequate information and those influenced by biases such as self-interest, and then formulating a set of general principles which explicates the considered moral judgments which emerge from the screening process."[1]

As a method, narrow reflective equilibrium balances the various judgments under consideration through a process of ongoing self-examination, comparison, and revision in which there is a mutual adjustment of principles and judgments and where the moral capacities of the decision-makers are displayed without distortion (Rawls 1971, p. 20 f, 47). A back and forth process, the idea is to shuttle "between particular moral judgments, general principles, medium-level moral rules, and moral practices, modifying, where there is an incompatibility, one or the other, until we have gained what we have good reason to believe is the most consistent and coherent pattern achievable at the time" (Nielsen 1997, p. 546).

---

[1] (DePaul 1986, p. 59). Norman offers a more abstract explanation:

(Narrow reflective equilibrium) consists of an ordered pair of (a) a set of considered moral judgments acceptable to a given person P at a given time, and (b) a set of general moral principles that economically systematizes (a). The set of considered judgments (a) is pared down from a set of initial moral judgments in two stages. First it is pruned to eliminate judgments that P is not confident of, has made without adequate information about the situation, or has made in a state of mind conducive to moral error. Second, the resulting considered judgments are further adjusted to eliminate irregularities that may block fit with the most desired set of principles. Such principles not only must economically systematize the considered judgments that result from the first stage of pruning, but if possible should somewhat extend the set of acceptable considered judgments to include some about which the person was not so confident or found indeterminate. The resulting set (b) might then be taken to characterize the moral views held by P. (Daniels 1980, p. 22)

When the process is complete, there is a coherence of the moral beliefs, considered judgments about what is good and bad, principles, and relevant background circumstances. This is called narrow reflective equilibrium and it is not only a balance, but also a product of reflection because it weighs the principles, judgments, and so forth in seeking equilibrium among competing moral claims.

As an exercise in deliberation, narrow reflective equilibrium can be thought of as the result of a screening process in which initial moral judgments are examined to eliminate those that are weak, formed on the basis of inadequate information, or influenced by biases such as self-interest (DePaul 1986, p. 59). Joseph Raz explains the culling process as follows:

> (It) begins with a person who accepts many moral judgments of various degrees of generality. He is confronted by all possible sets of moral principles and the philosophical arguments for them. In the process of considering them he may or may not abandon some or all of his initial moral beliefs and he may or may not accept other moral beliefs. The process is at an end when all his considered moral judgments are adequately supported by a set of principles that he accepts in combination with his other beliefs. (Raz 1982, p. 308)

Narrow reflective equilibrium is a dynamic or ongoing sort of balance. While it may come to completion with balance (or "equilibrium"), it is easily upset with the introduction of new and challenging situations, judgments, or moral beliefs. When this occurs, the process begins anew. Thus, reflective equilibrium may be achieved, but it is not absolutely finalized.

Wide Reflective Equilibrium

Although the process above leading to reflective equilibrium facilitates narrow consensus, it does not always recognize the broader important aspects of moral judgments. Consequently, a more sophisticated or wide form of reflective equilibrium is needed to account for background theories that influence the society where reflective equilibrium is sought.[2]

The process leading to wide reflective equilibrium, just as in the narrow version, attempts to resolve such conflicts on the basis of the individuals' degree of commitment to a belief. Here, the goal is to try to find coherence among a broader set of background theories held dear by society (DePaul 1986). As Norman Daniels explains,

> (W)ide reflective equilibrium is an attempt to produce coherence in an ordered triple of sets of beliefs held by a particular person, namely, (a) a set of considered moral judgments, (b) a set of moral principles, and (c) a set of relevant background theories. We begin by collecting the person's initial moral judgments and filter them to include only those of which he is relatively confident and which have been made under conditions conducive to avoiding errors of judgment....We then propose alternative sets of moral principles that

---

[2] (Holmgren 1989). Put another way, these background theories constitute the "best corroborated social-scientific theories and theories of human nature, firmly established social and psychological facts, and political realities, such as the extent and intractability of pluralism in the society or cluster of societies where the reflective equilibrium is sought" (Nielsen 1997, p. 547).

have varying degrees of "fit" with the moral judgments. We do not simply settle for the best fit of principles with judgments, however, which would give us only a narrow equilibrium. Instead, we advance philosophical arguments intended to bring out the relative strengths and weaknesses of the alternative sets of principles (or competing moral conceptions). These arguments can be construed as inferences from some set of relevant background theories. (Daniels 1979, pp. 258–259)

Accordingly, an attempt to achieve wide equilibrium has people choose among alternatives on the basis of arguments that reveal the strengths and weaknesses of competing moral views. Balance is reached, as DePaul explains, "when the considered moral judgments, and moral and background theories one accepts are coherent and seem more likely to be correct to one than any alternatives one has considered" (DePaul 1986, p. 59).

Put another way, wide reflective equilibrium is the coherence that results after a wide range of inputs containing multiple background sources are brought together and balanced. Numerous adjustments are required to achieve such coherence.[3] In this way, the balance achieved at the end of the process is more robust than that of the narrow sort.

In sum, reflective equilibrium is the balance and coherence reached through a deliberative process of mutual adjustments among general principles and particular judgments. As Nielsen explains:

(It) is not a person's sense of justice or the ensemble of his considered moral judgments, but rather the conception of morality and the moral sensibility he has after such an examination. What is crucial to obtain is a match between these complex clusters of considerations and his considered judgments. When we have this we have attained reflective equilibrium. (Nielsen 1982, p. 291).

While the narrow version concentrates on the moral judgments acceptable to a given person/society/cluster of societies at a given time, it is overly specific. The wide

---

[3] (Daniels 1979, pp. 258–259). In regard to this description's lack of structure, Daniels asserts:

The background theories in (c) should show that the moral principles in (b) are more acceptable than alternative principles on grounds to some degree independent of (b)'s match with relevant considered moral judgments in (a). If they are not in the this way independently supported, then there seems to be no gain over the support the principles would have had in a corresponding narrow equilibrium, where there never was any appeal to (c). (Daniels 1979, pp. 258–259)

In a subsequent piece, Daniels explains the process of seeking wide reflective equilibrium in this way:

The task for the person seeking wide equilibrium is to choose between such alternatives on the basis of philosophical arguments which reveal the strengths and weaknesses of the competing moral conceptions. Such arguments may be viewed as inferences from a body of relevant theories. They may include, for example, a theory of the person, a theory of the role of morality in society, a body of general social theory, and so on. (Moreover, to) establish wide equilibrium, of course, he must adjust his set of initial considered judgments, and, in turn, make further adjustments in his set of principles or even in the relevant theories. The wide equilibrium can now be characterized as an ordered triple of (a), the considered moral judgments, (b), the moral principles, and (c), the set of relevant theories invoked or presupposed by the winning arguments for (b), all duly 'adjusted' to be compatible with each other. (Daniels 1980, p. 25)

version attempts to offset this shortcoming by accounting for the facts and functions of human nature beyond the realm of narrow reflective equilibrium. Together, narrow and wide reflective equilibrium manifest a coherence and balanced state of beliefs that reflects the consensus of a pluralistic society.

Reflective Equilibrium and Casuistry's Similarities and Differences

As the result of a deliberative process of mutual adjustments of particular judgments resulting in coherence and balance, reflective equilibrium has a great deal in common with casuistry. Even so, the two processes are not identical. In the following we will examine how they are similar and dissimilar.

Similarities

If we set reflective equilibrium next to casuistry, we see similarities (see Table 5.2).

First, casuistry and reflective equilibrium are similar in that both seek to establish balanced judgments. Both processes weigh sometimes-conflicting alternatives in an attempt to settle on optimal outcomes and in this way accommodate the fine points of various perspectives without becoming bogged down in the nuances of each theory or perspective. In the end, the two processes similarly reach defensible judgments.

Second, casuistry and reflective equilibrium use methods that are similarly introspective and attuned to society's (or a cluster of societies') moral sensibilities. In this way, both turn inward in search of society's norms, that is, to find what a particular society considers valuable, good and bad, and right and wrong. In short, both are alike in searching out society's "shoulds" or the cluster of society's beliefs, practices, and moral rules that it holds dear. In this way, the two are alike in looking inward to the moral sensibilities promulgated within a given culture.

Third, casuistry and reflective equilibrium use similar processes to render moral judgments. Both have limited scope and reach judgments that are not necessarily applicable to societies other than those under direct consideration. The processes of both consider other societies only insofar as they factor into the considerations at hand or bring forth new information that is useful. Casuistry and reflective equilibrium are in this way alike in being narrow rather than universal in scope and in rendering moral judgments that pertain to a particular society or cluster of societies and not necessarily to others.

Fourth, casuistry and reflective equilibrium use similar reconciliation processes to bridge the sometime-conflicting moral processes at work in a society. Both use methods that emphasize coming to balanced judgments. So, too, both encourage competing parties to recognize the overlap of their moral views. In these ways, the two encourage understanding and compromise—or at least broker a cease-fire in the quest for

Table 5.2 Similarities: Casuistry and Reflective Equilibrium

Balance-seeking: both processes weigh alternatives and seek an optimal outcome

Introspective: both processes look within a society or a cluster of societies to understand its moral sensibilities

Narrow application: both processes render moral judgments that pertain to a particular society or cluster of societies and not necessarily to others

Reconciling: both processes seek to justify moral judgments to their society or a cluster of societies

Multi-directional: both processes render moral judgments through a back and forth process of confirmation and elimination of ideas that accommodates and captures unexpected yet important elements of a decision

Complex: both processes avoid over simplification and the quest for epistemic certainty

Ongoing and self-correcting: both are dialogical processes that invite new evidence to stimulate adjustment of judgments

Conventional: both processes uphold society's or a cluster of societies' traditional beliefs

Cumulative: both processes sum up various arguments in making a final judgment

supremacy in the battle of ideas that often rages within society. They remind competing individuals and groups that they are parts of a whole, intimately interconnected, and cannot exist or be understood independently of that whole. Put another way, the two processes are alike in facilitating reconciliation among competing moral views and in bringing about a holism and sense of moral integrity that is beneficial to society.

Fifth, casuistry and reflective equilibrium use similar multi-directional methods to render moral judgments by means of back and forth processes of confirmation and elimination. Rather than proceeding in a linearly sequential top-down manner, the two derive judgments by moving in a multi-directional manner among the various principles, theories, and practices of society. As the elements collide and interrelate in this process, they confirm, combine, and expand some judgments while also rejecting and eliminating others. In this way, the two processes forge judgments similarly in a multi-directional way that accommodates and captures unexpected yet important elements of a decision.

Sixth, casuistry and reflective equilibrium use complex processes that are alike in avoiding simplistic techniques that are more concerned with achieving epistemic certainty than with resolving pressing moral problems. Although the two processes seem to meander aimlessly along a trail of random connections, modifying, accommodating, and rejecting solutions along the way, their wanderings are actually purposeful and capable of accommodating complexity in ways that simpler methods cannot. Casuistry and the processes leading to reflective equilibrium can achieve in this way a balance that is defensible, reflective of various sources, and more applicable to practical situations than approaches that strive for epistemic certainty above all else. In this way, the two methods are alike in placing applicability and breadth of accommodation over epistemic purity.

Seventh, casuistry and reflective equilibrium have similar dialogical processes that invite in new evidence to stimulate the adjustment of judgments. Both use open-ended methods to promote the exchange of ideas and opinions. In this way, both are conversational and invite new evidence into the discussion with the intention of revising judgments.

As dialogical processes, casuistry and the methods to achieve reflective equilibrium are broadly conversational in that they allow input from the various diverse members of a pluralistic society. In this way they are what Richard Lewis calls "multi-active" and "reactive" approaches because they invite in multiple and divergent views.[4] As such, they differ from the "linear-active" Cartesian and dialectical reasoning methods put forward by most modern western European ethicists. In these latter processes, reason is applied in a straightforward (linear), prescribed, and sequential fashion—not unlike Descartes' rationalist methods or the multi-stage thesis-antithesis-synthesis processes promoted by Marx and Engles.[5]

While casuistry and reflective equilibrium are not strictly multi-active or reactive per the Lewis model, they are circuitous as these methods are. Both use back and forth deliberation and disputation and allow for multiple inputs and ongoing revision by various sources in reaching judgments. Their outcomes are therefore more accommodating to various perspectives within a pluralistic society and they are more facile and ready to accommodate revision. In the end, casuistry and reflective equilibrium rely on similar methods that are multi-active/reactive and somewhat at odds with pervasive linear-active methods used in the western ethics.

Eighth, casuistry and the methods to achieve reflective equilibrium are similarly conventionally normative. Both turn to traditional morality for guidance and do not attempt to forge altogether new theories or challenge the existing moral foundations of society. Casuistry does this by beginning with the prevailing notions of right and wrong embedded in cases and case taxonomies. Similarly, processes leading to reflective equilibrium begin by appealing to the principles, theories, and so forth that people already accept. Both methods then, rely on conventional norms (the *status quo*) and tend not to overhaul traditional moral sensibilities.

---

[4] The terms linear-active, multi-active, and reactive pertain to cultural distinctions. They are described in full by (Lewis 1999, 2003) and applied variously in business contexts by (Andersen et al. 2009; Aramo-Immonen et al. 2011) and others.

Although Lewis uses the terms linear-active, multi-active, and reactive to describe the preferences of people as they are influenced by their cultures, the terms are useful for our purposes to describe orientations to ethical decision-making.

According to Lewis' theory, linear-active individuals tend to be punctual, patient, introverted, and quiet. They are task oriented, prefer to plan things, live according to a set schedule, and do one thing at a time. They are rational and produce the sort of arguments and ethics advanced by Descartes, Marx, and others of the western Enlightenment.

Multi-active people, in contrast, tend not to be punctual and to be impatient, extroverted, and talkative. They can be unpredictable, avoid timetables, do several things at once, and pull strings and seek favors to get ahead. Their argumentation tends to be more roundabout than that of the linear active types. Reactive individuals, the third sort, tend to be punctual, patient, introverted, and silent. They tend to be quiet and caring, respectful, people-oriented, and good listeners. They also tend to analyze the general principles of a situation and react accordingly. Even so, they are not strictly principle-based but value harmony. As a result, their ethics tends to accommodate consensus in ways that linear-active types do not.

[5] Dialectical reasoning was popularized by Karl Marx (1818–1883) and Friedrich Engels (1820–1895) and commonly attributed to Georg Wilhelm Friedrich Hegel (1770–1831). Some have questioned the Hegelian roots of it, however (Mueller 1958). Cartesian reasoning is sourced in "Father of Modern Philosophy" René Descartes' (1596–1650) rationalism. For more, see (Buroker 1992; Grosholz 1991).

Ninth, casuistry and reflective equilibrium use similar processes of cumulative argumentation when making judgments. In casuistry, various cases are brought in sequentially to rebut or support a particular judgment. The decision-maker refers to a taxonomy of cases and draws upon as many cases as possible to advance or refute a particular position.

Reflective equilibrium, in like fashion, is derived by means of processes that consider the multiple background circumstances that influence decisions (Rawls 1955, p. 120). Not unlike casuistry, the methods leading to reflective equilibrium have the decision-maker search "all possible descriptions to which one might plausibly conform one's judgments together with all relevant philosophical arguments for them" (Rawls 1955, p. 49).

In both processes then, the decision-maker gathers arguments from a variety of sources to form particular judgments and in this way uses cumulative arguments in making judgments.

Differences

Although casuistry and reflective equilibrium are similar, they are not identical. They differ in the ways highlighted in Table 5.3.

First, casuistry and reflective equilibrium are dissimilar in their orientations toward principles. Casuistry's proponents, we have seen, are divided on the place of principles in moral reasoning. Some hold that narratives should replace principles as deliberative instruments because narratives serve as better guides in practical moral decision-making contexts (Hauerwas 1983, pp. 380–381). Others retain a place for principles, arguing that casuistry can frame moral judgments in terms of rules or maxims that are general but not universal or invariable (Jonsen and Toulmin 1988, p. 257). In either case, principles do not have a prominent place in casuistry. Either they are dismissed entirely or accommodated minimally and indirectly.

Reflective equilibrium, in contrast, is strongly principle-oriented. As a coherentist process for justifying moral principles, the derivation of reflective equilibrium balances beliefs by means of mutual adjustments among general principles and particular judgments (Rawls 1971, 1980; van der Burg and van Willigenburg 1998, p. 145). Although complicated and thought by proponents to be a pragmatic way to realize consensus in a pluralistic society, the process to derive coherence in reflective equilibrium is highly principle-oriented.[6]

An example from Rawls' "veil of ignorance" shows why this is so. An imaginative device to establish the Kantian objective of pure reason, the veil establishes an "original position" wherein people are ignorant of their particular differences. In this place, they forge an unbiased theory of justice and in so doing produce rules of justice that are reflective, balanced, and principle-imbued. The rules (principles) derived there apply once the veil is lifted, have embedded in them principles of equal opportunity and equal liberty as well as the difference principle (Rawls 1958, 1971, 1980, 1985, 1993).

---

[6] Coherentism, in simple terms, holds a belief to be true to the extent that it is logically consistent with a system of other beliefs.

The veil of ignorance example shows how the methods to produce reflective equilibrium focus on principle-imbued theories in ways that differ substantially from casuistry's nearly exclusively case based methods. In the importance they place on principles then, the two processes are notably dissimilar.

Second, casuistry and the processes to derive reflective equilibrium rely on different instruments when making moral decisions. As we saw, casuistry's tools of choice are paradigmatic and marginal cases. These are used in a back and forth way to forge agreements about the best course of action. Very little or no reference is made to principles nor is the development of a comprehensive theory a driving concern in this approach. Instead, almost all arguments are derived through the use of settled cases.

Casuistry also relies on case taxonomies as instruments for deliberation. This means that it uses ordered arrangements of settled cases in making judgments. These ordered cases are located within more or less formal classifications, yet they are not rigid and unchanging.

The methods to reach reflective equilibrium, on the other hand, rely heavily upon models and hypothetical constructs. These heuristic models provide a way to reason in a back and forth manner to forge consensus about the moral principles and theories that should guide action generally. Details about particular situations matter secondarily if at all and almost all argumentation is derived by means of general principles and concepts that can be extended to apply if not universally, at least generally to situations.

In the choice of instruments used in moral decision-making and in their emphasis on orderly procedure, casuistry and the processes leading to reflective equilibrium are significantly dissimilar.

Third, casuistry and the processes to achieve reflective equilibrium differ in regard to the emphases they place on abstractions and the concrete. As a case-based method, casuistry remains grounded in the concrete details of identifiable situations. As such, casuistry focuses primarily on the immediate experience of actual things or events. It does not set out to establish an abstract ideal, although it can support ideals as it does in certain religious contexts. For the most part, however, casuistry accepts ideals, principles, theories, models, hypotheticals, and other abstractions insofar as these have informative value and relevance to practical deliberations.

The processes used to achieve reflective equilibrium, on the other hand, minimize the role of concrete situations and concentrate instead on the principles, theories, and other background material at work in situations. In this way they are more focused on abstractions than on the concrete.

Proponents of this approach maintain that ideas, principles, and other abstractions contain the necessary information to forge an overarching theory to which the members of a pluralistic society can assent. The processes therefore need to value abstractions and deemphasize the importance of the concrete and the particulars of identifiable situations.

While this may be the case, it nevertheless sets the reflective equilibrium derivative process at odds with casuistry and so in regard to the value that the two place upon abstractions and the concrete, casuistry and the processes to achieve reflective equilibrium can be said to differ.

Table 5.3 Differences: Casuistry and Reflective Equilibrium

Casuistry	Reflective Equilibrium
Weakly principled: principles in casuistry, if they apply at all, are general and not universal or invariable, holding only in the typical conditions of the agent and circumstances of action	*Strongly principled*: principles in reflective equilibrium are of primary importance since it is a coherentist process for justifying broad ethical concepts
Cases and taxonomies as tools: casuistry uses paradigmatic and marginal cases to make judgments, cases are arranged in taxonomies	*Heuristic models as tools*: methods to reach reflective equilibrium use hypothetical constructs to settle on moral principles and achieve consensus about moral theories
Concrete: casuistry remains grounded in the situation at hand	*Abstract*: reflective equilibrium is concerned with abstractions as a balance of abstract principles, theories, and other background material
Specific: casuistry uses cases having meaning to a particular society, where judgments hold in the typical conditions of the agent and circumstances of action	*General*: reflective equilibrium concentrates on general principles, theories, and other background material relevant to a society
Analogy as method: casuistry compares cases to each other and to the situation at hand in deriving judgments	*Analogy as instrumental*: methods to derive reflective equilibrium compare principles, moral beliefs, and background material to each other and to reality to establish coherence and validity
Goal of judgment: casuistry establishes actionable moral judgments	*Goal of balance*: reflective equilibrium is a harmony of concepts and does not make judgments nor delineate specific actions to be taken
Easy to use: ordinary people can use casuistry	*Difficult to use*: deriving reflective equilibrium requires facility with moral theory and usually requires the input of moral experts

Fourth, casuistry and the processes to achieve reflective equilibrium differ in terms of their emphases on specifics and generalities. While the subject of specifics-generalities seems similar to the concrete-abstraction subject matter of the last point, the two concepts here have different foci and breadths of interest that set them apart.

Because casuistry is a case-based form of moral reasoning, it focuses on the particulars rather than the generalities of situations. The breadth of its interest is therefore not sweeping, but concerned with detail. Generalities matter insofar as they impinge on the events or sentiments that might sway a judgment. Details, in contrast, are important because they provide the basis for direction and effective case use. They indicate the sort of case that might apply in a particular situation and suggest through their inter-relationships where cases fit in a case taxonomy. In this way, they serve to fully inform casuistic judgments.

In the processes leading to reflective equilibrium, the situation is different. Here, details are minimized and focus is directed toward generalities that are expressed in wide-ranging principles, theories, and other background materials. Unlike casuistry, the breadth of interest is less concerned with the details that inform local judgments than the derivation of general consensus that results in the formation of general principles and theories.

Again, Rawls shows in his hypothetical veil of ignorance how this can be accomplished. There, participants stand behind an imaginary veil that deprives them of information about their particular characteristics. In this position of ignorance (the so-called "original position"), they must devise a social contract that they agree they will uphold after the veil is lifted. As part of this exercise, participants are pulled away from the details of their particular circumstances and asked to focus on the formal qualities they will use to forge general principles and theories, in this case, a theory of justice.[7]

Because the process leading to reflective equilibrium draws attention away from particulars, it neither delineates nor prescribes how individuals should act in specific circumstances. As a result, it does not render particular judgments in the way that casuistry does. The orientation toward detail and generalities of the two processes are therefore at odds and makes them dissimilar in regard to another important element of ethics.

Fifth, casuistry and the processes to achieve reflective equilibrium differ in terms of their use of analogy.

Casuistry, as we have seen already, is a case-based method that uses cases for comparison purposes and so it is an analogical process at heart. The processes that develop reflective equilibrium, on the other hand, use analogy to establish coherence among abstract concepts (principles, theories, and so forth) and to validate principles and theories by comparing them to the facts at hand. In the end then, the two processes use analogy, but do so in very different ways.

Sixth, casuistry and the processes to achieve reflective equilibrium differ in terms of their goals. Casuistry's main objective is actionable judgments that pertain to particular circumstances, that is, defensible verdicts related to real life present situations.

The goal of the process to achieve reflective equilibrium, on the other hand, is to establish is a harmony of concepts. Reaching judgments and delineating the specific actions to be taken in particular situations is not the main objective. Put another way, casuistry and the process leading to reflective equilibrium differ not only in terms of the stress they place on particulars and generalities, but also in terms of the ends or goals they strive to achieve.

Seventh, casuistry and the processes to achieve reflective equilibrium differ in terms of their ease of use. Casuistry is an easy-to-use method of moral discernment accessible by ordinary people. It is relatively straightforward and relies on story telling, traditional narratives, and truth-bearing cases that are familiar to people within a particular culture. It also uses maxims and other rhetorical devices that people easily recognize and use to express themselves. Finally, it emphasizes prob-

---

[7] Rawls states, "The notion of the veil of ignorance is implicit, I think, in Kant's ethics." (Rawls 1971, pp. 140–141). In this construct, Rawls has us pull away from the particulars of a situation to consider the form or essence of the matter at hand. This is evident, for example, in his development of the "justice as fairness" argument. Here, behind the artifice of a "veil of ignorance," rational agents make decisions about the rules to govern society. The general idea is to withdraw from particulars so as to establish a hypothetical original position wherein "parties do not know certain kinds of particular facts" so as to make more objective decisions (Rawls 1971, p. 137).

ability rather than certainty in judgments, thereby minimizing the onus of mistakes and encouraging ordinary people to make moral judgments in real contexts.

Reflective equilibrium, in contrast, does not appeal very strongly to ordinary users. As a "coherentist method of explanation and justification used in ethical theory, social and political philosophy, philosophy of science, philosophy of mind, and epistemology," it is geared to so-called moral experts who find it helpful for getting at the formal aspects of reality (Nielsen 1997, p. 546). Ordinary people, in contrast, are likely to find the process to be excessively abstract, complicated, and foreign. The notion of going behind a hypothetical veil to become ignorant and then make moral judgments is likely to seem cumbersome and strange to ordinary people and more of a luxury for speculative academicians with a lot of time on their hands.

In terms of ease of use then, ordinary people are more likely to casuistry than processes to achieve reflective equilibrium because casuistry is more accessible, accommodating of particulars, and easier to use in everyday contexts than the processes to derive reflective equilibrium.

Weighing the Disparities

Given all of the above, it seems that Sunstein's observation about casuistic reasoning being a kind of crude, incomplete version of reflective equilibrium is not entirely accurate (Sunstein 1993, p. 781).

As we have seen, casuistry is a self-standing moral approach that is not derivative of twentieth century constructs such as Rawls'. If anything, the opposite of Sunstein's observation seems to hold true—that reflective equilibrium is an unsophisticated (crude) form of casuistry—a form of casuistry that has excised details, exaggerated abstractions and principles, and turned away from the core of ethics as something chiefly concerned with how one ought to act in actual circumstances.

We have seen, too, how the processes leading to reflective equilibrium do not handle the complexity of specific circumstances very well. While they grapple adequately with the abstract aspects of reality (the general moral principles, middle-level moral rules, theories, and so forth operating behind the scenes), they are not as good at handling the practical and particular whole of reality as it is played out in everyday contexts. Thus, while reflective equilibrium processes possess an attractive epistemic purity, they fail to measure up to casuistry in terms of relevancy in concrete real-life decision-making situations.

Overall, casuistry and the process that result in reflective equilibrium share certain features and appear to be identical, but on further inspection, the two are vastly different. While the process that results in reflective equilibrium has a certain formal purity, casuistry comes out on top as a method for moral deliberation in real contexts and is a more appropriate way to derive defensible moral judgments in pressing real world contexts.

Chapter 6
Criticisms of Casuistry

A bad carpenter quarrels with his tools
(Japanese: こうぼうふでをえらばず, Koukou fude o erabazu)
—Japanese proverb

The previous chapters illustrated how casuistry is useful in practical settings. Chapter 1 explained casuistry's features and how it was used in the past in some of the world's most sophisticated secular and religious societies. Subsequent chapters detailed important elements of the method and compared them with other methods to show how casuistry is a fuller and richer method than newer and more popular approaches.

The obvious question at this point is: "Why was casuistry disparaged and mostly abandoned as a moral method?"

The answer to this question is complex. In some cases the objections to casuistry were valid but in others, objections were little more than bad carpenters quarrelling with their tools. We turn to these differences next.

To begin, casuistry was disparaged and displaced as certain religions communities grew larger and authority structures became more organized. As both advanced, religious leaders became more powerful and imposed rules on followers that required them to turn to authority figures for moral interpretations. Islam's so-called "closing of the gates of *ijtihad*" that replaced the practice of independent moralizing with "rightful interpreters" in the form of priests and clerics is a good example of this trend.

Second, casuistry was disparaged and weakened by the relentless and scathing criticisms directed against it, especially by Blaise Pascal. Although his critiques were as politically motivated as they were theologically/ethically oriented, Pascal's "gotcha" style of humor and ability to target casuistry's propensity to be used to foster moral laxity had widespread appeal and eventually undermined casuistry's reputation. The effect can be measured by the fact that today the term "casuistry" is mostly regarded as a pejorative.

Third, casuistry was displaced by principle-heavy theories in much of rapidly secularizing Western Europe during the period of the Enlightenment. As Newtonian physics and the scientific method took hold, society became increasingly disposed

Table 6.1 Casuistry: Criticisms and Rebuttals

Criticism	Rebuttal
Aimless and lacking moral force: casuistry wanders from case to case, has no moral grounding	*Singularly goal-oriented*: casuistry maintains the heart of ethics and has a single goal of establishing defensible moral judgments in particular situations
Unstructured: casuistry applies cases arbitrarily according to users' whims	*Highly ordered*: casuistry relies on taxonomies, is highly ordered, makes logical case connections, and is directed toward a single goal
Conventional and insular: casuistry is hidebound and defaults to tradition and formal authority	*Provides identifiable touchstones for subcultures*: casuistry enforces moral standards in subcultures that reside in pluralistic societies
Relies on arbitrary taxonomies and paradigm cases: casuistry's taxonomy is not based on identifiable norms and it elevates cases to paradigm status based on users' self-interests	*Taxonomies and paradigmatic cases remain valid until disproven*: casuistry's case order and paradigmatic cases stand until they are rebutted and are therefore similar to the rules of science and moral principles
Highly subjective: casuistry's criteria for identifying problems, naming cases, and establishing patterns are relativistic	*Bias is on par with other methods*: casuistry is no more relativistic than other means of moral decision-making
Lax: casuistic reasoning can be slipshod and high jacked by the unscrupulous who are prone to equivocation	*Laxity pertains as much to moral principles as to moral cases*: to be unscrupulous is to be unprincipled and equivocation occurs when the unscrupulous violate the form and spirit of moral rules

to the use of rules in moral decision-making. People also began to turn to recognized experts for judgments, just as in science. Old methods such as casuistry came to be viewed as traditional and comparatively inferior—as antiquated and inadequate vestiges of the past—and were let go.

Fourth and perhaps most important, casuistry was attacked from all sides and eventually displaced by a myriad of small claims against it. Not only Pascal, but Protestant Reformists criticized it, charging casuistry with being aimless, unstructured, conventional and insular, lax, and dependent upon specious taxonomies and paradigm cases that were subjective.

Although many of the objections were overblown and unfair, casuistry's reputation suffered and it took a long time before it was able to surmount many of the charges to reemerge as a viable method for moral decision-making. Table 6.1 lists some of the criticisms levied against casuistry and the rebuttals to support it.

Aimless and Lacking Moral Force

One of the most stinging criticisms of casuistry is that it is aimless and bereft of the moral force necessary for good ethical decision-making. It is thought to have no preconceived goals and to wander from one case to another until its users simply decide to quit analyzing a problem. Compared to applied principles methods that attempt to establish clear ends—say the greatest good for the greatest number (utilitarianism) or some overarching principle to protect human dignity (deontology's Categorical Imperative)—casuistry seems vacuous and pointless.

While it is true that casuistry does not have the prescriptive objectives of top-down methods such as utilitarianism or deontology, casuistry as a bottom-up process does have one overarching goal, that is, to establish defensible judgments in particular situations. This end serves to give casuistry both its moral force and its purpose.

Casuistry has as its end the establishment of a straightforward answer to the central question of ethics—"What ought I/we to do in this matter?" It does not bother to establish comprehensive theories nor try to derive conclusions having absolute certainty. Rather, casuistry draws upon previously settled cases to develop a defensible judgment about a contentious matter at hand. In this way, it is not a process that is aimless but one that is both purposeful and morally relevant.

In short, although casuistry seems aimless, its goal is direct and purposeful. It focuses on establishing defensible judgments in particular situations and in this way exercises a moral force greater than its critics are willing to admit.

Unstructured

Casuistry is also thought to lack structure and be an arbitrary process where cases are applied in a willy-nilly fashion without much logic or attention to form. This shapelessness, critics maintain, makes casuistry easy to manipulate and leads to moral prevarication.

While it is true that casuistry can be used as a tool for prevarication, the charge that casuistry lacks logic and dynamism misunderstands the method.

In casuistry, cases are applied by means of analogy and identifiable taxonomies, which means that the method proceeds in a methodical and prescriptive manner. While the application of cases can be fast paced and seem to zigzag in an arbitrary way to the point of appearing chaotic, the proper use of cases in casuistry is well-ordered and advances according to a predetermined taxonomy with a functional dynamic that is systematic.

How so? Let us consider these in turn.

Casuistry's Logic and Dynamics

As a bottom-up deliberative method, casuistry makes comparisons using cases that are retrieved from an ordered arrangement and then applied in a sequential way according to fit and relevance. In this way, not any old case will do. Rather, cases are selected and used in a logical and predictable manner.

The logic and dynamism of the casuistic process is not unlike that of billiards. There, hitting a cue ball causes it to roll in a prescribed way toward another ball that is hit in turn. One ball imparts force onto the other to achieve an objective—sinking a ball in the pocket. The movement is both logical and predictable.

In similar manner, with casuistry one case imparts moral movement to other cases for the purpose of advancing an understanding of right and wrong in a particular situation. The cases, not unlike the balls on a billiards table, are tapped sequentially, with each new case imparting a force on previous cases to advance an understanding of the issue and to move subsequent discussion in a new direction. Just as in billiards where the goal is to sink the ball in a pocket, so in casuistry the casuist has an outcome (here, a moral judgment) in mind prior to acting.

The billiards table example reveals both the external and internal dynamics of casuistry—how cases impart movement to other cases (external dynamic) and how cases are selected at the outset (internal dynamic). Throughout, there is a shifting dynamic wherein, as Jonsen explains, there is "a shift in moral judgment between paradigm and analogous cases, so that one might say of the paradigm 'this is clearly wrong' and of the analogous case, 'but, in this case, what was done was justified, or excusable'."[1]

In addition, insofar as the casuist recognizes a place for principles and theories in moral decision-making, there is an ordered dynamic to how these are used. As we learned earlier, the force behind casuistry is located in cases, not in rules, principles, and theories and so the mechanical application of principles and so forth has less moral bearing than cases as they are brought to bear on decisions. Principles, moral theories, and so forth can sometimes influence judgments, but do so indirectly because casuistry maintains "an invariant pattern of reasoning in which certain claims are related to grounds, warrants, backing and modal qualifiers."[2] In other words, casuistry's structure demands that users remain focused on the particular circumstances at hand and this grounding in reality helps users avert the tendency to lapse into the realm of abstractions, "good ideas," or other distractions based on self-interest.[3]

In the end, what appears as aimless and haphazard in casuistry is just the opposite. Casuistry is a systematic method that is goal-directed, logical, coordinated,

---

[1] (Jonsen 1991, p. 303). In this passage, Jonsen is describing the kinetics (forces on things in motion) behind the case movements in casuistry.

[2] (Jonsen 1991, p. 99).

Here, Jonsen explains that "claims" are judgments that one should or should not perform a specific action, "grounds" are statements that set out the factual circumstances in which claims are made, "warrants" are maxims that justify claims in those circumstances, "backing" consists of the theoretical arguments that support warrants, and "modal qualifiers" are mitigating provisions.

[3] Even skeptics of casuistry admit this orientation is valid. As Tom Tomlinson points out:

(S)kepticism and relativism are easier in moral philosophy than in real life, because in real life one has to actually make decisions which are justifiable to oneself and which survive scrutiny by others. One needs to be able to provide persuasive reasons for a course of action. If the core content of those reasons is not moral principles, then perhaps it should instead be our settled convictions about actual cases (Tomlinson 1994, p. 7).

fluid, and multidirectional. It is both purposeful and orderly and the criticisms of casuistry lacking these attributes are therefore unwarranted.

Conventional and Insular

Casuistry is sometimes thought to be conventional, insular, narrow, and hidebound because of its ties to tradition. Unlike those who assert that casuistry is aimless and lax (see Pascal below, for example), here critics maintain that casuistry is too restrictive because of its associations with religious dogma and authority.[4]

The charge of casuistry's narrowness can be traced to the early years of Protestantism and the observation that the Jesuits of the Roman Catholic Church used casuistry so frequently. While casuistry as a method was not particularly Jesuit or Catholic, its heavy use by Catholic clergy left it vulnerable to suspicion in Protestant circles. Critics pointed to stalemate situations where conflicts concerning morality defaulted to Church dogma and individuals in positions of formal authority when casuistry was employed. Casuistry came to be seen as little more than an instrument of authoritarian religious hierarchies. Its cases were viewed as tools of oppression designed to support the traditions of the Church and its taxonomies as nothing more than graded assessments of instances of conformity or abridgment of established dogma.

The charges of casuistry being narrow, conventional, and insular are not just historical. They persist to today. As Arras points out, without outside critique, casuistry can become prone to ideological distortions, lack a critical edge, and "tend to ignore certain difficult but inescapable 'big questions' (e.g., "What kind of society do we want?")" (Arras 1991, p. 48).

Conventionalism in case-based reasoning is a problem because, as Tomlinson explains, it "provides no way by which the settled paradigms themselves might be challenged" (Tomlinson 1994, p. 14). It simply accepts cases, the common understanding of the morality underlying them, and their ordered ranking as a given and this uncritical acceptance can lead to poor judgments. In short, casuistry can simply provide an elaborate refinement of our intuitions and superstitions and "merely refine our prejudices" (Arras 1991, pp. 44–45).

Casuistry's penchant to refine prejudices might not matter much but for the fact that people now live in pluralistic societies and need to understand and tolerate each others' moral perspectives. While a particular casuistry can be beneficial to a narrowly defined culture, religion, or society, its normative foundation will not likely be more broadly accepted. Outsiders are likely to question its notions of truth, the depth of meaning it attributes to cases, and the motives it has for adopting certain cases over others. They might also challenge the bases of a particular casuistry's

---

[4] Citing J. P. Sommerville, Tomlinson makes a similar point: "the worst excesses of casuistry, pilloried by Pascal, were the result not of any belief in the flexibility of principle … but quite the reverse." (Tomlinson 1994, p. 12).

traditions, its authority figures, and other subjectively determined components of the group that sponsors a particular casuistry.

Because casuistry is associated with relatively narrow groups of people, it is difficult to establish common moral values, rankings, and an authority widely recognized as responsible for interpreting case-based judgments. As a result, as societies become more diverse, it is unlikely that a single casuistry can perdure. Rather, as Kevin Wildes observes, it is likely that there will be "many casuistries not just one" within pluralistic societies (Wildes 1993, p. 33).

Not surprisingly, casuistry's proponents refute some of these assertions. James Tallmon, for one, responds to the last point by maintaining that a particular casuistry need not be as narrow as Wildes and others imagine it to be. Tallmon argues that the content of the casuistry must be distinguished from the casuistic method *per se*. In his and others' view, the charge that casuistry is insular is not so much a problem with the method of casuistry as it is problem with narrowly defined communities. If casuistry is perceived to be insular, it is because it reflects the insularity of a specific culture, society, or cluster of societies. When such distinctions are made, the casuistic method may be deployed successfully in morally pluralistic contexts.[5]

Second, although casuistry defers at times to formal authority in certain stalemate situations, it is not clear that this is always the case. In fact, it is likely to be the exception because casuistry emphasizes the decision-making capacity of ordinary people and sidelines the need to defer to authority figures or moral experts when making judgments.

The inclination to turn to moral experts is actually more in line with principle-based approaches because there one must submit to the authority of principles and determining the exact requirements of these principles is not always easy for ordinary people to do. Moral "experts" are either called in or insert themselves in the process to become the arbiters of legitimate judgments. In the end, deference to formal authority is not so much a problem with casuistry as a method as it is a pervasive problem in moral decision-making.

Third, the charge that casuistry is conventional is likely nothing more than code for objections to casuistry being associated with religious dogma and tradition. As we saw earlier, all moral norms are essentially conventional in that they reflect the

---

[5] (Tallmon 1994, pp. 103–104). In response to Tallmon, Wildes, states:

If casuistry were viewed as a method of reasoning then one could imagine how it could be transferred from a particular community to the context of secular bioethics. However, an important difficulty for the Jonsen-Toulmin model, and Tallmon's support of it, is that one cannot have pure method in casuistry without a commitment to some content.

Furthermore:

(T)he method of casuistry, as a form of rhetoric requires some subject matter. There must be some background theory about the moral life that enables the casuists to identify paradigm cases, case description, or maxims. If one draws the distinction between method and contend too sharply one will have a method that is empty and formal and therefore not applicable to all.(Wildes 1994, p. 115, 116).

moral standards of their societies. Targeting casuistry on the basis of it being conventional is therefore not a problem for casuistry *per se*.

In sum, charges that casuistry is conventional and insular are weak because other moral approaches also reflect society's conventions. If there is a problem with casuistry, it is with how the method is used rather than the method itself.

As other methods can be, casuistry can be used to exclude, insulate, promulgate prejudice, and harm outsiders. It need not be used in these ways, however. As a tool, it can be used for good or ill. As Arras explains, for all its usefulness as a method, casuistry "is nothing more (and nothing less) than an 'engine of thought' that must receive *direction* from values, concepts and theories outside of itself" (Arras 1991, p. 41). Thus, we are wrong to blame the tool for its misuse. People, not the instruments they wield, bear responsibilities for any harm perpetrated through casuistry's use.

Arbitrary Taxonomies and Paradigmatic Cases

Casuistry's establishment of taxonomies and paradigm cases are sometimes a concern to those who consider casuistry's ordering and elevation of particular cases to prominence as arbitrary and biased in favor of users' self-interests. These charges are serious because the form and structure of casuistry rely on a reliable system of cases organized according to likeness and grounded in the clearest possible examples of right and wrong. Because casuistry depends upon reliable taxonomies grounded in accepted paradigm cases, should these be considered weak, biased, or otherwise unreliable, then casuistry itself is in trouble.

Let us consider the structure and dynamics of casuistry's taxonomies next.

The Structure and Dynamics of Casuistry's Taxonomies

Taxonomies are important to casuistry because, as Jonsen explains:

> A taxonomy makes clear that an instant case is not unique. It allows the differences between the instant case and the paradigm case to dictate the judgment about moral propriety. The judgment is based, not on a principle or a theory, but upon the way in which circumstances and maxims appear in the morphology of the case itself and in comparison with similar cases. (Jonsen 1991, p. 303)

As we saw earlier, a casuistic taxonomy can be thought of as a pyramidal ordering of cases having a diamond-shaped ◊ hierarchy, with paradigmatic cases at the top and bottom and a wide set of marginal cases in the middle. At the top and bottom of the taxonomy, moral consensus about cases of right and wrong prevails and as analogous cases emerge, differences accrue, similarities become less acute, and the middle cache of cases increases (spreads out per the diagram).

In practice, a casuistic taxonomy acts like a file system where the strongest analogous cases are drawn upon first and then the less obvious cases are selected. Jonsen explains the nature of the draw in terms of Athenian warfare where, just as a general "might place his strongest and most aggressive soldiers in the forefront of the battle line, so the casuist seeks out those cases, within the type, that demonstrate the most obviously, unarguably wrong (or right) instance" (Jonsen 1991, p. 301). The strong cases to which Jonsen refers are paradigm cases—those manifesting the clearest sort of understanding of right and wrong. Next, are so called marginal cases that contain qualifications and rebuttals of the strong cases. These moderate references to the paradigm case and move deliberation away from it toward another case or series of cases.

Insofar as the case file system is set up in a haphazard fashion, casuistry's taxonomy can be charged with being arbitrary. In most instances, however, the system is constructed carefully with pieces of the taxonomy (the cases in the file system) ordered in a logical fashion. This order severely undermines the charge that casuistic taxonomies are capricious.

In addition, because the system of ordering reflects the conventions of society and not the preferences of a narrow group of users, charges that case-based taxonomies are biased in favor of users' self-interests are weak. On both counts then, the charges against casuistry's taxonomies largely fail.

Subjective Naming of Paradigm Cases

The charge that the naming of paradigm cases is arbitrary is also weak because case nomination typically derives from the consensus of users, not the whims of individual casuists.

As we have seen with other concerns about casuistry, paradigm cases are normative because they reflect society's preferences. This does not eliminate the subjective qualities of the cases. To the contrary, as Alasdair MacIntyre explains, "how particular cases are to be described and what it is in a particular case that makes it right to describe it in one way rather than another" is up for grabs (MacIntyre 1990, p. 635).

The nomination of a case as a paradigm moreover is the result of judgments based on "unanalyzable perception" (Tomlinson 1994, p. 11). Even the criteria for naming cases as paradigm can be said to be subjective, for the criteria also rests on the patterns of recognition of observers.[6]

---

[6] Tom Tomlinson notes the problem of subjectivity regarding paradigm case selection when he states, "(T)he appeal to paradigm cases assumes that the proper ones have been selected for comparison, and in any contentious ethical question, where there are competing ethical considerations or "maxims", there will also be alternative sets of paradigm cases to which analogies can be drawn." (Tomlinson 1994, p. 13).

Loretta Kopelman concurs, stating, "(to reach agreement) about what cases to use as core cases, then, does not necessarily show that they *ought* to be agreed upon as core cases or illuminate

In Loretta Kopelman's view, such subjectivity creeps in because of the need to identify the relevant features at each stage in casuistic problem solving. Bias surfaces, for example, "in describing what we take the case to be, stating the problem exemplified, choosing the cases used for comparison, and identifying the paradigms we select."[7]

Given these issues, would it be better for casuistry not to have paradigm cases at all?

Although it is tempting to *not* delineate cases as paradigmatic, doing so would undermine the casuistic taxonomy and casuistry as a method of moral deliberation would be weakened. As Tomlinson explains:

> (D)etermining whether the problem case fits closely with a paradigmatically right or wrong action is an essential first step in understanding the nature of the moral issue it presents .... (P)aradigm cases may also serve as a source of moral sentiment, and it is by association with conflicting sets of them that new cases present problems to be solved, even if the paradigms don't themselves provide the solutions (Tomlinson 1994, p. 19).

Naming cases as paradigm is therefore both a requirement and a challenge for casuistry. While it is true that unambiguous illustrations of circumstances of right or wrong are rare, it should also be recalled that casuistry does not aspire to absolute certainty. Clarity itself is a subjective quality and while they are not perfect, some cases are clear enough to be helpful in anchoring casuistic deliberations.

Oddly enough, sometimes a commonly held unambiguous case turns out to be less than clear. The Ford Pinto case is just such a case.

From Paradigm to Marginal Case: The Ford Pinto Case

The Ford Pinto case has been a *de facto* paradigm case for decades. A dramatic product safety story, it was included for many years in top business ethics textbooks and had an effect on public policy and the common perception of certain sectors of

---

what they are core cases of. Moreover, agreement about core cases does not show what criteria should be used to adopt core cases, or solve the problem of how to deal with marginal cases." (Kopelman 1994, p. 30).

Finally, Joseph DeMarco points out the main problem with appeals to practical wisdom by methods such as casuistry in noting that such appeals give, "little indication about how such wisdom may be recognized or instilled." (DeMarco 1991, p. 22).

[7] (Kopelman 1994, p. 33).

Elsewhere Kopelman states, "we must use general views about what is relevant; but some of our general views are biased, both in the sense of being unwarranted inclinations and in the sense that they are one of many viable perspectives. This reliance upon general views to determine relevancy creates difficulties for defenders who maintain that case methods of moral reasoning are not only useful, but more basic, reliable or prior to other forms of moral reasoning." (Kopelman 1994, p. 21).

the automobile industry.[8] It generated public outrage, helped facilitate changes in auto design, spurred on new forms of safety legislation, and led to the founding of government oversight agencies. Today, most people believe the case to be a land-mark narrative about a company that knowingly designed and marketed a car with structural deficiencies.

The problem with the Pinto case, however, is that the story's simplicity general-izes a complex situation, which turns out to be not so unambiguously wrongful as the paradigmatic case would suggest. Why is this so?

The story of Ford's alleged malfeasance began with an article by journalist Mark Dowie entitled "Pinto Madness" in *Mother Jones* magazine (Dowie 1977). There, Dowie contended that the Pinto had unique safety problems that key decision-mak-ers knew about but decided to overlook because of their overwhelming concern with profits. Ford Motor Company employees had allegedly made an informed, cynical, and coordinated decisions to remunerate burn victims' families because doing so would be more cost-effective than improving the car's fuel tank integrity (Lee and Ermann 1999). Readers, subsequent journalists, and case writers were hor-rified at the revelation and disseminated the story through successive articles and cases. With the passage of time, the story became enshrined in public lore.

Years later, however, Matthew Lee and M. David Ermann uncovered evidence that Ford managers made no such malicious choice with the Pinto design (Lee and Ermann 1999). Rather, Pinto's problems began long before safety was an overrid-ing social concern and consumer protection laws were in place. Faulty design and moral blindness rather than malevolence were the key causes of the Pinto's prob-lems. More precisely, an embedded unreflective atmosphere in Ford led to slipshod decisions that resulted in the dissemination of poorly designed products that could eventually harm people.

Although the manufacture and distribution of a shoddy product that can severely harm its users does not relieve Ford of blame and censure, there was no clear deci-sion at Ford to market an unsafe product, just as there was no decision to market a safe one. The sad reality of the situation is that there was little intentionality at all on the part of Ford's decision makers. The amoral nature of their decisions was therefore not unambiguously malevolent. As a result, the Ford Pinto case fails as a paradigm case.

Even so, the case still has merit as a marginal case. For one, it is a good reminder about the dangers of unreflective action and how companies can be exposed to extraordinary risk due to unforeseen liabilities related to shifting social and moral norms. We will explore these problems in later chapters on risk management, but for now we can see with the Pinto how certain features of a seemingly benign product (a small and inexpensive car) can result in significant financial and reputational li-abilities for a company and its managers.

---

[8] For early accounts of this case, see (Buchholz 1989, pp. 167–169; De George 1993, pp. 130–137, 1999, pp. 240–241; Hoffman 1995, pp. 552–559; Velasquez 1998, pp. 71–72, 73–74, 76, 81–82, 119).

For a complete analysis of the various Ford Pinto cases, see (Werhane 1998, pp. 189–197).

In addition, the Ford Pinto case highlights the fragility of paradigm cases and how even the most black and white case can become susceptible to new evidence that undermines its clarity. If nothing else, the Ford Pinto case reveals how paradigm cases are rare and not established or maintained easily.

Third and related to the last point, the Ford Pinto case illustrates one of Kuhn's central tenets—that rules remain authoritative only until they are disproven. Not unlike scientific rules, paradigm cases remain valid only insofar as they stand the test of inspection and cohere with reality (Kuhn 1970, p. 43). If they do not, they are discarded or made marginal—effectively kicked down the taxonomy to a less relevant position as more suitable cases replace them. In this way, case displacement mimics the rule displacement of science and the principle displacement in applied principles approaches. In all instances, the objects (case, rule, or principle) are replaced as better alternatives based on new evidence invalidate them.

Fourth, the Ford Pinto case's displacement from the pinnacle of the casuistic taxonomy is not to be mourned because its dislodgement effectively allows clearer cases to ascend to the top position. This, in turn, sharpens subsequent deliberations because the new cases are anchored more firmly in fact. Casuistry as a method is in this way purified and strengthened by tests that assure that paradigm cases are as close as possible to being clear-cut.

In the end, the Ford Pinto case shows that the nomination of paradigm cases is not arbitrary, but well considered and validated by comparisons to reality. It illustrates how paradigm cases, just as moral principles and the rules of science, are robust insofar as they stand up to inquiry and factual analysis and how, when they fail to measure up, they are either made marginal or discarded altogether.

Lax and Prone to Equivocation

Although critics have had longstanding concerns about casuistry's subjective propensities, their greatest concern has been casuistry's ability to facilitate moral equivocation and laxity. As we will see, Pascal used these charges to great success in his attempt to discredit his Jesuit foes and their casuistry. We turn to moral equivocation in regard to casuistry next.

A) Catholic Concerns with Casuistic Caginess: Blaise Pascal versus The Jesuits

To begin, equivocation is a form of evasion wherein one makes statements that are not literally false but cleverly avoid unpleasant truths. Equivocation has always been a problem in moralizing but was targeted as a special concern in Catholic Christendom during the era of high casuistry (1556–1656) when the opponents of casuistry's chief advocates, the Jesuits, highlighted it.

As we saw in Jonsen's comments in Chapter 1, the attacks against casuistry during its high era time were three-fold. They included the stinging critiques of Blaise Pascal's *The Provincial Letters* (French: *Lettres Provincials*), the dismissal of casuistry by mainstream post-Enlightenment moral philosophers, and the political antipathy directed toward its chief proponents, the Jesuits (Jonsen 1993, p. 56, 59, 62–63).

The first of these attacks, Pascal's highly popular and humorous *The Provincial Letters* were especially damaging to casuistry. Through these treatises, Pascal focused on instances of equivocation using casuistry to alert both the laity and the Church hierarchy to improprieties occurring within the Church.

The post-Reformation Catholic Church especially frowned upon equivocation and skepticism because of laxity's capacity to undermine lay confidence in the Church's sacramental (confessional) practices. Pascal, a highly conservative Catholic in the tradition of St. Augustine, was keen to protect the Church from what he saw as a human propensity to perversion.[9] Toward this end and as the following illustrates, Pascal lambasted the proponents of casuistry for sloppy case-based moralizing:

> If I had merely to reply to the three remaining charges on the subject of homicide, there would be no need for a long discourse, and you will see them refuted presently in a few words; but as I think it of much more importance to inspire the public with a horror at your opinions on this subject than to justify the fidelity of my quotations, I shall be obliged to devote the greater part of this letter to the refutation of your maxims, to show you how far you have departed from the sentiments of the Church and even of nature itself. The permissions of murder, which you have granted in such a variety of cases, render it very apparent, that you have so far forgotten the law of God, and quenched the light of nature, as to require to be remanded to the simplest principles of religion and of common sense. (Pascal 1941, *The Provincial Letters—Letter XIV*, 1999)

These sentiments are echoed in the following passage:

> Who, then, has given you a right to say, as Molina, Reginald, Filiutius, Escobar, Lessius, and others among you, have said, "that it is lawful to kill the man who offers to strike us a blow"? or, "that it is lawful to take the life of one who means to insult us, by the common consent of all the casuists," as Lessius says. By what authority do you, who are mere private individuals, confer upon other private individuals, not excepting clergymen, this right of killing and slaying? And how dare you usurp the power of life and death, which belongs essentially to none but God, and which is the most glorious mark of sovereign authority?" (Pascal 1941, *The Provincial Letters—Letter XIV*, 1999)

Jesuit casuists were especially prone to Pascal's challenges of moral laxity when they confused their role as pastor/confessors with their role as educator/theologians. On the one hand, as priests, pastors, and confessors, the Jesuits were charged with helping people discern important personal moral matters. On the other hand, as educators and theologians they were expected to act as responsible interpreters of

---

[9] Pascal disdained, for example, the sort of reasoning that attempts to avoid falsehood by swearing aloud, "I have not done that" only to "add in a low voice" "to day…(so) that this you perceive is the truth" (Pascal 1656).

the fine points of the Church's moral positions.[10] When Jesuits extended their pastoral duties beyond the confessional, especially when they weighed moral principles against their own concepts of the greater good of the individual (penitent), they sometimes made judgments that were at odds with the general tenets of the Church. At other times, the objectives of the two roles were unclear to the practitioners. In either case, they ran afoul of the norms of the Church.

To complicate matters further, Jesuit casuists often relied on probablism when attempting to resolve moral problems. Probablism—a doctrine that holds that moral certainty is impossible and that probability suffices in some circumstances—was especially risky because it allowed for leniency in moral judgments. It could allow, for example, that in situations where it was difficult to determine whether or not a moral rule held, that an opinion favoring free choice might be followed if that opinion commended itself to judicious minds or could be supported by authority.

Using this form of moral reasoning, Jesuit casuists sometimes got wrapped up in the details of moral laws and lost sight of the basic tenets of morality. In these instances, prevarication was not due so much to a disregard for moral norms as it was related to a dogged determination to maintain the appearance of adhering to the fine points of rules while finding exceptions to them. Casuists nitpicked and searched for loopholes in a drive to adhere to the letter of the law and in the end, drew conclusions that conformed to moral law but appeared cagey, self-interested, and hypocritical to outsiders.

Of course, some of the casuists of this era used any means they could find to dismiss moral rules that they found inconvenient. Others were simply dimwitted and equivocated because they did not know how to resolve moral problems well. In these instances (and there is little evidence to suggest how prevalent they were), simple corruption and ignorance were the problems.

Regardless of their reasons, Jesuit casuists appeared to be duplicitous and unwise—and Pascal made certain to highlight their foolishness. His onslaught of ridicule led to questions regarding the Jesuits' competency and propriety and because they were clerics holding positions of the authority in the Church, Pascal's questions stirred up calls for Church investigation.

Throughout this period, Pascal fueled his charges by means of humorous writings that appealed to a wide audience. Although doing so extended his fame, Pascal was not out to win a popularity contest. Rather, his objective was to cut down the influence of the Jesuits whom he considered too powerful within the Catholic Church. In his view, the Jesuits were "too politic," a "shrewd class of people," and "enemies of the Gospel"—and he felt obliged, for the sake of all pious persons, "to bring out that grand secret of (the Jesuits') policy" (Pascal, *The Provincial Letters—Letter II January 29, 1656*, 1999, *The Provincial Letters—Letter XV: To the Reverend Fathers, The Jesuits, November 25, 1656*, 1999). In his own words, Pascal designed to:

> (N)ot simply to show that your (the Jesuits') writings are full of calumnies; I mean to go a step beyond this. It is quite possible for a person to say a number of false things believing them to be true; but the character of a liar implies the intention to tell lies. Now I undertake

---

[10] For more, see (Jonsen and Toulmin 1988, p. 161, 164–175).

to prove, fathers, that it is your deliberate intention to tell lies, and that it is both knowingly and purposely that you load your opponents with crimes of which you know them to be innocent, because you believe that you may do so without falling from a state of grace. Though you doubtless know this point of your morality as well as I do, this need not prevent me from telling you about it; which I shall do, were it for no other purpose than to convince all men of its existence, by showing them that I can maintain it to your face, while you cannot have the assurance to disavow it, without confirming, by that very disavowment, the charge which I bring against you. The doctrine to which I allude is so common in your schools that you have maintained it not only in your books, but, such is your assurance, even in your public theses".(Pascal, *The Provincial Letters—Letter XV: To the Reverend Fathers, The Jesuits, November 25, 1656,* 1999)

The Jesuits were also Pascal's targets because they were central players in a larger Port-Royal Jansenist versus Jesuit dispute about Eucharistic practices that Pascal, a committed Jansenist, found unnerving.[11] Because the Jesuits were on the opposite side of a conflict of high importance to him, Pascal would use his talent to attack the Jesuits and their casuistry. He honed in on their equivocation with venom and his charges eventually led to theological debates within the Church. Subsequent papal decrees condemned certain individuals and their laxity and had the overall effect of dampening casuistry's use. Even so, the charges "could not destroy the plausibility of "case analysis" as an approach to the resolution of moral problems."[12]

In the end, the Jesuits won the theological dispute against Pascal's Jansenists—discrediting and disempowering the group and its theology—but Pascal managed to effectively damage the Jesuits' reputation and sully casuistry as a form of moral

---

[11] In essence, the Jansenist-Jesuit dispute concerned the role of grace (efficacious and sufficient) in salvation. Pascal summarizes the dispute in the following passage:

In one word, then, I found that their difference about sufficient grace may be defined thus: The Jesuits maintain that there is a grace given generally to all men, subject in such a way to free-will that the will renders it efficacious or inefficacious at its pleasure, without any additional aid from God and without wanting anything on his part in order to act effectively; and hence they term this grace sufficient, because it suffices of itself for action. The Jansenists, on the other hand, will not allow that any grace is actually sufficient which is not also efficacious; that is, that all those kinds of grace which do not determine the will to act effectively are insufficient for action; for they hold that a man can never act without efficacious grace.

Such are the points in debate between the Jesuits and the Jansenists; and my next object was to ascertain the doctrine of the New Thomists. "It is rather an odd one," he said; "they agree with the Jesuits in admitting a sufficient grace given to all men; but they maintain, at the same time, that no man can act with this grace alone, but that, in order to do this, he must receive from God an efficacious grace which really determines his will to the action, and which God does not grant to all men." "So that, according to this doctrine," said I, "this grace is sufficient without being sufficient." "Exactly so," he replied; "for if it suffices, there is no need of anything more for acting; and if it does not suffice, why- it is not sufficient." (Pascal, *The Provincial Letters—Letter II January 29, 1656,* 1999).

[12] (Jonsen and Toulmin 1988, p. 249). See, too (Jonsen, "Casuistry," 1986, p. 79).

deliberation. Pascal lost the larger religious war but won the battle against the Jesuits and casuistry.[13]

B) Protestantism Chimes In: Concerns with Casuistry's Link to Authority

Lutherans and Calvinists followed Pascal in criticizing casuistry and the Jesuits, but for reasons other than Pascal's. As Protestants, they disliked casuistry because of its roots in the confessional practices that, in their view, undermined the fundamentals of faith. In addition, they despised Jesuits as "malevolent and crafty agents of the pope" (Jonsen 1993, p. 62).

Anglicans, for their part, not only held these typical Protestant views about Roman Catholics and Jesuits, but were increasingly suspicious that their own casuists were equivocating as well (Jonsen 1993, p. 63). Although Anglican opposition to moral laxity was similar to that of the Catholics', Anglican dispositions to equivocation were unique. As Wenley explains:

> Anglo-Catholics would probably admit that, on the whole question of casuistry in morals, they have been too dependent upon Roman sources. For, consonant with the English, as contrasted with the Latin, temperament, they incline to deal as simply and plainly as possible with the issues raised, avoiding too curious subtleties. (Wenley 1911, p. 246)

Such widespread and varied opposition to casuistry within Christendom served to make for strange bedfellows. According to Jonsen, "(T)hose who embrace(d) a strict moral regimen dislike(d casuistry) because it…loosen(ed) obligations by clever reasoning. Those who favor(ed) liberty dislike(d) it because it can by punctilious logic, pull the strings of obligation tighter and cut off the flow of inspiration" (Jonsen 1993, p. 59).

Despite such differences, by working against casuistry from multiple fronts, Catholic and Protestant forces combined to make a potent and lasting force against it such that, at present, both "casuistic" and "Jesuitical" are regarded as pejoratives.

---

[13] Pascal capitulates, stating:

Reverend Sir,

If I have caused you some dissatisfaction, in former Letters, by my endeavours to establish the innocence of those whom you were labouring to asperse, I shall afford you pleasure in the present by making you acquainted with the sufferings which you have inflicted upon them. Be comforted, my good father, the objects of your enmity are in distress! And if the Reverend the Bishops should be induced to carry out, in their respective dioceses, the advice you have given them, to cause to be subscribed and sworn a certain matter of fact, which is, in itself, not credible, and which it cannot be obligatory upon any one to believe- you will indeed succeed in plunging your opponents to the depth of sorrow, at witnessing the Church brought into so abject a condition.

(Pascal, *The Provincial Letters—Fragment of a Letter XIX Addressed to Father Annat*, 1999). See also (Jonsen and Toulmin 1988, pp. 231–249)

Equivocation in Principle-Based Methods: Bill Clinton versus the American People

Although Pascal, the Protestants, and others made casuistic prevarication central to their attacks, the dubious judgments they highlighted could have been derived just as readily by other means, including highly respected principle-based methods. Casuistry, in short, was not the problem. Rather, duplicitous people used casuistry for their own devious purposes. They could have used any number of other means, but chose casuistry at this time in history.

Today, casuistry has been displaced by legalism and principles-based approaches by the less-than-honest.[14] Consider, for example, former American President William J. (Bill) Clinton's equivocation in a nationally televised speech on January 26, 1998, the day before his State of the Union address. There, at the end of his speech, Clinton spoke about his relationship with an intern named Monica Lewinsky. He pointed his finger at the camera and said:

> I want to say one thing to the American people. I want you to listen to me. I'm going to say this again. I did not have sexual relations with that woman, Miss Lewinsky. I never told anybody to lie, not a single time—never. These allegations are false. (Clinton, *Response to the Lewinsky Allegations (January 26, 1998)*, 1998)

Clinton made similar claims throughout the U.S. House of Representatives Committee on the Judiciary hearings of 1998. When pressed about conflicting statements, he typically quibbled about the fine points of words—even the meaning of the word "is."[15]

In an attempt to defend him, Special Counsel to the President Gregory Craig explained on December 8, 1998 that while defining simple words such as "is" might seem to be "a hair splitting evasive answer," in Clinton's mind there were important contextual differences in words, especially those related to sex acts.[16] Moreover, in

---

[14] Legalism in both the theological and secular sense, is the strict adherence to the law, with special attention given to the letter of the law rather than its spirit.

[15] In his testimony to the House of Representatives' Committee on the Judiciary in response to a question about whether or not Monica Lewinsky's statement that there was "no sex of any kind in any manner, shape or form, with President Clinton," was an utterly false statement, Clinton answered: "It depends on what the meaning of the word 'is' is. If the—if he—if "is" means is and never has been, that is not—that is one thing. If it means there is none, that was a completely true statement....Now, if someone had asked me on that day, are you having any kind of sexual relations with Ms. Lewinsky, that is, asked me a question in the present tense, I would have said no. And it would have been completely true." (Office of the Independent Counsel 1998).

[16] In answer to Rep. Bob Inglis' question "Did he lie to the American people when he said "I never had sex with that woman?" Gregory Craig said: "what he (Clinton) said, is that he did not have sexual relations and I understand you're not gonna like this, Congressman, because you will see it as a hair splitting evasive answer, but in his own mind his definition was not..." Inglis: "ok, I understand that argument..."(Sandel 2011, 16:54).

a written statement to the Committee, Clinton's attorneys pressed the distinctions between an ethical abuse and a legal violation.[17]

After hearing all the arguments, the Committee did not buy Clinton's argument and judged his prevarications to be part of an ongoing attempt to mislead. Because he violated a sworn oath at the advance of the proceedings "...to tell the truth, the whole truth, and nothing but the truth," Clinton was impeached on two charges, one of perjury and one of obstruction of justice.[18] He managed to avoid removal from office, however, when the Senate acquitted him on February 12, 1999.[19]

While the Clinton legal proceedings and political posturing were interesting on their own, the moral aspects of Clinton's position are more relevant for our purposes. Throughout the ordeal, Clinton never admitted to lying or encouraging others to lie on his behalf. Moreover, in his personal apology at the beginning of his lawyers' December 1998 written statement to the House Committee, he admitted to ethical but not legal wrongdoing. He confessed to abridging his religious beliefs ("I have sinned") and misleading his wife, his friends, and the Nation about the nature of his relationship with Ms. Lewinsky—but he insisted that he did not lie (Kendall and others 1998, Preface).

---

[17] (Kendall et al. 1998, Preface). In full:

> PREFACE In addition to the factual, legal and Constitutional defenses we present in this document, the President has asked us to convey a personal note: What the President did was wrong. As the President himself has said, publicly and painfully, "there is no fancy way to say that I have sinned."
>
> The President has insisted that no legalities be allowed to obscure the simple moral truth that his behavior in this matter was wrong; that he misled his wife, his friends and our Nation about the nature of his relationship with Ms. Lewinsky. He did not want anyone to know about his personal wrongdoing. But he does want everyone—the Committee, the Congress and the country—to know that he is profoundly sorry for the wrongs he has committed and for the pain he has caused his family, his friends, and our nation.
>
> But as attorneys representing the President in a legal and Constitutional proceeding, we are duty-bound to draw a distinction between immoral conduct and illegal or impeachable acts. And just as no fancy language can obscure the fact that what the President did was morally wrong, no amount of rhetoric can change the legal reality that the record before this Committee does not justify charges of criminal conduct or impeachable offenses.
>
> The Framers, in their wisdom, left this Body the solemn obligation of determining not what is sinful, but rather what is impeachable. The President has not sugar-coated the reality of his wrongdoing. Neither should the Committee ignore the high standards of the Constitution to overturn a national election and to impeach a President.

[18] The full rendering of the United States of America Solemn Oath states, "Do you solemnly swear or affirm that you will tell the truth, the whole truth, and nothing but the truth, so help you God?"

[19] Impeachment is a fundamental constitutional power belonging to Congress and a two-stage process that begins in the House of Representatives with a public inquiry into allegations and culminates with a trial in the Senate. It can be traced to ancient Greece and English Common Law and is reserved for grave offenses such as perjury—which is the deliberate and willful giving of false, misleading, or incomplete testimony after he or she has taken an oath to speak the truth.

Throughout his testimony, Clinton made legal distinctions based upon the fine points of the law, which brings up the interesting question: "Is there is a difference between an outright lie and a misleading truth from a moral perspective?"

In his televised "Justice" course, Michael Sandel poses just this question to a large group of students after they have engaged in a lengthy consideration of Immanuel Kant's Categorical Imperative and seen Clinton's testimony. The students use Kant's arguments to point out the difference between the unacceptability of a lie that violates the formal aspects of a rule about telling the truth as well as the acceptance of a misleading truth that retains the formal integrity of the truth telling mandate while deceiving others. In this way, the students reveal that they recognize that while the misleading truth and the lie have the same consequence, the motive behind the misleading truth acknowledges the duty to adhere to the formal aspects of truth telling whereas the outright lie does not.

The students then extend these ideas to show that Clinton did not necessarily violate the formal aspects of moral law as set out in Kant's absolutist deontology even though he effectively misled people.

Even so, as the students grind through their analyses, television cameras capture them giggling as Clinton obfuscates. As various members of the class present points of morality related to the case, they titter through what would otherwise be a serious discussion. This begs the question: "What is so funny?"

Student snickering seems to reveal a couple of important but unspoken aspects about the case related to truth telling. The intimate and embarrassing nature of the subject matter of the testimony is one factor, of course. Another is that people seem to have a timeless ability to spot duplicity when they encounter it. Put simply, twenty-first century Harvard students reflect a society ill at ease with this sort of subject matter and take perverse delight in witnessing a deceiver squirm when his prevarications are uncovered and held before him. In this latter sense, they are no different than the French provincial readers of Pascal's *Provincial Letters*.

What is interesting in all of this—especially the comparisons of Clinton to high era casuists—is the timelessness of the prevarication of those in positions of power. What is important for our purposes, however, is the way such duplicity is located in the perpetrator and not in the moral method *per se*. In the seveteenth century, casuistry was the scoundrel's method of choice. Today it is legalism and principle-based methods. In both, the method is merely a tool to deceive.

In the end, people and not the moral method are the source of equivocation because people can find loopholes in any moral method set before them. Jonsen and Toulmin say as much when they argue that it was not casuistry *per se* but the abuse of casuistry that led to moral laxity and casuistry's bad reputation (Jonsen and Toulmin 1988). That moralists of an earlier time chose to misuse casuistry rather than the rule-based methods that they misuse today is a matter of historical preference. Casuistry was and is not the source of prevarication…people are.

Modern Trends Toward Other Approaches

Finally, mainstream post-Enlightenment moral philosophers also rejected casuistry because they considered it to be at odds with the scientific processes they were trying to extend from the physical sciences to the moral realm.

The New Language of Modernity

Not surprisingly, Pascal was a member of this cohort by virtue of his being a prominent mathematician. He was unusual, however, in having the rare ability to frame his objections to casuistry in both the "religious-speak" of his Christian faith and the empirical language of his Enlightenment peers. These communication skills are clearly apparent in his following comments about casuistry's inability to uphold common moral principles:

> What a subversion of all principle is here, fathers! And who does not see to what atrocious excesses it may lead? It is obvious, indeed, that it will ultimately lead to the commission of murder for the most trifling things imaginable, when one's honour is considered to be staked for their preservation—murder, I venture to say, even *for an apple*! (Pascal 1941, *The Provincial Letters—Letter XIV*, 1999).

Aside from Pascal's objections to casuistry, modern philosophers tended to dislike casuistry for its lack of precision. Casuistry seemed "too disorganized, cluttered with maxims and definitions and distinctions, too probabilistic and prudential" for their tastes (Jonsen 1993, p. 59). In contrast to the pithy and precise rules of modern science, casuistry's methods seemed roundabout, antiquated, imprecise, unnecessarily fallible, and inconclusive. Worse, casuistry contained traces of tradition and religion. Modern philosophers could not tolerate these elements of religious-based morality because they were grounded in faith, which was unacceptable because belief could not be analyzed and verified.

As the Enlightenment movement expanded, so did the objections to casuistry such that it eventually became marginalized and replaced with principle-based methods. These latter methods placed greater emphasis upon rules, laws, and legal compliance monitored by institutions.

The Conflation of Ethics and Law

During the modern era there was a growing trend to conflate ethics and law and to accept the notion that law suffices to define ethics. In short, people began to think that if something was legal it was also ethical.

As many actionable elements of ethics were distilled to law, demands for compliance became more common. Today, this is evident in the ethics and compliance offices of many businesses. There, personnel target issues that are relevant to the organization and set up programs to disseminate ethics information. They also monitor adherence, make sure the information is integrated and coordinated throughout the organization, and retain documentation should the organization be challenged by outside agencies.

In addition, the advancement of ethics programs in this way provided new avenues to advance the competitive advantage of companies. Now they could not just stay within the laws and ethical customs of society, but could also demonstrate their ethical compliance for marketing purposes. Organizations could boast that they were now more ethical than they had been in the past and more socially responsible than their competitors.

The transformation of ethics in this way drew new attention to ethics, but led to some unforeseen problems. First, it aggravated the notion that ethics and law are identical—that what is ethical is what is legal. This perception led to ongoing concerns with legal compliance within every area of business. Ethics became more instrumental than guiding, something to caution rather than inspire. We will see how this plays out in risk management in the final Part of this book.

Second, the increased emphasis on law led to more quibbling about the fine points of formal adherence to rules. As ethics and law combined, certain elements of society became disposed to overlook notions of right and wrong in favor of strict adherence to law. For the most part, this trend provided helpful boundaries for people (especially businesses), but it also provided dangerous loopholes for rogues.

As the trend spread more widely to all elements of society, it reached the highest reaches of politics and society was faced with the most significant shortcoming of the conflation of ethics and law—a dangerous new form of equivocation.

The aforementioned Bill Clinton case is a good example of equivocation in terms of the formal elements of rules and laws. In this case, had the fine points of the rule of law not dominated discussions, the abridgment of ethics (misleading others) might not have been so readily overshadowed by arguments about how the President's acts were in conformity with the law's formal requirements. The consequences of misleading others, the general dismissal of right and wrong, the abridgment of the spirit of the law ("to tell the whole truth"), and so forth would have had more prominence in the Congressional hearings. Although the prevarication was eventually recognized in the judgment to impeach, the important point about the case for us is how legalism and the emphasis on law nearly eclipsed the larger ethical aspects of the case.

Third, the conflation of ethics and law and the institutionalization of ethics have led to greater acceptance of the notion that ethics is somebody else's problem (here, rule makers and ethics offices). With ethics' institutionalization, individuals have reason to act as if they merely need to comply with the rules established by someone else to remain ethical. Ethical responsibility is now someone else's problem and not the individual's concern. This leads to a general disassociation of the individual and a coarsening of the ethical environment of society.

Fourth, the conflation of ethics and law has led to a de-emphasis on the aspirational aspects of ethics. Discussions about the ways individuals might become "better" or more ethical within the context of their work become less pressing as people become preoccupied with ethics programs, ethical climate surveys, discussions about how to remain within compliance with laws and emerging social norms, and so forth. Academics, for their part, find that their normative considerations of "the good" are dismissed, but that empirical studies about the effectiveness of organizational norms on employee behavior are well received.[20] As a result, the big picture of morality, discussions about right and wrong, and other day-to-day aspirational aspects of ethics are overshadowed by compliance.

In the end, as ethics and law became more intertwined and compliance came to dominate ethical discourse, many of Pascal's and post-Enlightenment Reformists' criticisms found new relevance elsewhere. In the past, casuistry was the medium for equivocation. Today it is legalism.

As Jonsen and Toulmin have shown, in an earlier era casuistry was not the problem as people used it for dubious ends. Rather, it was the duplicitous and malevolent people who used casuistry as their tool of choice who were to blame. Casuistry was merely a tool that was badly misused ("abused") (Jonsen and Toulmin 1988). Today, the preferred instruments are rules and laws—and these are being manipulated ("abused") by the unscrupulous just as effectively as casuistry was in the past.

---

[20] For a good example, see (Treviño and Weaver 2001).

Chapter 7
Casuistry's Revival in Medicine and Now, Business

History doesn't repeat itself—at best it sometimes rhymes.
—attributed to Mark Twain

Discredited but not discarded, casuistry languished for centuries while analytic philosophical methods grew in prominence during the modern and contemporary eras. Interest in casuistry began to spark then gain momentum in the late twentieth century, however, as ethicists in specialty fields began to use it in problem solving. The timing and location of this resurgence was both unexpected and counter-intuitive. For one, casuistry reemerged at a time when rational methods were at their peak, implemented fully, and nearly universally accepted. Second, it reemerged within a most unexpected domain: medicine, a science-heavy discipline that would seem to be stridently opposed to casuistry.[1]

Why and how did casuistry return when and as it did?

Clinical Ethics: Casuistry's Restoration Begins

Casuistry reemerged in the specialty field of clinical ethics in large measure due to casuistry's compatibility with many of medicine's core practices. (Arras 1991, 1994, 2010; Blake 1992; Brody 1989; Calkins 2002; Hunter 1989; Jonsen, "Casuistry and Clinical Ethics," 1986, 1991; Kopelman 1994; Kuczewski 1997; Macpherson-Smith 1994; Tallmon 1994; Tomlinson 1994; Wildes 1993; Williams 1994) detail

---

[1] It should be mentioned at this point that case-based analysis also emerged recently, although with less vigor, within the disciplines of socio-political philosophy and the history of moral theology. Within the realm of business, while business ethicists Robert Jackall, Joanne Ciulla, Manuel Velasquez, and others have published essays concerning casuistry, their treatises are relatively short and have not sparked in business circles the sort of discussion about casuistry found in other disciplines.

For the most part, Ciulla's essay and Velasquez' response, go to original casuistic sources and debate the applicability of casuist history to business ethics (Ciulla, 1994; Velasquez, 1994).

In contrast, Robert Jackall's treatise uses the term "casuistry" to explain the efficiency-oriented occupational ethics operative in business (Jackall, 1987).

Finally, Velasquez and F. Neil Brady consider casuistry, but only as an aspect in a larger consideration of Catholic natural law's influence on business ethics (Velasquez and Brady 1997).

M. Calkins, *Developing a Virtue-Imbued Casuistry for Business Ethics,* Issues in Business Ethics 42, DOI 10.1007/978-94-017-8724-6_7, © Springer Netherlands 2014

aspects of casuistry's use in medicine and bioethics, showing how its adoption there was not universal nor altogether smooth.

Casuistry was brought into medical ethics because it blended well with standard medical decision-making processes. In medicine, critical judgments are made through an ongoing process of comparisons and decisions have to be made quickly without recourse to moral experts. Emergency rooms, battlefield medical situations, and confounding medical circumstances typify circumstances where these practices are most apparent.

In the emergency room, for example, standard practice holds for members of a medical team to venture an opinion as a patient is brought in for care. The team's objective is to diagnose the patient's problem as accurately as possible and then determine a course of treatment.

In complex situations where multiple doctors are needed, each practitioner advances an opinion based on his or her prior experience. Opinions are framed in terms of the similarity of the present situation to some case of the past. The reasoning used is therefore analogical and the opinion rendered is just that—an estimation or judgment based on what is probable but not absolutely certain.

If, for example, a patient is brought in with red spots on her body, one doctor might diagnosis the ailment as rubella (German measles) while another, noting the spots are bumpy rather than diffuse, might diagnosis it as hives. A third, seeing the spots are splotchier than rubella or hives might suggest that the problem is AIDS defining Kaposi's sarcoma. A fourth, observing that the spots trail along nerve routes might suggest the problem is shingles. Back and forth debate ensues drawing out new comparisons that support some diagnoses and eliminate others until consensus is reached about the nature of the ailment and its proper treatment.

Diagnoses are regularly made in medicine through this sort of analogical process, and not just in emergency room situations. In other medical venues as well—including each time a patient comes to a doctor with an ailment—the practitioner renders an opinion based on prior experience and settled cases.

As a "practice," medicine draws upon the practitioners' prior case experiences and ability to reason by means of analogy. Medicine is refined through repetition as doctors become increasingly expert at making defensible judgments through recognizing the similarities and differences between past and present events. Most important for our purposes, medicine is in this way compatible with casuistry.

That medicine is a case based practice is only part of the story because medicine is also highly rule oriented. Medical practitioners are trained in science as well as case usage and must comply with a host of rule-based regimens, oaths (the Hippocratic Oath being the most prominent), and principle-laden hospital codes. In addition, they must also be certified to practice medicine, are expected to approach problems dispassionately and with objectivity, to use justifiable treatment protocols, and to follow standard medical practices.

In short, medicine is an interpretative discipline and practice that relies on analogy and a hermeneutic that encompasses the entire framework of the interpretive process of case usage as well as the particular cases suited to immediate real world situations. At the same time, medicine is a science that relies upon the systematic study of the structure and behavior of the physical and natural world as encapsulated in rules and standards that are forged through an ongoing quest for objectivity.

That the case-based and scientific approaches are not entirely compatible makes for a tension in medicine. In many ways, this same tension is present in casuistry and helps explain why casuistry was revived in clinical medicine and why its reception there was not entirely smooth.

Elsewhere: Casuistry's Revival Continues

The revival of casuistry took place prominently in medical ethics, but casuistry was retrieved for use in other disciplines as well.

Casuistry and Law, Computer Ethics, and Journalism

Oddly enough, law was seedbed for casuistry because of casuistry's similarities to common law.

Common law—a type of law practiced in countries that trace their legal heritage to England—is a type of law based upon settled cases. Not unlike its portrayal in American television legal dramas, common law practice is one wherein cases are retrieved in sequence with the purpose of swaying listeners to a particular judgment, say, the establishment of the guilt or innocence of an individual.

When the common law process is complete, a verdict or judgment is reached that impinges on future court cases. In this way, the machinations within common law are not wholly unlike those of casuistry since in both cases are retrieved from a case taxonomy according to relevance and by means of analogy with the purpose reaching a defensible judgment. The new case then goes into the taxonomy to inform future case-based deliberations. In this way, the taxonomy of cases is built up and future deliberations are made more reliable.

Aside from law, casuistry has an affinity with certain areas of computer ethics and journalism (Boeyink 1992; Coleman 2007; McLaren 2006).

Casuistry and Business-Medicine Comparisons

In the past, (Brinkmann and Ims 2004; Calkins 2001, 2002; Ciulla 1994; Drucker 1981; McMahon 1986; Velasquez 1994) have considered casuistry for business ethics. Most did so, however, in terms of casuistry's history rather than its usefulness and applicability to business practice.

In business, not unlike medicine, casuistry dovetails with many core practices. Businesspeople, just as doctors, rely on case-based approaches to solve problems.

They, like doctors, are educated in legacy cases, the issues related to specific industries, and pressing aspects of decision-making.

Second, facility with case usage is helpful in business because it helps managers avoid mistakes in situations similar to those of the past. Precedent cases are particularly helpful in business as they are in medicine. In later chapters of this book we will see how case use has diminished in business practice and how this has turned out to be a disadvantage. For now, however, it is sufficient to recognize that certain areas of business—strategizing and risk management to name just two—benefit from case-based reasoning.

As Peter Drucker noted, success in today's "post capitalist society" depends on the ability of managers to bridge disciplines and use elements from disparate sources toward innovative and profitable ends (Drucker 1993). This means that managers must be able to see the similarities and differences among past and present events and then draw accurate and compelling analogies between these and the experiences drawn from other disciplines when making decisions.

Third, just as in medicine, business management demands that practitioners sometimes make quick decisions without recourse to experts. While outsiders sometimes think of managers as lone rangers, they are more accurately individuals forced to make solitary decisions by virtue of their work situations. Not unlike doctors, they often do not have the luxury of engaging in drawn out collective consensus seeking nor do they always have access to experts when faced with a problem. They must make decisions immediately and alone. Usually they can make their decision through analytic means, but sometimes circumstances contain a moral component and casuistry becomes an easy-to-use method to aid problem solving.

Fourth, business and medicine have similar analytical components, yet the two differ in terms of the analytic specialties. Business decision-making is typically statistics driven since it is concerned with probable risks, market trends, and so forth. Medical decision-making, in contrast, is often based on the findings of natural sciences. Accordingly, businesspeople are required to have familiarity with economics, accounting, finance, marketing, operations/engineering, and other technical discipline. Doctors, on the other hand, typically train in the natural sciences of biology, chemistry, or physics.

While the nature of the analysis of the two disciplines differs, business managers and doctors share an approach to problems that emphasizes objective and rational analysis and provable consistency with fact. Casuistry's precedent cases aids this reasoning process by bringing to bear relevant facts rooted in the past.

Fifth, business managers and doctors operate within similar highly organized and regulated environments. Both work in environments with established rules, codes of conduct, mission statements, and explicit and implicit standards of behavior. Both sets of practitioners must also conform to the standards of certifying agencies and/or government regulators and, in some cases, be familiar with and conform to international codes and foreign regulations.

Milton Friedman calls these formal and informal boundaries the "rules of the game" and emphasizes that their understanding is crucial to successful business management (Friedman 1970). Not surprisingly, these rules are taught (or should be taught) in business education programs, even alongside or embedded within the cases of case-based teaching.

Casuistry and Business: The Road Ahead

As we have seen, business management is inclined toward analysis and rules compliance, yet reasoning by analogy and the lessons of settled cases have particular relevance to business decision-making. At present, contemporary business ethicists have done a good job of assisting organizations in monitoring and advancing their ethical compliance systems and have proffered helpful principle-based ethical pluralistic schemas for managers. They have done little to further casuistic moral reasoning, however.

What is needed therefore is an effective casuistry for business that takes "seriously even small distinctions in circumstances that may affect application."[2] While it might be the case that casuistry is not "an alternate model of moral reasoning preferable or superior to principle-based approaches," its starting premise "that our understanding of our moral principles is rooted in paradigmatic cases—is nevertheless appealing" (Tomlinson 1994, p. 18).

Advancing an effective casuistry for business is worthwhile because it would round out ethical analysis in business. Nevertheless, casuistry cannot be brought in and applied in the way it was in the past. Its reputation is too tarnished for direct historical application.

Rather, if casuistry is to be implemented effectively, it will need to be bolstered and protected by other measures. These might come via the addition of rules or laws, but the Bill Clinton example shows how rules can be twisted to suit the interests of ne'er-do-wells.

Another, simpler, approach might be the infusion of virtue into the casuistic mix. After all, virtue is necessary to both adhere to rules and utilize cases responsibly. Accordingly, the following sections will show first the benefits of virtue ethics and then how that ethic can be used with casuistry to create "virtue-imbued casuistry."

---

[2] (DeMarco 1991, p. 21). He goes on to say, "Casuistry, at its best, promises (a) to show how principles or maxims should be applied to particular cases, (b) to show how particular cases may fix the meaning of principles, and (c) to show how more difficult cases can be solved by examining their relationship to less complex, paradigmatic cases." *Ibid.*

Part II
Virtue Ethics in the Context of Business

Chapter 8
Aristotle's Virtue Ethics

> *Different men seek after happiness in different ways and by different means, and so make for themselves different modes of life.*

(Aristotle 2009a, VII. 8.1328b)

Virtue ethics is a branch of normative ethics that holds the virtues or characteristic habits of excellence of the soul as its highest value. As a normative approach, virtue ethics advances habits that both identify the person as a moral agent and motivate the individual to become a better human being. In this sense, virtue ethics is unusual in emphasizing the character of the decision-maker rather than the rules or theories of moral decision-making.

A consideration of virtue ethics is particularly important for our purposes—the establishment of a virtue-imbued casuistry—because its addition to casuistry can bolster the likelihood of casuistry being used responsibly.

As we saw at the end of the last chapter, one of casuistry's weaknesses was its tendency to be misused by ne'er-do-wells. With the incorporation of virtue, casuists are more likely to embrace cases conscientiously. This should offset some of casuistry's perceived weaknesses and allow for it to be used more effectively as a form of moral reasoning in business.

Background and Influence

To begin, what is virtue ethics and what has its influence been on ethics?

The most common form of virtue ethics today was forged by Plato (c. 428/427–c. 348/347 BC) and Aristotle (384–322 BC) and summarized in Aristotle's *Nicomachean Ethics* (Aristotle 1962). Aristotle's treatise, in particular, established the basics of a virtue-based teleology that concentrates on the choices of the individual and the ways these choices advance the person toward his or her final good end (Gk. *telos*). Aristotle also explained how the motives of the individual to do the right thing relate to a life well lived.

Aristotle effectively established by means of his ethic a unique branch of normative ethics that concentrates on the person making moral judgments rather than the processes of moral decision-making. In this way, he neither exalted nor dismissed moral rules but shows how the individual fulfills the demands of rules by acting upon them habitually such that they become characteristic of him or her.

Because of its unique approach to moralizing, others have scrutinized, adapted, integrated, and applied Aristotelian virtue ethics variously. Modern philosophers such as David Hume and Adam Smith have adapted it, it has been integrated into Christian teaching with the works of Aurelius Ambrosius, Augustine of Hippo, Thomas Aquinas, and others, and it has been used in most contemporary fields of applied ethics.[1] Even so, other moral perspectives grew to overshadow it until its late twentieth century revival by Alasdair MacIntyre with *After Virtue* (MacIntyre 1984).

Today, Aristotelian virtue ethics is found in nearly every type of applied ethics, including business ethics. It has been applied to business in general by (Collins 1987; Hosmer and Kiewitz 2005; Jensen 2009; Koehn 1992; Maguire 1997; Meikle 1996; Mintz 1996; Moore 2005a, b; Morris 1997; Morse 1999; Whetstone 2001) and applied to various facets of business by (Berry 1992; Cavanagh and Bandsuch 2002; Hartman 1996; Koehn 1995; May 1995; McCloskey 1994; Moberg 1999; Moore and Beadle 2006; Murphy 1999; Riggio et al. 2010; Shanahan and Hyman 2003; Solomon 1992a, b, 1994, 2003; Stone 1982). In addition, its relationship to the common good in the context of business has been explored by (Alzola 2012; Arjoon 2000; Audi 2012; Beabout 2012; Beadle and Knight 2012; Dierksmeier and Celano 2012; Moore 2012; Sadler-Smith 2012; Sison and Fontrodona 2012; Sison et al. 2012; Wells and Graafland 2012).

This ancient Greek virtue theory is therefore valuable because it is a unique and valuable approach to moralizing and has much to contribute to contemporary ethics in general, business ethics in particular, and to making casuistry more robust.

General Features of Virtue Ethics

In general, an Aristotelian ethic of virtue is an approach to moralizing that advances the personal characteristics of excellence of the soul (Gk. *aretê*).[2] These qualities have been translated to mean "virtues" from the Latin *virtus*, the stem of which, *vir*, (meaning "man") is also central to the word "virile." In Aristotle's view, a virtue is:

> A characteristic involving choice, and that it consists in observing the mean relative to us, a mean which is defined by a rational principle, such as a man of practical wisdom would use to determine it. It is the mean by reference to two vices: the one of excess and the other of deficiency....but in regard to goodness and excellence it is an extreme. (Aristotle 1962, II.6 1106b 1136–1107a 1108)

---

[1] For examples of these points, see (Aquinas 1984; Aristotle 1962; Donahue 1990; Keenan and James 1996; Porter 1990; Statman 1997).

[2] The references to virtue throughout are to moral virtues and not intellectual or other sorts of virtues.

As Plato's student, Aristotle was steeped in the role-based castes of *The Republic* and thought that some people were more disposed to virtue than others. His audience was mostly male and aristocratic, but his association of virtue to manliness was not meant to emphasize male physical qualities but how virtue brings a man to the fullness of his being.

Today, virtue is more broadly conceived and thought to be common to anyone who is not "maimed with respect to excellence" (Nussbaum 1990, p. 378). The use of the term "virtue" today therefore associates the ancient Greek notion of excellence of the soul with the perfected nature of the human being.

The Final Good End and Striving for Perfection

Virtue ethics stresses the characteristic habits that enable a person to become his or her best, that is, wholly actualized. These habits or virtues do so by aligning the individual in accordance with right reason to a proper human end (Gk. *telos*) of happiness (Gk. *eudaimônia*), the highest good that can be attained by a person through his or her own efforts and "that at which all things aim."[3]

Following Plato, Aristotle defines the notion of "the good" as either things pursued without regard to additional benefits (intrinsically good) or things conducive to the intrinsically good (Aristotle 1962, I.6 1096b 1011–1015). He goes on to describe the good end (Gk. *telos*) in *The Rhetoric* in the following way:

> We may define a good thing as that which ought to be chosen for its own sake; or as that for the sake of which we choose something else; or as that which is sought after by all things, or by all things that have sensation or reason, or which will be sought after by any things that acquire reason; or as that which must be prescribed for a given individual by reason generally, or is prescribed for him by his individual reason, this being his individual good; or as that whose presence brings anything into a satisfactory and self-sufficing condition; or as self-sufficiency; or as what produces, maintains, or entails characteristics of this kind, while preventing and destroying their opposites. One thing may entail another in either of two ways—(1) simultaneously, (2) subsequently. Thus learning entails knowledge subsequently, health entails life simultaneously. Things are productive of other things in three senses: first as being healthy produces health; secondly, as food produces health; and thirdly, as exercise does-i.e. it does so usually. All this being settled, we now see that both the acquisition of good things and the removal of bad things must be good; the latter entails freedom from the evil things simultaneously, while the former entails possession of the good things subsequently. The acquisition of a greater in place of a lesser good, or of a lesser in place of a greater evil, is also good, for in proportion as the greater exceeds the lesser there is acquisition of good or removal of evil. The virtues, too, must be something good; for it is by possessing these that we are in a good condition, and they tend to produce good works and good actions. They must be severally named and described elsewhere.

---

[3] *Telos* means "end" or "conclusion." It is the perfection or complete actuality of a thing. Applied to the human being, the proper *telos* is happiness (Aristotle 1962, p. 315). Aristotle defines the good "as that which all things aim" (Aristotle 1962, p. 1094a). Martin Ostwald suggests, however, that Aristotle was not the first to frame the concept: "we do not know who first gave this definition of the good" and suggests that it is implied as well in the Platonic dialogues, especially in *Republic* VI. (Aristotle 1962, 3 ftn 3).

Pleasure, again, must be a good thing, since it is the nature of all animals to aim at it. Consequently both pleasant and beautiful things must be good things, since the former are productive of pleasure, while of the beautiful things some are pleasant and some desirable in and for themselves.

The following is a more detailed list of things that must be good. Happiness, as being desirable in itself and sufficient by itself, and as being that for whose sake we choose many other things. Also justice, courage, temperance, magnanimity, magnificence, and all such qualities, as being excellences of the soul. Further, health, beauty, and the like, as being bodily excellences and productive of many other good things: for instance, health is productive both of pleasure and of life, and therefore is thought the greatest of goods, since these two things which it causes, pleasure and life, are two of the things most highly prized by ordinary people. Wealth, again: for it is the excellence of possession, and also productive of many other good things. Friends and friendship: for a friend is desirable in himself and also productive of many other good things. So, too, honour and reputation, as being pleasant, and productive of many other good things, and usually accompanied by the presence of the good things that cause them to be bestowed. The faculty of speech and action; since all such qualities are productive of what is good. Further-good parts, strong memory, receptiveness, quickness of intuition, and the like, for all such faculties are productive of what is good. Similarly, all the sciences and arts. And life: since, even if no other good were the result of life, it is desirable in itself. And justice, as the cause of good to the community.

The above are pretty well all the things admittedly good. In dealing with things whose goodness is disputed, we may argue in the following ways: That is good of which the contrary is bad. That is good the contrary of which is to the advantage of our enemies; for example, if it is to the particular advantage of our enemies that we should be cowards, clearly courage is of particular value to our countrymen. And generally, the contrary of that which our enemies desire, or of that at which they rejoice, is evidently valuable. (Aristotle, 350 BC, I. 6)

The virtues, Aristotle maintains, facilitate attainment of the good because they enable the individual to flourish as a human being. Unlike other good things, the virtues "render good the thing itself of which it is the excellence…caus(ing) it to perform its function well."[4]

Interestingly, Aristotle, following Plato, does not include money making as something related to the good because money making and the life surrounding it "is led under some kind of constraint: clearly wealth is not the good which we are trying to find, for it is only useful…a means to something else" (Aristotle 1962, I 5 1096a 1096).

As characteristics, the virtues distinguish and identify the individual. While they are unique as attributes, they are alike in sharing the same end of working to perfect the individual by aligning him or her in accordance to right reason to a proper human end. They do this by regulating and motivating the individual and having him or her act (and intend to act) appropriately in the situations at hand (Audi 2012, pp. 274–275). The overall effect of this process is to enable the person to constantly strive to become better and to flourish as a human being.

---

[4] (Aristotle 1962, II 6 1106a 1115; Broadie 1991, pp. 24–25).

Elsewhere Aristotle claims that "well-doing (*eupraxia*) is the end we seek: action of some sort or other is therefore our end and aim." (Aristotle 1995, VII 3 1325b 1319).

Habits that Define

As characteristic habits, the virtues are practiced activities that identify the person. That they are "characteristic" means that they are habitual ways of acting that are recognized by others. In practical terms, we know people by their habits, including their moral habits such that we can say, for example, "Tom is a courageous young man" or "Mary is a just woman."

As any other habit, the virtues are learned and fostered through repetition. They are taught by others and then repeated by the individual until they become internalized. As Thomas Wells and John Graafland explain, virtues are internalized by means of "the regular repetition certain (good) actions and thinking, often originally motivated by extrinsic motives" (Wells and Graafland 2012, p. 324). They are, at the same time, "not easily acquired or maintained" (Sison et al. 2012, p. 209). Much like the (bad) habit of smoking or the arguably not-so-bad habitual preference for Scotch, virtues are learned and are acquired tastes.

Virtues are not just discrete acts but patterned behaviors that are, "constitutive of how a person perceives situations and reasons for actions" (Wells and Graafland 2012, p. 319). As outwardly manifested behaviors, they are associated with the reputation of the individual. They identify the individual as a particular sort of moral human being, that is, the sort of moral person one is in the minds of others.

Flow State and Flourishing in the Present

Virtues are patterned behaviors that result in happiness to those who practice them. As we saw, they bring about happiness as an end by facilitating the *telos* (happiness or *eudaimônia*), which is the highest good for the human being.

Equally important, the practice of the virtues brings about happiness in the doing—as the individual exercises the habits of moral perfection. The virtues do this by insisting on moderation or mean-seeking.

Mean-seeking is related to the immediacy of happiness by means of its capacity to develop a golden mean of perfection that is at once fulfilling. One experiences the golden mean of perfection as a "sweet spot" or sense of bliss and well-being. This experience is immediate, not delayed.

The sweet spot of the golden mean is not unlike the joy of the emotional flow state described by positive psychologist Mihaly Csikszentmihalyi. It is the joy of being oneself at one's best—a condition of being completely involved in an activity for its own sake such that one is so enraptured with an activity that nothing else seems to matter (Csikszentmihalyi 1991; Geirland 1996). When experienced, the individual experiences the blissful feelings associated with a highly energized focus on the process.[5]

---

[5] Daniel Goleman describes the flow state in terms of emotional intelligence and as a critical component of managerial success (Goleman 1995).

In Aristotle, today's notion of an emotional flow state is described differently and in terms of the happiness associated with moral actions that optimize the individual's flourishing as a human being of a particular sort. Even so, the same feelings of being oneself at one's best and the same positive, exuberant, and delightful outcomes are conveyed. In both Aristotle and today there is the recognition of the experience of a state of harmony and self-satisfaction that is at once profoundly exciting and somewhat fleeting. In both, there is the timeless recognition that one experiences bliss when at the top of one's "game" and that the shining moments of one's life are rare, to be sought after, and to be cherished.

Moderation and the Shifting Golden Mean

Although the state of happiness described here is experienced in the immediate, it does not come about instantly through reckless and headlong pursuit. Rather, it is the product of deliberate wise choices, self-command, and a host of restraints that curb unbridled passions for the sake of gratification in the future. It comes about, in other words, by means of long-term practices of moderation. A life of mean-seeking moderation then, is key to bringing about the joy of fulfillment both as an end and in the doing in virtue ethics.

Although virtue impels the individual to strive for excellence, it seeks the *telos* by, "observing the mean relative to us, a mean which is defined by a rational principle, such as a man of practical wisdom would use to determine it. Virtue, in other words, is derived through seeking the mean of two vices: one of excess and the other of deficiency. In regard to goodness and excellence, however, virtue itself is an extreme" (Aristotle 1962, II.6 1106b 1136–1107a 1108).

The mean of virtue is a state of character relative to the acting or choosing agent—something that inclines the individual toward the midpoint between deficiency and excess as these relate to the individual exercising the virtue.

As a quality related to the acting or choosing agent, virtue operates differently from person to person. This means that there is no singular universal conception of virtue. Rather, virtue varies such that one person's virtue can be another person's vice. This is so because one person's moderation can be deficiency or excess for another.

Let me explain. Consider two athletes (a man and a woman) who are training for a bench press competition. The man is an elite athlete and the woman is a novice. To be successful in their upcoming events, both need to become stronger, avoid injury, and train wisely. This means that they both need to push themselves in their training. They will need to train with heavy weights, but their workout weights cannot be so heavy that lifting them will tear a muscle or a ligament. So, too, the training weights cannot be so light that the training effort is wasted. How should the two train for their events?

To be successful, each needs to set up a training regimen that will optimize his or her lifts at the competition. For the elite athlete, the regimen might involve bench-press workouts at weights to 340 lbs. (154 kg.) because that athlete knows that training at such a heavy weight will enable him to lift a maximum weight of 440 lbs. (200 kg.) or more on the day of competition and allow him to win his class. To him, 340 lbs. (154 kg.) is moderate compared to the extreme of 440 lbs. (200 kg.) on competition day.

Moderate training for the novice, on the other hand, might involve bench-press workouts at 45 lbs. (20.4 kg.) because training at that weight ensures she will achieve her best lift of 90 lbs. (40.8 kg.) at the competition. She, too, might win her class at this weight.

For the two athletes then, the middle ground and notions of excess and deficiency differ according to the abilities and natures of the individuals. The middle ground of one cannot be switched for that of the other for if the two were swapped, the novice's training at 340 lbs. (154 kg.) would turn out to be excessive, if not fatal and training at 45 lbs. (20.4 kg.) would be of no use to the elite athlete.

In addition, the end goals of the two (the maximum lifts at competition time) differ and cannot be interchanged because doing so would not demonstrate the capabilities of the two athletes. In fact, if the ends were switched and the two attempted them, one (the novice) would fail in the attempt or be injured and the other (the elite athlete) would so easily achieve the weight that the attempt would confound the judges and the competitor would fail to measure up to the performance standards of his peer group (here, his weight class).

In both, sensitivity to the middle ground in light of the end is key. So, too, in virtue ethics the middle ground between excess and deficiency is relative to the agent and determined by means of wisdom and an eye on the end state.

Moreover, just as in physical training, the middle ground changes over time and what was moderate at the outset is insufficient later. This is why athletes train. They attempt to become better than they were at the outset. If the two train year after year at 340 lbs. (154 kg.) and 45 lbs. (20.4 kg.) respectively, they will plateau and not become better athletes. Their performances will not improve and they will stagnate. To become "better" weight lifters, they need to push themselves to lift progressively heavier weights while recognizing the limits of their physical being.

The notion of a progressive mean in virtue theory, not unlike in weight training, is commonly termed the "shifting mean." Determining it is not easy, but once found it is "golden"—valuable because it leads to perfection or the final end. For these reasons, Aristotle emphasized that virtue is "defined by a rational principle, such as a man of practical wisdom would use to determine it" (Aristotle 1962, II 6 1106b 1136).

Virtue and Personal Integration: The Competitive Runner

The exercise of moderation also brings about the final good end or *telos*, which is the highest good for a human being. We have seen this concept described as a sort of flow state of personal happiness. Here, we will consider it as a sort of personal integration wherein the individual strives toward coordinated and complete person-hood.

Aristotle captures the notion of the *telos* as personal integration with the example of the competitive runner. The runner (as well as the wrestler and boxer) was a model of virtue because he displayed the full spectrum of mean-seeking, goal-oriented, and deliberate behaviors related to human perfection and fulfillment.[6] The runner was a paradigm not because he was especially morally upstanding, but because he possessed an "excellence of the soul" that inspired him to shine at something that suited him best as a person. He also knew himself so well and possessed such a well-honed spirit that he could align all of his personal attributes in a way to maximize his running abilities.

Why is such roundness of attributes important to a life of virtue? Consider what it takes for a competitive runner to achieve peak performance.

When the competitive runner performs well—even if he does not win—he (or she) displays not just expert footwork, athleticism, drive, and enthusiasm for a sport, but a host of other animating personal attributes.[7] He acts not as a machine, but as a man (or woman) driven by the desire to achieve. He marshals all his resources and combines them in such a way as to maximize the chances of success. In doing so, he exposes himself as a person who is singularly focused and driven toward a goal related to himself at his best.

More important, when he runs well he strips himself bare to expose how integrated and ingrained his practices of moderated striving over time have become. He shows not just how hard he has trained, but how much he wants to be the best he can be. Even if he does not win, his effort shows who he is as a person and how much he values his own final good end.

Aspiration and Nature's Limits

The competitive runner in running well displays himself as willful, fully engaged, integrated, and whole (Sison and Fontrodona 2012, p. 231). Moreover, he exposes a spirit directed properly to his final end (*telos*) and that he is, as Sarah Broadie phrases it, "*such as to* (and *disposed to*, act well" when occasion arises (Broadie 1991, p. 58). He possesses "appropriate thoughts, motives, and reactive feelings" that incline him to act correctly in general (Nussbaum 1990, p. 378). He is fully committed and decisive.[8]

---

[6] In describing the mean of virtue in Book II, Aristotle uses the example of a famous wrestler named Milo. He then states, "the same applies to running and wrestling." For this reason, I will use the example of the runner here (Aristotle 1962, II 6 1106b 1105).

[7] Philippa Foot argues that because virtues engage the will, they are more than mere individual skills evoked by habit (Foot 1978). See also (Meilaender 1984, p. 9).

[8] "Virtuous states do not correspond perfectly with a disposition to any set of acts and, in addition, the virtuous act may be achieved without the virtue. I may face danger without fleeing, but this

In running at his best, the competitive runner manifests an integrated and broad array of dispositions having to do with his ability to engage his will properly so it is directed toward the final good end.

As Robert Solomon observed, such a person has an integrity and wholeness to his life such that his practice, roles, duties and responsibilities seamlessly come together (Sison and Fontrodona 2012, p. 231; Solomon 1992a, pp. 328–329). He shows "right motivation and emotion" and a willingness and ability to deliberate well about his own abilities and goals (Sison et al. 2012, p. 209).

At the same time, the runner operates within the narrow limits of nature, his particular gifts, and the circumstances at hand. He recognizes his physical boundaries, which is important because, as Martha Nussbaum explains:

> Human limits structure the human excellences, and give excellent action its significance. The preservation of the limits in some form…is a necessary condition of excellent activity's excellence. And concerning excellence in the universe in general, apart from the contexts of specific forms of life, we can, as Aristotle argues well, say nothing with real content. (Nussbaum 1990, p. 378)

For all of these reasons, we laud the competitive runner when he or she puts forth maximum effort. Whether he is a world class Kenyan who wins a prestigious marathon or a Special Olympics girl who crosses the finish line despite all sorts of physical disabilities, we recognize the gifts and limits of nature as well as the amount of effort the athlete has to put forth to become his or her best in a race. More important, we applaud the inspiration afforded us by one so steadfast and appropriately determined. The runner, in other words, does not just show us his or her best self, but reminds us of our own potential.

The Social Aspects of Virtue

As we have seen with the examples of the weightlifter and competitive runner, virtue is integrated and becomes habituated and internalized after being stimulated by extrinsic factors. Virtues, in simple terms, are learned traits—taught by others and nourished by society. They become habituated and internalized by individuals through use and by means of continuous stimulus from outside sources.

That society has a role in facilitating individual virtue suggests that society possesses virtue and has the mechanisms to define, retain, and promulgate virtue to its members. Moreover, it suggests that society as an entity is virtuous—for how can a society impart something it does not already possess? How does this come about?

On the one hand, society imparts virtue to individuals through prudent mentors such as Aristotle's person of practical wisdom (Gk. *phronimos*), and by means of everyday life in societies directed toward advancing the good life.[9] In this sense,

---

does not make me courageous. It may, as Hobbes knew, only show that I am still more fearful of some other danger." (Meilaender 1984, p. 8).

[9] For more on the development of virtue, see (Broadie 1991, pp. 72–74).

virtue is not a birthright or a talent, but something developed through interaction with virtuous others.

As Nussbaum explains, "Aristotle's ideal person of practical wisdom is no solitary Jamesian heroine, but a politically active citizen of Athens" (Nussbaum 1990, p. 98). This means that the individual learns virtue within society or the city-state (Gk. *polis*) for the Greeks (Aristotle 1995, 1252a1251). The lessons are learned by means of communication with the prudent people and other members of society who teach individuals the meaning of virtue by modeling it and helping the individual understand, refine, apply, and integrate it appropriately.

Society is capable of doing this because society itself is virtuous—as Aristotle clearly articulated in *The Politics*. In Aristotle's view, the *polis* itself was a virtuous gathering because it could be properly directed to a *telos* or good end.[10]

Properly understood, the *polis* was "an association of households and clans in a good life, for the sake of attaining a perfect and self-sufficient existence"—an entity in itself and not just a collection of individuals.[11] It was a "species of association (Gk. *koinōnia*)," a shared enterprise undertaken by citizens (Aristotle 1995, 1252a 1251.1251 ftn 1251). It was so important that civilized human existence was possible only within it (Aristotle 1962, 1094a 1027 ftn 1098). Quoting Homer, Aristotle exclaims, "clanless and lawless and heartless is he" who is without a city by reason of his own nature and not of some accident (Aristotle 1995, 1253a, pp. 1254–1255).

Because life within society was important, the study of political science (Gk. *politikē*) was crucial for the individual so that he or she could carry out his or her civic duties.[12] Familiarity with society's moral norms was important not only for the individual to advance in society, but also for the shared enterprise (*polis*) whose norms were perpetuated by knowledgeable individuals. In addition, society's merit in the view of outsiders was upheld (or not) as outsiders encountered and interacted with members of the *polis*.

Taken together, Aristotle forged a normative theory that concentrates on individual character while advancing social benefits. While this association has been close, the emphasis of late has been on the individual such that the social aspect

---

[10] It should be noted at this point that Aristotle's conception of virtue as something formed by and for society derives from even earlier notions of virtue in Greek society. Prior to Aristotle, in Homeric conceptions of virtue, for example, virtue's social aspect was emphasized even in a conception of virtue as something associated directly with one's role in life. While the example of the runner suggests that a remnant of this role-specific conception of virtue remains, Aristotle shifted the focus of attention from the role to the character of the person filling that role. In making this shift, however, he did not espouse a highly individualistic notion of virtue. Instead, he maintained that virtue was constructed by and for society as well as by and for the individual (Nussbaum 1990, p. 378).

[11] (Aristotle 1995, 1280b, 1231). In the passages surrounding this quote, Aristotle argues that a city-state cannot be forged through intermarriage or "matters of exchange and alliance" (commerce), but that the *polis* itself has a purpose—the good life, which "consists in living a happy and truly valuable life" (Aristotle 1995, 1280b 1212- end).

[12] See "Politics as the master science of the good" in (Aristotle 1962, 1094a 1018–1094b 1012, glossary, 1311–1313) and (Rawls 1993, p. xxi).

of virtue has been overshadowed. Even so, it continues to survive, as Gilbert Mei-laender explains:

> Character seems to suggest those cardinal virtues of our time, sincerity and authenticity—in short, being true to oneself. 'Virtue', by contrast, may still carry a little of its older meaning: standards by which to measure and evaluate the self we are.[13]

Despite a dilution of interest in virtue's older social dimension, the consideration of this aspect is important for our purposes because it draws attention to matters beyond individual character development. Since virtue is constructed by and for society and because it can only be realized by the individual within the context of the *polis* or shared enterprise, individuals and society alike have an interest and obligation to facilitate society's attainment of virtue as it helps perfect the collective enterprise.

Managers as participating members in the *polis* and key figures in a microcosm of the *polis* in form of business enterprises, therefore have duties to consider society's good ends as well as their own individual interests and the profits of companies when they conduct their daily affairs.[14]

Summary: General Virtue

To recapitulate, virtue is a characteristic of excellence of the soul that enables the individual to flourish. It does this by regulating and motivating the individual in such a way that right action and right motives become habituated and integrated as identifiers of the person. In practice, it has the individual seek the golden mean of extremes and strive toward the *telos* or final good end. This results in personal flourishing and happiness.

Virtue is an individual trait but is constructed by and for society and only realized within the context of the *polis* or shared enterprise of households and clans. Consequently, virtue brings about happiness in the doing and as an end for individuals and society alike. Table 8.1 summarizes most of these concepts.[15]

---

[13] (Meilaender, 1984, 4–5). He quickly admits, however, that virtue need not be strongly normative and its weak normativity might be attributable in some cases to its "uncodifiability" or inability to provide detailed guidelines for action (Meilaender 1984, p. 4).

[14] These ideas are supported in large measure by the common good arguments related to business by (Alzola 2012; Audi 2012; Beabout 2012; Beadle and Knight 2012; Dierksmeier and Celano 2012; Moore 2012; Sadler-Smith 2012; Sison and Fontrodona 2012; Sisonet al. 2012b; Wells and Graafland 2012).

[15] Robert Audi lists six dimensions of virtue (field, target, beneficiaries, agential understanding, motivation, grounding), explaining each in turn (Audi 2012, pp. 274–276).

Table 8.1 Aristotle's General Notion of Virtue

A characteristic habit of excellence of the soul
A moderating or mean-seeking state of character relative to the acting or choosing agent
A characteristic habit that perfects one's nature and renders good the thing itself of which it is the excellence
A characteristic habit that aligns the individual in accordance to right reason to a proper human end (*telos*) of happiness (*eudaimônia*)
A characteristic habit that has the individual do the right thing for the right reasons
An individual trait constructed by and for society and realized within the context of the *polis*, which has its own end of perfection as well

Application to Business: The Tylenol Crisis and Virtue-based Management

Having established the general tenets of virtue theory, how do they apply to business? In particular, how might a teleological perspective such as this influence the way a manager does business?

Consider the now familiar example of James E. Burke's Johnson & Johnson (J&J) executive team's during that company's struggle with the 1982 cyanide tainting of Extra-Strength Tylenol capsules.[16]

An unresolved crime that resulted in the deaths of seven people in the Chicago area, the Tylenol-tainting incident led to federal anti-tampering laws, reforms in the packaging of over-the-counter products and demonstrated how a major business should handle a disaster involving one of its products.

Throughout the ordeal, Burke (J&J Chairman and CEO 1976–1989) and others on the executive team remained connected with J&J stakeholders. When the outbreak of deaths occurred, they immediately halted production and advertising and directed the company to distribute warnings to hospitals and distributors to cease product use. At the same time, they assured the public that tampering had not taken place at J&J plants and conducted a widespread recall of about 31 million bottles of the product at a loss of more than $ 100 million (over $ 223 million in 2010 dollars).

With the product off store shelves and its name tarnished, Tylenol's demise seemed inevitable, but such was not the case. The public responded favorably to the J&J team's sympathetic approach to the crisis as well as its assurances that Tylenol's reformulation and more secure packaging would prevent a repetition of the tainting. Within a short time, Tylenol rebounded, recovered most of its market share, and eventually built to its current high levels.

Today, most assessments conclude that the J&J leadership team performed well during the crisis (Larsen 2007; Smith 1989; Time.com 2007). Although some fault the company for using its advertising and marketing areas for media relations and not having a proactive public affairs program before the crisis hit, these critics fail to appreciate the newness of the tainting phenomenon and the standards for

---

[16] For summaries of the Johnson & Johnson Tylenol case, see (Buchholz 1989, pp. 212–232).

business behavior at the time (Kaplan 2005; Snyder 1983). Overall, the J&J team's approach to the surprise tainting of one of the company's products generated a positive response.

For our purposes, Burke and the J&J executive team's handling of the crisis demonstrated not just responsible business behavior, but also Aristotle's general features of virtue.

First, the team demonstrated that it was *telos*-directed by responding to the Tylenol tainting crisis appropriately and in accordance with stated aspirations of the company's "Our Credo" (Johnson and Johnson 2012a, b). Throughout the ordeal, the executive team acted in terms of the company's final end and thereby manifested proper motives related to the company's notion of its best self. The team demonstrated a willingness to act to further the unique qualities of the company and revealed a propensity to strive to achieve J&J's notions of excellence. In this way, the team exhibited the ends-driven heart of Aristotelian virtue theory.

Second, the J&J executive team demonstrated its habit of turning to the company's code of ethics ("Our Credo" ") during crises. In this way, it revealed how deeply ingrained its inclination was to turn to the *telos*. Not unlike the weightlifters and runners previously mentioned, the management "athletes" here were familiar with the goals and aspirations set out in J&J's stated mission. As the team honed its decision-making and leadership skills over time, it integrated these values such that when the tainted Tylenol incident occurred, it did not have to think about the starting point of crisis management. It almost instinctively acted in terms of the company's end values as they were distilled in the credo. As a result, the team not only was not paralyzed with uncertainty, but was able to respond quickly in a sympathetic and proactive manner that reflected the best of J&J.

Third, J&J executives acted moderately, neither denying the product-related problem nor over reacting to it. The team did not attempt to take the easy way out by shirking responsibility for the Tylenol tainting. Rather, it stood by J&J's product and agreed to coordinate its removal from public access. At the same time, the team held in check a tendency to act aggressively. It did not meddle in investigations nor did it thwart law enforcement inquiries. To the contrary, the executive team chose a middle-ground by working closely with law enforcement officials and the media, listening to others with knowledge about such matters, keeping the public informed, and responding when it was appropriate to do so. Thus, just as a winning athlete does, the J&J executive team pushed itself at times and held itself in check at other times so as to forge ahead toward the goals set out in "Our Credo." In this way, the executive team tempered inclinations to act extremely and manifested Aristotle's golden mean.

Fourth, the Burke-led J&J executive team persevered in a quest to achieve its final end (*telos*). It marshaled the resources available to it and endured a harsh situation in the ways that competitive athletes must when they are striving for success. The team thereby demonstrated tenacity and a will to hold in check its appetites for the extreme to more likely achieve its own and J&J's final good ends. All of these are demonstrations of virtue in action.

Fifth, the Burke-led J&J executive team demonstrated a sense of social respon- sibility in its ongoing concern for public safety. As active participants of the *polis*, team members realized and exercised their moral duties to consider society's good ends as well as those of the team members as individuals and as those charged with advancing J&J's profits. They did not prevaricate in a Bill Clinton manner nor did they look for ways to sidestep the law to relieve the company of its responsibilities. To the contrary, the team established a new benchmark for corporate performance within the pharmaceutical industry that spilled over to new American expectations of corporate social responsibility. In this way, the team effectively broke new ground for managing crises and, at the same time, advanced the interests and well being of society. They demonstrated not just how a management team can lead a company, but how a team can make a good company even better, even under circumstances of extreme duress.

For all of these reasons, society applauds Burke and the J&J executive team. In management as in athletics, we recognize in their example the trying circumstances and the amount of effort put forth by people to become their best. Moreover, we see in their actions not just good character but also how we might strive in our own circumstances to measure up to the virtuous performance standards they have set.

The Particular Virtues

To this point we have considered the general attributes of Aristotelian virtue theory. Now we turn to his explanation of the particular ways that virtue can be achieved. Here, we will concentrate on the relatively narrow range of moral virtues that Aris- totle considers in *The Nicomachean Ethics*. These are listed and briefly summarized in Table 8.2.

Prudence

Prudence is arguably Aristotle's most important virtue because "virtue in the full sense cannot be attained without practical wisdom" (Aristotle 1962, VI 13 1144b 1118–1119). In simple terms, prudence is the characteristic habit of deliberating well about what is good and advantageous for oneself in practical affairs. It is prac- tical wisdom (Gk. *phronēsis*) or sound judgment in everyday life, a trait of good deliberation, excellent understanding, and an ability to judge well (Aristotle 1962, VI 9–13).

Although prudence is practical wisdom, it is not simply a set of practical skills or proficiency within a craft (Gk. *technê*) nor is it the disinterested and objective knowledge of science (Gk. *epistémé*). Rather, it is an ability to "calculate well with respect to some worthwhile end, one that cannot be attained by an applied science

Table 8.2 Aristotle's Particular Virtues

Prudence
- Deliberating well about what is good and advantageous for oneself in practical affairs
- Sound judgment in everyday life, excellent understanding, and the ability to calculate well with respect to a worthwhile end
- Practical wisdom (Gk. phronēsis). Not attained by means of an applied science or art
- The guiding virtue that enables the individual to "do the right thing for the right reason" by finding the mean of extremes and to recognize and accept his or her moral duty
- Necessary for the virtuous life. Virtue cannot be attained without it
- Involves moral prescience (forethought)
- Has individual and social dimensions: individuals learned it from prudent others and society benefits from prudent members as its norms and moral standing are advanced

Justice
- Highest of all the virtues, a complete virtue, an excellence in the fullest sense because the one who possesses it can make use of this virtue not only alone, but also in relation to others
- An excellence of the soul that distributes to each according to his or her desert, treating equally those who are equal
- A characteristic habit enabling the individual to direct his or her will appropriately to relate properly to others
- Orders and regulates proper conduct within society. Is the bond that holds together the shared enterprise of households and clans (the polis)
- The whole of virtue, but not identical to virtue

Courage (Fortitude)
- Moderates feelings of fear and confidence (the irascible appetites)
- Perseverance and confidence in withstanding danger, fear, or trying circumstances
- The mean of cowardice and recklessness

Temperance (Self-Control)
- Soundness of mind, discretion, or the habit of controlling the pleasures of the body (including the concupiscible appetites)
- The mean of insensitivity and self-indulgence

Other Virtues
- Generosity (Liberality) : an excellence of the soul by which an individual gives appropriately, to the right people, the right amount, at the right time. The mean of extravagance and stinginess
- Magnificence: an excellence of the soul by which an individual spends grandly and freely on uncommon but worthwhile things. The mean of vulgarity and tightfistedness
- High-mindedness (Magnanimity) : greatness of soul, an excellence by which an individual takes what he deserves and is willing to bear good and bad fortune appropriately. The mean of pettiness and vanity
- Unnamed Virtue: The mean of ambition and lack of ambition. It is unnamed because the man who occupies the median position is unremarkable, does not have a name
- Gentleness: an excellence of the soul by which an individual becomes difficult to stir to anger. The mean of short-temperedness and apathy
- Friendliness: an excellence of soul by which an individual puts up with and refuses to put up with the right things in the right manner. The mean of obsequiousness and grouchiness
- Truthfulness: a characteristic habit of excellence of the soul whereby the individual speaks the truth, avoids falsehood, and is honest. The mean of boastfulness and self-deprecation
- Wittiness (Tactfulness) : an excellence of the soul that enables an individual to be tactful and fun because relaxation and amusement are a necessary part of life. The mean of buffoonery and boorishness

or art."[17] It is a quality that has the individual do the right thing for the right reasons. As such, it is about correctness "in assessing what is conducive to the end" that results in "true conviction" (Aristotle 1962, VI 9 1142b 1135–1139).

Prudence has long fascinated moralists. Philosophers such as Adam Smith extracted the aspect of conviction from prudence to construct a new virtue called "self-command" with an emphasis on sagacity (levelheadedness) and caution ("the prudent traveler takes an umbrella"). Similarly, contemporary business ethicists such as Robert Solomon focus on the demanding qualities of prudence to formulate "toughness" as a virtue (Solomon "Corporate Roles, Personal Virtues: An Aristotelian Approach to Business Ethics" 1992, p. 337). Still others concentrate on prudence's attention to discernment and its mandate to do something "for the right reasons" (Melé 2010; Moberg 2007; Schwartz and Sharpe 2006, 2010).

While these are certainly traits of prudence, prudence itself is expansively dispositional. It is, as are all virtues, a characteristic trait and this means that it is constitutive of the person. When it is exercised, it is drawn from within and colors one's interpretation of one's role in life and understanding of the circumstances at hand. As something directive (do things for the right reasons), it requires that one not just muse on oneself, but choose to act rightly because to do otherwise would be uncharacteristic and deeply troubling.

Because prudence is subject related, what is prudent for one person might not be prudent for another. The measure of prudence is, as all other virtues, the mean of excess and deficiency. Here, however, the measure is related to the purpose of understanding the notion of sound judgment in everyday life. This means that prudence effectively regulates the other virtues in that it determines the wise middle ground of temperance, courage, and so forth. As a result, prudence is essential to the virtuous life.

Although prudence is dispositional and characteristic of the individual, it is learned or, conversely, taught by others. This means that while it is a habit or internalized practice, it is something that originates outside of the individual and sourced in external motivations. For Aristotle, prudence is constructed by and for society and realized only within the context of a specific *polis*. More to the point, it is acquired through exposure to social forces, society's ethical customs, laws, and so forth—but most importantly, it is conveyed by means of prudent teachers.

For Aristotle and the other ancient Greeks, prudence was thought to be conveyed best by means of prudent figures. As a result, young people were placed alongside men of practical wisdom (Gk. *phronimos*) who taught them the ways of the world. Mentor was this sort of prudent figure. A trusted advisor and wise friend of Odysseus, Mentor and Odysseus developed a *phronimos-protégé* relationship that effectively transferred an understanding of practical wisdom from the elder to the younger.

---

[17] (Aristotle 1962, VI 5 1140a1128–1130). The contemporary understanding of Gk. *phronēsis* as "prudence" derives from Cicero's Latin translation of the Greek term as *providentia*, meaning a sort of divine foresight. This term was subsequently interpreted as cautiousness, circumspection, and care. For more, see (Beabout 2012, p. 420; Hariman 2003).

In business, *phronimos-protégé* (mentoring) relationships are quite common. Sometimes they are formalized in programs, but most often an older person who sees vitality and promise in a youngster initiates the relationship. If it works well, the relationship is symbiotic, with both parties mutually satisfied. The elder takes satisfaction in passing on his or her wisdom and witnessing the growth of a youngster while the youngster learns the pitfalls and opportunities associated with the work environment.

Not surprisingly, mentoring has a strong political component since conveying practical wisdom involves educating youth in the machinations of the world (firm, industry, community, and so forth). Some mentors do this better than others and some mentors are simply good at politics and are not very wise. Dennis Moberg found, for example, that mentoring in business can range widely and that sometimes those who mentor are just more politically skilled and not necessarily more practically wise than non-mentors (Moberg 2008; Moberg 2008). Lily Orland-Barak concurs, arguing in the context of education that the mentor's role is mainly "to promote and respond to teachers' continuous deliberations and critical discussion of how political and social structures relate to and influence educational aims and practices."[18] In the end, the mentoring relationship of business and the *phronimos-protégé* relationship of Aristotle are closely related but not identical.

The *phronimos-protégé* relationship of Mentor and Odysseus can be thought of as a friendship-based relationship of journey (Awaya et al. 2008). Not unlike parenting, it involves modeling whereby the young learn from the older and wiser by means of word and deed over a long period of time. Moreover, the young learn not just how to be politically skillful and how social structures function toward certain narrow ends, but how one can actually "do the right thing for the right reason" by being insightful, reflective, contemplative, rational, and able to bridge or draw distinctive differences among experiences. In this way, they learn to do more than survive. They learn how to live fuller lives.

Practical Wisdom and the Final Good End

Prudence, as all other virtues, is *telos*-directed, which means that it has the individual strive toward the final good end. This idea is not entirely new with Aristotle. Sophocles ends *Antigone*, a play written around 442 BC, with the line, "Wisdom is the supreme part of happiness."[19] Aristotle, however, develops the notion to mean both an immediate quality of practical discernment (a characteristic habit of the

---

[18] (Orland-Barak 2010). Orland-Barak argues further that, mentoring involves "learning to plan and improvise; observing the consequences and sources of participation systematically; appreciating the contexts within which others work; responding to the situational constraints of a particular strategic action; and improvising conditions of free open dialogues to promote practitioners' self-understandings" (Orland-Barak 2010).

[19] The full quote is "Wisdom is the supreme part of happiness; and reverence towards the gods must be inviolate. Great words of prideful men are ever punished with great blows, and, in old age, teach the chastened to be wise" (Sophocles 2000).

individual) and a future oriented trait that results in the individual's flourishing. In other words, prudence is wisdom practiced here and now and having a goal to be attained later.

Example: The Prudent Runner

To illustrate these concepts, consider again Aristotle's example of the competitive runner who, as a prudent athlete, deliberates well about how to train so as to achieve his or her final good end, especially as it relates to competition.

What does prudent deliberation in this sense entail?

For one, prudent deliberation demands that the runner determine the mean of excess and deficiency as it applies to him or her. This, in turn, requires that he or she possess self-knowledge and be reflective, contemplative, shrewd, insightful, rational, and capable of assessing his or her natural limits. It also requires that the individual understand the similar and distinctively different features of the current race compared to those of the past. Then, this combined knowledge is used to discern temperance (how much one should eat, sleep, and so forth), fortitude (how early one should get up to run, how hard to train, and so forth), justice (how one should treat competitors fairly), and so forth in terms of a training regimen.

Second, prudent deliberation requires that the individual keep an eye trained on the *telos* and strive for constant improvement. With this ideal self-image in mind, the runner can better weigh the circumstances at hand and the limits of his or her own natural talents and attempt to run farther, faster, and with more endurance without injury than he or she did in the past. In doing so, he or she becomes a more excellent runner. Thus, the prudent runner determines the mean of excess and deficiency as it applies to him or herself, keeps an ideal self-image in mind, and better exercises all the other virtues with the objective of becoming the best runner he or she can be.

A Goal in Itself

With this in mind, it is not surprising that Aristotle considered prudence to be a goal in itself. This is because a person of practical wisdom (Gk. *phronimos*) understands and can act in terms of the golden mean of perfection as well as the final good end relative to him or herself. Put another way, becoming practically wise is a goal because it is part of what it means to be a perfected individual (or virtuous).

In addition, prudence is a goal because a practically wise person (Gk. *phronimos*) perfects society by his or her interaction with it. In understanding and acting in practically wise ways, the prudent person is both disposed favorably toward society's moral norms and able to advance and disseminate them effectively. For these reasons, society needs the support of prudent people for its survival because without such people, society's moral identity and norms wither and die. Thus, as we saw in the Mentor-Odysseus *phronimos-protégé* relationship, society encourages prudent people to transfer their wisdom to others (especially the young) by means of personal relationships, formal mentoring programs, and so forth.

Prudence's Place in Business

Finally and related to the subject matter of this book, prudence/practical wisdom is a goal important to good business management.

As in life in general and the experience of the competitive runner, business managers must keep an eye on the *telos* of the firm and similarly weigh the circumstances at hand, know the natural talents of the firm (and themselves), and strive to perform better, faster, and with more endurance without exposing the firm to unacceptable risk than they and others did in the past. Prudence in the context of business as elsewhere therefore demands that managers exceed past performances and perfect themselves as managers and their firms as productive communities.

Drucker captures many of these ideas in the concept of the "post capitalist society" wherein success is determined by the ability of managers to discern the positive features embedded in seemingly unrelated areas for the purpose of advancing innovation, productivity, and profits (Drucker 1993). Here, as others have noted, managers must be able to handle knowledge that is "mediated, situated, provisional, pragmatic and contested" (Blackler 1995, p. 1021). They must be "knowledge workers" and yet comfortable with a prophetic role as they shape collective actions (Kitay and Wright 2007; Sousa and Hendriks 2007). They must exercise, as Paul Gibson observes, practical wisdom in dealing with the "dynamic interaction between perception, experience, character, and an insightful vision of what is proximately and ultimately good for people, organizations, and business" (Gibson 2008). Put another way and following the lead of Gregory Beabout, they must possess a sort of "domain-relative" prudence (Beabout 2012).

Moral Prescience

Thus far we have considered the functional aspects of prudence, but prudence functions as a virtue only when it is future (*telos*) focused. This means that the prudent individual must strive for something not wholly at hand and must discern in terms of potentialities. This mindset, in turn, requires that the individual exercise forethought or what I will call "moral prescience."[20]

Moral prescience is simply the ability to think about the moral aspects of a present situation as it extends into the future. Its content is moral (or ethical), but the act itself is a process of forward thinking. It is a cognitive process that begins with a mental picture or image. Why? Because as Aristotle explains in *De Anima*, "the soul never thinks without an image" and "the faculty of thinking…thinks the forms

---

[20] (Dierksmeier and Pirson 2009) considers the future orientation of business by contrasting Aristotle's theory of household management to the management of modern corporations. Otherwise, the term "prescience" is not used much in business except in the context of planning. See (Waitman 2008). "Moral prescience" is used mostly in passing in healthcare literature as in (Lundberg 2002).

in the images."[21] Contemporary ethicists have called this starting point "moral imagination."[22] Moral prescience, however, goes beyond the starting point of imaging and visualization to cognitive processes directed toward particular ends.

In being focused on ends, moral prescience is not just a variant of consequentialism nor is it a derivative of utilitarianism or pragmatism. It is distinct from these other methods because it does not rest upon nor does it advocate identifiable moral principles (usefulness or practicality as examples). Moreover, it does not advance narrow notions of happiness as other theories do (Bentham 1781; Mill 1979). While it admittedly shares a focus on ends with utilitarianism, consequentialism, and pragmatism, it lacks the prescriptive qualities of these ends-oriented normative approaches.

Moral prescience is nevertheless instrumental to Aristotelian ethics in that it directs attention toward a final good end that is not yet realized. In doing so, it directs deliberation toward the future and has the individual forge practically wise judgments now while keeping an eye trained on the future. In this way, it requires that the individual mentally remove him or herself from the immediate (at least in part) so as to reflect upon the repercussions of today's decisions on the future.

Moral prescience is not only important to moral theory and virtue ethics; it is essential to good management. Most business ethics violations occur because managers lacked foresight. They could not (or refused to) "think through" the implications of their decisions or failed to consider the ramifications of decisions in light of the company's objectives.

In the later chapters of this book, we will see how a lack of forethought resulted in smallpox vaccines being diminished to dangerously low levels and how managers need to think though the moral hazards associated with decisions to go ahead (or kill) a rapidly aging pharmaceutical product. We will see, too, how moral prescience is critical to strategic planning and risk management; especially as processes become more statistic and model driven.

Summary: Prudence

In the end and to recapitulate, prudence is a characteristic habit of deliberating well. As practical wisdom, it is characterized by shrewd, insightful, reflective, contemplative, and rational thinking—where the individual is able to bridge or draw distinctions among experiences.

As a virtue, prudence motivates the individual to do the right thing for the right reasons and is focused on the final good end. It also relies heavily on moral imagination and moral prescience and clarifies the notion of the mean more broadly than

---

[21] Aristotle explains in full: "To the thinking soul images serve as if they were contents of perception (and when it asserts or denies them to be good or bad it avoids or pursues them). That is why the soul never thinks without an image" (Aristotle 1928). For more, see (Lowe 1983).

[22] For more on moral imagination, see (Johnson 1993; Kekes 1991; Moberg 2002, 2003; Moberg and Calkins 2001; Moberg and Seabright 2000; Seabright and Schminke 2002; Tierney 1994; Vidaver-Cohen 1997; Werhane 1999, 2002).

other virtues. For this reason, it is key to understanding and attaining all other moral virtues or, as Aristotle says, "virtue in the full sense cannot be attained without practical wisdom" (Aristotle 1962, VI 13 1144b 1118–1119).

Justice

Although prudence is most important as a guiding virtue, justice is the highest of all the virtues in Aristotle's view.

The Complete Virtue

For Aristotle, justice is complete virtue and excellence in the fullest sense because the one who possesses it can make use of it "not only by himself but also in his relations with his fellow men" (Aristotle 1962, V 1 1129b 1128–1130). In general, justice is identified by its abridgment, that is, we know justice when we see it violated in an injustice—when someone takes more than his or her share, treats others unfairly, or some such (Aristotle 1962, V 1 1129b 1121).

Although justice is the whole of virtue (complete), it is not identical to virtue. As J.A. Stewart explains, whereas "virtue is the state conceived simply as a state; justice is the state conceived as putting its possessor in a certain relation to society" (Stewart 1892, p. 401) In other words, the difference between justice and virtue *per se* is the difference between things assigned to the category of *quality* and to the category of *relation* respectively (Stewart 1892, p. 401). Thus, insofar as justice is exhibited in relation to others it is justice, but insofar as it is simply a characteristic of moderation it is a virtue (Aristotle 1962, V 1 1130a 1111–1116).

As Aristotle's translator Martin Ostwald observes, justice (Gk. *dikaiosynē*) is the same as righteousness and honesty. Justice "regulates all proper conduct within society, in the relations of individuals with one another, and to some extent even the proper attitude of an individual towards himself" (Aristotle 1962, p. 304).

How does justice accomplish these feats? At the beginning of Book V of *The Nicomachean Ethics*, Aristotle details the features of justice and how it derives the various median positions between extremes (Aristotle 1962, V 1 1129a).

First, justice is an individual trait that has the person perform just actions, that is, act justly (Aristotle 1962, V 1 1129a 1128). These acts of the individual seek the good of others and not just that of the actor. In this way justice differs from other virtues that regulate the behavior of the individual alone.

Because of its other-oriented perspective, justice was considered the "social virtue" by modern ethicists. While the moderns were correct in their observation of justice's social nature, justice is first and foremost a characteristic of the individual. Thus, we know Mary to be a just woman or Danny to be an unjust man, that is, we identify individuals by the habits of justice (or injustice) that they manifest as individuals.

While it exhibits the social aspects of virtue in general, justice is different from other virtues in being "complete" virtue, that is, excellence in the fullest sense. It is considered so because the one who possesses it can make use of it not only by him or herself but also in his or her relations with other people (Aristotle 1962, V 1 1129b 1131–1132).

A Social Virtue

More than a trait of the individual, justice perfects a man or woman in terms of their relations with others and in this way, makes society better off (Aristotle 1962, V 1 1129b 1133–1135). As a result, justice is a social virtue that produces and preserves happiness for society or, in Aristotle's terms, the *polis* or political community (Aristotle 1962, V 1 1129b 1116–1119).

Justice's social aspects have intrigued people for centuries. Today, the social dimension of justice tends to dominate. It is often found in the term "social justice," which attempts to capture the notion of fairness in the distribution of society's benefits and burdens. Even so, the term "social justice" is relatively new, emerging from mid-nineteenth century collectivist/communitarian calls for the redistribution of individual wealth holdings. Now firmly entrenched, the term is typically used as a moralistic rallying cry within discussions about distributive, retributive, compensatory, and (more recently) restorative justice.

As a term, however, social justice is meaningless as a redundancy because justice itself is a social virtue. As Friedrich Hayek observed, social justice is nothing more than a mirage, an empty formula, a quasi-religious belief with no content, "a sign of the immaturity of our minds…a direct consequence of that anthropomorphism or personification by which naïve thinking tries to account for all self-ordering processes," and "a will-o'-the wisp which has lured men to abandon many of the values which in the past have inspired the development of civilization" (Hayek 1978, pp. 62–63, 67).

The basis of social justice is problematic, Hayek holds, because it shifts moral demands from the individual to society and gathers a collective force beyond that of the individual to convey an understanding that "members of society should organize themselves in a manner which makes it possible to assign particular shares of the product of society to the different individuals or group" (Hayek 1978, p. 64).

Put another way, the concept of social justice seeks to take decision-making power and hence autonomy from the individual and give it to a select group of people who will then take it upon themselves to redistribute society's benefits and burdens according to a particular pattern that is regarded as "just" (Hayek 1978, p. 64). In this way, others and not the individual determine where one will work, where one's earnings will be allocated, what obligations one has to others, and so forth. In this way, the concept of social justice diminishes individual autonomy and the central feature of the virtue of justice as a characteristic habit of the individual.

Moreover, because social justice is framed in the language of the common good, the redistribution it strives to achieve is determined by the few. These distributions (more properly understood as redistributions) will be regarded as more "just" than the distributions based upon the many choices of individuals who work, earn wages, and fulfill their individual moral obligations. Now, with calls for "social justice," individuals have a moral duty to submit to the collective power of an elite group that will coordinate the efforts of individuals toward some set of ends that their cohort determines to be worthwhile.[23] To enforce these moral imperatives, the teachers and preachers of morality, especially large sections of the clergy, are enlisted to enshrine social justice in the official doctrines of all Christian denominations.[24]

Not surprisingly, these modern notions of social justice are far removed from Aristotle's notions of justice as an individual and social virtue. In *The Politics* he explains his idea of the social dimension of justice in the simple phrase, "justice belongs to the city" (Aristotle 1995, I.2 1253a 1244).

For Aristotle, justice as a social virtue is an ordering mechanism of political associations, which determine what is fair within the relations of the city-state. Within the context of the city, in other words, justice regards matters of common concern and addresses the various forms of goodness perceived by members of the community (Aristotle 1995, III.13 1283a 1246). Justice is essential to a functioning society, as Ernest Barker explains, because a shared conception of what is good and just makes political life possible (Aristotle 1995, p. 361).

Even so, justice is primarily a characteristic habit of the individual having to do with the individual's "relations with his fellow men" (Aristotle 1962, V 1 1129b 1128–1130).

For Aristotle, justice is the bond that holds society together. Central to this concept is fair dealing and equality, but not in the way that we think of these concepts today. In Aristotle's time, equality was reserved for those who were equal and not for all (Aristotle 1995, III.9 1280a 1213–1215). Similarly, inequality was considered just, again for those who were unequal and not for all (Aristotle 1995, III.9 1280a 1216–1217).

Put another way, Aristotle was not an egalitarian in the modern sense of the term. Rather, he held that justice demands that we treat our equals equally and not treat those who are not our equals equally. Distributive justice, in this sense, would mean not giving everyone exactly the same privileges. Rather equal privileges would be given to those who are equal and unequal privileges to those who are unequal (Aristotle 1995, p. 357).

Of course, there are problems with such a system as Aristotle himself recognized. For one, people can be equal in one respect but not in others. People also

---

[23] Hayek argues further that such a system governed by "planners" ultimately leads to the individual being enslaved by powerful overseers. *The Road to Serfdom*, as he calls it, is the final end of a system in which the individual is made subservient to the collective (Hayek 1945, 2007).

[24] In this way, Hayek concludes, church leaders increasingly evidence a loss in faith in supernatural revelation and "appear to have sought refuge and consolation in a new 'social' religion which substitutes a temporal for a celestial promise of justice" (Hayek 1978, p. 66). Even if this is not the case, the prevalent use of the term "social justice" by religious leaders suggests that the redistributionist ideals of socialism have found a moral imperative with strong support within large segments of Christendom.

tend to be self-referential and make bad judgments where their own interests are involved (Aristotle 1995, 357 and III.359 1280a 1219–1221). As Aristotle observed, "(e)veryone agrees that in distributions the just share must be given on the basis of what one deserves, though not everyone would name the same criterion of deserving" (Aristotle 1962, V 3 1131a 1125–1127).

Worse, the propensity toward self-interest could be institutionalized in government where people might seek their own interests by attempting to establish governments to secure equalities. "Democrats reply by saying that justice consists in the will of a majority of person. Oligarchs reply by saying that it consists in the will of those with greater wealth, and that decisions should be taken on the basis of weight of property."[25]

In short, Aristotle recognized that people have a propensity to use the concept of justice to further their own political ambitions and that "while everybody is agreed about justice, and the principle of proportionate equality, people fail to achieve it in practice" (Aristotle 1995, V.1 1301a 1327).

The Organizing Virtue

For Aristotle, justice is a virtue that orders and regulates proper conduct within society, especially in regard to the relations of individuals with each other. Justice is "the bond that holds the association (the *polis*) together" (Aristotle 1962, V 5 1132b 1132–1133). It is the reciprocal return of what is proportional to what one has received that binds together the people of the shared enterprise of households and clans. Without it, society dissolves because of dissention. Justice therefore orders and regulates society and thereby preserves society's existence.

Justice's ordering and regulatory aspects have special relevance to business within capitalist systems because they inform what Friedman calls "the rules of the game" by which business affairs must be conducted (Friedman 1970). Although it is true that Aristotle thought commerce to be an illiberal occupation, his ideas regarding the formation and ends of justice as a virtue as well as his views on household management, the fairness of exchanges, and other justice-related aspects of common business practice are important to business' proper role in society. Not surprisingly, others have detailed many of these subjects (Cordero 1988; Dierksmeier and Pirson 2009; Duska 1993; Koehn 1992; Meikle 1996).

For our purposes, Aristotle's understanding of justice is important to business management because it establishes justice as something more than a principle. With Aristotle's justice, justice is deeply embedded in the practices of the individual (a

---

[25] (Aristotle 1962, V 3 1131a 1127–1128, 1995, VI.3 1318a 1325–1329). Aristotle observes further that inequalities and injustices will inevitably emerge in the formation of political systems. In the first case, if justice consists of the will of the majority, the majority will consider their own interests and act unjustly by confiscating the property of the rich minority. In the second case, if justice consists in the will of the few, the oligarch who owns more than all other owners of property will claim to be the sole ruler and tyranny will result (Aristotle 1995, VI.3 1318a 1330–1337).

characteristic habit), and both borne of and nurtured within the structures of civil society.

Summary: Justice

To summarize, justice is the highest of all the virtues, complete virtue (an excellence in the fullest sense) because the one who possesses it makes use of it not only alone, but also in relation to others. Justice places demands on the individual—that he or she distribute to each (self and others) according to desert. In this way, justice enables the individual to direct his or her will to relate properly to others and thereby advance fairness within society. For Aristotle, justice means equality for those who are equal and not for all. Thus, while it is not identical to virtue, justice is the whole of virtue and the bond that holds society together.

Courage (Fortitude)

Courage or fortitude (Gk. *andreia*), the mean of confidence and fear, is an important virtue of moral strength for Aristotle because it is a characteristic habit that enables the individual to persevere in adversity and withstand danger, fear, or trying circumstances.

Courage is a habit of mind that empowers the individual to regulate pain and strive toward the mean of cowardice and recklessness. It is a sort of willfulness that, as Thomas Aquinas explains, allows one to control the irascible appetites having to do with anger (Aquinas 2008, I 20 21 ad.22).

In short, courage governs the feelings of fear and confidence and allows the individual to remain poised yet forceful in fear inducing circumstances.

Confidence: Keen in the Thick of Action But Calm Beforehand

Aristotle provides numerous examples of both real courage and false courage in Book III of *The Nicomachean Ethics* (Aristotle 1962, III 7–9). Genuine courage, he maintains, quells a hot temper at times and encourages the timid to take action at other times. It is regarded as a virtue because it has the individual take reasonable risks in pursuit of a noble end.

In this sense, courage is the sort of self-possession that enables the individual to remain composed in the face of adversity. "A coward, a reckless man, and a courageous man are all concerned with the same situations," Aristotle observes (Aristotle 1962, III 7 1116a 1115). What differentiates the three is the ability to find the middle ground between extremes and remain poised yet able to act forcefully in fear inducing circumstances.

As Aristotle explains, the coward fears the wrong things in the wrong manner and is pessimistic and deficient in confidence (Aristotle 1962, III 7 1115b 1135). The reckless man, at the other extreme, is impetuous and often eager before danger arrives but stays out of it when it is there (Aristotle 1962, III 7 1116a 1118–1110). Aristotle goes so far to say that there is no name for a man who exceeds in a lack of fear because only a madman is so immune to pain that he fears nothing (Aristotle 1962, III 7 1115b 1126). The reckless man is boastful and imitates the courageous man, but does not stand his ground when there is something really to fear (Aristotle 1962, III 7 1115b 1130). Indeed, the most reckless men are reckless cowards (Aristotle 1962, III 7 1115b 1134).

The courageous man, in contrast to the other two, is keen in the thick of action but calm beforehand, confident and ready to endure hardship "because it is noble to do so or base to refuse" (Aristotle 1962, III 7 1116a 1115 and 1112).

In sum, the courageous person is "dauntless as a human being" and "will fear what is fearful; but … will endure it in the right way and as reason directs for the sake of acting nobly: that is the end of virtue" (Aristotle 1962, III 7 1115b 1112).

Example: The Courage of the Boxer

Although courage involves withstanding pain and sometimes abstaining from things that are pleasant, the end toward which courage is directed is pleasant, "obscured though it is by the attendant circumstances" (Aristotle 1962, III 9 1117b 1111). Aristotle draws on the example of the boxer to illustrate this relationship of the happy end to the pain associated with courageous acts.

For the boxer, the end of a fight is pleasant because there s/he receives adulation and fame—"the wreath and the honors," in Aristotle's words (Aristotle 1962, III 9 1117b 1113). S/He seeks this end despite the fact that the punches s/he receives hurt, as does the exertion associated with fighting. In fact, the painful elements are so great in number that the happy end appears small and devoid of pleasure (Aristotle 1962, III 9 1117b 1115). Yet, the boxer gets into the ring and boxes. Why does s/he do this?

The answer to this question is simple: the boxer endures hardships of the ring because s/he is a boxer and "it is noble to do so or base to refuse" (Aristotle 1962, III 7 1116a 1112).

Put another way, the boxer endures the punishment of his or her opponent because it is the right thing to do if s/he is to be a boxer. Should s/he fear the anticipated blows so much that s/he cannot enter the ring or shirks from his or her opponent when s/he is in the ring, then s/he does not actually spar and cannot be considered a boxer. Even if s/he is well trained in the art of pugilism and can display fancy footwork and strong punches against a speed bag, s/he does little more than show the extent of his or her training and the level of fitness. S/He remains untested and dissociated from the actual act of boxing. S/He is, in short, a cowardly person—fearful in the wrong manner, at the wrong time, in the wrong place.

On the other hand, the one who gets into the ring and proceeds to swing his or her fists madly without any sense of fear, wearing him or herself out against an opponent more skilled than s/he is, and then finds that s/he has become so exhausted that s/he can do nothing but stand and take a pounding, is not a real boxer. In being one so reckless to allow him or herself to be pounded to a bloody pulp such that s/he is sidelined with debilitating injuries, s/he has demonstrated that s/he is an emotion-driven street thug and not a real boxer.

The true boxer is one who is willing and able to conquer certain of his or her fears related to pain while remaining coolheaded in the pursuit of the good end. S/He is a person who steels him or herself to meet the adversary head on and with a firm sense of purpose—one who remains coolheaded and confident, able to conquer his or her fears and face the danger, pain, and adversity s/he will surely find in the ring (Aristotle 1962, III 9 1117b 1112–1120). S/He is a person who gets into the ring knowing s/he will meet the blows of an adversary, but soldiers on wisely against the opponent.

As ringside witnesses of such a boxer, we properly praise his or her demonstrations of courage as s/he boxes well.

Example: The Courage of the Whistleblower

The same sort of courage that the boxer displays in the ring is found in the courage of the business manager who must similarly display confidence, an ability to withstand fear, and perseverance in the face of adversity in trying circumstances. In business practice as in the boxing ring, the manager must understand his or her fear, address it in the right manner, in the right place, and at the right time while remaining coolheaded and focused on the good end.

Harris describes courage in the context of management, Treasurer explores it in relationship to leadership, and Naughton and Cornwall consider it in relation to entrepreneurship and the business life cycle (Harris 1999; Naughton and Cornwall 2006; Treasurer 2009, 2011). In all, the idea is the same—that moderation in handling fear, the determination of the mean of cowardice and recklessness, and the necessity of remaining poised while acting forcefully in an appropriate manner are important.

Perhaps the clearest illustration of courage in business is whistleblowing and cases such as that of Cynthia Cooper's at WorldCom. A great deal has already been written about Cooper and the WorldCom fraud and how Cooper's detective work as an internal auditor at WorldCom exposed some of the accounting irregularities there intended to deceive investors (Moberg and Romar 2003; Romar and Calkins 2008).

In a nutshell, Cooper and her staff conducted a secretive internal investigation at night and uncovered hundreds of millions of dollars of wrongful entries that resulted in the largest financial fraud in history. The discovery eventually led to massive layoffs at WorldCom, depressed share prices for ancillary telecommunications equipment manufacturers, and destruction of the firm's accounting firm, Arthur Andersen as well as the arrest and conviction of the chief perpetrators of the fraud.

Before she acted, however, Cooper considered the consequences of her actions, weighing them against the interests of the public. She also made sure she had all the facts and that they were accurate, sought outside advice, and explored alternative solutions to the problems she unearthed.[26] In the end, she realized that the bad behavior would continue to corrupt the company and all those touched by it if she did not act. Moreover, she realized that if she did not blow the whistle on the fraud, then she would become a collaborator in the corruption as well.

Throughout the ordeal, Cooper remained dauntless despite requests from her superiors to delay reports. She also faced resistance by her staff as they became concerned that they might end up being blamed for the mess. In the end, however, Cooper conquered her fears and remained coolheaded in the pursuit of a good end. She prepared well, met her adversaries head on with a firm sense of purpose and while she did not ignore or dismiss her fears, she was not crippled by them. In these ways, Cooper did the right thing, in the right way, at the right time, and was ultimately successful in advancing the betterment of herself and her community. She was courageous and we applaud her as we would the boxer in the ring. Not surprisingly, Cooper was one of three women nominated as Time Magazine's "Persons of the Year" in 2002 (Lacayo and Ripley 2002).

Temperance (Self-Control)

A fourth important virtue for Aristotle is temperance or self-control (Gk. *sōphrosynē*), which is the characteristic habit of moderation in the indulgence of the passions for pleasure.

Although typically thought to mean abstention from intoxicating drink, temperance is more accurately the mastery of oneself—the soundness of mind and discretion that allows one to be in control of the body's appetites for pleasurable satiation, stimulation, or relaxation (Aristotle 1962, 79 ftn 29 and III 10 1118a 1112).

Temperance is properly understood to be a moderating trait that governs what later moralists called the concupiscible appetites. It is self-control in regard to the appetites for food, drink, and sex and a virtue that seeks the middle ground between profligacy and dissipation on the one hand and insensitivity to pleasure and delight on the other.

Self-Control and Adulthood

For Aristotle, temperance is a characteristic habit that enables the individual to hold in check certain lustful and desirous pleasures—those that are "slavish and

---

[26] For a good summary of whistleblowing and its criteria, see (Dasgupta and Kesharwani 2010; Near and Miceli 1996). Other excellent whistleblowing resources include (Bok 1980; Callahan et al. 2004; Chertow et al. 1993; Davis 1989; Miceli and Near 1992; Near and Miceli 1985; Painter 1995; Radin and Calkins 2004).

bestial"—so as to seek the mean of insensitivity and self-indulgence (Aristotle 1962, III 10 1118a 1125). It is manifested when the individual follows right reason to "take() no pleasure in what is most pleasant to the self-indulgent, but rather finds it disgusting; in general, he takes no pleasure in what he should not, and no excessive pleasure in touch and taste" (Aristotle 1962, III 12 1119a 1111–1120).

Temperance is therefore a virtue of the mind as well as the body and the mark of an adult. In Aristotle's view, only children are intemperate and self-indulgent. When an adult gives in to self-indulgence, he or she becomes like a child, a whining slave to his passions and out of control in an unacceptable way.

Whereas children can be forgiven for their excesses because they have parents to discipline them (and parents should do so, in Aristotle's view, because "what grows wild needs to 'checked' or 'pruned'"), adults must show self-restraint by monitoring and curtailing their propensities to overindulge. In controlling themselves in this manner, mature individuals advance in virtue and toward their proper human end (Aristotle 1962, III 12 1119b 1111–1117).

Advancement in temperance in this way means that the individual must seek the middle ground of extremes related to attractive things. Because people are so drawn to pleasures, the notion of moderation itself has often been described by means of examples of temperance. We learn, for example, what moderation is early in life through tales such as *The Story of Goldilocks and the Three Bears* (Oral Tradition 2013). This and other similar stories reveal the importance of moderation. Through them, we learn early in life of the value of sensitivity to the middle ground in regard to food, drink, and sleep.

The same notion of moderation in regard to the concupiscible appetites is then carried forward variously into the adult realm and even into business. Carr has explored temperance in general Morse has considered it in terms of business practice (Carr 2002; Morse and Morse 2002).

Example: Temperance and Physical Fitness

Temperance is, in many ways, not unlike courage. Consider, for example, how it similarly applies to athletic training and performance.

For the weight lifter, competitive runner, or boxer to train effectively and compete well (which is the athlete's end or goal), he or she must work within his or her abilities to strive toward the middle ground of excess and deficiency. To do so, the athlete must train prudently and demonstrate courage, to be sure, but also moderate the inclination to over or under indulge the appetites for pleasure.

In addition, temperate training demands an understanding that the mean of one athlete cannot be exchanged for that of another and that temperate behavior varies from individual to individual. This means that the novice's intake of food, drink, sleep, and so forth cannot be extended to the elite athlete and vice versa if the two athletes are to advance in their sport. So, too, it means that both will need to understand the shifting nature of the middle ground in relation to the final good end.

Consistent betterment over the span of a lifetime for the athlete demands that he or she recognize that advancing age, physical deterioration, illness, lifestyle changes, changing training and fitness levels, and so forth will moderate the notion of the mean. Yesterday's temperance will not necessarily be today's or tomorrow's and the food and other intake that was appropriate for an individual as a young athlete will become excessive as that person ages to become a more sedentary adult.

In the end, while not easy to achieve, temperance is crucial to the individual's attainment of the good life and final end. Settling on a notion of right reason and exercising it to find the mean of insensitivity and self-indulgence related to the individual's current condition and particular circumstances are not easily achieved but are nevertheless crucial to the individual's current sense of joy and his or her attainment of fulfillment and happiness.

Other Virtues

Thus far we have considered Aristotle's four main virtues, described by later moralists as the cardinal virtues since other virtues hinge or turn (Lat. *cardo*) on them.[27]

Aristotle identifies these other virtues in Book IV of *The Nicomachean Ethics* (Aristotle 1962, p. IV). They include generosity, magnificence, high-mindedness, the mid-range of ambition, gentleness, friendliness, truthfulness, and wittiness. All of them, as virtues, contribute to the good life and becoming one's best.

Generosity

Generosity might seem to be an odd choice for a virtue, but Aristotle begins Book IV with it and contrasts generosity with magnificence, which we will treat presently.

Generosity or liberality is an excellence of the soul by which an individual gives appropriately the right amount, to the right people, at the right time (Aristotle 1962, IV 1 1120a 1125). It is the mean of extravagance and stinginess and involves the giving and taking of material goods. By "material goods," Aristotle means everything whose value can be measured in money (Aristotle 1962, IV 1 1119b 1125).

For Aristotle a generous act does not depend on the amount given, but on the characteristic of the giver and his or her relationship to property. A person can therefore be considered generous if he or she gives less than others but does so out of smaller resources (Aristotle 1962, IV 1 1120b 1110).

---

[27] As John Rickaby explains, "The term *cardo* means a hinge, that on which a thing turns, its principal point … The origin of the fourfold system is traceable to Greek philosophy; other sources are earlier, but the Socratic source is most definite. Among the reporters of Socrates, Xenophon is vague on the point; Plato in *The Republic* puts together in a system the four virtues adopted later, with modifications by St. Thomas." (Rickaby 1999).

Magnificence

Magnificence, on the other hand, is giving on a grand scale. Again, "scale" is relative to the individual, but the idea here is similar to generosity in that the nature of the virtue hinges on the ability of the giver to spend greatly on worthwhile things (Aristotle 1962, IV 2 1122b 1110–1115).

Unlike generosity, magnificence has the individual spend greatly on things that produce splendid results, things that are uncommon but valuable. Spending on things related to the common good or that happen only once such as a wedding constitute magnificence (Aristotle 1962, IV 2 1122b 1120–1123a 1125). Outlandish spending that leaves one destitute or penny-pinching are vices because they result in unhappy ends—poverty on one hand and ruin of the grand gesture on the other (Aristotle 1962, IV 2 1123a 1125–1130).

High-mindedness

High-mindedness or magnanimity is similar to magnificence, but the two differ in terms of the locus of greatness. Whereas magnificence is about greatness befitting an occasion, magnanimity is about greatness of spirit or high-mindedness (Aristotle 1962, 89 ftn 10 and 93 ftn 18).

Aristotle values high-mindedness such that he calls it "the crown of the virtues" because high-mindedness magnifies the other virtues. In this regard, magnificence cannot exist without the other virtues (Aristotle 1962, IV 3 1124a 1121).

For Aristotle, magnanimity is the greatness of soul that enables the individual to take what he or she deserves, whether good fortune or misfortune (Aristotle 1962, IV 3 1124a 1125). It is the mean of pettiness and vanity and is manifest in the individual bearing good fortune with grace and without becoming haughty and arrogant.

Magnanimity is also displayed by the individual in unfavorable situations when he or she does not overly lament his or her position and cry for help when encountering unavoidable misfortune.

Magnanimity is the sweet spot between small-mindedness and vanity. It is the middle ground between the sort of insensitivity that would result in a person depriving him or herself of the good he or she deserves and the conceit that would result in a person displaying him or herself with ostentation so as to boast about his or her good fortune (Aristotle 1962, IV 3 1125a 1115–1135).

Ambition and the Lack of Ambition as the Extremes of an Unnamed Virtue

Perhaps the strangest of all of Aristotle's virtues is one that is unnamed and only described in terms of its extremes. This so-called "unnamed virtue" is the mean of ambition and lack of ambition and is unnamed because the person who possesses it is unremarkable, that is, does not have a name (Aristotle 1962, IV 4 1125b 1121–1125).

A virtue related to the drive for success, the unnamed virtue holds it to be wrongful for one to strive for honor more than one should or to derive honor from wrong sources. It also holds it to be improper to deliberately desire not to be honored even for noble achievements.

The individual who manifests the unnamed virtue appears to lack ambition, but in comparison to a person who actually lacks ambition, appears ambitious. In the end then, one who possesses this virtue appears to be neither ambitious nor unambitious and therefore seems unremarkable to others (Aristotle 1962, IV 4 1125b 1120–1125).

Gentleness

Gentleness is also a virtue for Aristotle because it enables the individual to show anger under the right circumstances, with the right people, in the right manner, at the right time, and for the right length of time (Aristotle 1962, IV 5 1125b 1132).

It is noteworthy that Aristotle considers gentleness to be the mark of a man—a concept sometimes overlooked by modern males. For Aristotle, gentleness facilitates the good life and is the mean of short-temperedness and outright apathy. It is that virtue that allows an individual to be unruffled and not driven by emotion (Aristotle 1962, IV 5 1125b 1135).

Friendliness

The virtue of gentleness is similar to friendliness, another of Aristotle's virtues. A characteristic habit that has an individual put up with or refuse to put up with the right things in the right manner, friendliness is the mean of obsequiousness and grouchiness (Aristotle 1962, IV 6 1126b 1110–1115 and 1118).

Friendliness resembles friendship but it is not identical to friendship in that it does not involve emotion or affection for associates (Aristotle 1962, IV 6 1126b 1122). Nevertheless, friendliness is important to social relations and living together in the shared association of the *polis*.

Truthfulness

Truthfulness, too, is important to life in common because it assures honest relations. As the mean of boastfulness and self-deprecation, truthfulness is a characteristic habit of excellence of the soul whereby the individual speaks the truth, avoids falsehood, and is honest.

Here, Aristotle is not concerned with truthfulness in contracts, which would be a matter more relevant to justice, but the truthfulness of one who "is truthful in his speech and in his life simply because it is part of his character to be that kind of man" (Aristotle 1962, IV 7 1127b 1121–1123). Again, Aristotle does not define truthfulness *per se*, but describes it in terms of its abridgments.

Wittiness

Last and as sort of a finale, Aristotle identifies wittiness as virtue. The mean of buffoonery and boorishness, wittiness is a form of thoughtful humor that allows the individual to be tactful and fun.

Because relaxation and amusement are integral to the good life, Aristotle considers wittiness to be an important characteristic of the individual. He explains at length the nature of true wit by contrasting it with attempts to be funny at any cost, jokes at the expense of others, and dourness (Aristotle 1962, IV 8 1128a 1121–1115, 1117, and 1131). People who lack wit are buffoons, slanderers, or sourpusses. People who possess wit listen to others and engage in repartee that is thoughtful, tactful, and pleasurable—and so with wittiness we end the consideration of Aristotle's virtues on a fitting pleasant note.

Chapter 9
Building a Virtue Theory for Business

Ability will enable a man to get to the top, but character will keep him from falling.

—Chinese Proverb

Virtue's Various Expressions

Aristotle's virtue theory is foundational to western ethics. Understanding it is helpful because, as Charles Larmore explains, it increases our self-understanding and enables us to know better "how we have become what we are" (Larmore 1992, p. 191). Perhaps more important, understanding Aristotle's virtue ethics helps us "remember what we have had good reason to leave behind" as our moral theories developed over subsequent centuries (Larmore 1992, p. 191).

Contemporary moralists have massaged Aristotle's ideas, modifying and adapting them to fit contemporary settings, including business. Keenan, for one, draws from Aristotle to identify self-esteem, hospitality, wisdom, gratitude, sympathy, humor, and physical fitness as important virtues for contemporary life (Keenan and James 1996). Similarly, Robert Solomon relies on Aristotle to recommend honesty fairness, trust, and toughness as basic virtues for business as well as friendliness, honor, loyalty, and shame as important virtues for the corporate self (Solomon, *Ethics and Excellence: Cooperation and Integrity in Business*, 1992).

In general, these and other contemporary moralists build on a legacy of interpretations and adaptations that began not long after Aristotle's ideas began to proliferate. The following distils some of these theories, culminating in Adam Smith's ideas about virtue in the context of free-markets.

Stoicism

Stoicism, which developed around 300 BC and shortly after Aristotle's death in 322 BC, was one of the first departures from Aristotle's virtue theory. Stoicism held that emotions like fear or attachments to pleasures either were, or arose from, false judgments and that the sage—a person who had attained moral and intellectual

M. Calkins, *Developing a Virtue-Imbued Casuistry for Business Ethics,* Issues in Business
Ethics 42, DOI 10.1007/978-94-017-8724-6_9, © Springer Netherlands 2014

perfection—would control them (Baltzly 2010). Today we understand stoicism to be synonymous with calm endurance.

Not unlike Sophocles, Plato, Aristotle, and the other early Greeks, the Stoics focused on the end of happiness and attempted to systematize ethics and establish what was to count as the final good or end of human action.[1]

As Gisela Striker explains, early Stoics proposed that the proper human end was a consistent life or life in agreement with nature, where "nature" was conceived to be a rational being. According to this rationale, natural things were thought to exist in a hierarchy in conformity to divine reason and human beings, because they possessed a god-like ability to think, were thought to hold a position just below the gods. The human "good" then, was thought to consist in the perfection of human reason. By extension, human virtue was thought to be more than acting correctly: it was first and foremost a matter of acting reasonably and for the right reasons.

For the Stoic, the paradigmatic virtuous person was a sage (a mature or venerable person of sound judgment) whose every action was informed by insights into the will of Zeus and whose only desire was to conform to nature's laws.

As Athens declined and greater pluralism ensued after Rome's conquest of Greece, more emphasis was placed on natural law and the human ability to discern right from wrong. Duty, control of the passions, and "equality before a universal moral law" began to take root in Western culture (Stackhouse et al. 1995, p. 132).

Shortly thereafter, skeptics began to criticize stoicism for its coolness and insensibility. Even so, as Max Stackhouse, *et al.*, point out, "Ideas of modern democracy, human rights, and mass markets might not have developed without the Stoics' moral challenges to the ancient tribal societies, the state-dominated political philosophy of Plato, or the household-dominated political philosophy of Aristotle" (Stackhouse et al. 1995, p. 132).

Influential Moderns

Stoicism's emphasis on natural order combined with its inward-directed and unworldly morality influenced certain early Christian moralists and Enlightenment philosophers (Striker 1992).

The ancient Greeks introduced the notion of striving for personal excellence for society's male elite, but as the idea spread it gained popular appeal. With time it was extended outside the top echelons of society to the lower ranks and by the modern era with its emphasis on equality of persons, it was applied generally. As Larmore notes, "One of the great insights of modern times, beginning in the Reformation, has been an appreciation of the moral possibilities of ordinary life: moral excellence

---

[1] Stoicism can be divided into Early, Middle, and Late forms. Early Stoa dates from 300 BC to the middle of the second century BC Middle Stoa dates from the middle of the second century BC and is represented by Panaetius (c. 180–109 BC) and Posidonius (c. 135–151 BC). The Stoics of the Roman Empire represent late Stoa. For more, see (Striker 1992, vol. II, pp. 1208–1213).

is not reserved for the hero or the saint, but is achievable even by the humblest of us, in the everyday areas of work and family" (Larmore 1992, p. 190).

The following sections show how ancient Greek philosophy was selectively embraced, modified, and at times discarded by key figures of the Enlightenment. It addresses only three figures from this era and concentrates on Adam Smith to show the progression of views on virtue and the ways it was incorporated into the moral conventions related to free markets.

Thomas Hobbes

Many of Aristotle's and the ancient Greeks' fundamental notions about the human being and final good end were called into question or discarded altogether during the Enlightenment because they could not be verified by means of reason alone. Thomas Hobbes' (1588–1679) was key in this movement and questioned the fundamental notions of morality.

In *The Leviathan*, Hobbes argued that moral philosophy was "nothing else but the Science of what is *Good* and *Evill*, in the conversation, and Society of mankind," where good and evil "signify our appetites and aversions, which in different tempers, customs, and doctrines of men are different" (Hobbes 1988, I, XV, p. 82). Aristotle's concept of an overarching *telos* was effectively removed with this assertion and in its place the idea that when man is in a state of nature—a condition of war—private appetite becomes the measure of good and evil (Hobbes 2012, I, XV).

Hobbes draws these conclusions first by arguing that nature makes all people equal but endows them with variously stronger and weaker faculties and a competitive nature (passion) such that there are three main causes of quarrel: competition, diffidence, and the quest for glory (Hobbes 1988, I, XIII, pp. 63–64). In the state of nature, these passions lead to a condition of "war of every man against every man" (Hobbes 2012, I, XIII and XIV and II, XIX). As Hobbes explains:

> In such condition there is no place for industry, because the fruit thereof is uncertain: and consequently no culture of the earth; no navigation, nor use of the commodities that may be imported by sea; no commodious building; no instruments of moving and removing such things as require much force; no knowledge of the face of the earth; no account of time; no arts; no letters; no society; and which is worst of all, continual fear, and danger of violent death; and the life of man, solitary, poor, nasty, brutish, and short. (Hobbes 1988, I, XIII, pp. 64–65, 2012, I, XIII)

In the state of war of all against all, nothing can be unjust and notions of right and wrong, justice and injustice, have no place (Hobbes 2012, I, XIII). "Where there is no common power, there is no law; where no law, no injustice. Force and fraud are in war the two cardinal virtues. Justice and injustice are none of the faculties neither of the body nor mind" (Hobbes 2012, I, XIII).

Out of fear of death and a desire for the opportunity to live comfortably, people therefore enter into agreements with each other and forge a compact to assure peace. The articles of peace that they drawn up, the "Lawes of Nature," are limiting precepts or general rules of restraint that men find by reason. The most essential of these laws is that of the liberty (the absence of external impediments) to preserve one's own life. The liberty to exercise this liberty or to forbear against those who would violate it is what Hobbes takes to be a "right."[2]

Hobbes then goes on to argue that "it is necessary for all men that seek peace to lay down certain rights of nature; that is to say, not to have liberty to do all they list" (Hobbes 2012, I, XV). They must, in other words, limit their liberties for the sake of peace and thereby agree to obey the laws of a sovereign or "Leviathan" that has absolute control. This "covenant" as it was called, rests on the premise of mutuality, that "every man should say to every man: I authorise and give up my right of governing myself to this man, or to this assembly of men, on this condition; that thou give up, thy right to him, and authorise all his actions in like manner" (Hobbes 2012, II, XVII). The sovereign, even if he or she is a despot, has absolute power as a result.

Liberty and the freedom to divest oneself of a right to all things were therefore the first two of general rules from which justice, gratitude, "compleasance" or accommodation to society, pardon, and a host of others, flowed (Hobbes 1988, XIV, pp. 66–67 and XV, pp. 78–79). Unlike Aristotle, "justice, equity, modesty, mercy," and, in sum, doing to others as we would be done to, of themselves, without the terror of some power to cause them to be observed, are contrary to our natural passions, that carry us to partiality, pride, revenge, and the like (Hobbes 2012, II, XVII). Moral virtue, in other words, does not exist except under the power of the sword.

It is an understatement to say that Hobbes' worldview was bleak and that his notion of humanity emphasized self-interest while overlooking other important human attributes such as sympathy or what Adam Smith calls, "fellow feeling." Even so, Hobbes' ideas carry forward many of Plato's ideas from *The Republic* and set the ground for the contractarianism we saw earlier in Rawls' veil of ignorance.[3]

David Hume

Hobbes's ideas about natural rights, liberty, and political structures are typically compared to those of John Locke (1632–1704) whose arguments against absolute monarchies not only countered Hobbes' but also influenced America's founders and later philosophers such as David Hume and Immanuel Kant. While Locke is a primary figure of the era and critical to an understanding of rights—especially the property rights that are essential to free markets—he is overshadowed by David Hume (1711–1776) as a virtue theorist.

---

[2] In Hobbes' words, "right of nature, which writers commonly call jus naturale, is the liberty each man hath to use his own power as he will himself for the preservation of his own nature" (Hobbes 2012, I, XIV).

[3] The moral theory of contractarianism claims that moral norms derive their normative force from the idea of contract or mutual agreement.

Demonstrating an extensive familiarity with the virtue theories of the ancient Greeks (Plato, Homer, Cicero, and others), Hume was not unlike others of the Enlightenment era in concentrating on the roots of morality.[4] In *An Enquiry Concerning the Principles of Morals*, he argues that, "reason and sentiment concur in almost all moral determinations and conclusions" (Hume 1983, I, p. 15). Our moral distinctions cannot be discerned by pure reason nor can they be resolved into sentiment. Rather, Hume argued, moral reasoning is a confluence of sentiment and reason that occurs in the following way:

> The final sentence, it is probable, which pronounces characters and actions amiable or odious, praise-worthy or blameable; that which stamps on them the mark of honour or infamy, approbation or censure; that which renders morality an active principle, and constitutes virtue our happiness, and vice our misery: It is probable, I say, that this final sentence depends on some internal sense or feeling, which nature has made universal in the whole species. For what else can have an influence of this nature? But in order to pave the way for such a sentiment, and give a proper discernment of its object, it is often necessary, we find, that much reasoning should precede, that nice distinctions be made, just conclusions drawn, distant comparisons formed, complicated relations examined, and general facts fixed and ascertained. (Hume 1983, I, p. 15)

Hume also considered the origin, usefulness, and agreeableness of morality. The qualities in morality that he deemed "useful to ourselves" included discretion, industry, reasonable frugality, honesty, fidelity, truth, and endowments "a thousand more of the same kind, no man will ever deny to be excellencies and perfections" (Hume 1983, VI, I, pp. 51–57). Qualities "agreeable to ourselves," he thought, included "chearfulness," greatness of mind or "dignity of character," courage, tranquility, benevolence, and delicacy of taste (Hume 1983, VII, pp. 61–68). Finally, "qualities agreeable to others," the so-called companionable virtues, included good manners or politeness, wit and ingenuity, a generous spirit and self-value, decency, cleanliness, and so on (Hume 1983, VIII, pp. 68–72).

These and other like qualities, virtues and vices, and morality itself, Hume maintained, were "recognized" (Hume 1983, IX, I, p. 76). Some virtues, such as justice, he considered to be "artificial" and formed out of necessity. The constructed laws of justice, for example, are artificial and allow us to live together and to flourish individually and collectively. The utility of these laws, Hume thought, "pleases us" for without them wagoners, coachmen, and so forth, "cannot even pass each other on the road" (Hume 1983, IV, p. 38).

In these ways, Hume argued for "artificial virtues" and while he probed certain qualities of character at length, he avoided the traditional terms of "virtue" and "vice."[5] Not unlike Larmore's point about the foreignness of Aristotelian ethics to contemporary culture, Hume thought that the ancient Greek notions of virtue and vice could not be rendered accurately into modern English. He preferred to sidestep the concept and instead identify objects of praise as "talents" and blamable or censurable qualities as "defects" (Hume 1983, Appendix IV, pp. 98–99). Accordingly, he main-

---

[4] For examples, see (Hume 1983, Sect. II, Part I, 17, Sect. III, Part I, 24 f, and Sect. VII, 63).

[5] (Kline 2012; Vanderschraaf 1999) extend Hume's ideas into institutions and commercial practices.

tained that there can be no greater philosophical truths more advantageous to society than those which "represent virtue in all her genuine and engaging charms, and make us approach her with ease, familiarity, and affection" (Hume 1983, IX, II, p. 79).

In Hume's view, virtue was simple and recognizable. At its core, when "(t)he dismal dress falls off, with which many divines, and some philosophers have covered her…nothing appears but gentleness, humanity, beneficence, affability; nay even, at proper intervals, play, frolic, and gaiety" (Hume 1983, IX, II, p. 79). Thus, similar to Aristotle's runner,

> (Hume's figure of truth and virtue) talks not of useless austerities and rigours, suffering and self-denial. She declares, that her sole purpose is, to make her votaries and all mankind, during every instant of their existence, if possible, cheerful and happy; nor does she ever willingly part with any pleasure but in hopes of ample compensation in some other period of their lives. The sole trouble, which she demands, is that of just calculation, and a steady preference of the greater happiness. (Hume 1983, IX, II, p. 79)

As we can see from this quote, neither the boundaries between virtue theories nor the boundaries between virtues and talents, vices and defects can be fixed precisely (Hume 1983, Appendix IV, p. 99). Rather, virtues and virtue theories overlap and influence each other. It is this overlap that Alasdair MacIntyre explored in *After Virtue*, a text that helped to renew interest in virtue ethics. As Janet Coleman explains,

> In *After Virtue* MacIntyre outlines a history of apparently incompatible and changing notions of virtue as these related to changing social orders from Homer, to Aristotle, the New Testament, Aquinas, to Jane Austen and the modern liberalism of Ben Franklin and beyond. He asked: can we disentangle from these rival versions a unitary core concept of the virtues? He believed we could and so sought to give an account of a unitary core which would be more compelling than *any* of the rival versions discussed. (Coleman 1994, p. 65)

MacIntyre concludes from this exercise that a virtue can be thought of in at least three different ways:

> (A) virtue is a quality which enables an individual to discharge his or her social role (Homer); a virtue is a quality which enables an individual to move towards the achievement of the specifically human *telos*, whether natural or supernatural (Aristotle, the New Testament and Aquinas); a virtue is a quality which has utility in achieving earthly and heavenly success (Franklin). (MacIntyre 1984, p. 185)

Whether or not MacIntyre successfully was "able to disentangle from these rival and various claims a unitary core concept of the virtues of which we can give a more compelling account than any of the other accounts so far," he renewed interest in the various virtue theories of the past and inspired queries into their applicability to contemporary society (MacIntyre 1984, p. 186).

The Virtues of Commerce of Adam Smith

As we have seen, Hobbes and Hume established many of the basic notions of modern virtue theory. While their contributions have been significant, they pale in comparison to those of Adam Smith (1723–1790) in terms of linking virtue to free markets and business.

In the following, we will consider what Christopher Berry calls "the virtues of commerce" and Smith's reworking of Aristotelian virtue theory for modern business (Berry 1992). In doing so, we will also review and further Patricia Werhane's and my earlier work, see (Calkins and Werhane 1998).

To begin, when describing the theoretical underpinnings of Western business, commentators typically reference Adam Smith's *The Wealth of Nations* (Smith, *The Wealth of Nations*, 1976). Even so, as economic historian Joseph Schumpeter observes, "the *Wealth of Nations* does not contain a single analytic idea, principle, or method that was entirely new in 1776" (Schumpeter 1954, p. 184, italics omitted).

Despite its lack of originality on some levels, as a collective analysis of eighteenth-century thinking, *The Wealth of Nations* is almost inexhaustible in its richness and has influenced economic theory for over two centuries. In the following we will see how Adam Smith's account of the virtues enjoys a fate similar to that of his account of economics.

In general, Smith's account of the virtues derives from his knowledge of Aristotle and the Stoics, was influenced by his reading of Samuel von Pufendorf (1632–1694), and molded by the thinking of his mentor, David Hume. While these others helped form his thinking, Smith and not Hume elaborated the role of the virtues in commercial society, and that elaboration, however intellectually derived, has had an important influence on what later came to be called the "bourgeois virtues" (McCloskey 1994).

In two of his main treatises, Smith made the important point that people engaged in commerce could be virtuous and that the virtues of prudence, justice, and self-command were critical to a well-functioning commercial and free enterprise-based political economy.[6]

Unlike his predecessor Bernard Mandeville (1670–1733), whose views are often attributed erroneously to Smith, Smith argued against the thesis that private vices are public virtues, and that greed, avarice, and selfishness can contribute to the public economic well being.

In Smith's view, commerce is a morally decent activity and people who engage in commerce have the capacity to be morally virtuous while engaged in economic activities. In this way, Smith departs significantly from Aristotle on the topic of commerce.

Sympathy of Fellow-Feeling

Although *The Wealth of Nations* was Smith's most popular work, he developed many of his ideas there as well as his moral philosophy in an earlier treatise entitled, *The Theory of Moral Sentiments* (Smith, *The Theory of Moral Sentiments*, 1976, *The Wealth of Nations*, 1976). In this earlier book Smith argues against Hobbes'

---

[6] In addition to the two books mentioned here, Smith's other major accomplishment was (Smith 1982).

pessimism and authoritarianism and proffers sympathy as an alternative and basis of a virtue ethic compatible with individual enterprise, opportunity, and responsibility.

As Robert Boyden Lamb has argued, in Smith, sympathy stands in contrast to self-interest as a motivating force in morality (Lamb 1974). For Smith, sympathy—an "original passion of human nature" or "fellow-feeling" that develops through "changing places in fancy" with someone else—is the ground of morality and a universal trait of human nature (Smith, *The Theory of Moral Sentiments*, 1976, I.i.1.1 and I.i.1.3).

Sympathy employs the copying capacity of our imaginations and is a latent capacity wherein we imagine ourselves to be in another's situation, even in another's body. It is the manner by which we "form some idea of (someone's) sensations, and even feel something which, though weaker in degree, is not altogether unlike them" (Smith, *The Theory of Moral Sentiments*, 1976, I.i.1.2).

As fellow-feeling, sympathy explains how we can have affection for others and how we can share a passion of concern *for* others *with* others. As Smith explains: "How selfish soever man may be supposed, there are evidently some principles in his nature, which interest him in the fortune of others, and render their happiness necessary to him, though he derives nothing from it except the pleasure of seeing it" (Smith, *The Theory of Moral Sentiments*, 1976, I.i.1.1).

Sympathy is the means whereby we understand the feelings of another, for example, a murderer, and not share in or even necessarily be repulsed by them (Heilbroner 1987, p. 58; Smith, *The Theory of Moral Sentiments*, 1976, I.i.1.10, I.i.11.12, I.i.13).

Although Smith regards sympathy to be a natural trait of the subject, a "sentiment" and an "original passion of human nature," he nevertheless relates it to objects (Smith, *The Theory of Moral Sentiments*, 1976, I.i.1.1). An individual who is sympathetic (the subject) looks to something other than himself or herself (an object) for a measure of affective propriety. Accordingly, sympathetic propriety or suitability hinges on how well a person's sentiments correspond to an objective stimulus. Moreover, sympathetic propriety relies on the ability of spectators to go along with the passions of the person principally concerned. Thus, when the principal person's passions are suitable to their objects, spectators approve of the passions and claim that they are in "entire sympathy" with the principal person. As Smith explains:

> He who admires the same poem, or the same picture, and admires them exactly as I do, must surely allow the justness of my admiration. He who laughs at the same joke, and laughs along with me, cannot well deny the propriety of my laughter. On the contrary, the person who, upon these different occasions, either feels no such emotion as that which I feel, or feels none that bears any proportion to mine, cannot avoid disapproving my sentiments on account of their dissonance with his own. (Smith, *The Theory of Moral Sentiments*, 1976, I.i.3.1)

Despite these proclivities, because the degree of passion that animates the person principally concerned can never be imagined completely by someone else for more than a moment, the person principally concerned who nevertheless longs for the relief of the complete sympathy of others must lower the level of his passions "to harmony and concord with the emotions of those who are about him" (Smith, *The Theory of Moral Sentiments*, 1976, I.i.4.7). The principal person must modify or vary his or her sentiments, in other words, if he or she hopes to attain the sympathy of others.

These characteristics of sympathetic propriety form the basis of Smith's notions of virtue. For Smith, virtue involves the same suitableness, proportion, and propriety associated with sympathy. Instead of being a sort of emotional harmony, however, virtue has to do with causes and the consequences, the decency, or "ungracefulness" of action. As Smith explains:

> The sentiment or affection of the heart from which any action proceeds, and upon which its whole virtue or vice must ultimately depend, may be considered under two different aspects, or in two different relations; first, in relation to the cause which excites it, or the motive which gives occasion to it; and secondly, in relation to the end which it proposes, or the effect which it tends to produce. (Smith, *The Theory of Moral Sentiments*, 1976, I.i.3.5 and II. i. Introduction, 1)

As a result, someone who practices virtue (Smith's "virtuous man") is an individual "whom we naturally love and revere the most" (Smith, *The Theory of Moral Sentiments*, 1976, III.3.35). According to Smith,

> (A virtuous person) joins, to the most perfect command of his own original and selfish feelings, the most exquisite sensibility both to the original and sympathetic feelings of others. The man who, to all the soft, the amiable, and the gentle virtues, joins all the great, the awful, and the respectable, must surely be the natural and proper object of our highest love and admiration. (Smith, *The Theory of Moral Sentiments*, 1976, III.3.35)

Self-Command

In Smith's view, a perfectly virtuous person "acts according to the rules of perfect prudence, of strict justice, and of proper benevolence" (Smith, *The Theory of Moral Sentiments*, 1976, VI.iii.1). Such a person acts "with cool deliberation in the midst of the greatest dangers and difficulties" (Smith, *The Theory of Moral Sentiments*, 1976, VI.iii.11). He or she observes "religiously the sacred rules of justice in spite both of the greatest interests which might tempt, and the greatest injuries which might provoke (him or her) to violate them" (Smith, *The Theory of Moral Sentiments*, 1976, VI.iii.11). At the same time, he or she is never discouraged "by the malignity and ingratitude" of others (Smith, *The Theory of Moral Sentiments*, 1976, VI.iii.11).

For Smith, self-command is a great virtue because anyone who possesses it is able to set aside selfish interests for the sake of peaceful coexistence with others and thereby achieve magnanimity. He or she is continent and capable of controlling his or her passions through a combination of knowledge, foresight, self-reliance, and self-control (Smith, *The Theory of Moral Sentiments*, 1976, VI.iii.1 and IV.ii.6). The self-commanded person is therefore capable of integrating into society and participating in the community's fruitful or productive interactions.

In Smith's view, self-command is so great that "all the other virtues seem to derive their principal lustre" from it (Smith, *The Theory of Moral Sentiments*, 1976, VI.iii.11). As a virtue, it enables other virtues to be exercised and thereby allows a person to be something other than a well-intentioned bystander.

Self-command helps the individual control the passions that tend either toward excessive fear and anger or toward excessive ease, pleasure, applause, and self-grat- ification. In this regard self-command is sort of a combined Aristotelian temperance and courage that enables the individual to regulate the passions (Smith, *The Theory of Moral Sentiments*, 1976, VI.iii.3).

According to Smith, all great men possess the virtue of self-command. Follow- ing the lead of the Stoics and the archetype of the warrior-hero, self-command is a virtue that enables the warrior to face danger or torture yet "preserves his tranquil- lity unaltered, and suffers no word, no gesture to escape…which does not perfectly accord with the feelings of the most indifferent spectator" (Smith, *The Theory of Moral Sentiments*, 1976, VI.iii.5). More than mere bravado, however, the hero's greatness here is related to an ability to combine knowledge of the rules of justice with a personal sense of duty and a commitment to act wisely (Smith, *The Theory of Moral Sentiments*, 1976, VI.iii.1 and 11).

Such action is rare and hard won and so we laud the self-commanded person as we would Aristotle's boxer and wish him or her to be rewarded with "all sorts of honours and rewards" and crowning him "with wealth, and power, and honours of every kind" (Smith, *The Theory of Moral Sentiments*, 1976, III.5.9).

Proper Wealth Acquisition Versus Greed

Given this background, Smith goes on to conceive of wealth as the material evi- dence of industriousness and moral greatness. Following the lead of the early Greeks, Smith thinks that wealth has no moral worth of its own and can be acquired rightly or wrongly. When it is acquired wrongly it is debilitating, as evident in the idle rich who revel in unearned riches, yet are incapable of achieving real magna- nimity because of their unwillingness to risk embarrassment or distress related to the undermining of their social status. When wealth is properly acquired, however, it can be used as a measure of happiness and industriousness (Smith, *The Theory of Moral Sentiments*, 1976, I.iii.2.4 and 2.5). In these latter observations, Smith's views deviate from Aristotle's.

For Smith, wealth acquisition and self-command are especially linked because when we seek wealth at any cost we eventually lose our virtuous qualities. The cor- ruption is not immediate but the result of a series of personal compromises related to unrestrained wealth seeking. It begins with undue admiration of the condition of the rich and misappropriated sympathy. By this, Smith means that in state of head- long pursuit of wealth we are inclined to sympathize more with joy than with sor- row, desire to appear lovely to others, and inclined to look to the rich as the model of happiness (Smith, *The Theory of Moral Sentiments*, 1976, I.iii.2.1, III.2.1, and I.iii.2.2). Smith suggests,

(The rich seem to us to have attained a perfect state of happiness) in all our waking dreams and idle reveries, we had sketched out to ourselves as the final object of all our desires. We feel, therefore, a peculiar sympathy with the satisfaction of those who are in it. We favour all their inclinations, and forward all their wishes....We could even wish them immortal; and it seems hard to us, that death should at last put an end to such perfect enjoyment. (Smith, *The Theory of Moral Sentiments*, 1976, I.iii.2.2)

In pursuing wealth in this manner, those of modest means not only emulate the rich, but also become increasingly fearful of the obscurity of poverty. They grow to despise their modest circumstances and become like the poor man's son who finds his father's cottage unbearably small in comparison to the rich man's castle. They huddle under the flimsy umbrella of power and riches—that "immense fabric" that keeps "off the summer shower, not the winter storm"—and in the end, grow fatigued from trying to acquire labor-saving devices and other things that they think will bring them comfort (Smith, *The Theory of Moral Sentiments*, 1976, I.iii.2.1 and IV.1.8). In doing so, however, they end up sacrificing real tranquility and trade their original state of calm for one of obsequiousness and mental turmoil.

In exercising self-command, however, Smith believes people will "strain with every nerve" to achieve wisdom and virtue, "those ends which it is the purpose of (our) being to advance" (Smith, *The Theory of Moral Sentiments*, 1976, II.iii.3.3 and I.iii.3.1 and 2). Those who are self-commanded will not be greedy, since rapacity evidences a lack of control. They will be rational and exercise a modicum of self-denial (Schelling 1984). The self-commanded will seek wealth in a self-disciplined manner, acquiring things yet remaining modest and plain in the pursuit. Those in possession of this virtue will be known for their probity, prudence, generosity, and frankness. Their lifestyle will avoid the extremes of Spartan discipline with its abnegation of the passions as well as the inactivity of the polite and idle rich. They will, in the end, have an acquisitive yet moderate demeanor reflective of the natural beauty that pertains to the customary human form. Their virtuous demeanor will be reflected in their flourishing and will bring about "the greatest applause" from others who will recognize them as persons "who can acquit (themselves) with honour" (Smith, *The Theory of Moral Sentiments*, 1976, I.iii.2.5, VI.iii.3, and V.2.9).

Prudence and Assiduity

Smith recognizes that the ability to distinguish between industriousness and avarice is difficult because it requires prudence, which he regards as, "the best head joined to the best heart" (Smith, *The Theory of Moral Sentiments*, 1976, VI.i.15).

In Smith's view, prudence in action has an end in sight, which is "the care of the health, of the fortune, of the rank and reputation of the individual, the objects upon which his comfort and happiness in this life are supposed principally to depend" (Smith, *The Theory of Moral Sentiments*, 1976, VI.i.5). Unlike Aristotle, however, the principal object of prudence is security. Here, prudence combines knowledge and skill in an effort to promote assiduity, industry, frugality, and parsimony. The prudent person, in other words, is sincere, if not always open and frank. He or she is friendly, if not ardently passionate and sociable. Finally, he or she is content to live within a certain income and to serve his or her country when asked to do so (Smith, *The Theory of Moral Sentiments*, 1976, VI.i.6, VI.i.8 and 9, and VI.i.12 and 13).

Justice and Natural Jurisprudence

Whereas Smith's notion of prudence regulates an individual's self-interested behavior, his notion of justice regulates an individual's other-interested behavior deriving from social passions.

Smith considers justice to be a social virtue and the proper object of resentment and punishment that are the results of harm. Justice is also concerned with security, but whereas prudence is concerned with an individual's security, justice is concerned with society's security (Smith 1978, B, pp. 5–15).

Believing that "there can be no proper motive for hurting our neighbour, there can be no incitement to do evil to another, which mankind will go along with, except just indignation for evil which that other has done to us," Smith held that violations of the "sacred laws of justice" call for vengeance and punishment (Smith, *The Theory of Moral Sentiments*, 1976, II.ii.2.1 and 2.3). Justice "prompts us to beat off the mischief which is attempted to be done to us, and to retaliate that which is already done; that the offender may be made to repent of his injustice, and that others, through fear of the like punishment, maybe terrified from being guilty of the like offence" (Smith, *The Theory of Moral Sentiments*, 1976, II.ii.1.4).

For Smith, justice is a negative virtue that "hinders us from hurting our neighbour" (Smith, *The Theory of Moral Sentiments*, 1976, II.ii.1.9). Although Smith does not spell out clearly the differences between individual and social virtues, it is evident that for Smith just as for Aristotle justice has both individual and social qualities. As an individual virtue, justice is a characteristic of restraint. As a social virtue, justice is that "consciousness of ill-desert" implanted by nature in the human breast to safeguard the association of humankind (Smith, *The Theory of Moral Sentiments*, 1976, II.ii.3.4).

According to Smith, justice is a social virtue deriving from natural jurisprudence. Justice, he asserts, is "the main pillar that upholds the whole edifice" of society (Smith, *The Theory of Moral Sentiments*, 1976, II.ii.3.4). As Smith explains, "(S)ociety cannot subsist unless the laws of justice are tolerably observed, as no social intercourse can take place among men who do not generally abstain from injuring one another" (Smith, *The Theory of Moral Sentiments*, 1976, II.ii.3.6).

Justice is a kind of social prudence that preserves a harmonious system of passions, interests, and sympathy. As the virtue of prudence induces an individual to protect his or her own interests, natural beauty, and customary form, so justice induces an individual to protect the life, property, and rights of others. As prudence preserves an individual's natural form, so justice preserves the ideal natural social order. Prudence and justice differ in terms of their original concerns. Prudence is concerned first with the protection and preservation of an individual's well-being as he or she moves about in society whereas justice is concerned first with the protection of society's welfare and integrity as potentially disruptive individuals move about within it.

Universal Benevolence or Social Sympathy

Benevolence is another virtue related to the social passions and not unlike sympathy, derives from our "interest in the fortune of others" (Smith, *The Theory of Moral Sentiments*, 1976, I.i.1.1).

Benevolence at first glance appears similar to justice but is unlike justice in that benevolence is not necessary for the continued existence of society as justice is. Campbell explains the distinctions among justice, prudence, and benevolence, but Smith himself explains the distinction as follows: "(B)eneficence, therefore, is less essential to the existence of society than justice. Society may subsist, though not in the most comfortable state, without beneficence; but the prevalence of injustice must utterly destroy it" (Campbell 1967; Smith, *The Theory of Moral Sentiments*, 1976, II.ii.3.3).

In Smith's view, universal benevolence (benevolence extended broadly) is a key social virtue. It is a sort of social sympathy and relates to sympathy in the way justice relates to prudence. As justice and prudence share a concern for security, so universal benevolence and sympathy share a concern for the locus of an individual's interest. As sympathy is the fellow-feeling that we have for another, universal benevolence is the fellow-feeling that we have for society.

Universal benevolence is a virtue for Smith because it is a personal characteristic tied to both good human ends and the natural order of things. As Smith states, "(There is) no solid happiness to any man who is not thoroughly convinced that all the inhabitants of the universe, the meanest as well as the greatest, are under the immediate care and protection of that great, benevolent, and all-wise Being, who directs all the movements of nature" (Smith, *The Theory of Moral Sentiments*, 1976, VI.ii.3.2).

Universal benevolence also contains the self-denial prevalent in self-command and prudence as well as the social concerns of justice. As Smith argues, "(T)he wise and virtuous man is at all times willing that his own private interest should be sacrificed to the public interest of his own particular order or society" (Smith, *The Theory of Moral Sentiments*, 1976, VI.ii.3.3). Thus, the virtue of universal benevolence shares an affinity with sympathy in its concern for others, with self-command and prudence in terms of the control of personal desires, and with justice in respect to a concern for society.

In sum, for Smith, sympathy and the virtues of self-command, prudence, justice, and universal benevolence are interrelated personal characteristics that serve to maintain an individual's natural order. They also contain a social aspect, with justice as the premier social virtue. Table 9.1 summarizes Smith's unique virtues.

Table 9.1 Adam Smith's Main Business Virtues

Self-Command
- A habit of self-discipline where one is continent and capable of controlling the passions by means of a combination of knowledge, foresight, self-reliance, and self-control
- A great virtue: "all the other virtues seem to derive their principal lustre" from it
- Helps the individual sympathize with others and control the passions that tend either toward excessive fear and anger or toward excessive ease, pleasure, applause, and self-gratification
- Regulates wealth maximization. Has the individual seek wealth in a self-disciplined manner, acquiring things yet remaining modest and plain in the pursuit

Prudence
- Sagacity and good judgment in regard to practical ends having to do with the prevention of harm to the individual
- Combines knowledge and skill with the object of promoting security and preserving the individual's well being
- "The best head joined to the best heart."
- Regulates an individual's self-interested behavior and promotes assiduity, industry, frugality, and parsimony
- Has the individual remain content to live within a certain income and to serve his or her country when asked to do so

Justice
- A social virtue concerned with society's security and the proper object of resentment and punishment that are the results of harm
- Regulates the individual's other-interested behavior deriving from social passions
- A negative virtue that "hinders us from hurting our neighbor."
- "The main pillar that upholds the whole edifice" of society
- Preserves a harmonious system of passions, interests, and sympathy

Universal Benevolence (Social Sympathy)
- The individual's willingness that his own private interests be sacrificed to the public interest of his own particular order or society
- The fellow-feeling that we have for society
- A sort of social sympathy that preserves "interest in the fortune of others."
- Related to justice: society may subsist without it, but injustice will destroy it

Comparison: Smith and Aristotle on Virtue in General

Some early interpretations of *The Theory of Moral Sentiments* maintain that Smith's virtue theory relies on stoicism, but contemporary virtue theorists as well as Smith himself consistently turn to Aristotle when commenting on virtue.[7] Ryan Hanley, for one, explains the "resurgence in neo-Aristotelianism" in Smith's ethic and his "alternative approach" to prior rules-based approaches (Hanley 2006, pp. 17–39). Wells and Graafland explain further how this approach was used by Smith to forge an ethic relevant to commercial society (Wells and Graafland 2012, pp. 321–326).

In general, Smith adapted Aristotelian virtue theory to fit the commercial life of Western Europe as it industrialized. Many of Smith's virtues therefore resonate

---

[7] Athol Fitzgibbons mourns the fact that few commentators on Smith write about the Stoic origins of his virtue theory, but there may be good reason for this (Fitzgibbons 1995, pp. 104–106).

strongly with the attributes of the virtuous man portrayed by Aristotle above, but do not dovetail entirely with Aristotle's worldview.

In terms of their consonance, Smith's notion of the "perfectly virtuous man" as a magnanimous warrior, for example, agrees with early Greek concepts of heroic virtue. So, too, Smith's moral views reflect many of the characteristics of Aristotle's teleology, if not the universal and final end he proffered.

As we saw, in Aristotle's ethic the *telos* of happiness or *eudaimônia* is the highest good that can be attained by a person through his or her own efforts and is brought about by virtuous action and the proper functioning of the person (Aristotle 1962, I 7 1097b pp. 1021–1025 and II 1096 1106a 1015). Virtue, in Aristotle's words, "renders good the thing itself of which it is the excellence, and causes it to perform its function well."[8]

With Smith there is a similar relationship of virtue to ends, but not in terms of an overarching *telos*. Instead, Smith eliminates the Aristotelian notion of a comprehensive end and replaces it with a sort of harmonious order to nature that virtue facilitates. Put another way, in Smith virtue aligns us with the natural order and is the means whereby we cooperate with the plans of the so-called author of nature (Viner 1927). In this regard, Smith agrees with Aristotle's idea of virtue as something related to proper human functioning but he avoids the notion of striving toward a single good end of happiness.[9]

In Smith's view, we draw from a pool of goods that are maintained by the "great, benevolent, and all-wise Being" (Smith, *The Theory of Moral Sentiments*, 1976, VI.ii.3.2). Human flourishing therefore has to do with the acquisition of good things in accordance with a standard order of being rather than the attainment of a certain high standard associated with a complete life.

Although Smith agrees with Aristotle that virtue causes us to function well, he does not advocate Aristotle's idea of virtue as something having a preconceived ultimate end. Instead, he focuses on how things work well practically in the present and proposes practical ends having to do with the satisfaction of our natural desires.

Smith points out, for example, how our desire to be beloved impels us to adjust our actions in virtuous ways. By this he means that because we desire to be the proper object of someone else's love, we lower our emotional level to garner another's sympathy and present a modest and plain image that makes us appear more temperate, self-disciplined, and generous. Similarly, we are inclined to accumulate wealth because in doing so we become more visible and attractive.

Smith captures these ideas in his powerful comments about ambition:

> It is because mankind are disposed to sympathize more entirely with our joy than with our sorrow, that we make parade of our riches, and conceal our poverty. Nothing is so mortifying as to be obliged to expose our distress to the view of the public, and to feel, that though

---

[8] (Broadie 1991, pp. 24–25). and (Aristotle 1962, II 6 1106a 1115). Elsewhere, Aristotle claims that "well-doing (*eupraxia*) is the end we seek: action of some sort or other is therefore our end and aim." (Aristotle 1995, VII 3 1325b 1319).

[9] Recall the Latin *virtus'* rooted is *vir*, meaning "a man." See also (Smith, *The Theory of Moral Sentiments*, 1976, VI.iii. pp. 1–12).

our situation is open to the eyes of all mankind, no mortal conceives for us the half of what we suffer....For to what purpose is all the toil and bustle of this world?...From whence, then, arises that emulation which runs through all the different ranks of men, and what are the advantages which we propose by that great purpose of human life which we call better-ing our condition? To be observed, to be attended to, to be taken notice of with sympathy, complacency, and approbation, are all the advantages which we can propose to derive from it. (Smith, *The Theory of Moral Sentiments*, 1976, I.iii.2.1)

Smith—the supposed foremost advocate of wealth seeking—argues here that the real reason for people striving to accumulate things is to get attention and avoid becoming invisible to others.

Smith does not make this claim in passing. Rather, he reiterates it in different form in a later passage about the poor man's son who exhausts himself in the pursuit of riches only to find in the last dregs of life "that wealth and greatness are mere trinkets of frivolous utility" and that he has sacrificed "a real tranquility that is all times in his power" to possess for things that are simply more "observable" than those simple things he had as a poor man (Smith, *The Theory of Moral Sentiments*, 1976, IV.i.8).

Smith argues elsewhere that we act virtuously because we are concerned with rewards and their utility, not because we are concerned with achieving an ultimate end tied to a conception of our humanity.[10]

In these ways, Aristotle and Smith disagree on the nature of ends, but agree on certain foundational matters. The two concur on the experiential ethical starting point, believing that ethics begins with the familiar and an active and emotion-laden person. Both hold that ethics starts not with first principles or "with what is intel-ligible in itself but with what is familiar to us, that is, with the bare facts, and works back from them to the underlying reasons."[11] Both agree that ethics proceeds from the fact that some people possess characters that love what is noble and hate what is base.

Both agree, too, on the need for moderation. As we saw in Smith's comments on wealth seeking, much of Smith's ethic fits Aristotle's mean-driven notion of virtue. Smith's "poor man's son" is not just about the need for visibility, but also about the need for moderation in regard to ambition, that "unnamed virtue" that Aristotle considers in *The Nicomachean Ethics* (Aristotle 1962, IV 4 1125b pp. 1121–1125). Especially on a practical level, moderation is important to Smith's concept of hu-man flourishing as something related to upholding certain standards of restraint.[12]

Smith and Aristotle also agree that individual virtue has a social dimension. Ar-istotle emphasizes this point in his treatment of politics and the explanation of how

---

[10] Compare (Aristotle 1962, II 6 1106a 1115) with (Smith, *The Theory of Moral Sentiments*, 1976, III.2.1, III.5.8, III.5.9, and IV.1.1).

[11] (Ross 1960, p. 185). In sum, Aristotle's *Ethics* begins with the *arché*, "the that," and not "the because." For more, see (Burnyeat 1980, p. 71 and 75).

[12] Smith asserts that the "deformed," those not in accord with their natural form, are "monsters." (Smith, *The Theory of Moral Sentiments*, 1976, V.1.8). Also see (Smith, *The Theory of Moral Sentiments*, 1976, III.5.6 and 5.7). and (Aristotle 1962, I 7 1097b 1030, I 1096 1096b 1034, and I 1094 1095a pp. 1016–1019).

the *polis* presupposes *philia,* the human relational bond of friendship that holds together all associations.[13] Similarly, Smith begins *The Theory of Moral Sentiments* with the argument that morality begins with sympathy and the disposition to consider the interests of others as well as our own. He then goes on to argue that the connection that individuals have to one another brings about virtuous behavior and the ability to interact well with others.

In both perspectives, social considerations are fundamental to the concept of a virtue.[14] As Laurence Berns explains, Aristotle and Smith are so similar on this point that Smith's sympathy can be interpreted as a social psychological explanation for Aristotle's worldview:

> (Smith) gave impressively plausible psychological accounts of things, especially the sentimental side of ethics, that Aristotle observed, noted, and alluded to, but did not elaborate. In this sense he could be thought of as "working together" with Aristotle, working together to make the same things more understandable. (Berns 1994, p. 75)

Comparison: Smith and Aristotle on Particular Virtues

Not only did Smith rework some of Aristotle basic notions of virtue, he also reworked many of Aristotle's particular virtues. Prudence, justice, courage, and other key virtues are modified with Smith to be more concerned with self-restraint than in the past. These, we will see, serve the individual particularly well in the realm of business.

Aristotle's prudence, as we saw earlier, is a characteristic habit of "deliberating well about what is good and advantageous for oneself" in terms of practical affairs (Aristotle 1962, VI 5 1140a 1125). It utilizes practical wisdom or *phronēsis* and is action-oriented, concerned with what is to be done in terms of a human *telos*, and is displayed in good deliberation, excellent understanding, and an ability to judge well.[15]

In Smith's interpretation, prudence is also a deliberative habit, but instead of being directed toward a unified complex excellence, it is concerned with individual security and self-restraint. It utilizes good deliberation, sagacity, and good judgment for practical ends having to do with the prevention of harm to the individual. As a result, it is not so much a noble virtue as it is a protective and respectable habit that

---

[13] See "Politics as the master science of the good" in (Aristotle 1962, 1094a 1018 to 1094b 1012, glossary, pp. 1311–1313). and (Rawls 1993, p. xxi).

[14] MacIntyre suggests this about Homeric societies (MacIntyre 1984, p. 184).

[15] Broadie observes that Aristotle recognized that sometimes an agent reaches a rational choice but fails to act on it due to moral weakness or incontinence (*akrasia*). This incontinence is not a vice nor is its opposite, continence, a virtue, "for the continent person enacts his choice but not without a struggle against bad impulses, whereas the truly good person is free from these." See (Aristotle 1962, VI 5 1140b 1145, VI 1149 1142b pp. 1141–1135, VI 1110 1143a pp. 1141–1117, and VI 1111 1143a pp. 1118–1124 and pp. 1129–1132; Broadie 1991, pp. 266–267).

"commands a certain cold esteem" (Smith, *The Theory of Moral Sentiments*, 1976, VI.i.1 to 6 and VI.1.14).

A second important virtue, justice, is more difficult to compare because Aristotle and Smith emphasize different functional aspects of the virtue. Aristotle considers justice to be the highest virtue and devotes all of Book V of *The Nicomachean Ethics* to it. It is, in his words:

> (T)he highest of all virtues, more admirable than morning star and evening star, and, as the proverb has it, "In justice every virtue is summed up." It is complete virtue and excellence in the fullest sense because it is the practice of complete virtue. It is complete because he who possesses it can make use of his virtue not only by himself but also in his relations with his fellow men. (Aristotle 1962, V 1 1129b pp. 1128–1132)

For Aristotle, justice is a moral ordering quality of a person that enables the *telos* to flourish within the context of society. It is an interior ordering quality of the will that manifests itself in an exterior ordering in respect to others. It is excellence in the fullest because it is wholly consonant with our human *telos* in allowing us to live well as individuals in society.

In Smith's perspective, justice is a practical virtue to ensure society's security (Smith 1978, B, pp. 5–15). While he, too, consider justice to be an ordering characteristic, he deviates from Aristotle in considering just ordering to have no single and ultimate end. Here, justice, not unlike prudence, is a characteristic habit of concern with practical affairs having to do with fairness and proportionality in practical matters. The order, however, protects society from the harm that would result from unbridled self-interest.

In Smith, justice is a commutative construct and does not promote social or individual welfare beyond certain negative requirements. Again, there is no sweeping notion of "social justice" for Smith. Rather, the social dimension of justice rectifies inequities and sets boundaries for acting fairly and not harming others. It is also reflective of the hierarchy of natural laws that protect the life, property, and rights of persons (Smith, *The Theory of Moral Sentiments*, 1976, II.ii.2.2).

It should be noted here that Aristotle and Smith do not disagree entirely on justice's protective role. To the contrary, both hold justice to be essential to the longevity of a viable society.

In Aristotle's view, civilized human existence takes place only within the context of a *polis* and justice regulates proper conduct within society as well as "the relations of individuals with one another."[16] What is just in the practical social context is "what is lawful and fair" (Aristotle 1962, V 1 1129a 1135). Accordingly, politics is important because it is the means whereby society "legislates what people are to do and what they are not to do" in terms of their ends as individuals and social beings (Aristotle 1962, I 2 1094b pp. 1095–1097). As Berns explains,

> (T)he secondary order of commutative, or rectifying justice, the civil and criminal law, then, is derivative from the more fundamental order of distributive justice. That is, laws

---

[16] See editor's comments in (Aristotle 1962, I 2 1094a 1027, f1098, 1094 and V 1091 1129a 1091, f1091, 1111).

are laid down in accordance with the operative principles of distributive justice. Civil and criminal laws promote those principles and rectify their violations. (Berns 1994, p. 81)

In Smith's view on the other hand, society is a sort of tapestry and justice secures its structure. Justice is "the main pillar that upholds the whole edifice of society" for without it, society would "in a moment crumble into atoms" (Smith, *The Theory of Moral Sentiments*, 1976, II.ii.3.4). Society cannot subsist,

> (U)nless the laws of justice are tolerably observed, as no social intercourse can take place among men who do not generally abstain from injuring one another; the consideration of this necessity, it has been thought, was the ground upon which we approved of the enforcement of the laws of justice by the punishment of those who violated them. (Smith, *The Theory of Moral Sentiments*, 1976, II.ii.3.6)

Although Smith does tackle issues involving distributive justice in *The Wealth of Nations*, he is mostly concerned with the practical aspects of distributive justice rather than the concept as a whole. He considers, for example, the impact of poverty on the family, not poverty's relationship to happiness (Smith, *The Wealth of Nations*, 1976, I.viii. pp. 37–38).

Similarly in *The Theory of Moral Sentiments*, he focuses almost exclusively on commutative justice and the need for justice as it relates to society's security needs. Hobbes' influence is undoubtedly the subtext of this emphasis and concern. Thus, while Aristotle and Smith agree on the importance of justice as a virtue, they regard it differently in terms of justice's ends and purposes.

A third virtue of self-command is most closely associated with Smith but it, too, has roots in Aristotle's ethic. It simply bears less direct correspondence to it than the previous virtues.

Self-command for Smith is a characteristic habit of discipline regarding passions that tend either toward excessive fear and anger or toward excessive ease, pleasure, and self-gratification. It is, moreover, a form of moderation that enables the individual to become magnanimously self-possessed (Smith, *The Theory of Moral Sentiments*, 1976, VI.iii.5 to 6). As such, it melds aspects of Aristotle's virtues of courage, temperance, and magnanimity.

In Aristotle's ethic, control of the irascible and concupiscible appetites is governed by the distinct virtues of fortitude and temperance. These virtues guide the individual's "sphere of operations" toward different middle grounds.[17] Fortitude, for example, moderates the feelings of fear and confidence and induces the individual toward the mean of cowardice and recklessness. Temperance, in contrast, moderates the appetites related to pleasure and pain and impels the individual toward the mean of insensitivity and self-indulgence.

Although Aristotle recognizes that fortitude and temperance proffer similar ends related to control of individual inclinations, he maintains the distinctiveness of the two virtues (Aristotle 1962, II 7 1107a 1133 to 1107b 1103, III 1107 1115b 1106 to

---

[17] Aristotle uses the terms courage and self-control. However, to distinguish more easily between Aristotle's self-control and Smith's self-command, we follow the lead of Aquinas' terminology. See (Aquinas 1984, q.56 a.54 and q.60 a.54).

1116a 1115, II 1107 1107b pp. 1104–1107, and III 1111 1118b 1108 to 1112 1119b 1119).

Smith effectively does away with many of these bright line distinctions and conflates certain functional aspects of Aristotle's separate virtues into a single virtue of self-command that he then highlights as a preeminent individual virtue for those engaged in commerce.

Universal benevolence, a fourth virtue constructed by Smith, reworks Aristotle's distinct virtue of generosity (liberality) and then mixes it with aspects of justice to derive a new virtue that he calls "universal benevolence."[18] Smith adds to this combination certain elements of other parts of his ethic such that in the end sympathy, self-command, prudence, and justice, as well as Aristotle's notion of generosity form a ubiquitous and altruistic virtue concerned with the interests of society and human relational bonds.

Comprehensive in scope, universal benevolence reflects the characteristics associated with Smith's "benevolent, and all-wise Being, who directs all the movements of nature" (Smith, *The Theory of Moral Sentiments*, 1976, VI.ii.3.2). This Being, godlike in its strength, is not a divine entity but the ordering mechanism of nature. It is called the "invisible hand" because it is an irrefutable force that drives self-interested, rational, wealth-maximizing people to truck and barter.

Distinctly anti-Hobbesian in these perspectives and starting point, Smith argues that people come together not out of fear and need for security, but to engage in commerce and to build things to their mutual benefit. "Give me that which I want, and you shall have this which you want, is the meaning of every such offer; and it is in this manner that we obtain from one another the far greater part of those good offices which we stand in need of" (Smith, *The Wealth of Nations*, 1976, I.ii).

Smith goes on to argue against exchanges dependent upon benevolence ("it is not from the benevolence of the butcher, the brewer, or the baker, that we expect our dinner, but from their regard to their own interest"), but his underlying message is that individuals set aside some of their private interests for the sake of social order (Smith, *The Wealth of Nations*, 1976, I.ii).

The invisible hand "common to all men" and "found in man alone" has people divide their labor and truck and barter to mutual advantage (Smith, *The Wealth of Nations*, 1976, I.ii). While it does rely on individual self-interest, the invisible hand of the market does not advocate unbridled greed. Rather, it has the individual set aside certain private interests for the sake of a market order that benefits society. Thus, out of "social sympathy" and a sense of universal benevolence we restrain ourselves to comply with the market mechanism. Jonathan Wight captures these sentiments in both novel and academic form and Peter Harrison gives an excellent account of the history of the invisible hand, effectively conveying the moral context of Smith's construct that guides modern economic systems (Harrison 2011; Wight 2001, 2007).

---

[18] For more on Aristotle's notions of generosity or liberality, see (Aristotle 1962, IV 1). Aristotle's notion of generosity in regard to the use of property can be found in (Aristotle 1995, II 5 1263b 1213 and II 1266 1265a 1230).

In the end, Smith holds that, "one has perfect duties not to harm another," but not necessarily a perfect duty to charity or benevolence.[19] Even so, universal benevolence is important in communicating Smith's support of the civility necessary for ordered life in society and for commercial exchanges.

Virtues Specific to Commerce

So far we have seen how Adam Smith redescribed Aristotle's understanding of virtue to produce a practical theory devoid of a *telos* while maintaining Aristotle's notion of virtue as a personal characteristic of flourishing reliant upon reason, self-control, and affiliation with others. Smith also retained Aristotle's concerns for balancing self-interest and altruism as well as the individual's proper relationship to society.

Interestingly, the two treatises of Smith covered here are remarkably consistent in terms of their moral underpinnings and notions of social obligation. In many ways, *The Wealth of Nations* applies the virtue theory Smith developed in *The Theory of Moral Sentiments*.

Berry maintains that "Smith's general argument…is that the postclassical world is irretrievably a world of strangers and that in this world we must look to the public realm for rules to govern us and to the private for virtue" (Berry 1992, p. 84). The text of *The Wealth of Nations*, however, belies that conclusion.

Berry's contention may be based on two passages from *The Wealth of Nations* where Smith writes, for example, "Every man, as long as he does not violate the laws of justice, is left perfectly free to pursue his own interest in his own way, and to bring both his industry and capital into competition with those of any other man, or order of men" (Smith, *The Wealth of Nations*, 1976, IV.ix.51).

As we have seen here, however, Smith maintains that strangers cannot expect benevolence from each other but he does not advocate unrestrained self-seeking nor does he advocate that the commercial world is devoid of virtue. To the contrary, Smith maintains that it is always wrong to harm another and that the social virtue of justice requires us in commercial settings to be fair even to strangers (Smith 1978, A, pp. 9–15 and B, pp. 16–11). Indeed, we have a perfect duty to be just in every circumstance because being unfair, like harming another, is always a moral violation. The beggar cannot expect benevolence nor should she depend on it. However, she can expect not to be maligned and to be treated fairly. Similarly, in commerce a businessman need not be benevolent to his competitor or even to an employee, though he has perfect duties not to harm others and to compete fairly.

Furthermore, the world of commerce is not merely a collection of strangers, nor is justice limited to civil law. Wells and Graafland explain how some but not all of Smith's virtues (prudence, temperance, civility, industriousness, and honesty) oper-

---

[19] For more on the distinction of virtues in terms of the good, see (Aquinas 1984, q.54 a.53). For Smith's view, see (Smith 1978, A, pp. 9–15).

ate in competitive circumstances such as business and how Smith's sympathy-based ethic was not exclusively competitive (Wells and Graafland 2012, pp. 326–341). Smith's claim in *The Theory of Moral Sentiments*, for example, that human beings are intrinsically social beings is reiterated in his analysis of a political economy in *The Wealth of Nations*.[20] This is evident in particular in Smith's description of the division of labor as "the necessary, though very slow and gradual consequence of a certain propensity in human nature…to truck, barter, and exchange one thing for another" (Smith, *The Wealth of Nations*, 1976, I.ii.1). Trade is impossible, and commerce cannot flourish without cooperative agreements, coordination, and mutual respect for individuals with whom merchants and manufacturers trade and compete. Thus, while benevolence is seldom evident or expected in commerce, justice and mutual respect make manufacture and trade possible, and the vices of malevolence and injustice are equally vices in business.

Unbridled self-interest, in other words, is not something Smith advocates. Because commerce is a social activity, fair play is required. Smith writes,

> In the race for wealth, and honours, and preferments, he (the competitor) may run as hard as he can, and strain every nerve and every muscle, in order to outstrip all his competitors. But if he should justle, or throw down any of them, the indulgence of the spectators is entirely at an end. It is a violation of fair play, which they cannot admit of. (Smith, *The Theory of Moral Sentiments*, 1976, II.ii.2.1)

Smith criticizes injustices of price or wage conspiracies, unfair labor practices, parties who do not honor contracts, and unfair laws as detriments to a well-working commercial society (Smith, *The Wealth of Nations*, 1976, I.x.c.27, I.viii.13, and I.viii.13).

Smith does not, however, advocate broad notions of today's common notion of "social justice" or "distributive justice." Rather, his notion of the justice of the market is spare and devoid of the primitive, immature, and anthropomorphic concepts of justice proposed by nineteenth to twenty-first century political philosophers. Instead, Smith argues that fair employers and merchants enhance commerce (or conversely, that injustices hinder commercial progress) and that fair play is a virtue and injustice is an enemy to commerce.

Because such an ethic for commerce depends on the virtue of prudence, Smith repeatedly extols prudence and identifies greed as a key vice in business. He says, for example, "(e)very prodigal appears to be a publick enemy, and every frugal man a publick benefactor" (Smith, *The Wealth of Nations*, 1976, II.iii.25). Prudence is sometimes framed in terms of the wisdom of saving. Smith writes, for example:

> Parsimony, and not industry, is the immediate cause of the increase of capital…Parsimony, by increasing the fund which is destined for the maintenance of productive hands tends to increase the number of those hands….It tends therefore to increase the exchangeable value of the annual produce of the land and labour of the country. (Smith, *The Wealth of Nations*, 1976, II.iii. pp. 16–17)

---

[20] "It is thus that man, who can subsist only in society, was fitted by nature to that situation for which he was made. All the members of human society stand in need of each others assistance, and are likewise exposed to mutual injuries." (Smith, *The Theory of Moral Sentiments*, 1976, II.ii.2.1).

Greed, on the other hand, is to be avoided: "People of the same trade seldom meet together…but the conversation ends in a conspiracy against the publick, or in some contrivance to raise prices" (Smith, *The Wealth of Nations*, 1976, I.x.c.27). In addition, "merchants and master-manufacturers…say nothing concerning the bad effects of high profits. They are silent with regard to the pernicious effects of their own gains. They complain only of those of other people" (Smith, *The Wealth of Nations*, 1976, I.ix.24). With regard to profit, Smith comments: "The high rate of profit seems every where to destroy that parsimony which in other circumstances is natural to the character of the merchant…(As a result) (t)he capital of the country… gradually dwindles away" (Smith, *The Wealth of Nations*, 1976, IV.vii.c.61). Smith also discusses avarice: "(A)varice and ambition in the rich, in the poor the hatred of labour and the love of present ease and enjoyment, are the passions which prompt to invade property" (Smith, *The Wealth of Nations*, 1976, V.i.b.2).

Even Smith's famous construct of an invisible hand is not impervious to the influence of the virtues. In a free market, Smith observes, the "whole of the advantages and disadvantages of the different employments of labour and stock…be either perfectly equal or continually tending to equality" (Smith, *The Wealth of Nations*, 1976, I.x.a.1). This is an ideal, but even so, Smith notes that the market is most efficient when there is a competitive but level playing field. In fact, it works best when merchants and manufacturers cooperate as well as compete and when they engage in fair play. Monopolies, trade restrictions, unduly low wages, dishonored contracts, unfair banking practices, and price conspiracies adversely affect market exchanges and competition, thus upsetting optimal market equilibrium.[21] Unfair practices, in other words, hamper rather than facilitate the workings of the free market and so should be avoided.

In the end, Smith argues that virtues play a central role in free enterprise and that prudent and fair merchants, manufacturers, and employers who respect each other enhance commerce. Conversely, he maintains that greed, selfishness, harmful activities, and injustices negatively affect market exchanges and hinder economic progress.

While most of Smith's ideas about virtues and vices were drawn from Aristotle and other early figures, Smith extends these prior notions to apply to the commercial realm, thus contextualizing the virtues in new and practically useful ways. He also effectively raises the stature of the merchant because with Smith's justifications now the person of commerce can be regarded as virtuous while engaged in his or her chosen work. Moreover, because the rest of us truck and barter with merchants, we, too, share in the ethical restraints associated with proper commercial interchanges.

In the end, Smith shows how moral virtue contributes to economic well-being and in this way, infuses Western thought with the notion that attempts to separate virtuous conduct from commerce result not just in bad behavior, but in the decline of business success.

---

[21] See examples in (Smith, *The Wealth of Nations*, 1976, I.xi.10, I.viii.13, IV.ii.21 and v.a.23, I.ix. pp. 16–17, II.ii.94, and I.x.c.27).

Chapter 10
Virtue Ethics' Value

> Watch your thoughts for they become words. Watch your words
> for they become actions. Watch your actions for they become
> habits. Watch your habits, for they become your character.
> And watch your character, for it becomes your destiny. What we
> think we become.
> —Margaret Thatcher (played by Meryl Streep) in "The Iron
> Lady" (Lloyd 2011)

Virtue Ethics' Strengths and Weaknesses

To this point, we have seen how contemporary western notions of virtue developed from ancient Greek and modern Enlightenment ideas about morality. Next, will go further to assess the strengths and weaknesses of virtue ethics as a moral method. The salient points made in this chapter are listed in Table 10.1.

Strengths

Perhaps virtue ethics' greatest strength is that it is ends-driven with a focus on moral development. Virtue ethics is a method that promotes characteristic habits directed toward human perfection and flourishing, that is, practices directed toward a final good end appropriate to one's humanity (ancient Greeks) or, alternatively, a set of ends deemed "good" (the moderns).

While virtue ethics has a consequentialist orientation, it is unlike other consequentialist ethics in its focus on ongoing moral character development. Throughout its application, the explicit or implicit question virtue ethics poses to the individual is, "What sort of person will I become with this choice?" In focusing on ends in relation to character in this way, virtue ethics has the individual not simply consider the outcomes of an action, but also how those outcomes relate to the person's greater purposes in life and the degree to which judgments advance or deteriorate the person's overall moral bearing.

Although other methods hone in on the results of moral judgments (utilitarianism, for example), they do not consider the influence of those ends on the character

Table 10.1 Strengths and Weaknesses: Virtue Ethics

Strengths	Weaknesses
Ends-driven with a focus on moral development: virtue ethics concentrates on consequences and their influence on the individual's character	*Vague ends*: ends are ambiguous, immeasurable, and lack strong moral imperative
Felicity producing: virtue brings about happiness as an end and in the doing	
Personal: virtue ethics links moral judgments to individual character and emphasizes the importance of being ethical	*Overly subjective*: virtue ethics lacks the objectivity necessary for widespread application
Provides security and moral order: virtues provide a useful protective function that advances order and morality in society	*Does not rectify structural deficiencies*: virtue ethics is unable to address moral deficiencies of a structural or a societal nature
Grounded in the practical: the virtues remain embedded in the concrete rather than the abstract and thereby broaden the scope of moral discourse in helpful ways	*Easy to apply inappropriately*: virtue ethics' vocabulary can be easily but wrongly extended to institutions and other entities that are incapable of bearing moral responsibilities
Fortifies and expands conventional morality: virtue ethics secures and advances society's moral norms, increasing the likelihood that morality will be contextualized and passed on to future generations	*Unable to challenge conventional morality*: virtue ethics cannot determine if and when an enduring morality is antiquated or wrong
Inspirational: virtue ethics reveals how individuals can become better through the development of habits of moral excellence	*Overlooks the unmotivated*: virtue ethics presumes everyone seeks betterment whereas some people merely want to avoid punishment or social sanctions
An alternative to principle-based approaches: virtue ethics enriches moral deliberations by accounting for moral integration as other approaches do not	*Weakly normative*: virtues lack clear measures for making moral judgments even within a particular social group
Broadly reflective: virtue ethics is a reflective process that relies on prudence to have the user consider a wide range of ethical aspects when making judgments	*Can facilitate self-absorption*: virtue ethics' introspection can lead to ego-centrism and self-centeredness
Individual betterment: virtue ethics advances the moral bearing of the individual through internal incentives to improve one's self	*Ill-defined ideal image*: virtue ethics does not adequately help the user discern the propriety of the ideal image of self or whether or not it is even partly attainable
Betters society: virtue ethics not only betters the individual, it also betters society as conventional norms are solidified within it	*Provides little means for social censure*: virtue ethics does not provide a way to levy moral demands or censure individuals
Convenient: anyone can use virtue ethics to improve and flourish	*Unclear*: virtue ethics provides little clarity about the right time, right place, and right way to apply the virtues or how to assess the disparities of virtues displayed by an individual

of the person nor do they concentrate on the relationship of results to the person's larger (final) purposes the way virtue ethics does. Virtue ethics therefore holds a unique position of strength among moral methods in its focus on ends and the larger purposes of life.

A second strength of virtue ethics is its ability to bring about happiness as an end and in the doing. In this sense, it is a felicity-producing ethic unlike other moral approaches.

In virtue ethics, the end state of each of the virtues is either the final good end (*telos* per the ancient Greeks) or a set of good ends (the moderns) that bring about a sense of fulfillment or flourishing as well as a profound sense of happiness or *eudaimônia*. In this sense, the exercise of virtue brings about happiness as an end state.

At the same time, however, the exercise of the virtues brings about happiness immediately, that is, in the practice of the virtues. Not unlike the positive psychological flow state wherein an individual becomes fully immersed in the blissful feelings associated with an energized focus and involvement in a process, the exercise of the virtues brings about a deep satisfaction and sense of fulfillment and joy as one performs the virtuous act.[1] In this sense, the exercise of virtue brings about happiness in the doing.

With virtue ethics then, the individual experiences happiness or flourishing as an end and as he or she exercises the virtues. While other moral methods advance ends of happiness (again, utilitarianism, as an example), they do not consider happiness in the twofold manner that virtue ethics does—as something that produces happiness as a final end as well as in practice.

A third strength of virtue ethics is its ability to emphasize the personal nature of morality. Virtue ethics links moral judgments to individual character and suggests that one can *be* ethical, not just act ethically according to some outside criteria. This gives virtue ethics a special personal relevance that makes it more likely to be used in real contexts.

Since virtue ethics is not wedded to external objective principles and because its judgments depend heavily on the practical reasoning capabilities of individuals, virtue ethics produces subjective determinations that reflect the moral bearing of the deciding agent. The morality associated with these judgments is therefore personally relevant to the individuals making decisions. The relevance is further enhanced by the awareness of the long-term formative abilities of moral judgments, that is, by the realization of the cumulative effect of judgments on the moral development and reputation of the individual.

Unlike other moral methods that attempt to excise the individual (the subject or agent) from the process so as to analyze problems in isolation along one or two lines of inquiry, virtue ethics considers moral problems in terms of both the actions under consideration and the impact of those actions on the individual making the judgment. In these ways it establishes awareness that the individual's choices have consequences on others as well as the moral character of the person making the choice. Both of these are important because, as William May notes, "ethics must

---

[1] Again, see (Csikszentmihalyi 1991; Geirland 1996; Goleman 1995).

deal with virtues as well as principles of action, with *being* good as well as *producing* good"(May 1995, p. 693).

A fourth strength of virtue ethics is its ability to provide security and moral order in society. The virtues of justice, courage, truthfulness, and self-command, are especially useful in "protecting us from the harms, dangers, temptations, and distractions that threaten the elements of a flourishing life" (Sher 1992, p. 99). As we saw with Hume and Smith, justice is a social virtue that preserves social order thereby allowing society to exist. Without it, society dissolves into a Hobbesian war of all against all.

In addition, the virtues are useful in enhancing morality's effectiveness in society. As Hume noted and George Sher explains, "people tend to be better off when they develop and exercise some subset of their intellectual and physical powers, and when they pursue with some success an integrated, realistic, and moderately complex plan of life."[2] Thus, the virtues provide a useful protective function for society and are a helpful way to advance morality's order and effectiveness.

A fifth strength of virtue ethics is its ability to stay grounded in the practical and avoid lapses into abstraction. This allows virtue ethics to broaden the scope of moral discourse in helpful ways by moving it away from a strict concentration on theory-based principles.

Virtue ethics' focus on the concrete aspects of moral decisions means that it remains grounded in reality and does not get sidetracked easily by irrelevant abstractions and theoretical details. Moreover, its focus on moral development—how the aggregate of moral decisions can change the individual and society for better or worse—inclines the user away from legalisms and reminds the person of the practical consequences of the decision at hand on his or her reputation and moral standing within a community.

Together, these two features keep moral discourse grounded in the situation at hand and lead to judgments that are both meaningful and likely to be applied effectively.

Virtue ethics' sixth strength is its ability to fortify conventional morality and expand the likelihood that society's norms will be meaningfully contextualized and passed on to future generations.

As we saw in the sections on Aristotelian virtue, virtues are characteristic habits of the individual that are taught to the individual by society's prudent representatives. These prudent figures help the individual understand and contextualize society's norms and moral practices until such time as the individual is able to habituate them. In this way, the development of individual virtue secures the conventional morality of society and enhances the likelihood that moral norms will be rooted more deeply within society and passed on to future generations.

---

[2] Sher goes on to state, "Of course, some people are happy without attachments or complicated plans, and some plans actually preclude close personal ties. But because both generalizations contain ceteris paribus clauses, and because happiness is in any case only one index of flourishing, such facts do not undermine what has been said. By collating and integrating these and related observations, we can piece together a loose-jointed and imprecise, but still contentful, characterization of the conditions in which humans tend to thrive." (Sher 1992, p. 100).

Seventh, virtue ethics is beneficial because it inspires people to develop habits of moral excellence. This is important, as James Donahue explains, because it "widens the scope of moral analysis…offers a rich theory of the moral self…(and) accounts for development and change within a moral life" (Donahue 1990, pp. 232–233).

Virtue ethics presents to the individual an ideal image of him or herself and suggests how much better and happier the person might become through the exercise of particular habits of moral excellence.[3] It paints a picture of the sort of person one is now and indicates the sort of person one might become after making certain choices. In this way, virtue ethics inspires people by reinforcing the inclinations they already have that they are capable of doing more than they are doing now and should strive harder to reach their full potential as moral beings.

An eighth strength of virtue ethics is its ability to enrich moral deliberations by providing an alternative to principle-based approaches. By concentrating on the influence of moral decisions on character development, virtue ethics sidesteps concerns with adherence to moral principles and the theories upon which they are based and focuses instead on the subject and the ways moral judgments can advance or inhibit the moral standing of the person.

This ability to remain focused on the impact of moral judgments on the person making the decision is important, as Meilaender explains, because there is "widespread dissatisfaction with an understanding of the moral life which focuses primarily on duties, obligations, troubling moral dilemmas, and borderline cases" (Meilaender 1984, pp. 4–5). David Solomon echoes this sentiment, asserting that virtue ethics has reemerged because recent moral philosophy has not paid sufficient attention to moral criticism and deliberation that centrally involves virtue concepts—concepts essential to any developed ethical theory (Solomon 1988, pp. 428–429).

Virtue ethics therefore provides a positive alternative to rules-based approaches by allowing the individual to consider morality in terms of the impact on him or herself and not just in terms of adherence to abstract norms and theories.

A ninth benefit of virtue ethics is its ability to have the user reflect broadly on a wide range of ethical aspects when making judgments. The source of this strength is virtue ethics' reliance on practical reasoning (prudence) and its mandate that the user deliberate about a wide range of integrated issues.

As we have seen, while virtue ethics does not discount principles *per se*, it contextualizes and combines norms in a way that enables the individual to determine the best course of action to advance the *telos* of human perfection and flourishing. In this way, virtue ethics is a reflective process that emphasizes prudence and accommodates a wide range of ethical concerns when making judgments.

A tenth strength of virtue ethics is its ability to highlight the internal incentives that enable the individual to improve him or herself. Put simply, virtue ethics has the

---

[3] David Solomon makes a similar argument, claiming that an ethic of virtue serves:

1. to develop and defend some conception of the ideal person;
2. to develop and defend some list of virtues that are necessary for being a person of that type;
3. to defend some view of how persons can come to possess the appropriate virtues. (Solomon 1988, p. 429).

individual strive to become better by holding before the person an ideal image of him or herself. This image incentivizes the person in ways that are more meaningful and effective than sources from without. It also increases the likelihood that the person will act ethically and in this way makes it more likely that ethics will be considered in moral-laden contexts.

Eleventh, virtue ethics is beneficial because it facilitates society's betterment as the exercise of the virtues increases the aggregate sum of moral individuals.

As we have seen, virtues are characteristic habits of the individual but they are not drawn from the air. Virtues are taught and nurtured by the members of society who view the moral betterment of the individual as beneficial to society. With more morally upright individuals in society, society benefits as its moral norms are solidified and embedded more deeply and as moral order is secured and expanded.

Twelfth and finally, virtue ethics is beneficial because it is convenient and broadly suitable to those who are likely to use it. Unlike other moral approaches that are forbiddingly complicated and can only be divined by means of so-called moral experts, virtue ethics is understandable by the ordinary people who need to use it. Because ordinary people can be virtuous and virtuous action befits everyone from every walk of life, virtue ethics is uniquely accessible for everyday use and is "achievable even by the humblest of us, in the everyday areas of work and family" (Larmore 1992, p. 190).

In this sense, virtue ethics is not otherworldly and part of an exclusive domain of philosophers or moralists. Rather, it is easily understood and therefore more likely to be used than methods that are more complicated, abstract, foreign, and off-putting.

Weaknesses

Although virtue ethics has these and other strengths, it also has some significant shortcomings.

First, virtue ethics' ends can be vague. Aristotle describes the good final end in detail, but the practical manifestation of this end state is ambiguous and immeasurable. It therefore lacks strong moral imperative. The same holds for other virtue theories. All put forward a goal for virtue that is a mix of elements that are often ill defined or added in unequal measure. Prudence, for example, is a governing virtue that determines the mean and is described as a common sense reasoning approach, but it is ill defined, not easy to communicate, and applied in different measure according to circumstances.

Bentham, Mill, and other utilitarians picked up on these nebulous notions of happiness as an end and subsequently distilled happiness to mean feelings of pleasure or the absence of pain. As rational Enlightenment philosophers, they could not encapsulate the old notions of happiness for rational scrutiny and so they proposed a "useful" approach to ethics that would recognize and maximize the actual experiences of the happiness of people.

The broad notion of flourishing central to Aristotelian virtue theory and the vague results (ends) of subsequent theories are therefore virtue ethics' most glaring shortcoming in the view of its critics.

A second weakness of virtue ethics is its high levels of subjectivity that make it difficult to apply widely.

Although virtue ethics affirms society's moral norms, the values it upholds might not be shared beyond a particular community. In addition, the virtues themselves can be interpreted variously from place to place. Courage, for example, is defined differently in secular and Muslim contexts. Even modern virtues such as self-command, universal benevolence, and so forth are expressed differently in different places. As a result, the application of the virtues is difficult to extend beyond the narrow boundaries of a particular society and they thereby remain subjectively bounded rather than universally germane.

A third weakness of virtue ethics is that it is ineffectual against moral deficiencies of a structural or societal nature. While virtue ethics is expedient in advancing morality within a particular society, it has little wherewithal to question the moral deficiencies of the prevailing institutions and organizations of society.

Virtue ethics' weakness in this regard is particularly troublesome because the ethic can overlook the wrongs that have been perpetrated by multifaceted, integrated, long-enduring, and respected organizations. This is especially relevant in commerce where, as May notes, the traditional "virtues of the marketplace" (industry, honesty, and integrity) can fail to account for the full scope of contemporary, highly bureaucratic, large-scale organizations (May 1995, p. 693). There, conventional ways of doing business can span a length of time such that those responsible have died, left the organization, or become inaccessible.

In addition, organizations can be so byzantine and interconnected that locating responsible parties and encouraging virtue (or apportioning blame) is impossible. Thus, while virtue ethics can be helpful in advancing morality in individuals who engage in business, it is not so helpful in addressing the shortcomings of structures with well established ways of doing things or foundational structures that might be flawed.

A fourth weakness of virtue ethics is that the language it uses to describe the benefits to the individual can be wrongly extended into inappropriate realms, especially into institutions and other entities that cannot properly be asked to bear moral responsibilities. This is not so much an indictment against virtue ethics as it is an observation of the easy misuse or sloppy application of virtue theory.

As we have seen, the virtues are mean-seeking qualities that lead to the perfection or happiness of the person. They are proper to the human being *per se* and so when they are extended outside of the person or community (*polis*), they are attributed wrongly to things incapable of fulfilling the demands of virtue. For this reason, as Donahue notes, "little has been said to how institutions and collectivities within a community can be said to have character" (Donahue 1990, p. 234). There is good reason for this silence.

Nevertheless, virtue ethics' vocabulary continues to be applied to all sorts of institutions and non-human entities. When this happens, it is extended inappropriately to realms that are incapable of bearing moral responsibilities.

A fifth weakness of virtue ethics is that it is not very good at challenging conventional morality. Not unlike its weakness in terms of addressing the shortcomings of longstanding organizations and structures, virtue ethics is not very good at tackling aspects of conventional morality that might be antiquated or wrong.

Although virtue ethics is effective at fortifying the moral *status quo*, it is unable to unravel and expose the underlying problems that might exist in conventional morality. As a result, it can be used to justify specious moral positions and can be vulnerable to upset by other, particularly principle-based, approaches.

A sixth weakness of virtue ethics is that it begins with the notion that people aspire to become morally excellent and want to develop habits of moral excellence. In reality, some people are not so motivated. Many are content to simply avoid the stick and are unwilling to strive for the carrot, that is, they wish to avoid punishments, social sanctions, or inconvenient forms of disapproval and are not inclined to aspire to become their best selves.

Although it is true that virtue ethics "offers a rich theory of the moral self… (and) accounts for development and change within a moral life," some people are unambitious and just do not care about such things (Donahue 1990, pp. 232–233). While this might seem to be a sad commentary on the human condition, it bears mentioning that people are not entirely alike and that they sometimes respond to different moral incentives. While the good end of virtue ethics inspires some, it can be less inspiring to others.

A seventh weakness of virtue ethics is its lack of clear normative criteria for decision-making. Although it is good at enriching moral deliberations, virtue ethics mostly fails to provide objective moral criteria by which to make concrete ethical decisions (Donahue 1990, p. 228).

Not unlike the prior weaknesses about the vague nature of virtue ethics' ends and the variance of virtue from place to place, here the charge is that virtue ethics does not provide clear standards for moral decision-making even within a particular social context.

Sarah Conly argues this point, claiming that the idea of flourishing "will not provide a standard that successfully distinguishes virtue from vice" (Conly 1988, p. 84). Rather than proposing a basis for ethical deliberation, she maintains, virtue ethicists typically appeal to classical moral virtues such as justice and courage, to Bradleyesque notions of self-realization, to Kantian notions of respect for persons as ends in themselves, and to the added notion "that the flourishing life must…be pleasant for the person who lives it" (Conly 1988, p. 88). These sorts of appeals, she believes, do not provide "an independent explanation of function" (Conly 1988, p. 88). Virtue ethicists' accounts of flourishing, when "specific enough to support claims about what traits will or will not contribute to it (are) unacceptable (and when) broad enough to be acceptable (are) too broad to entail that any specific traits will contribute to, or detract from its achievement" (Conly 1988, p. 84). What we need to understand, she maintains, is that human flourishing has a wide range of characteristics with concomitant excellences and that these broad notions cannot serve as independent explanations of function.

Donahue, in response, addresses the concern that virtue ethics fails to provide normative criteria by arguing that a virtue approach yields some central moral norms that have identifiable components or essential values "that are constitutive of and necessarily entailed by the concept of character and…(that) these values can be articulated as formal, processive norms that provide guidance for making moral decisions in applied settings" (Donahue 1990, p. 228). An interplay of essential values such as consistency, coherence, continuity, communication, conviction, and creativity "offers a framework that will yield movement and direction" in moral deliberation.[4] Resounding Edmund Pincoffs' critique of "Quandary Ethics,"[5] Donahue maintains that the debate over foundationalism "casts a shadow on the ethics of character" (Donahue 1990, p. 235).

Overall, it seems that virtue ethics does lack the strong normative and prescriptive imperatives of other methods. While virtue ethics has the individual adhere to standards befitting the good life as defined by practical reason, the duties and obligations that attend to the virtues are largely subjectively determined and so vary

---

[4] The essential values entailed by character and narrative that can be formulated as action-guiding moral norms include those listed below (Donahue 1990, pp. 238–243). These values, Donahue maintains, "at least suggests that character ethics and an ethics of norms are indispensable to one another." (Donahue 1990, p. 243).

1. Consistency (that one can be counted on to act in distinctive ways): to have character and to be virtuous means that one has developed certain habits and that one acts consistently with the virtues one has developed.

2. Coherence (the unity of the moral self in a distinctive and particular way): to have character implies that there is an integration and unity within the self and that the parts of the moral personality are related to one another in an integrated way.

3. Continuity (the ability to locate moral choices within the context of a "unified life story"): to have character means that one is able to see how a choice "flows out of" or "fits into" the history of a person or community.

4. Communication: since moral decision-making requires conversation among all the relevant actors in the moral environment, virtue ethics' narratives provide such a means of communication.

5. Conviction: those beliefs that a person or community possesses that identify the person or in such a way that to change those convictions would make the person or community distinctly different.

6. Creativity: there is no reason to assume that the criticisms of character ethics is that it cannot account for newness and change in the identity and direction of a person or group is accurate because apprehension of the moral good entails being open to having one's perception and vision affected by the revelation of the good in the newness of each moment.

[5] Pincoffs raises questions about the so-called "Quandary Ethics" that conceives ethics to be concerned "with 'problems,' that is, situations in which it is difficult to know what to do." According to this ethic, the ultimate beneficiary of ethical analysis is the person who, in one of these situations, seeks rational ground for the decision he or she must make. Thus, the goal of ethics here is concerned primarily with finding the grounds of moral deliberation, often conceived of as moral rules and the principles from which they can be derived. Meta-ethics, in turn, here consists in the analysis of the terms, claims, and arguments that come into play in moral disputation, deliberation, and justification in problematic contexts (Pincoffs 1983).

in strength from individual to individual even within a relatively small circle of people. Thus, in comparison to principle-based ethics that emphasize duties and strive for objectivity and universalizability, virtue ethics is subjective, particularized, and weakly normative.

An eight weakness of virtue ethics is its unhelpful tendency to foster self-absorption and excessive introspection. As Meilaender explains, "concentration upon the virtues may tempt us to self-indulgence by leading to what Williams calls a reflexive concern. That is, not only do I act with gratitude, but I act from a conception of myself as one who acts gratefully" (Meilaender 1984, p. 14). This tendency is problematic because it may "divert our attention from others to self—and once our attention is diverted, our action may be as well" (Meilaender 1984, p. 15).

The heart of this objection is that the concentration on individual characteristics of excellence, on the mean relative to the acting agent, and so forth, inclines the individual to egocentrism, excessive self-centeredness, and perverse and delicate forms of moral temperature taking.

As these might be played out in the case of our aforementioned athletes (runners, weight lifters, or boxers), for example, one might become overly concerned with *his* performance, *his* regimen, *his* feelings of accomplishment, flow, and so forth and be less concerned about others' well-being. Since ethics attempts to check the normal human tendencies toward ego centrism and seeing oneself as an exception to the norms that would apply to others, virtue ethics' propensity to facilitate self-indulgence can be a problem.

In fairness to virtue theory, it should be noted that this sort of propensity to self-indulgence is not so much a weakness of the theory as it is a misuse of the theory. As David Solomon notes, the truly virtuous person attempts to embody not just self-regarding traits, but also other-regarding traits such as charity (Solomon 1988, pp. 434–436). Accordingly, there is no reason to assume that virtue theory as such contains more imbalances regarding the self than other theories.

In addition, the astute reader will recall that Aristotle was adamant that the virtues remain socially contextualized. They are forged within the community (*polis*) and strengthen the moral norms of society. Modern renderings of virtue such as those of Hobbes, Hume, and Smith also stress this social dimension, especially with the social virtue of justice. Thus, in concentrating so much on the individual, naysayers neglect the fact that virtues are formed and nurtured within society and so not quite as obsessively self-absorbed as virtue ethics' critics suggest.

A ninth weakness of virtue ethics is that it does not adequately help the user discern the propriety of the ideal self that it recommends. Similar to the argument about the subjective nature of its ends, the objection here is that virtue ethics provides no way of knowing if the ideal image of ourselves toward which we strive is even attainable. All we know is that it *seems* valid after the application of individual practical reasoning.

In addition, virtue ethics' mapping function—its ability to provide a vision of how much better and happier we might become through the exercise of virtue—is questionable. It is not clear how virtue ethics helps us discern whether one course of action (one road on the map) is any better than another other than through appeals to individual practical reason, which one may or may not possess.

A tenth weakness of virtue ethics is its inability to hold a person accountable for a lack of virtue. Because virtues are traits of the individual and are subjective, others have difficulty scrutinizing the individual or making moral demands on him or her from a virtue perspective. While it is relatively easy to charge a person with breaking principles, the rules of justice for example, it is difficult to charge a person for failing to have or exercise virtue. Consequently, virtue ethics is not very helpful in facilitating society's ability to make moral demands or censure individuals.

Eleventh and finally, virtue ethics is weak because it provides little clarity about the right time, right place, and right way to apply the virtues or how to balance the disparate virtues displayed by an individual.

While virtue ethics is helpful in practical circumstances, the exercise of traits in the right time, right place, and right way can be difficult to ascertain. In addition, the unequal manifestation of the virtues by an individual can cloud assessments and add to virtue ethics' uncertain value.

Ambiguities such as these become especially problematic when a person exercises only some of the virtues or manifests them in wildly unequal measures. An individual can be courageous in a fight, for example, but a drunkard (intemperate) otherwise. Another might be temperate, but unjust in dealing with others. In these cases, the individual exhibits virtue in one respect, but vice in another. This calls into question whether or not the person is virtuous or vice ridden overall.

While the virtue/vice imbalance can be seen as a simple problem of ambiguity, some claim that such disparity is not a problem for virtue ethics because it indicates a general lack of virtue. There is, they maintain, a "unity of the virtues" that is regulated by the guiding virtue of prudence that secures the overall virtue of the individual. When disparities such as those above arise, there is sufficient evidence to suggest a general lack of virtue. The courageous drunk, in other words, is not virtuous despite his or her valor.

Whether or not one would go so far as to castigate a drunken war hero as wholly vice ridden, it seems evident from this line of argumentation that virtue ethics' ambiguity regarding the right time, place, and way to apply the virtues and how to reckon with imbalances of virtue and vice are weak spots in virtue ethics.

In the end, virtue ethics is similar to other moral approaches in having significant strengths and weaknesses. Fortunately, as Pincoffs observes, however, "there can be more than one door" through which to enter ethics (Pincoffs 1983, p. 111). Virtue ethics is one such entryway.

Part III
Overlaps and Synergies of Methods

Chapter 11
The Synergy of Casuistry and Virtue Ethics

> *Synergy: A Code Word Lazy People Use When They Want*
> *You to Do All the Work. (Despair 2012)*
> —Demotivator by Despair, Inc.

In Part 1, we saw how casuistry can be used to resolve pressing moral problems and how it can inspire us to make tough moral decisions without turning to moral experts.

In Part 2, we saw how moral decisions are character forming and how certain moderating and end-seeking virtues can help us attain a better life. With the J&J Tylenol tainting example, we saw how "excellence of the soul" can be developed within the context of business and how character matters in business decision-making.

Now in Part 3 we will consider combining casuistry and virtue ethics to take advantage of their benefits and offset the drawbacks of each when used separately. The purpose of doing so is to establish a new method for moral problem solving called "virtue-imbued casuistry." We will also compare and contrast casuistry and the business case method here with the goal of establishing a rationale for using virtue-imbued casuistry in the management areas explored in subsequent sections of the book.

Casuistry and Virtue Ethics' Similarities

Casuistry and virtue ethics share a number of positive characteristics, many of which are summarized in Table 11.1.

First, casuistry and virtue ethics are methods grounded in the concrete rather than the abstract. Unlike other approaches that begin by applying abstract principles, concepts, or theories to present circumstances, casuistry and virtue ethics begin, remain, and end with the particular circumstances and individuals at hand.

As a method that relies on truth-bearing cases, casuistry is rooted in comprehensive independent accounts of situations wherein a variety of moral precepts have been applied. These detail real events and circumstances in which judgments have been rendered. Most important, they stick close to actual events and are not general summaries, compendiums, hypotheticals, or stories to highlight abstract principles or theories. They are concrete, relevant, and not made up.

M. Calkins, *Developing a Virtue-Imbued Casuistry for Business Ethics,* Issues in Business Ethics 42, DOI 10.1007/978-94-017-8724-6_11, © Springer Netherlands 2014

Table 11.1 Similarities: Casuistry and Virtue Ethics

Concrete: casuistry and virtue ethics are grounded in the concrete rather than the abstract
Practical: both methods rest on precedence and accumulated learning and forge judgments that are practical to employ in everyday settings
Social group specific: both methods operate under the premise that the ability to deliberate well is learned, constructed by and for society, and realized only within the context of a specific social context
Oblique use of abstractions: both methods refer indirectly to abstractions, principles, and theories by upholding ideals as valuable ends and reflecting the abstract conventions of society's notions of right and wrong
Form character: both methods emphasize the effects of judgments on those making the judgments
Elastic hermeneutics: both methods allow for the flexible interpretation of principles
Reflective and imaginative: both methods foster discernment and understanding of the present circumstances
Narrative-based: stories are central to casuistry's truth-bearing cases and virtue ethics' formation of character and definition of the virtues
Convenient, easy to use, and understandable: both methods are accessible to the ordinary people who actually must make moral decisions in the real world

Similarly, virtue ethics is also grounded in the concrete. Since the virtues are habits learned and performed in real world settings, they account for the unique differences of specific situations and avoid the sweeping generalizations of theories and universal principles. In addition, as mean-seeking habits of moderation, the virtues are defined and honed through direct interface with the real world and everyday circumstances. Both casuistry and virtue ethics are therefore firmly grounded in the concrete in ways that theory-based methods are not.

Second, casuistry and virtue ethics are alike in being practical methods to derive moral judgments. Casuistry, for one is a practical method for decision-making in situations where timeliness is important. Because it turns to previously settled cases rather than complicated dogmas, theories, or universal principles, casuistry can derive judgments relatively quickly, which makes it a good method for situations that demand expediency. Casuistry is also practical because it goes quickly to the heart of the moral mission—that is, to a useful answer to the question, "what ought I/we do" in this or that particular situation.

Virtue ethics, in like manner, is practical because the notion of moderation that defines virtue is determined by means of practical wisdom or prudence (Gk. *phronēsis*). Unlike other normative methods that sideline practical wisdom in favor of the quest to derive epistemic certainty and coherence with theories or universal principles, virtue ethics focuses on practically wise decision-making. In this sense, virtue ethics is similar to casuistry in resting on precedence, accumulated learning, and judgments that are employable in practical settings.

Third, casuistry and virtue ethics operate under the similar premise that the ability to deliberate well is learned, constructed by and for society, and realized only within specific social contexts.

As we have seen, both methods are social group specific in that casuistry's settled cases and virtue ethics' moral norms are tied to identifiable groups of people—to particular religious groups, tribes, cultures, or communities. In both approaches, morality is learned, promulgated, and extended into the future within specific social contexts.

The specificity of this alignment serves a number of important functions. For one, it helps to identify the operative morality of a particular group of people and thereby signal the moral norms that have significance within the community in which the methods are practiced. This has the effect of informing members and outsiders alike of the moral boundaries of a particular society. Perhaps more important, it aids in the formation of the moral culture of a community by ensuring that particular moral norms are promulgated widely throughout the membership and to new generations who will carry them into the future.

Fourth, casuistry and virtue ethics are alike in not appealing directly to abstractions, principles, and theories. Rather, they do so indirectly by referring to ideals as valuable ends or by turning to the conventional but abstract notions of right and wrong embedded in settled cases.

In both processes, the reference to abstractions is oblique. In virtue ethics the reference is more obvious than in casuistry because virtuous action itself is directed toward the formal but highly abstract final good end. Abstractions also underpin the notion of the ideal proffered in the perfection of the individual as well as the notion of "excellence of soul" that motivates the individual. Abstract ideals, in other words, are not highlighted *per se*, but they are nevertheless important as goals and motivators in virtue theory. As Aristotle notes, virtues are mean-seeking activities relative to us "defined by a rational *principle*, such as a man of practical wisdom would use to determine it."[1] This means that virtues do not appeal first to narrowly defined and abstract principles, but they do appeal to them indirectly via the wider rules of reason.

With casuistry, the reference to abstractions is more deeply embedded in the settled cases and taxonomies reflective of society's notions of right or wrong. Casuistry's positive and negative paradigm cases, for example, expose the abstract moral norms of society in a clear way. As manifestations of unambiguous instances of right and wrong, they rest on normative criteria that are essentially abstract. Marginal cases that manifest right and wrong do the same thing albeit less clearly. They, too, reflect the moral norms of society and so similarly rest on abstractions. In both paradigm and marginal cases then, the appeal is not to abstract first principles but to cases that contain oblique references to abstract moral concepts.

In addition, casuistry's taxonomies are abstract because they are ordered hierarchies based on prearranged conceptual criteria. Even the notion of "fittingness" of cases—the tacit or explicit agreements about the degree of compatibility of a present situation with one of the past—is based on harmonies and dissonances that are essentially conceptual and abstract. In both casuistry and virtue ethics then, abstractions are deeply embedded and obliquely referenced rather than points of direct and first appeal.

Fifth, casuistry and virtue ethics are alike in emphasizing the effects of judgments on those making the judgments.

---

[1] Emphasis (italics) mine (Aristotle 1962, II 6 1106b 1136).

As a method, casuistry appeals to past decisions having relevance to the deci-sion-maker(s). This relevance is revealed at the outset when an individual or group chooses one case among many and is carried forward with subsequent cases that are employed in a comparative process that reflects the values and priorities of the decision-maker(s). Put another way, the individual or group goes through a sequen-tial process of choosing one case over another and in this way makes a series of subjective choices that reveal a hierarchy of values and a great deal about the moral character of those making choices.

For its part, virtue ethics links moral choice and character even more clearly than casuistry. Here, virtue itself is built up by means of an accretion of decisions that reflect the hierarchy of values and choices of the individual. These choices lead to habits that define the individual so that we know him or her as just, temperate, courageous and so on.

To recapitulate the point, casuistry and virtue ethics are alike in emphasizing choices that bring about moral judgments having a formative capacity on the char-acter of those making judgments.

Sixth, casuistry and virtue ethics are alike in having hermeneutics that allow for an elastic interpretation of principles.

As we saw, casuistry leads to "expert opinions about the existence and stringency of particular moral obligations, framed in terms of rules or maxims that are general but not universal or invariable, since they hold good with certainty only in the typi-cal conditions of the agent and circumstances of action" (Jonsen and Toulmin 1988, p. 257). This means that casuistry uses principles without becoming overly reli-ant on them. The method allows—indeed, encourages—the interpretation of moral principles. This is beneficial because it makes principles more relevant to people and the situation at hand.

Virtue ethics is also flexible in its interpretation of principles, but in a different way. Aristotle's definition of virtue as something "defined by a rational principle, such as a man of practical wisdom would use to determine it," proffers that princi-ples are interpreted by *people*, especially "the man of practical wisdom," rather than rules having separate authority (Aristotle 1962, II 6 1106b 1136). In virtue theory then, principles are not regarded as impervious to human intervention but are guides for action and useful to the agent making a decision. In the end then, casuistry and virtue ethics similarly hold that principles are interpretable, flexible, adaptable, and thus more applicable to practical situations.

Seventh, casuistry and virtue ethics are alike as reflective and imaginative pro-cesses. Both have the individual reflect upon the present circumstances for the pur-pose of coming to a better understanding of the context of a decision. Through such a mental exercise, the individual takes account of reality more fully and is more likely to make a better judgment.

Casuistry relies on reflective discernment by having the individual muse upon the situation at hand and then compare it to a collection of truth-bearing cases. Re-flection here focuses on the underlying dynamics of a situation and the similarities and differences between the present and the settled cases of the case taxonomy.

Virtue ethics similarly relies on reflective discernment by having the individual consider his or her intended actions in light of a personal history of such moral decision-making. In doing so, it has the individual consider his or her intended actions within the context of his or her final end or set of ends.

In addition, both processes (casuistry and virtue ethics) are imaginative in that they have the individual form mental images of the underlying situation at hand as well as the outcomes of intended judgments. In this way, both approaches tap the creative abilities of people by having them conjure up pictures (images) of what is and what might be as a consequence of a judgment.

Eighth, casuistry and virtue ethics are alike in being narrative-based methods. Casuistry's truth-bearing cases are accounts of situations in which people faced moral quandaries and made moral judgments. As stories, they attempt to capture the user's imagination so the person can place him or herself in the shoes of one or more of the characters of the story. In this way they convey the nuances of a situation and the characters involved in it and thereby aid in the resolution of a real-life moral dilemma.

Virtue ethics also uses narratives, but does so to emphasize the development of character or to illustrate the nature of the virtues. As we have seen, one of the goals of virtue ethics is to advance the individual's moral character toward the final good end (*telos*). This is accomplished through repetitive practices that become habitual. The practices are kept alive and made relevant by means of narratives that enrich the virtues on an ongoing basis.

In addition, virtue is defined by means of narratives. Through stories we learn, for example, how Mary became the courageous woman we know her to be. Narratives recount how she took risks, blew the whistle on a wrongdoing in the workplace, stepped up to defend a friend who was accosted on the street, walked out on an abusive husband, and so forth. Narratives reveal, in short, how she became the courageous woman we know her to be today.

Both casuistry and virtue ethics rely heavily on narratives to convey the truth-bearing aspects of settled cases and the formation of character and definition of virtue.

Ninth, casuistry and virtue ethics are alike in being convenient and understandable and so easy to use by ordinary people. Because of their practicality, use of familiar narratives, and all the other qualities mentioned above, both processes are easy to use in real-world settings. As a result, the two processes are alike in being viable and effective methods for moral decision-making in practical situations because they are readily accessible to the ordinary people who actually must make moral decisions in the real world.

Casuistry and Virtue Ethics' Differences

Although casuistry and virtue ethics share certain features, they do not always manifest features to the same degree or in the same way. The following considers how the two differ. A summary of the most relevant points can be found in Table 11.2.

Table 11.2 Differences: Casuistry and Virtue Ethics

Function: the two processes function differently. Casuistry functions as an instrument for moral
  decision-making while virtue ethics functions as a normative approach to ethics that emphasizes the character of the moral agent

Use of principles: the two methods use principles differently. In casuistry principles are embedded in maxims and case narratives that provide moral meaning without unnecessary concerns
  about epistemic purity whereas in virtue ethics principles frame the reasoning process to help
  inform the individual on how to act morally

Use of abstractions: the two methods accommodate abstractions differently

Direction: the two methods direct moral deliberations differently. Casuistry directs the user
  according to the values of a particular culture or tradition while virtue ethics directs in terms
  of a final end that acts as both a motivator and a lifetime goal

Foci of reflection: the two methods focus reflective discernment differently. While casuistry has
  users reflects upon the reality at hand to be able to understand it and then make good judgments about it, virtue ethics encourages self-reflection so as to come to a better understanding
  of oneself and fitting ends

Scrutiny of ends: the two methods scrutinize ends differently. Casuistry takes the particular ends
  of a society, culture, or religion as given while virtue ethics modifies ends to make them more
  meaningful and motivating to the individual

Limits of cultural influence: the two methods differ in terms of the influence of culture on the
  method. Casuistry is bounded by the cultures and traditions of the groups that maintain cases
  while virtue ethics is more broadly appealing because of the timelessness of the virtues

Time orientation: the two methods emphasize different aspects of time. Casuistry turns to long-
  enduring, oft-beloved, truth-bearing cases that are time bound in a previous era while virtue
  ethics examines a current situation so as to be able to know to best carry forward into the future

First, casuistry and virtue ethics have different functions. Casuistry functions
as an instrument for moral deliberation and is a comparative process that relies on
resemblances to work outward from unambiguous to more problematic cases. As
such, it is a tool to help individuals and groups clarify and resolve moral dilemmas.

Virtue ethics, in contrast, functions mainly as a system to describe human character and the qualities of the person that are necessary for right decision-making.
As an ethic, it attempts to account for moral dispositions and the impact of those
dispositions on the self and others. It articulates the various traits of excellence one
possesses or needs to possess to be morally praiseworthy and reveals how one becomes better through right or wrong actions. In this way, it derives its moral normative strength by describing the attributes of character that will enable the individual
to strive optimally toward his or her final good end.

Put another way, the two processes function differently in that casuistry acts as
an instrument for moral decision-making while virtue ethics acts to frame morality
in terms of character and the proper ends of the moral agent.

Second, casuistry and virtue ethics differ in their use of principles. Casuistry, if it
uses them at all, relies on principles that are deeply embedded in maxims and case
narratives. Principles are not emphasized but instead are deeply rooted and inter-
mixed in cases, giving cases moral meaning without being obvious and sidetracking
the process with concerns about adherence to epistemic purity.

Virtue ethics, on the other hand, relies differently on contextualized principles.
As we have seen, virtues are "defined by a rational principle, such as a man of

practical wisdom would use to determine it" (Aristotle 1962, II 6 1106b 1136). The emphasis here is not on principles as such because throughout, the focus remains trained on mean seeking and the quest for perfection of the individual. Even so, principles are important because they frame the reasoning process that helps inform the individual on how to act. In virtue ethics, it is the practical person of wisdom who chooses when and how to implement principles and principles *per se* remain instrumental rather than central to the ethic.

Third, although casuistry and virtue ethics similarly rely on ideas generalized from particular instances, they differ in regard to their use of abstract concepts. In casuistry, the user understands a case to be relevant because he or she sees in the account of facts some immaterial (abstract) elements with meaning. There is, in other words, recognition of a similarity of a situation to cases, an evaluation of that situation in terms of the merits of options, and then a forging of judgments based on the findings. At each step of the process there is an engagement of abstractions.

In addition, casuistry relies on cases placed within a taxonomy that is abstract at its core. The very notion of "order" upon which taxonomies rest is conceptual and abstract. So, too, are the understandings of particular cases as either paradigmatic or marginal. At these and other levels, the cases' delineation, ranking, and moral relevance are established by means of criteria that are abstract.

Virtue ethics also relies on abstractions, but does so differently and for different purposes. Here, the notion of "excellence of soul" that defines virtue and motivates the individual to develop particular characteristic moral habits is fundamentally abstract.

Moreover, all of the virtues are directed toward "the good," which is an abstract notion expressed in other abstract notions such as the final end, perfection, happiness, thriving, and so forth.

Finally, virtue ethics relies on the abstract notions of moderation, mean-seeking, and excess. Each of the virtues (temperance, fortitude, justice, and prudence) is determined as the middle point between two extremes and is therefore reliant upon these three abstract notions. At a number of levels then, virtue ethics is dependent upon abstractions in important ways.

Fourth, casuistry and virtue ethics provide different sorts of direction to moral deliberations. For its part, casuistry directs the user according to the values of a particular culture or tradition. This is clearly evident in religion-based casuistries where paradigmatic and marginal cases are used to direct the user to specific ends (salvation, for example). In Christian casuistries, for one, paradigm cases are located in parables and other truth-bearing narratives of Scripture. Marginal cases of less importance are located in authoritative teachings. Together, both sorts of cases impart a sense of obligation in followers and forge the identity of the group. Both also serve to promulgate the religion and regulate how one should think and act when making moral decisions as a member of that organization.

Virtue ethics, on the other hand, also provides direction but does not have casuistry's formal ordering mechanisms. Rather, it directs by providing the user with a final end that acts as both a motivator and a lifetime goal. This end admittedly remains always out of reach, but it nevertheless keeps the individual directed toward perfection.

Fifth, casuistry and virtue ethics have different foci of reflection. In casuistry, the user reflects upon reality to be able to understand it as fully as possible and then make good judgments about it. In virtue ethics, the user is encouraged to reflect upon reality in much the same way and toward similar ends, but one is also encouraged to self-reflect to thereby come to a better understanding of oneself, especially in relation to one's final good end(s). Thus, while both are similar reflective processes, casuistry and virtue ethics differ in terms of the direction of reflection.

Sixth, casuistry and virtue ethics differ in terms of their scrutiny of ends. Casuistry takes the particular ends of a society, culture, or religion as given. These are neither questioned nor necessarily developed further. People simply assume the validity of norms and ends and then attempt to remain in alignment with them by means of judgments based on certain accepted cases. In casuistry, in other words, there is little scrutiny of ends.

Virtue ethics, in contrast, constantly scrutinizes ends. As in casuistry, virtue ethics assumes the end as a given, but unlike casuistry virtue ethics, refines and expands the end as the individual practices the virtues. As the individual advances in virtue, his or her final good end is reviewed, amended, and nuanced to become more meaningful to the individual. In other words, in virtue ethics the end is tweaked and scrutinized regularly to remain effective as a moral motivator and in this way virtue ethics differs significantly from casuistry.

Seventh, casuistry and virtue ethics differ in terms of the influence of culture on the method. As we saw, ancient Greeks, Jews, Christians, Muslims, western moderns, and others have casuistries that appeal to people within those specific groups. The casuistries associated with these cultures are relatively simple instruments for moral decision-making because they rely on familiar stories and norms.

Virtue ethics, on the other hand, expresses virtues in ways meaningful to a local culture, but also maintains elements embedded in the virtues that are long enduring, timeless, and recognizable outside the narrow parameters of culture. As a result, virtue ethics is not as culturally bounded as casuistry.

While context matters to a degree, people can recognize courage, temperance, prudence, and justice in examples that are culturally foreign. They can see, for example, the virtue of men such as Odysseus, Moses, Jesus, and Muhammad despite the fact that these men lived long ago and in environments quite different than today's. Although the accounts of their lives are unlike our own, the qualities of character that they displayed are not that different than those we experience today. Odysseus' courage in the *Odyssey*, for example, is easily comprehensible. As a result, it can be reformatted to suit contemporary tastes. Odysseus' voyages can be "retooled" to become Captain Kirk's ongoing intergalactic adventure, *Star Trek*. Thus, while virtues reflect certain social values rooted in a specific culture, the breadth of their appeal is wide—and certainly wider than that of casuistry.

Finally, casuistry and virtue ethics are oriented differently toward time. Casuistry relies on narratives rooted in the past (i.e. precedent cases) and has the user look for resemblances between the present circumstances and past incidents. These past incidents are recounted in truth-bearing cases that are time bound. Even so, they are not passé. Rather, they are long enduring and oft beloved.

Virtue ethics, on the other hand, is forward directed. Even when it turns to the past for guidance, virtue ethics does so to inspire future excellence on the part of individuals.

In virtue ethics, past incidents are used to frame a vision about a current situation so as to be able to know how to best act now and in the future. Inspirational, virtue ethics reminds us of the sorts of people we might become by our actions. Thus, while it respects the past, virtue ethics is mostly concerned with the future and individual betterment, that is, how one can become better as one progresses in life.

Casuistry-Imbued Virtue Ethics Versus Virtue-Imbued Casuistry

From the above, it seems that bringing casuistry and virtue ethics together should leverage the two methods' similarities and differences in positive ways by taking advantage of the beneficial qualities or offsetting the negative features of each in isolation. The combination of the two in a new method for moral problem solving should create a synergy that makes the approach more robust than other methods or either component method used alone.

Given this possibility, the question is whether to attempt to create a method based on casuistry imbued with virtue ethics or virtue ethics imbued with casuistry. To answer this question, we need to review the primary role of each method.

Casuistry functions as an instrument for moral problem solving that is dependent upon its users for good direction. As we saw in the earlier section on casuistry's critics, users can wield casuistry for good or ill. As a consequence, casuistry depends upon the good character of its users to be a legitimate tool for moral decision-making.

Virtue ethics, on the other hand, is a normative moral theory that emphasizes character by holding before the individual an ideal image of him or herself and suggesting how one might develop habits of moral excellence through moderation and the exercise of the virtues. It does this well but does not have the effective decision-making instrumentality of casuistry.

If the intention is to establish a new and more robust method for moral problem solving, then it would seem more logical to forge a new sort of casuistry imbued with virtue ethics rather than vice versa. This is because virtue ethics brings moral rigor to a method already designed for problem solving. Although casuistry can enhance deliberations about virtue, virtue ethics as an approach is not structured as a decision-making tool as casuistry is. Thus it can modify and enhance but not replace casuistry as a decision-making tool.

Virtue-Imbued Casuistry's Synergies

In the following, we will see how a virtue-imbued casuistry can be established to leverage the similarities and differences of casuistry and virtue ethics to take advantage of their strengths and to neutralize their shortcomings. The argument will establish the synergy of the two approaches and then construct virtue-imbued casuistry as an alternative method for moral decision-making.

Synergy of Strengths

To begin, casuistry and virtue ethics can be combined to take advantage of their similarities. This combination creates a synergy along the lines summarized in Table 11.3.

First, the combination of casuistry and virtue ethics in virtue-imbued casuistry will further emphasize the concrete and thereby enable users to make even more defensible moral judgments about specific situations than other methods or casuistry or virtue ethics used in isolation.

As we have seen, casuistry and virtue ethics are alike in emphasizing the concrete rather than the abstract. As individual processes, each trains the user's attention on the situation at hand rather than abstract principles, theories, and concepts. Casuistry does this by using settled cases that are accounts of actual events while virtue ethics does it by having the individual practice the virtues in real-world contexts.

The combination of the two methods to form virtue-imbued casuistry therefore underscores the preferences of the two methods to not stray into abstract theorizing but remain with the concrete reality at hand. It also focuses the user's attention on the details of a circumstance from more than one perspective and in this way accounts for the particulars of a moral problem more thoroughly than might occur otherwise.

Second, the combination of casuistry and virtue ethics in virtue-imbued casuistry is likely to produce judgments that are more realistic, relevant, and useful than those derived by other methods or casuistry or virtue ethics in isolation.

Casuistry strives for relevancy by using settled cases that recount real world judgments. It then uses these cases in a cumulative way to form a practically implementable judgment about a present problem. In both orientation and practice then, casuistry exerts practical moral force on judgments.

Virtue ethics does something similar, but relies on prudence or practical wisdom to determine a course of action rather than cases. At its core, virtue ethics appeals to real world experiences much as casuistry does but its practically deliberative orientation sets it apart from casuistry. As a method, virtue ethics appeals to judgments made by wise individuals and in this way exerts a practical moral force on judgments that differs from casuistry's in important ways.

When put together in virtue-imbued casuistry, the combination of methods underscores the practical relevance of particular judgments made with them. Because

Table 11.3 Synergy of Strengths: Casuistry and Virtue Ethics

Strengths		Synergy
Casuistry (C)	Virtue ethics (V)	(C + V)
Settled cases are concrete accounts of actual events	Virtue is honed through practice in real-world contexts	Virtue-imbued casuistry further emphasizes the concrete rather than the abstract more strongly than either method in isolation
Casuistry is a practical method for making moral judgments	Virtue is derived by means of practical wisdom (prudence)	Virtue-imbued casuistry underscores the practical relevance of a course of action from more than one moral perspective
Casuistry's settled cases are significant to members of the particular communities that retain them	Virtues are taught, defined, and promulgated by members of specific social groups	Virtue-imbued casuistry further nuances, solidifies, and advances society's moral norms more effectively than either method in isolation
Casuistry's cases can appeal indirectly to moral principles	Virtues are mean-seeking activities that account for rational principles defined by the practically wise	Virtue-imbued casuistry enhances the advancement of ideals, principles, and notions of right and wrong in strong but indirect ways to the benefit of society
Casuistry's case selection depends on individuals of good character	Virtue ethics links ongoing moral choices with the development of good character	Virtue-imbued casuistry enhances the likelihood that people will make moral judgments that will better themselves and society
Casuistry allows for flexible interpretation of moral principles	Virtue ethics holds that principles are flexible in that "the man of practical wisdom" interprets them	Virtue-imbued casuistry advances a helpful flexible hermeneutic for the interpretation of principles
Casuistry has the individual reflect upon a situation and its underlying dynamics to find similarities between present circumstances and settled cases	Virtue ethics has the individual reflect upon intended actions in terms of a personal history of such decisions and the final good end of the person	Virtue-imbued casuistry amalgamates the reflective and imaginative aspects of each method to expand the overall reflection within moral decision-making and thereby bring about more deeply thought out and defensible moral judgments
Casuistry cases enrich the prudential reasoning processes of virtue ethics	Virtue ethics' moral analysis enriches the moral content of casuistry's truth-bearing cases	Virtue-imbued casuistry enriches the moral content of casuistry's narratives resulting in more robust moral judgments
Casuistry encourages ordinary people to make moral judgments without appeals to moral experts	Virtue ethics encourages people to adopt moral habits and act rightly within the confines of their particular abilities and constraints	Virtue-imbued casuistry enhances the likelihood that the ordinary people charged with making moral decisions in real contexts will do so

the judgment is the result of more than one practical perspective, it produces outcomes that are more realistic, relevant, and useful than those derived by means of other methods or casuistry or virtue ethics used in isolation.

Third, the combination of casuistry and virtue ethics in virtue-imbued casuistry should further nuance and solidify society's moral norms and in this way make society's moral environment more robust.

As we saw, both methods are social group specific, which means that the two processes have relevance to the societies that use the specific iterations of the methods. Casuistry does this by turning to settled cases having significance to members of an identifiable community that not only cherishes the cases, but also ranks them according to a hierarchy of moral relevance reflecting society's preferences.

Similarly, virtue is taught, defined, and promulgated by identifiable communities of people. Although there are overlaps and similarities among virtue theories, the specific iteration of what it means to be virtuous and what each of the virtues (courage, temperance, prudence, etc.) means is determined by particular social groups and reflects their preferences.

When combined to form virtue-imbued casuistry, the different iterations of society's moral preferences embedded in casuistry and virtue ethics will merge to further nuance and better solidify society's moral norms and, in the end, make society's moral environment more robust.

Fourth, a combination of methods in virtue-imbued casuistry is likely to better draw out, nuance, support, and promulgate abstract notions within society and thereby advance society's ideals, principles, and notions of right and wrong.

Both methods refer indirectly rather than directly to moral principles. This makes them good ways to disseminate moral norms within society. While each refrains from lecturing about principles, each nevertheless incorporates moral principles in decisions.

Virtue ethics does so by construing virtue as a mean relative to the agent as well as something defined by a rational principle as a person of practical wisdom would determine it.

Casuistry, in contrast, often avoids principles altogether, but when it does recognize them, does so indirectly and by means of cases.

In both methods then, abstract ideals and notions of right and wrong are embedded within the methods in ways that enable norms to function well within real situations. When the two methods are combined in virtue-imbued casuistry, these abstract notions are drawn out, nuanced, supported, and promulgated within society even better and as they are, society's moral norms and identity as a community are advanced.

Fifth, a combination of casuistry and virtue ethics in virtue-imbued casuistry increases the likelihood that people will make responsible moral judgments because they see them as personally beneficial.

Although each method emphasizes the effects of judgments on the moral character of the individual, their combination makes this influence even more apparent.

Used in isolation, casuistry appeals to past decisions having relevance to those making judgments. The act of selecting one case over another—or engaging in moral deliberation at all—thus reflects the moral dispositions of individuals.

Virtue ethics, on the other hand, emphasizes character formation explicitly by linking daily choices and the development of characteristic habits to the quest for moral betterment or perfection.

When the two methods are combined in virtue-imbued casuistry, these aspects of character formation and character-at-work come together to highlight the importance of good moral character in decision making even more than the two methods do in isolation. The imbuement of casuistry with virtue ethics therefore underscores the effects of decision-making on the character of the individual and increases the likelihood that people will make responsible moral judgments because they see them as personally beneficial.

Sixth, the imbuement of casuistry with virtue ethics advances a flexible hermeneutic in regard to moral principles that is more helpful than other methods or casuistry or virtue ethics in isolation.

Insofar as it admits of principles at all, casuistry advances flexible interpretations of moral principles. It does this firstly through its promotion of individual choice in case selection. Although casuistry's taxonomy of cases and paradigm cases are set and while the moral principles embedded in cases are well established in theory and tradition, casuistry allows the individual to choose among cases, determine the nature of the moral issue at hand, and then settle on an interpretation of the moral principle(s) involved in the dilemma.

In addition, casuistry has the individual determine how and where to apply cases and in this way frees the individual to interpret the importance and applicability of the moral norms embedded in select cases. In these ways, casuistic choices evidence the exercise of a flexible hermeneutic in regard to principles.

Virtue ethics, for its part, promotes flexibility in interpreting moral principles by maintaining that principles are to be interpreted by "the man of practical wisdom." Because prudence defines each of the virtues and guides the individual to a proper final end, it emphasizes the ability of individuals to interpret not just the situation at hand, but also the moral norms at work there. In these ways then, virtue ethics stresses flexibility in the hermeneutics of moral norms, including principles.

Combined in virtue-imbued casuistry, these notions of flexibility in interpreting moral principles are advanced beyond that of each method singly. With virtue-imbued casuistry, each method's influence in adapting principles to make them more relevant to practical problem solving is made stronger and more effective.

Seventh, the combination of virtue ethics and casuistry in virtue-imbued casuistry advances the reflective and imaginative processes of each method that are crucial to making good moral judgments.

As we have seen, each process has the individual mentally reflect upon the present circumstances for the purpose of coming to a better understanding of the context of a decision. Each does so to enable the individual to account for reality more fully and thereby make better judgments.

When the two methods are combined in virtue-imbued casuistry, the reflective and imaginative aspects of each method singly amalgamate to expand the overall reflection within moral decision-making. This fusion widens the user's perspective to enable him or her to consider potential outcomes that might otherwise be overlooked. In this way, it facilitates the development of more deeply thought out and defensible moral judgments.

Eighth, the combination of casuistry and virtue ethics in virtue-imbued casuistry enriches the cache of narratives available to moral decision-making.

As we saw, casuistry's truth-bearing cases that recount situations in which people made moral judgments in the past provide meaningful stories that help in moral decision-making. Often, these narratives contain examples of prudential reasoning, moderation, courage, temperance, or justice in action.

Virtue ethics provides these same benefits, but in a different manner. To explain prudence, moderation, and so forth, virtue ethics must rely on truth-bearing narratives. In other words, to make its central concepts sensible, virtue ethics draws upon narratives to illustrate the theory's abstract qualities.

When combined in virtue-imbued casuistry, this sort of back-and-forth flow of meaning and narrative advances to better ends. There is an enrichment of the process that each method uses singly and, as a result, users have a better tool to make defensible moral judgments.

Ninth, although each method is convenient, easy to use, and understandable on its own, the combination of casuistry and virtue ethics in virtue-imbued casuistry enhances the ease of use and likelihood that the method will be employed by the ordinary people charged with making moral judgments in real contexts.

As we saw earlier, casuistry relies on narratives that are accessible and relevant to ordinary people. Similarly, virtue ethics concentrates on the various ways ordinary people can perfect themselves and their societies through good moral choices.

The combination of the two methods in virtue-imbued casuistry therefore enhances the positive qualities of each and increases the likelihood that those charged with making moral decisions in real contexts will actually do so.

Synergy of Offsetting Limitations

The combination of casuistry and virtue ethics can take advantage of the similarities of the two, but linking them can also leverage their differences to neutralize their respective shortcomings and create a similar synergistic dynamic. The ways that this can be accomplished are summarized in Table 11.4.

First, the combination of casuistry and virtue ethics to form virtue-imbued casuistry is likely to create cases richer in content and normative direction.

Although casuistry's settled cases account for the facts and judgments associated with problems, they do not always provide normative direction. They sometimes just reiterate the *status quo* morality of a society—and this limits their effectiveness. In contrast, virtue ethics provides good normative content and direction, but often fails to emphasize virtue in the context of particular practices.

Combining virtue ethics and casuistry can neutralize these weaknesses by creating a dynamic synergy that advances not just the *status quo* morality, but also a deeper understanding of the virtues as they apply to practical situations. In this way,

Table 11.4 Synergy of Offsetting Limitations: Casuistry and Virtue Ethics

Differences and Limitations		Synergy
Casuistry (C)	Virtue ethics (V)	(C + V)
Settled cases record events and judgments, but lack normative direction	Virtues offer normative direction, but not much context	Virtue-imbued casuistry enriches case content and casuistry's normative direction
Case taxonomies suggest moral strength, but do not indicate how moral weight is derived	Virtues are normative, but not case based	Virtue-imbued casuistry can make cases taxonomies more useful as moral deliberative instruments
Case taxonomies provide rich examples of morality in action, but little scrutiny of the underlying morality	Virtues are important to individual flourishing, but can seem vague if not contextualized well	Virtue-imbued casuistry widens the understanding and appreciation of the virtues
Casuistry's cases support the moral *status quo* of a social group or culture, but can lack widespread appeal	Virtues are defined by and have relevance to specific groups of people, but are not accepted in the same manner everywhere	Virtue-imbued casuistry can help translate the existing morality of a society, making it more relevant to those inside and outside the host community
Casuistry helps people discern a best course of action, but does not define the end	Virtue ethics defines the end of virtue as the final good end(s), but does not give particular ways to get to that end	Casuistry and virtue ethics combine to perfect the individual through practical means

the method can provide greater normative direction to the case-based process and help users make better moral judgments. Combining the two, in other words, enables each method to offset the shortcomings of the other and in this way offer more effective direction than other approaches or either component method used singly.

Second, combining casuistry and virtue ethics in virtue-imbued casuistry can help make case taxonomies more useful as moral deliberative instruments. At present, casuistry's case taxonomies indicate a case's strength by the case's proximity to a paradigm case (one with an incident that is unambiguously right or wrong). There is no indication of how or why the original case is so relatively strong or weak from a moral perspective.

Virtue ethics can relieve some of this ambiguity by providing a flexible normative component that hones moral distinctions, refines the weighing of the moral features of cases, and aids in the comparison of cases in terms of their moral content. In this way, the inclusion of virtue ethics can strengthen casuistry by helping its case taxonomies become clearer and more useful to moral decision-making.

Third, the combination of casuistry and virtue ethics in virtue-imbued casuistry can bring about a better understanding of the nature of virtue and can widen the scope of the applicability and relevance of the virtues.

As we have seen, cases are rich illustrations of morality in action. They are also sometimes repositories of instances of virtue—examples of how virtue is practiced in real life settings. Cases are not always very good at deeply scrutinizing the underlying morality embedded in the cases, however.

Virtue ethics, in contrast, scrutinizes moral problems well, but can seem vague if the virtues are not contextualized in meaningful ways. Unless they are framed well, the virtues can seem abstract and foreign. Their meaning remains largely hidden unless they are placed in recognizable circumstances.

Combining casuistry and virtue ethics in virtue-imbued casuistry can relieve these deficiencies by widening the general understanding and appreciation of the virtues. Enriching casuistry's cases with virtue ethics can help users understand the moral depth of the judgments within settled cases. It can also help users appreciate how the virtues are contextualized in relevant circumstances. In these ways, virtue-imbued casuistry can enrich both methods individually and facilitate more robust moral judgments.

Fourth, the combination of casuistry and virtue ethics in virtue-imbued casuistry can help translate the existing morality of a society to make it more relevant to insiders and more understandable to those outside the community in which the ethic resides.

As we have seen, casuistry supports the moral *status quo* of a particular social group or culture. Its moral foundations are conventional and largely unquestioned. While it can be significant to the members of a particular community, it might not resonate very well with outsiders. It can therefore lack widespread appeal.

Similarly, virtue ethics' virtues are defined by and have relevance to specific groups of people. They, too, are culturally interpreted, defended, and promulgated by limited numbers of people and are not necessarily universally accepted.

Virtue-imbued casuistry can relieve some of these tensions related to ignorance or misunderstanding of a conventional morality by helping to translate the morality to make it more palatable. For one, the use of casuistry alongside virtue ethics can advance a wider understanding of the particular iterations of virtue in a society, thereby making the virtue ethic more likely to be accepted, relevant, and applied. When used well, cases can also help frame the interpretation of rather universal concepts such as recklessness, courage, temperance, injustice, and so forth. In this way, cases can facilitate the familiarity if not the complete acceptance of particular renderings of virtue outside the community that formulated it.

For its part, the use of virtue ethics can explain the underlying values and reasons behind the judgments in casuistry's settled cases. It can help outsiders understand why a particular group of people cherishes the narratives that it does. Just as with cases helping the understanding of virtue, the use of virtue ethics can facilitate the familiarity if not the complete acceptance of the particular judgments made in settled cases to those outside the community that reveres the cases.

In combining casuistry and virtue ethics and applying virtue-imbued casuistry in these ways, the moral norms and truth-bearing cases of a society are nuanced, supported, and advanced both within and outside the society that initiated them in ways that neither method can do singly.

Fifth, the combination of casuistry and virtue ethics in virtue-imbued casuistry can help perfect people. As we have seen, casuistry helps people discern their best course of action by having them consider a range of options expressed in terms of precedent cases. It does not specify an explicit end, however.

Virtue ethics, in contrast, defines the end (or ends) of virtue but does not give practical ways to get there. It sets out the final good end(s) as an objective of virtue, but does not provide specific ways to achieve this end other than through the exercise of practical wisdom (prudence) and the mean course of action among extremes.

When casuistry and virtue ethics are combined in virtue-imbued casuistry, the limits of each method in regard to ends are moderated significantly. The two approaches can combine in such a way that the individual is perfected by means of the practical examples provided by cases. Here, the end(s) of virtue (the *telos*) is furthered by means of comparisons to previous incidents where judgments were more or less correct. More important to the overall thrust of ethics, the person making the judgment is helped in this way along the road to personal perfection.

To summarize, although people can engage casuistry without attending much to virtue and can act virtuously without engaging in casuistic deliberations, the combination of casuistry and virtue ethics can help them produce more robust moral judgments than either method alone.

As shown here, virtue ethics and casuistry are compatible methods that when brought together produce a *pousse-café* of synergistic advantages that enhance the effectiveness of moral decision-making. Together, they are more effective than other methods or either method alone and can help people make good moral judgments in everyday circumstances. For these reasons, virtue-imbued casuistry is worth pursuing.

Chapter 12
Bringing Casuistry and the Business Case Method Together

> *Coming together is a beginning; keeping together is progress; working together is success.*
>
> —attributed to Henry Ford

Because casuistry's and virtue ethics' histories are replete with accounts involving business, no book advocating virtue-imbued casuistry in the context of business would be satisfactory without a consideration of the ways the basic method (casuistry) and cases in general have been used to advance an understanding of morality in commerce.[1]

Casuistry and Cases in Business

In the past, particularly during the high era of Christian casuistry, businesspeople were exposed to casuistic disputations through the advice of priests, the religious sacrament of confession, and the sermons of itinerant preachers. Through these means businesspeople learned how to reason similarly and came to a deeper understanding of the moral significance of their daily affairs.

One of the most contentious business-related moral issues of this time was that of money lending at profit and the prohibition of usury. This issue was particularly pressing then because of the increased demand for capital as European centers of influence expanded their reach abroad, built cities, and established more intricate commercial ties. As a result and as Jonsen and Toulmin note, "from the eleventh to the eighteenth century, the problem of usury exercised the finest theological and canonical minds" (Jonsen and Toulmin 1988, p. 181).

Casuistry was useful in bringing people to a deeper understanding of the roles of money and profit in generating wealth and social prosperity. It also helped refine the term "usury" so that the term could better capture the intention of thwart-

---

[1] A less advanced version of sections of this chapter was originally published in (Calkins 2001) and then reprinted in (Calkins 2007).

M. Calkins, *Developing a Virtue-Imbued Casuistry for Business Ethics,* Issues in Business Ethics 42, DOI 10.1007/978-94-017-8724-6_12, © Springer Netherlands 2014

ing moneylender abuses yet accommodate reward for risk to enable lenders to underwrite capitalist initiatives. As a result of these deliberations, the definition was changed from the Middle Ages' notion of "where more is asked than is given" to St. Alphonsus Ligouri's (1696–1787) "interest taken where there is no just title to profit" (Jonsen and Toulmin 1988, p. 193).

In general, the back and forth of casuistic discussions of the past served to advance the understanding of the moral underpinnings of commerce so it could better accommodate "the explosion of new data from an expanded vision of the world"(Keenan S.J. and Shannon 1995, p. xvi).

Unfortunately, the use of casuistry in business died out in business as it did elsewhere. Even so, case use continued in a different manner—in the business case method of business education.

Today, cases and the business case method are used extensively as part of a formulaic andragogy to advance the analytic skills of emerging managers. As we will see next, case use is the basis of many business education programs and an integral part of most business courses, especially at the graduate level.

Lamentably, case use tends to meet an abrupt end for business students upon graduation. For some reason or combination of reasons, managers or case providers have not carried forward the case use techniques of business education into business practice. This phenomenon and its resolution will be considered in the last chapters of the book, but for now it is helpful to consider how cases are used at present and how this case use compares to casuistry.

The Business Case and Case Method

Many of today's business managers have been educated by means of a business case method in which cases are used to solve complex problems. At first glance, this method appears identical to casuistry, but as we will see, the two are not the same.

The Business Case

The use and format of cases in the business case method are well established and longstanding in business education. In general, the process relies on business cases that are open-ended narratives designed "to give each individual student a practical and professional training suitable to the particular business he (or she) plans to enter."[2] They differ from the cases used in other disciplines—medicine, biology, law, and so on—in terms of its length, purpose, use, and usefulness. The general features of the business case are summarized in Table 12.1[3].

---

[2] C. R. Christensen quoted in (Lundberg 1993, p. 45).

[3] The points in this table are sourced in the following:

    Point 2: P. Lawrence quoted in (Vance 1993, p. 46).

Table 12.1 The business Case's Characteristics

A tool for deliberation
A vehicle for classroom discussion
A record of a real-life managerial dilemma
A clinical study of events
Focused on a specific time
Focused on particular facts
Emphasizes decision-making
Short and lightly footnoted
Open-ended
Concerned with human relationships
Controversial and pertinent
A mini-drama, but not "just a story"

The business case is a tool for deliberation that serves as a vehicle for classroom discussion. It is essentially an account of a real-life situation—an in-depth exploration of an incident that is rich in detail. While it is usually based upon firsthand experience, it may be derived from another's account.[4] In almost all instances, it is concrete rather than abstract and focused on the particular problems faced by managers.

The business case is typically short—15 to 20 pages in length—and lacks the heavy footnoting of cases in disciplines such as law, for example.[5] The ideal case is

---

Point 3: (Gragg 1954, p. 46).

Point 5: (Rotch 1996).

Point 6: (Bruner and Paddack 1996).

Point 7: J. A. Erskine et al., quoted in (Vance 1993, p. 47).

Point 12: (Abell 1997, p. 4–7). Abell sites ten features of a good case. His recommendations follow:

1. Make sure it is a case and not just a story.
2. Make sure that the case tackles a relevant, important issue.
3. Make sure that the case provides a voyage of discovery—even some interesting surprises.
4. Make sure that the case is controversial.
5. Make sure that the case contains contrasts and comparisons.
6. Make sure that the case provides currently useful generalizations.
7. Make sure that the case has the data required to tackle the problem—not too many and not too few.
8. Make sure that the case has a personal touch.
9. Make sure that the case is well-structured and easy to read.
10. Make sure that the case is short (no more than 8–10 pages).

[4] As noted earlier, there is disagreement over whether true cases must be based *solely* on firsthand experience.

[5] Michael Leenders and James Erskine suggest further that a good business case supports the adage, "if you can't say it in ten to fifteen pages, it's probably not worth saying." (Leenders and Erskine 1978, p. 43).

William Rotch backs up Leenders and Erskine in asserting that, "many faculty believe seven pages of text is maximum." (Rotch 1996).

The University of Virginia's Darden Case Production and Style Manual, moreover, recommends that case writers use appendixes rarely and that "bibliographies be added only if a case makes many references to works of interest to a student." (Reisler et al. 1994, pp. 24–25).

of sufficient length to describe a problem without providing a solution, containing enough data to be useful without being so detailed that context is lost.[6] Although some cases are more elaborate and lengthy than others, the business case's relative brevity is due to its "open-endedness," which is useful as a teaching instrument to elicit student situational analysis and judgment.

Of late, the business case has become lengthier due to the increasing complexity of contemporary business and the demands of publishers that cases be scientifically and analytically more rigorous than they were in the past.[7] This combination has resulted in a wider range of case lengths, with simple, single-issue cases having sparse material tending to be short and more complex cases covering multiple issues tending to be longer.[8]

Aside from case length, business case content tends to be about human relationships. The reason for this, as Charles Gragg pointed out, is that:

> (B)usiness management is not a technical but a human matter. It turns upon an understanding of how people—producers, bankers, investors, sellers, consumers—will respond to specific business actions, and the behavior of such groups always is changing, rapidly or slowly.[9]

The business case strives to capture the complex human interactions at work in a given situation by distilling and synthesizing the seemingly disparate components that comprise an event into a compelling narrative that acts as both an action-drama and a fable. Its vivid account of managerial actions establishes certain business leaders as "characters" (think James Burke) who then become memorable such that they can be recalled and emulated later in similar real-world situations.

Although such features identify the business case as such, individual cases can vary according to andragogical purpose. These can be grouped or "typed" according to the list in Table 12.2.

That business cases vary along functional lines is not a new concept. The first four points in Table 12.2 are from (Lundberg 1993, p. 49) while the fifth to ninth are from (Rotch 1996). They are included here to underscore the point that the business

---

[6] Leenders and Erskine observe that, "the present committee at Harvard, which investigates the types and uses of case materials, is in general agreement not to include solutions." (Leenders and Erskine 1978, p. 44).

[7] To be published, case-based articles increasingly must not only persuade, they must also withstand the epistemic scrutiny proper to science. One academic business journal's article review sheet, for example, asks the reviewer whether or not the article in question manifests sound judgment based upon data and a measure of "scientific quality." While this requirement makes sense for scientific articles, it may not befit case-based articles. To the contrary, instead of strengthening case-based articles, this requirement may weaken these sorts of articles by relegating the cases therein to the status of examples. In emphasizing principles or points of argument in a manner befitting science, abstraction is emphasized and cases become mere illustrations of theories. This changes the case's function, demotes the case, and undermines the role of narrative in argumentation. In the end, the scientific requirement weakens an instrument that expresses human relationships that are not quantifiable but nevertheless fundamental to business.

[8] Leenders and Erskine affirm this notion when they observe that, "during the past ten years cases have been getting longer (and) (t)he content is becoming more complex and the descriptions more elaborate." (Leenders and Erskine 1978, p. 45).

[9] (Gragg 1954, p. 7). Note: originally published in 1940.

Table 12.2 Business Case Types

Iceberg cases: those that offer a sample of a situation
Predictive series of cases: those in which "the diagnosis and action recommended of the first case may be compared with the reality of the chronologically next case."
Multimedia cases: those that rely on audio-visual augmentation
Living cases: those where "one or more executives are questioned by the class to discover the facts of the situation before analysis and action planning."
Focused decision cases: those where the decision to be made is fairly clear and the task is to analyze alternatives and decide the best course of action
Unfocused decision cases: those where the task is to discover and define the problem and then decide the best course of action
Implementation cases: those that include the question of how the favored decision is to be implemented, *i.e.*, who should say or do what to whom?
Appraisal cases: those where the immediate problem is not readily apparent and where one has to ask penetrating questions to uncover the assumptions, processes, and characteristics of the organization and situation that are under investigation
Simple or complex cases: those that vary according to student capabilities and where they are used in a course of study

case is an identifiable sort, but also one that has multiple purposes and functions. In this regard, it is not wholly unlike business itself—identifiable as a certain sort of entity but variable according to need and function.

The Business Case Method

In America, business case use typically follows a method developed at Harvard University's law and business schools in the late-nineteenth and early-twentieth centuries.[10] This method emerged, as Michael Davis points out, from faculty members' accounts of incidents and were akin to professorial "war stories" (Davis 1997, p. 354). Later, the stories and story telling were refined and used in a more systematic way.

As Arthur Dewing explains, today's business case method involves the "class discussion of possibilities, probabilities, and expedients—the possibilities of the combinations of very intricate facts, the probabilities of human reactions, and the expedients most likely to bring about the responses in others that lead to a definite end" (Dewing 1954, p. 4).

The purpose of the method is to help managers sharpen their analytical skills, enhance their ability to put order into unstructured situations, identify problems, develop conclusions, and recommend actions in complex business situations (Rotch 1996). In line with these objectives, the case method encourages its users to develop habits of discernment and other important personal traits. A list of these can be found in Table 12.3.

---

[10] For excellent summaries of the early history of the business case method, see (Barnes et al. 1994, pp. 38–50; Beauchamp 1998; Copeland 1954, pp. 25–33).

Table 12.3 Business Case Method Objectives

Greater Knowledge: helps individuals gain an understanding of a particular subject
Technical Expertise: provides a forum to practice and master particular analytic techniques
Good Habits of Analysis: stimulates clear thinking, analysis, and curiosity so that these may become natural and automatic with time and practice
Manager's Perspective: encourages the broad, entrepreneurial, and administrative perspective essential to effective business management
Problem-Solving Skills: helps individuals sharpen their analytical skills and ability to put order into unstructured situations and helps individuals identify problems, develop conclusions, and recommend actions in complex business situations
Communication Skills: facilitates communication and stresses the importance of good questioning in the analysis of business data
Consensus-building: stimulates consensus in the face of individual differences
Personal Development: strengthens the individual's sense of internal security and facilitates leadership, assertiveness, personal responsibility, active learning, and a realistic assessment of one's own abilities and expertise
Risk Management: strengthens the ability to deal successfully with an unpredictable future

Just as in the penultimate Table, the points in the last Table are derived from others' work, specifically that of Rotch and Donham.[11] Their explanations need not be replicated here but are referenced to underscore the ways the case method advances the critical thinking, reflection, and communication skills of its users.

In general, the case method helps the user become more confident in handling business problems by allowing him or her to develop analytical and critical thinking skills within the context of a relatively non-threatening educational environment. It is a method that helps the user order unstructured situations, identify problems, develop conclusions, manage risk, and recommend actions in complex business environments. In this way, it enables the user to advance beyond his or her current limits of assertiveness, personal responsibility, abilities, and expertise.

Perhaps most important, the business case method facilitates the user's development of good communication skills. Because the method is dialogical, it stresses listening and verbalization and thereby helps the individual improve his or her interpersonal and communicative skills. It also facilitates the development of an appreciation of the importance of consensus-building and good questioning in the analysis of business data (Rotch 1996).

Given these benefits, most case method business schools today—those that use cases primarily or exclusively as andragogical tools—stress student participation in class discussions. School leaders understand that hands-on use is how students demonstrate and hone their interpersonal communicative skills, ability to question effectively, and organize and analyze data quickly and correctly.

---

[11] Points 1–4: (Rotch 1992).
    Points 5–7: (Rotch 1996).
    Point 8: (Rotch 1992, 1996).
    Point 9: (Donham 1954, p. 245).

Table 12.4 Similarities: the Business Case Method and Casuistry

Instrumental: both are tools for deliberation
Comparative: both use analogy to determine the fit of past and present circumstances
Cumulative: both build cumulative arguments to establish the high probability of accuracy of their judgments
Probable, not certain: both emphasize the probability rather than the certainty of judgments
Relevant: both methods account for actual events and produce actionable results for practical situations
Distil: both methods draw out the salient elements of complex situations and then frame them simply in shortcuts to expedite the reasoning and decision-making processes

At the University of Virginia's Colgate Darden Graduate School of Business Administration, for example, teaching relies heavily on cases (some of which are drawn from the School's extensive case catalog) and students are graded on the basis of how well they grapple with the nuance of narratives and their embedded issues. As part of this process, students are critiqued in terms of their interpersonal skills, ability to reach consensus with other students, and capacity to derive an acceptable course of action in terms of the case. The development of these skills facilitate, in turn, what Wallace Donham calls, "a sense of internal security, assurance in their capacity to get on with people collaboratively and to deal successfully with the unpredictable future" (Donham 1954, p. 245).

The Business Case Method and Casuistry Compared

The astute reader will recognize at this point certain similarities between the business case method and the casuistic approach to moral problem solving described earlier. While it would be tempting to leap to the conclusion that the two methods are the same, in fact they are not.

In the following we will see how the business case method and casuistry are alike and different. We begin with a consideration of the ways the two methods are alike.

Similarities

The business case method and casuistry share a number of key features, many of which are summarized in Table 12.4.

First, because the business case method and casuistry help the user reflect upon the situation at hand, they are alike as instruments to facilitate deliberation. While the case method generally focuses on the immediate concerns of stakeholders and the bottom line, casuistry focuses on the moral hazards and opportunities of a particular circumstance.[12]

---

[12] The term "moral hazard" refers to threats of a moral nature, that is, the risks associated with the violation of moral norms. The use of the term here differs from economics where moral hazard

Second, the business case method and casuistry are alike in being comparative processes. Both use analogy to determine the fit of past and present circumstances. Although the case method remains with one particular incident and casuistry brings a number of incidents to bear on deliberations, both look for the similarities between past and present events and therefore are alike as processes of comparison.

Third, the two methods are alike in similarly building cumulative arguments to establish the high probability of accuracy of judgments. Both aggregate or sum up arguments to justify their judgments and in this way convince by means of a collection of forceful arguments.

Fourth and following from the last point, both methods similarly account for actual events and produce relevant and actionable results for practical situations. Neither is an intellectual pursuit to satisfy the curiosity of academics. Neither strives for epistemic certainty or attempts to derive "formal proofs of a kind that can be judged by anyone with an eye for 'necessary connections'" (Jonsen and Toulmin 1988, p. 257). Rather, each attempts to establish the "licitness or permissibility of acting in one particular way or another" (Jonsen and Toulmin 1988, p. 256). In this way, the two methods remain grounded in the reality at hand and produce relevant and actionable results.

Fifth, the business case method and casuistry are alike in that both draw out the salient elements of complex situations and then frame the elements simply in maxims to expedite the reasoning process.

Not unlike Immanuel Kant's insistence on the Categorical Imperative being framed in shortcut form ("Act only on that *maxim* whereby thou canst at the same time will that it should become a universal law"), the case method and casuistry reduce much of the complexity of moral reasoning to rules of conduct rule expressed in sententious form, that is, maxims (Kant 1785, 1964, 1990). The use of maxims or shortcut phrases with embedded rules is helpful because it distils complex notions to a manageable level. Moreover, the pithiness of maxims convinces and inspires people to act in the way recommended. Maxims are therefore effective ways to communicate and convince others about the rightness or wrongness of something.

The distillation of norms to maxims is especially useful in business practice because it helps managers make more timely decisions. Because managers typically work under time pressure, they must eschew long and wordy deliberations framed in abstract and theoretical terms. Their position statements (arguments) must be framed simply and be easily understood. Business people consequently rely on code phrases, industry-specific jargon, and shortcut statements to facilitate the flow of discussion. At times, as we will see in a later chapter, they rely on paradigmatic and marginal cases when making decisions. All of these skills are honed in the case method approach and they are enhanced through the use of maxims.

In like manner, as we saw earlier, casuistry relies on maxims and ordered arrangements (taxonomies) of paradigmatic and marginal cases. As in business

---

refers to third party risks. It also differs from its use in business, especially insurance, where moral hazard refers to risks that are incurred by an insurance company with respect to a lack of honesty or prudence among policyholders.

Table 12.5 Differences: the Business Case Method and Casuistry

Hazards: the two methods differ in terms of the sorts of hazards they consider. Whereas the case method addresses the threats (hazards) to profit in an environment of competing stakeholder interests, casuistry addresses the moral hazards associated with the possible abridgement of society's ethical norms

Resolution: the two methods differ in terms of the degree of resolution of their cases. The business case method's cases tend to be open-ended or unresolved while casuistry's cases are settled or resolved

Order: the two methods differ in terms of their propensity to order cases. While casuistry maintains a strict taxonomy of cases, the business case method's cases float freely without order

Nomination: the two methods differ in regard the way they value and nominate particular cases. While particular business cases can become paradigmatic in case method teaching, they are not named such as they are in casuistry

practice, casuists use code phrases, jargon, and shortcut statements to facilitate the flow of the discussion regarding a moral issue.

In both the business case method and casuistry then, the salient elements of complex situations are drawn out and framed simply in shortcuts (maxims) to expedite the reasoning and decision-making processes.

Differences

Although the business case method and casuistry share certain features, they do not always demonstrate these features to the same degree or in the same way. In other words, they appear alike in some ways but are not identical.

In general, the two methods differ in regard to their purpose and use. Table 12.5 summarizes the salient points of the two processes' differences.

First, the business case method and casuistry differ in terms of the hazards they regard as most important. Whereas the case method focuses on the threats (hazards) to profit in an environment of competing stakeholder interests, casuistry concentrates on the moral threats associated with the possible abridgement of society's ethical norms.

When managers fail to account for moral threats as they strategize to maximize profits and balance stakeholder demands, they can risk overlooking significant liabilities to their companies. We will explore this problem in detail in a subsequent chapter but for now, it is sufficient to recognize that the case method and casuistry differ in terms of the hazards they concentrate upon.

Second, the business case method and casuistry differ in terms of their emphasis on case resolution. While the business case method's cases tend to be open-ended or unresolved, casuistry's cases are settled or resolved. Both are designed this way to be better able to fulfill their central purposes.

As we have seen, the business case lacks closure. It contains enough information to make a decision and concludes just before the central character renders a judgment. This "open-ended" quality allows the reader/student to figure out the right judgment and practice being a manager without taking on the risks associated with real problematic situations.

Casuistry's cases, on the other hand, are already resolved or settled. Their value lies in the fact that they *are* settled because the success of past judgments affirms the likelihood of the validity of a similar decision in the present. Casuistry's cases therefore have an authority and prescriptive quality that is useful in deliberations involving moral hazards.

Third, the business case method and casuistry differ in terms of their propensity to order cases. While casuistry maintains a strict taxonomy of cases, the business case method's cases float freely without order. Careful arrangement of cases is not a goal of the business case method because multiple cases are rarely used. In casuistry, however, the ordered arrangement of a distinctive case taxonomy is central to the method and its usefulness.

Fourth, the business case method and casuistry differ in terms of the way they value and nominate particular cases. Particular cases in the business case method can act as paradigms, but typically are not named as such because there is neither a naming body nor consensus about the stated value or relevance of the cases.

In casuistry, in contrast, cases are named as paradigmatic or marginal and there is agreement (at least within a narrow community) on the value and moral significance of the cases in question.

To explain further, recall that in casuistry settled cases are ordered according to their ability to inform the user about right and wrong. Casuistry's cases, in other words, have a recognizable moral content and are named as paradigmatic or marginal according to their ability to exhibit right and wrong in particular situations.

The business case method has no such protocol for its cache of cases. Although some of the cases can be *de facto* paradigmatic, they are not categorized as such and there is no established order about right and wrong. Cases simply float around in a cache with each case remaining distinct and unrelated to others.

Synergies: Bringing the Methods Together

We have seen how the business case method and casuistry share and differ in regard to particular features and how they have significant benefits and shortcomings that aid or limit their usefulness in isolation.

The following will show how the two methods can be brought together to create a synergy that takes advantage of their benefits while minimizing their individual shortcomings. The highlights of the points here can be found in Table 12.6.

First, bringing the case method and casuistry together deepens the understanding of the case at hand, the cache of cases, and the case taxonomy used in making judgments.

Table 12.6 Synergies: the Business Case Method and Casuistry

Case method (B)	Casuistry (E)	Synergy (B + E)
Provides helpful single case analysis	Multiple cases that serve as resources for case analysis	Bringing the two methods together deepens the understanding of the case at hand, the cache of cases, and the case taxonomy used in making judgments
Probable rather than certain judgments	Probable rather than certain judgments	Bringing the two methods together enhances the probability that the judgments will be right or at least more defensible than those derived by each method in isolation
Practically relevant cases	Practically relevant cases	Bringing the two methods together enhances the practical relevance of a judgment
Stakeholder hazard management is the main concern	Moral hazard management is the main concern	Bringing the two methods together allows for consideration of a wider range of hazards to a business
Open ended cases	Settled cases	Bringing the two methods together nuances and informs the decision process and leads to more defensible judgments
Cases are loosely identified and isolated from each other	Cases named as paradigm or marginal and ordered in distinct taxonomies	Bringing the two methods together in a clearly named and orderly way enhances case use effectiveness
Highly relativistic	Moderately relativistic	Bringing the two methods together results in more convincing judgments that help reduce the prevalence of stalemates borne of relativism
Business case use is a group effort and requires good communication skills	Casuistry is a bottom-up, cross-disciplinary, deliberative process that facilitates communication	Bringing the two methods together advances communication across academic disciplines and in business practice

From the perspective of business case method users, case analysis typically concentrates on the single case at hand. The user investigates all the facts of the case then applies outside information (typically theory) as needed. Incorporating casuistry allows the business case user to draw on case-based information as well as theory and thereby draw on information that might not otherwise be available.

Casuists, too, can benefit from the synthesis of the two methods as the in-depth analysis that business case method users employ refines the information in the cases of the cache of cases used by casuists. The business case users' analysis also helps refine the case taxonomy as it clarifies elements of the cases and makes them more apparently right or wrong.

In the end then, the combination of the case method and casuistry results in a deeper understanding of the case at hand, the cache of cases, and the accuracy of the case taxonomy in which cases are included.

Second, because the business case method and casuistry similarly strive for highly probable rather than certain judgments, bringing the two methods together enhances the probability that the judgments reached are the best ones, or at least more defensible than those derived through either method in isolation.

As we saw earlier, both processes sidestep the inclination to validate theory first and strive for epistemic certainty. Rather, they use theory insofar as it aids in the formation of a practical judgment. This leaves the two processes open to accusations of laxity but even so, the judgments that each produces are more nuanced, multi-perspectival, and practically useful than those derived from a single theoretical source. The combination of the two methods therefore enhances the probability that the judgments derived by means of their combined use will be right or at least more defensible than those derived by each method in isolation.

Third, bringing the case method and casuistry together expands the practical relevance of the judgments rendered. As we have seen, both methods are practically oriented in their own way. When the two are brought together, the likelihood that the judgments they render will be practically applicable is enhanced. Judgments are therefore likely to be more relevant than other methods and either component method used in isolation.

Fourth, bringing the case method and casuistry together widens the range of risks of a moral and social nature considered in deliberations. Because the business case method is concerned with the issues of a single case, it can focus exclusively on a relatively narrow set of stakeholder concerns. These usually have to do with profit making in the context of some stressor—a catastrophe or unplanned event that upsets the normal course of business. Balancing these stakeholder concerns in light of the case's risks to profit is therefore the chief focus of those employing the case method.

In casuistry, cases concentrate on some sort of threat of an ethical abridgment that makes a business vulnerable to loss of some sort. Because violations of the ethical customs of society are generally regarded as violations of the social contract between business and society and because these risks can impact the bottom line negatively, managers are as concerned with avoiding moral threats as they are with avoiding other sorts of risks to the company. Thus, bringing the case method and casuistry together allows for the consideration of a fuller range of hazards to a business and strengthens the likelihood of defensible moral and business based judgments by managers employing them in tandem.

Fifth, bringing the case method and casuistry together resolves those aspects of business cases that are intentionally or unintentionally incomplete. As we saw, business cases are open ended to allow the user to figure out the next step in managing a dilemma. As such, they leave out certain judgments that might give direction to the decision-maker.

Casuistry, in contrast, uses settled cases in which judgments have already been rendered. In fact, its cases are useful precisely because they are not open ended in the way business cases are.

When the two methods are brought together, casuistry's settled cases aid business case users in forming more defensible judgments. Although the business case is not necessarily resolved any quicker, certain aspects of the decision-making process are nuanced and informed by judgments already rendered by means of casuistry. These can facilitate the formation of a better informed and more defensible judgment about the situation portrayed by the case.

Sixth, bringing the case method and casuistry together in a clearly named and orderly way enhances case use effectiveness.

As we saw, the business case method's cases are loosely identified and isolated from each other. They are discrete and largely separate from other cases. Such individuality and isolation makes them difficult to locate and use together.

On the one hand, that business cases are discrete and isolated enhances their distinctiveness and tendency to be remembered. At the same time, case individualism undermines their effective use in situations where combined case use might be helpful. Addressing these concerns is not easy because, in part, of the way case providers maintain cases. Let me explain.

Major case merchants (Harvard Business School, Richard Ivey School of Business, Darden School/University of Virginia, MIT Sloan Management Review, IESE, IMD, INSEAD, John F. Kennedy School of Government, the European Case Clearing House, and so on) maintain searchable case databases, but their effective use is limited by labeling that makes searching difficult. One can search databases by key words, but the words associated with cases tend to be company names, products, industries, dates, or general phrases. Particular topics, unless they are named explicitly in the case, can become invisible. This is especially true of cases having moral content. In these cases, terms such as "social responsibility" or "ethics" or even very general terms such as "stealing," "lying," or "cheating" are common, but helpful only to facilitating a general search. They are not very helpful to locating, collating, and combining cases as is necessary in multi-case deliberations.

The difficulty of naming and tagging cases precisely is not as easily remedied as one might imagine. For one, doing so demands that authors and database maintainers agree upon case descriptions and, in the case of moral cases, the cases' normative criteria. Those unfamiliar with norms and (especially) those who regard such nomination as rigid, anti-intellectual, authoritarian, or antiquated have difficulty settling on descriptions.

An additional problem with the lack of business case nomination is the inability to order cases effectively. Without clear identifiers, cases float in a miasma of like cases with little arrangement and no hierarchical taxonomy.

Casuistry, we have seen, has strong nomination and ordering features. It names cases as paradigm or marginal and sets them in a hierarchy according to their ability to convey certainty about rightness or wrongness.

Bringing the case method and casuistry together should address many of these concerns by allowing singular business cases to be ordered in more helpful ways. The inclusion of casuistry's ordering propensity can give clear direction to users by providing them with a map to cut through ambiguity while deciding. In this way, the addition of casuistry's ordering mechanisms can lead to stronger and more defensible judgments, especially those that involve moral hazards.

Seventh, bringing the case method and casuistry together can result in more convincing judgments and help reduce the prevalence of stalemates borne of relativism.

As we have seen, the case method was developed at Harvard during the late-nineteenth and early-twentieth centuries when American Pragmatism was also being advanced within the tightly knit local scholarly communities. The business case method therefore reflects Pragmatism's action-orientation and can-do matter-of-fact spirit. It also manifests its pervasive relativism.

While Pragmatism's action-inspiring attributes are helpful to management, its relativism and insistence that there are no right answers to moral dilemmas and no agreement on methods to decide whether one decision is better than another sometimes results in problematic irresolvable stalemates.

Although casuistry has also been charged with being relativistic, its content-rich and clear taxonomy can advance discussions beyond mere emotional preferences or beliefs. The synthesis of the two methods therefore might not eliminate relativism entirely, but it at least enhances the strength of judgments made using the combined methods.

Eighth, bringing the case method and casuistry together can advance communication across academic disciplines and within business practice.

As we saw, casuistries are based on meaningful narratives (truth-bearing cases) reflective of collective notions of right and wrong. Casuistries emerge through the efforts of many, are reflective of particular cultures, and not necessarily delimited by particular academic disciplines.

When applied to business problems, casuistic inputs can be drawn from a wide range of academic disciplines including those outside the realm of business. This enriches discussions immeasurably by more accurately reflecting the overall values of society. It also strengthens the decision-making and judgments that are rendered.

In addition, the incorporation of casuistry's ordering mechanism can facilitate a helpful bottom-up deliberative practice that lessens the isolation of managers (and would-be student managers) as they make tough decisions.

As a consensus-driven bottom-up process of moral deliberation, casuistry allows managers who use it to find support for their decisions (or be cautioned against mistakes) by others.

The overall effect of both the inclusion of inputs from various sources and the enhancement of communication through the combination of the two methods is support for those who make decisions in business or business classes.

Conclusion

The combination of casuistry and the case method offers the opportunity to use business cases in a more orderly and thorough fashion and can facilitate more robust case-based judgments. Even so, implementation will not be achieved easily. If an effective taxonomy of cases for business is to emerge, managers and academics will have to come together to settle on the particular cases that hold meaning for them and agree on the cases that fit the criteria of paradigm and marginal. They will also have to collectively review maxims and analogies for accuracy and then gather, code, and order the existing cache of cases for more efficient and meaningful use.

While this task is large, it is not insurmountable. With today's advanced technology, academic disciplines are easier to bridge, ethical and business language is more commonly held, and case databases are easier to use. Those who are interested in doing so, need only build upon what is already present in nascent form. The real challenge is the willingness to engage the process and marshal those who find casuistry to be a practically useful and meaningful tool for combined moral and managerial deliberation.

Part IV
Using Virtue-Imbued Casuistry in Business Practice

Having seen how casuistry and virtue ethics and casuistry and the business case method can be brought together positively, we turn next to how virtue-imbued casuistry can benefit particular aspects of business practice.

In the following chapters, we will consider how virtue-imbued casuistry can help break ideological stalemates, caution against unreasonable optimism and vicious people, and be integrated into scenario-based strategic planning in businesses that need to assess their risk exposures.

The latter sections will also provide a summary assessment of the status of case use in business practice and make recommendations for ways cases might be expanded and used advantageously there.

Chapter 13
Breaking Stalemates: Using the Method to Upset the Genetically Modified Foods Impasse

> *Up till now I always thought bickering was just*
> *something children did and they outgrew it. Of course,*
> *there's sometimes a reason to have a 'real' quarrel,*
> *but the verbal exchanges that take place here*
> *are just plain bickering.*
>
> —Anne Frank (Frank, 2010, 42)

One of the appeals of virtue-imbued casuistry is that it can moderate emotions and advance reconciliation among people opposed to each other on the basis of ideologies or principles. The benefits of this contribution should not be underestimated because the alternative of non-stop argumentation based on energized opposition to ideological starting points can appear to be, as Anne Frank observed above, nothing more than endless childish bickering. Even so, it can escalate to an intensity that brings about dire consequences. No one experienced this escalation of ideology-driven hatred more forcefully than Ms. Frank.

Casuistry is especially helpful in stopping ideology-based squabbling because it sidesteps concerns with ideological purity and limits discussions to the practical matters contained in cases. Virtue ethics, for its part, is helpful because it reminds people of the value of moderation and the need to keep an ends perspective before them in discussions. Together, these and other positive features of virtue-imbued casuistry enable people to moderate their simmering antipathies and avoid unhelpful long-term disagreements based on principles, theories, or other abstractions.

In the following, we will see how these ideas play out in the longstanding stalemate over the proliferation of genetically modified (GM) foods. We will see in particular how GM foods proponents and opponents have rooted themselves firmly in theoretical and principle-based positions, how the disagreements have been disruptive at times, and how the impasse has lasted well over 15 years. The suggestion will then be made that virtue-imbued casuistry can help break the stalemate by changing the tenor of discussions from norms and theories to mutually acceptable case-based virtue-grounded methods.[1]

---

[1] An early version of the following was published in (Calkins 2002). My thanks to Svetlana Shatalova for research assistance on the update of this chapter.

Background: Building to a Stalemate

In 1999, the so-called "Battle in Seattle" captured worldwide attention for its protests and street theater. Violence, property destruction, and injury marked demonstrations that brought GMOs as well as the deeply entrenched ideology-based controversies surrounding them to public attention.[2]

Although the protests seemed new at the time, the disagreements about GMOs did not begin in Seattle but were rooted in the successes of other street protests (the race riots of the 1960s and the anti-war protests of the Vietnam War era as examples) and fueled by European skepticism of science and an entrenched American preference for pragmatic problem solving. Moreover, the protests were not resolved in Seattle, but continued in other locations for years.

The widespread nature and long duration of protests against GM food products produced a chilling effect on the businesses associated with developing or promulgating bioengineered wheat, rice, tomatoes, and other basic fruits and vegetables. Even so, the chill did not dissuade companies from pursuing what they saw as an emerging and lucrative new industry (Hindo 2008). They quickly adapted by devising new strategies and turning their focus away from GM fruits and veggies and toward less obvious crops—seed for industrial purposes, animal feed, ethanol, textiles, and so on (Hindo 2008). The general plan was to wait out the hubbub and then return to put GM foods directly back on store shelves.

By 2009 (just 10 years after Seattle), the bioengineering companies' plan was successfully implemented in full. They not only managed to weather the storm of controversy, but also successfully transitioned from experimenting on simple foods such as tomatoes and wheat to advancing fully cultured GM meat, milk, and fish for consumer markets. They also began to experiment with products that even the most alarmist protesters could not have imagined in 1999. They started developing GM salmon that could produce less waste and require less water and feed than natural varieties as well an "EnviroPig" that could produce less waste and phosphorus than ordinary swine.[3]

Proponents' Arguments

For more than a decade after Seattle, agricultural-biotech proponents maintained a consistent argument for the ongoing development of genetically altered foods using

---

[2] I will use the legal definitions of terms found in Article 2 of the Official Journal of the European Communities directive 90/220/EEC. Hence, "organism" will mean any biological entity capable of replication or of transferring genetic material and "genetically modified organism (GMO)" will mean an organism in which the genetic material has been altered in a way that does not occur naturally by mating and/or natural recombination (Council of the European Communities 1990). For more information and a good description of the way crops' genes are altered, see (US Food and Drug Administration 2000).

[3] (Temple 2009; Warner 2009). While this prospect pleased animal rights advocates, it further aggravated hardcore GMO opponents who disparaged the idea of introducing such manufactured foodstuffs into the public realm.

utilitarian and pragmatic arguments. A summary of their main arguments is listed in Table 13.1.

For the most part, GM food proponents maintained that the positive aspects of genetically altered products outweighed the shortcomings associated with them. As late as December 2012, they offered compelling step-by-step reasons for GM crops and modern farming methods as the best hope to feed the world's billions (Block 2012).

While GM food proponents did admit of certain dangers associated with the misuse of genetically "enhanced" products (sometimes called "novel foods"), they asserted strongly that these products were overwhelmingly beneficial to society because the foods have higher concentrations of nutrients, reduced maturation times, require less land, and produce more abundant yields than regular crops. Consumers were better off because GM crops could be designed to have higher concentrations of nutrients such as Vitamin C, Vitamin E, and beta-carotene than natural varieties, thereby helping to reduce the prevalence of certain cancers and heart disease in people.[4] GM varieties could better withstand rot, be formulated to be less sensitive to damage in transit, and have certain desirable aesthetic qualities. Peas, for example, could be designed to be sweeter, melons to be smaller (single serving size, for example), bananas and pineapples to have delayed ripening qualities, peanuts to have improved protein balance, and rice to have enhanced Vitamin-A levels.[5] Temperate-climate plants could be modified to grow in hostile environments with low rainfall or extremely high temperatures, thereby bringing a more varied diet to people in remote locations.[6]

Proponents bolstered their arguments for GM crops with claims that the products were better for the natural environment than the alternatives. Proponents argued that genetically modified crops could be formulated to be less disruptive to the soil, more drought and flood tolerant, and to need fewer applications of herbicides and pesticides than natural strains.[7] In fact, they argued, the *real* threat to the natural environment was the continued use of outdated traditional farming methods that rely on "yesterday's genes cultivated by yesterday's farmers, on endlessly spreading acres of what was yesterday's wilderness" (Huber 1999, p. 26).

Finally, GM food proponents maintained that the human propensity to manipulate the genes of foodstuffs is not new—that people have been modifying food for a long time and have found the process to be safe. Today, the practice of genetically modifying food is so sophisticated that gene-modified soybeans account for about

---

[4] Even tobacco might be designed to be less harmful than it is now (Fairclough 2001, p. R15).

[5] Vitamin-A enhanced rice is thought to be an effective way to lessen the prevalence of premature blindness in the people of less developed countries.
For more on the benefits of GM foods, see (American Dietetic Association 1998; International Food Information Council Foundation (IFIC), *Benefits of Biotechnology—Just Around the Corner, Food Biotechnology*, 1999, *Food Biotechnology: Health & Harvest for Our Times* 1999).

[6] Tomatoes, for example, might be developed from stock infused with a gene from the arctic flounder to be less susceptible to cold than natural strains, thereby enriching the diets of people who reside in colder climates with shorter growing seasons.

[7] GM crops often can withstand salts and metals better than regular crops and can be modified to fix nitrogen from the soil, thereby reducing the need for fertilizer.

Table 13.1 GM Food Proponents' Main Arguments

Proponent	Argument	Examples
Monsanto	GM foods help alleviate world hunger	Vitamin A-enhanced rice Drought-resistant corn and wheat
Novartis	GM technology enhances the taste and longevity of products	Sweeter peas Cold-climate tomatoes
A.G./AstraZeneca/ Syngenta	GM products are better for the environment	Less tillage and pesticide and herbicide use
DuPont	Already in use and found to be safe	Current percentages of wheat and soybean plantings in US are high
Others	GM foods are not new	Corn hybrids have been around for years

half the US crop and some part of this soybean crop can be found in 60% of our processed foods (Jenkins 1999).

In fact, as Michael Fumento asserts, "virtually everything we eat has been 'genetically modified' by the hand of man through selective breeding, beginning thousands of years ago" (Fumento 2000, p. A14). If we need an issue to rally around, proponents counter, we should consider the ability of naturally occurring bacteria to mutate in a relatively short period of time with deadly consequences. In contrast to these organisms, genetically altered foods and GM foods are rather benign (Huber 1999).

In sum, for over a decade proponents consistently reasoned that consumers and the natural environment are better off with GM products than without them and that human manipulation of the fundamentals of nature is nothing new—and that it is not nearly as bad as opponents claim.

Opponents' Arguments

During this period, opponents of agricultural-biotechnology neither agreed with the agriculture industry's rosy utilitarian/pragmatic outlook nor consented to the notion that scientists should be the final arbiters in decisions involving permanent changes to the basic structures of living organisms.

Unlike GMO proponents, GMO opponents were never a cohesive group. From the outset they remained loosely organized, approached issues from different ideological perspectives, had divergent concerns, and not spoken with a single voice. A summary of their main arguments is listed in Table 13.2.

Today's GM food opposition coalition can be summarized in the following way.

At one extreme is a group opposed to any sort of modification of the genetic code of organisms. Its members are passionate in their beliefs about the violation of the laws of nature and views genetic engineering, transgenic experimentation, and gene-splicing as egregious abridgements of the natural order. Any replication or transference of genetic material that does not occur naturally by mating or natural forms of recombination is wrongful in the view of this group.

Table 13.2 GM Food Opponents' Main Arguments

Opponent	Argument	Example
European greens	GM food producers are invading our turf	European food bureaus German brewers Italian pasta makers
Organic farmers	GM foods put us out of business	Taints organic corn farms next to GM corn farms
Environmentalists and Naturists	GMOs disrupt natural processes	DDT example
European folklorists	GMOs are ghoulish, shades of Frankenstein and Nazis	Creep factor: vegetables infused with animal genes
Anti-tech political groups and anti-capitalists	GM foods represent a rotten capitalist system	Demonstrations in conjunction with WTO meetings

A second and more strident GM food opposition group, the radical environmentalists, is opposed to agricultural-biotech not so much out of a concern for nature but from a deep disdain for capitalism *per se*. Less identified with a distinct moral position, it typically argues from a vague notion of "sustainability" and is adamant about what is *not* acceptable, that is, any sort of profit-driven use of resources that supports a consumerist, capitalist society. With great fervor, it targets agri-businesses along with paper producers, testing facilities that use animals, and other similar industries. Not surprisingly, some of its members—which include groups such as the Earth Liberation Front—are not above committing criminal acts to advance their agenda.[8]

Despite the extreme stance this group sometimes takes, the radical environmentalists are similar to the natural law group in opposing current food engineering practices as wrongful. Unlike the natural law people, however, radical environmentalists envision an altogether different world—one that is less consumerist and distinctly non-capitalistic.

A third and less obvious opposition group is one with strong ties to European folklore. It taps into powerful stories of past abuses by scientists and draws upon old stories such as Mary Wollstonecraft Shelley's *Frankenstein* (Shelley 1831). It also sometimes bridges from lore of the distant past to more recent historic accounts, such as the barbaric scientific practices of the Hitler regime's experimentation on human beings during World War II.[9]

---

[8] The Earth Liberation Front (a breakaway group from Earth First!) not only claimed responsibility for the break-in to the University of Minnesota lab to uproot oat plants used in a genetic engineering experiment, it also caused $ 400,000 damage to Michigan State University's Agriculture Hall in the name of combating genetic engineering (Editor 2000, p. A26).

[9] Thomas DeGregori argues that the Nazis were the first antitechnology postmodernists. Their emphasis on racial purity, commitment to vegetarianism and organic agriculture, love of animals, and preference for holistic medicine and natural healing over so-called Jewish scientific medicine, were part of a quest for wholeness and a revolt against the modernism of Germany's Weimar culture. Their preferences, DeGregori maintains, resonate with many of today's protests against GM food technology (DeGregori, *Agriculture and Modern Technology: A Defense*, 2001, pp. 149–155).

Using a collection of horror stories, European folklorists attempt to undermine the public's notions of science and scientists as benevolent. Casting a glassy eye on the notion of "better life through science," the group portrays GM foods as "frankenfoods" with all the creepy associations the term implies. The goal of doing so is to undermine the portrayal of GM products as safe and "enhanced," heighten fears about GM foods, and stir public sentiment against GM products the way legendary citizenry did against Frankenstein's monster and his progeny—Wolfman, the Werewolf, and the beast in the *Beauty and the Beast*.

While the European folklorists' portraits seem silly to some, the imagery the group uses is hard to forget and is therefore effective in bringing the notion of science and GM technology into question.

A fourth group—a European food coalition composed of farmers, food producers, politicians, and bureaucrats—is not so much opposed to GM science as it is frustrated with the political and economic changes wrought by European economic unification.

As a group, the European food coalition is complex, somewhat disparate, but united in a struggle to maintain a power base in the face of Europe's attempt to become more market oriented. Predominantly populated by farmers and farm bureaucrats, the coalition has long been a powerful influence in national and regional politics and now has a particular interest in maintaining the *status quo*.

With European economic integration, the food coalition, not unlike other groups, has been forced to examine its operational efficiencies more closely. New farming techniques that produce higher volumes of crops with less fertilizer and tilling have pushed the coalition to look at its methods and the outcome of this scrutiny has challenged its prevailing notions of stable incomes, smaller farm sizes, and assured profit levels. In addition, Asian, North American, and Latin American competition has forced the coalition to defend its markets and at the same time highlighted the inefficiencies of longstanding farming techniques.

While these movements have affected farmers directly, they also indirectly affected the politicians and bureaucrats tied to farmers. With European integration, local farm bureau personnel, for one, found their jobs consolidated or eliminated altogether on the grounds of inhibiting free trade. So, too, politicians who were backed by local farmers found their support diluted as economic unification diminished the prominence of local political forces.[10]

At the same time, however, the Nazi regime cannot be said to be entirely technophobic. Their efficient war machine and experiments involving human subjects attest to the their embrace of science and engineering. In the end, it may be that their conflicted approach to science is reflected in today's European anxiety about GMOs.

[10] These issues seem to have been present in the December 1999 Montreal discussions about the Cartagena Protocol on Biosafety as well as in the court proceeding about gene patenting that eventually found in favor of Novartis. In the Novartis case, judges allowed, for the first time, biotech inventors to establish patents on genetically modified plants. In both cases, the European food coalition struggled to define itself vis-à-vis larger corporate interests concerned with protecting open markets and promoting free trade.

(Pollack 2000, A1 and A6).(Reporter 1999, p. A10).

Politicians and bureaucrats therefore joined farmers in opposing GM and other emerging farm technologies, acting together to appeal to national sentiments and against what they saw as a harmful homogenization movement sweeping throughout Europe. Claiming that certain foods produced in a region were cultural identifiers sufficiently unique to warrant protection (Champagne wine with a region of France, German beer, or parmesan cheese with Parma, Italy, as examples), the coalition offered colorful if not entirely convincing opposition to GM food proliferation in Europe.[11]

In the end, the European food coalition's doomsday projections about the demise of locally identifiable foods failed to materialize. So, too, the group's self-interestedness became increasingly apparent and unpalatable to the public. Combined, the lack of apparent harm and the obvious self-interestedness of a small group of people undermined the coalition's prominence and effectiveness.

A fifth opposition group, the organic farming community, raises some of the thorniest questions of all because it focuses on what agricultural-biotech has not yet been able to resolve. This group targets the technical aspects of GM crop production such as plant proliferation that depends upon wind-born pollination. It questions how organic products such as corn can withstand the cross-pollination from proximate fields planted with GM varieties. It also questions the industry's proliferation of so-called "terminator gene" technologies that prevent plants from self-regenerating and asks how poor farmers can remain solvent when they have to purchase GM seed each year because they cannot collect a portion of their current crop for next year's planting.[12]

Although the organic farming group is as critical of GM crops as other groups, it is the most palatable to pro-agricultural-biotech representatives because it advocates the use of pragmatic reasoning and respects scientific explanations as the proponents do. Not insignificantly the group also recognizes the importance of niche markets, profit making as a business concern, and the value of open markets. Thus, while the organic farming group questions the risks associated with GM organism proliferation, it at least speaks the same practical language of GM food proponents.

Entrenching the Stalemate

Having established the cohorts of the two sides, we can see how the debate about GM food proliferation spiraled to become a battle of ideas with intransigent and polarized positions.

---

[11] German brewers, for example, have long relied on strict definitions of what may and may not be used in producing beer.
For details about Germany's (Bavaria's) beer purity rules (*reinheitsgebot*), see: (Editor 1998, p. 23; Reporter 1996, p. A5).

[12] Interestingly, this group finds itself torn on the issue of terminator genes because such genes can be used to eliminate the problematic cross-pollination of corn described here.

The standoff began as the critics of GM crops—informally known as "cropatis-tas"—initiated confrontations with small but peaceful protests. Dressed as Monarch butterflies and chanting in the streets, the so-called "seeds of resistance" rallied against GM crop "pharmers" and seed producers whom they dubbed "Monsatan" and "Mutanto."[13]

Monsanto seemed to be a special target of protesters for two likely reasons. First, opponents saw it as a large and visible company, a leader in its industry with deep pockets that might be tapped by successful lawsuits. Second, because Monsanto produced Agent Orange, one of the herbicides and defoliants used by the U.S. military as part of its chemical warfare program during the Vietnam War from 1961 to 1971, anti-war activists of the past brought with them a special antipathy toward the company.[14] Not surprisingly, Monsanto responded by becoming a leader in the defense of GM technology.

In general, the GMO opponents' strategy was to mobilize colorful and noisy demonstrations at a major international meeting (a World Trade Organization meeting, for example), publish position pieces in full-page advertisements in nationally circulated newspapers and electronic media, and assail responsive politicians with anti-GM position statements (Stecklow 1999, p. A1).

At the beginning, protests were local and peaceful but they quickly grew clamorous, violent, and destructive so that by the time of the Seattle ruckus, violence was well established. Media was more than happy to cover the confrontations because the activists visibly shunting peaceable "butterfly people" to the sidelines made good news.[15]

Throughout, demonstrations were staged to seem serendipitous but were well-orchestrated and consistent with prior protests in Europe where aggressive and violent tactics (including outright sabotage) were commonplace (Barboza, "Biotech Companies Take On Critics of Gene-Altered Food," 1999, p. A1). Not surprisingly, shortly after Seattle, violence began to proliferate in America, with the Earth Liberation Front's break in and extensive damage to US university labs conducting genetic engineering research being just one example.[16]

Oddly enough, violence did not squelch the opponents' appeal. Some saw it as a form of righteous indignation and reflective of genuine fear of GM foods. Camera hungry politicians and celebrities in search of a cause attached themselves to the cause and began to echo the coalition's doomsday message.[17]

---

[13] Variations on the Monsanto name come from (Barboza, "Biotech Companies Take On Critics of Gene-Altered Food," 1999, A1).

[14] For more on Monsanto's position on Agent Orange, see (Monsanto Company 2013).

[15] The so-called "butterfly people" were mostly children dressed up as Monarch butterflies, the emerging symbol of the anti-biotech movement in the US.

[16] The Earth Liberation Front allegedly did extensive damage to a University of Minnesota lab by uprooting 800 oat plants that were part of a genetic engineering experiment to improve plant resistance to disease. For more, see (Editor 2000, p. A26).

[17] Organic farmer Nell Newman (actor Paul Newman's daughter and head of the organic division of Newman's Own Inc.) and Elizabeth Wilcox (director of a consortium of small family philanthropies) became two of the opposition force's better-spoken critics (Lagnado 1999). Wilcox, for one, crystallized the opposition view when she stated, "We talk about creating the perfect food, and

Not surprisingly, GM food opponents were particularly effective in swaying political opinion as politicians found a role for themselves in calling for more regulation of GM foods. Leveraging this sentiment, opponents lobbied government agencies around the world to work in their behalf. In America, for example, they pressured U.S. Food and Drug Administration representatives to extend the degree to which the federal government oversees genetically altered food. They also gathered outside the meeting place in Chicago where U.S. Environmental Protection Agency representatives were deciding whether or not to tighten restrictions on the planting of genetically altered corn. Similarly in Canada, they pressured the representatives of 130 nations gathered in Montreal in late-January 2000 to sign the Cartagena Protocol on Biosafety, the first global treaty to regulate trade in genetically modified products that had languished in heated debate for a long time until its ratification (Fialka 2000, p. B12; Kilman, "FDA Signals Tighter Biofood Oversight As Pressure From Opponents Increases," 1999, p. A8; Pollack 2000, A1 and A6).

In tandem with these actions, GMO opponents also tapped various legal systems to work in their behalf. In mid-December 1999, just two weeks after the Seattle demonstrations, they filed a class-action suit against Monsanto in the federal district court in Washington. Brought at the urging of activist Jeremy Rifkin and supported by an alliance of populist farm groups, the lawsuit alleged that Monsanto did not adequately test the safety of its genetically modified corn and soybean plants. It also maintained that Monsanto's patented genes gave the company too much control over how staple crops are used and that Monsanto was heavily involved in an international cartel to fix the prices of soybean and corn seed (Barboza, "Monsanto and Pharmacia to Join, Creating a Pharmaceutical Giant," 1999; Kilman, "Monsanto Is Sued Over Genetically Altered Crops," 1999).

Proponents of GM foods immediately downplayed the class-action lawsuit, arguing that it was just another high-profile complaint against GM foods along the lines of those rejected earlier by the FDA and the Justice Department. Even so, they admitted that the suit's timing was perfect—that it could not have been timed better to annoy their businesses (Kilman, "Monsanto Is Sued Over Genetically Altered Crops," 1999). Opponents were pleased at such news, hoping their suit would not just annoy companies, but scare them away from further GMO research and development (Huber 1999).

Outside America, GM food critics were successful in numerous countries, especially in India and Australia (Bolton 2008). That they were successful in India is particularly noteworthy because the modern agricultural technology movement called the "Green Revolution" took root there and served to thwart what was thought to be inevitable widespread malnutrition (Easterbrook 1997). If any place benefitted from GM crop technology, it would seem to be India and here around 50 years later objections to the technologies were emerging.

In any event, by mid-December 1999 a series of pending lawsuits, widespread demonstrations, and negative media attention focused on GM businesses induced many investors to distance themselves from biotech companies involved in

---

the perfect body and don't want to cry eugenics, but this issue is really scary." Elizabeth Wilcox quoted in Lagnado, A1.

GM ventures. In response, companies de-emphasized their GM product involvements and, in a series of mergers, began to retreat to their core pharmaceutical businesses.[18]

Despite an apparent retreat from GM business, however, many corporate directors remained optimistic about the future of GM crops. Fred Hassan, Pharmacia's chairman and chief executive officer, for one, was "very enthusiastic about the agricultural business" and "impressed by the amount of research assets" accumulated by Monsanto. Conceding, "We have some public relations issues," he nevertheless expressed confidence that the underlying science and technology of the Pharmacia-Monsanto merger was sound.[19]

GM technology, others argued, was necessary to stem expected food shortages. Citing United Nations experts, Monsanto, for one, maintained that the industry needed to double food production by 2050 to feed an anticipated population of 9.3 billion people (Monsanto Company, *Sustainable Agriculture*, 2009). In short, GM technology was necessary to feed those who would otherwise not survive (Monsanto Company, *Sustainable Agriculture*, 2009).

As it turned out, Hassan and the others' projections and optimism about the future of GM crops were well founded. With time, anti-GM food sentiment cooled and production resumed and increased about 60-fold from 1996 to 2006, from 4.2 million acres (1.7 million ha) planted in 1996 to 250 million acres (102 million ha) planted in 2006.[20]

Even so, the successes of the GM food industry neither satisfied nor silenced GM food opponents who continued to claim that the benefits of GM crops were groundless. To bolster their assertions, they brought more class action suits against the

---

[18] The Anglo-Swedish pharmaceutical company AstraZeneca PLCand Swiss drug giant Novartis, for example, announced a merger through which they would spin off their respective agricultural-chemical businesses. Similarly, Pharmacia & Upjohn Inc. and Monsanto Co. agreed to an initial $ 27 billion "merger of equals." As part of this deal, the two companies planned to return to their core competencies and lessen the merged entity's exposure to agricultural-biotech with a public offering of as much as 19% of Monsanto's agricultural interests. (Deogun and Langreth 1999, p. A3; Deogun et al. 1999, p. A3; Lipin et al. 1999, p. A3).
Founded in Stockholm, Sweden, in1911, Parmacia merged with Upjohn in 1995 to form Pharmacia & Upjohn. In April 2000, Pharmacia & Upjohn completed a merger with Monsanto and Searle creating Pharmacia. In August 2002, Pharmacia completed the spin-off of its agricultural subsidiary, Monsanto Company (Pfizer Inc. 2013).

[19] Fred Hassan quoted in (Deogun et al. 1999, p. A3). Monsanto chairman Robert B. Shapiro echoed this sentiment in pronouncing agriculture-biotech to be "the most successful launch of any product in agriculture since the plow." Not all shared Shapiro's optimism, however. In the midst of the merger announcements, a front-page story in *The Wall Street Journal* detailed Shapiro's tunnel vision about the benefits of biotechnology as well as his inability to account for consumer attitudes toward GM food products. Robert B. Shapiro quoted in (Deogun et al. 1999, p. A3). See (Barboza, "Monsanto and Pharmacia to Join, Creating a Pharmaceutical Giant," 1999, A22; Kilman and Burton 1999, p. A1).

[20] Monsanto estimates the cumulative area planted to biotech crops during that period was 1.43 billion acres (577 million ha) (Monsanto Company, *Increasing Farm Prosperity with Innovation*, 2009). By 2006, the reach of GM crops in wealthier developed countries was extensive and growth in the next decade is now expected to occur in developing countries (Human Genome Program 2008).

industry and kept up their pressure on the U.S. Department of Agriculture (USDA) to remain vigilant in its monitoring of the safety of GM foods (Anslow 2008). Their tactics worked such that in 2007 US federal district judge Harold Kennedy ruled that the USDA must halt approval of all new field trials until more rigorous environmental reviews are conducted (Ho et al. 2007).

After more than a decade, polarization was nearly complete with both sides firmly entrenched in their positions. Unfortunately, the mutual stridency distracted both sides from considering one key player in the issue—the farmers who planted seeds for a living.

When the incidents in Seattle began, farmers were the staunchest proponents of GM seed because they considered it to be easier to grow, better resistant to pests, and capable of producing higher yields than regular seed. In fact, they preferred GM seed so much that they were willing to pay a 25% premium for it because it produced higher rates of income than traditional crops.[21]

After the Seattle skirmish, however, projections were revised and farmers were in a quandary about what to plant. Subject to the whims of the market and shifting public sentiment, many farmers abandoned GM seed and returned to traditional products and farming techniques. Others simply decided to do nothing and wait until the furor over gene-altered foods ran its course.[22]

At present, the stalemate is complete but the ordinary farmer remains caught between two feuding forces with little sanctuary offered by either side. The question remains, how could this have been avoided?

Defusing the Stalemate

As we have seen, GM food proponents and opponents have argued their positions to a standstill. For years, they have framed their positions in terms of their favored ethical worldviews, principles, and beliefs—relying on well-worn arguments based on the practical benefits of GM foods, certain laws of nature, and particular notions of the good life. Not surprisingly (and for all the reasons explained in previous chapters), they have mostly employed principles-based approaches and thereby failed to resolve their dispute satisfactorily.[23]

---

[21] Monsanto estimates that it brought in $ 27 billion in additional income in 2006 (Monsanto Company, *Increasing Farm Prosperity with Innovation*, 2009). Other sales figures supported farmers' stated preferences, as GM seed sales, first available in 1996, grew to $ 1 billion by 1998 (just two years later) (Kilman, "Once Quick Converts, Farmers Begin to Lose Faith in Biotech Crops," 1999, A1).

[22] For an excellent history of this issue from a mostly European perspective, see (DeGregori, *Genetically Modified Nonsense*, 2001).

[23] As we saw earlier, broad and abstract approaches are insufficient in dealing with particular moral problems such as this one because these approaches tend to rely on principles and theories that are often in conflict with each other, hidden, or so deeply embedded as to be impractical. Even exercises that seek normative consensus through a process of reflective equilibrium are likely to be

What seems clear at this point is that a new approach is needed to break the longstanding deadlock—one that recognizes the distinctiveness of business, the practical difficulties of a wide range of stakeholders, and the widely divergent moral perspectives of those engaged in the issues. This new approach must also be one that is understandable and meaningful to people while at the same time capable of enabling people to resolve their differences in ways that are mutually satisfying. This new approach is, of course, virtue-imbued casuistry.

How might virtue-imbued casuistry help to advance discussions about GM foods?

First, virtue-imbued casuistry's emphasis on virtue can draw attention to the relevance of character in decision making and help raise the moral tenor of discussions, challenge proponents and opponents to think more creatively, and encourage the members of both sides to bring new and more positive suggestions to the discussions.

From the start, proponents and opponents have relied almost exclusively on arguments based on principles and because their starting points were often at odds, each grew to see the other as an enemy. Each became unable or unwilling to address the strengths of the others' views or to acknowledge the shortcomings of their own. Eventually, the situation deteriorated to one of non-stop bickering, negativity, intransigence, and resentment—with each side largely viewing the members of the other side as selfish ne'er-do-wells.

While this poisonous situation continues unabated, it is possible that the introduction of virtue-imbued casuistry can break the cycle of negativity by encouraging both parties to manifest their best intentions by means of meaningful and uplifting stories (cases). It can do this by encouraging both sides to moderate their antipathies and draw on their best intentions and those meaningful cases that inspire hope rather than doom. In this way, it is hoped, both sides might better strive for collective betterment.

Second, virtue-imbued casuistry's emphasis on case use should help relieve the dissonance that results from over reliance on principle-based theories and abstractions.

As we saw in Jonsen's and Toulmin's meeting of the National Commission for the Protection of Human Subjects of Biomedical and Behavioral Research, case use can change the tenor of discussions by keeping talks trained on practical conclusions rather than the principles or definitions of abstract concepts that underlie

---

found lacking because of the emphasis placed on agreement to far-reaching principles. As a result, approaches that emphasize broad moral principles, theories, and normative consensus-building such as Rawlsian reflective equilibrium are likely to be found insufficient in resolving the GM foods problem. For more on the place of principles in moral problem solving, see (Bowie 2000, pp. 7–20).

In addition, approaches that rely on good character can influence how individuals approach moral problems but cannot adequately resolve problems of a systemic nature, that is, those that extend beyond the concerns and control of the person or group. For more on the issue of the extent of influence of individual character in business ethics, see (Boatright 1999, pp. 583–591; Phillips and Margolis 1999, pp. 619–638).

specific positions.[24] This shift in focus can enable members to get around the insurmountable differences related to conflicting fundamental principles and help the parties advance toward mutually satisfying conclusions. Jonsen and Toulmin have shown how this sort of case-based approach worked well in a real-world biomedical setting. There is good reason that it can work in the GM food debate as well.[25]

Third, because virtue-imbued casuistry emphasizes cases, its use should revive certain cases that are now dormant but likely to be helpful to the GMO deliberations.

The current state of bickering over this issue has distracted proponents and opponents from seeking out virtue and vice-laden cases that might be relevant to ongoing discussions. Because of their entrenchment, both parties have been hindered from thinking creatively and discovering the wisdom contained in stories about past incidents similar to the GM food issue.

This ignorance has not been shared equally, however, as GM food opponents have been more skillful at using case-like stories in their arguments than proponents. The opponents' story of the "butterfly people," for example, has been effective in dramatizing the negative impact of GM crops on nature—conveying an emotional narrative by means of colorful costumes on innocents (children and young people) of the impact of harmful farming practice on the Monarch butterfly. Through this imagery, opponents have effectively drawn attention to cases of abuse of beautiful and not-so-beautiful creatures now extinct (snail darters, passenger pigeons, Carolina parrots, and so forth) or threatened by industrial processes.[26]

Proponents of GM technology, on the other hand, have been slow to develop compelling stories. Although they have impressive informational web sites, they have not constructed moving narratives on par with those of GM food opponents.[27] As a result, they have not assuaged fears of certain GM foods nor offset the concerns put forth by GM food opponents.

That GM food proponents have not advanced compelling stories to advance their cause is curious because they have so many rich stories at their disposal. Former secretary of the Department of Agriculture from 1981 to 1985 John Block, for one, paints a vivid picture of life without modern agricultural techniques in his narrative about his experiences of growing up on a farm in Knox County, Illinois and watching his family's fields of corn, soybeans, and wheat repeatedly decimated by corn borers and rootworms. His story, if dramatized on par with that of the butterfly people, would drive home the felt impact of life without modern agricultural technology. It might also give pause to today's politically correct urban dwellers

---

[24] (Jonsen and Toulmin 1988, pp. 16–19). See above notation about Jonsen's and Toulmin's description of the debate within the 1974 US Congressional National Commission for the Protection of Human Subjects of Biomedical and Behavioral Research.

[25] Few expected the group to have much basis for agreement, but insofar as members were able to stay on the taxonomic or casuistical level, they were able to agree to practical conclusions (Jonsen and Toulmin 1988, p. 17).

[26] This movement can be traced to 1962 and the controversy over DDT that concentrated on the chemical industry's abuse of the environment. For more, see (Raloff 2000).

[27] See, for examples, (BioValidity 2000; Council for Biotechnology Information 2001; Greenberg and Graham 2000; National Agricultural Library 2001). Also, for information on the ag-biotech industry's ad campaign, see (Kilman 2000, p. B6).

who insist on buying organic vegetables, but run to phone the exterminator at the first sight of a bug in their apartments (Block 2012).

Even institutions such as Monsanto have compelling stories to offset those that paint the company so negatively. Its "Story of Sweet Potatoes," for example, shows how Monsanto was successful in engineering potatoes to protect themselves against several key viral diseases (Monsanto 2001). Monsanto also has the gripping narrative about how it has shared its viral disease resistance technology with scientists from the Kenyan Agricultural Research Institute (KARI) since the early 1990's—long before the debate of GM foods took center stage (Monsanto 2001). Finally, Monsanto has a persuasive account of how it is developing customized GM corn for Africa and offered not to charge royalties for the use of its GM corn technology there. This product, it should be noted, is expected to be ready by 2017; about 5 years after drought-tolerant corn will be made available to American farmers (Pollack 2008).

Had proponents of GM foods been willing to bring these stories forward more forcefully, they might not only have calmed fears about GM foods and advanced their corporate reputations by now, but also might have changed their public image from one that can be caricatured so readily as steely and cold. Moreover, had they used virtue-imbued casuistry, they might have recalled other useful yet dormant cases and framed their current narratives in ways to highlight their good intentions. Together, these strategies might have taken the GM foods discussion in new and positively productive directions.

Fourth, a focus on virtue-imbued casuistry would spur the development of a functional taxonomy of cases pertinent to the GM food issue and helpful to other similar business deliberations.[28]

Until now, GM food proponents have tended to rely on a string of unrelated anecdotes related to their philanthropic activities and opponents have drawn on meaningful but unconnected stories to advance their positions. Neither has turned to an ordered set of cases because at present there is no established taxonomy of settled cases.

The virtue-imbued casuistic approach suggested here would spur on the development of such a case taxonomy for business. Today's case database maintainers would recognize in more case use the greater demand for their services. They would see the potential for greater profits in the expansion of their offerings outside of academia to the private business sector.

To bring about an effective case taxonomy, case warehouses would need to reframe some of their activities. First, they would need to locate, settle on, and nominate certain *de facto* paradigm cases. Then, they would need to grade the remaining cases according to their ability to convey moral propriety or abridgment. Next, they would need to make their services easy-to-use and readily accessible from both technology and price standpoints. Finally, they would need to expand their marketing to highlight the ways cases can help account for moral hazard in business strategy.

These suggestions seem daunting but are not unreachable because much of the work has already been done informally. As the following table suggests, there is already a tacit taxonomy of cases relevant to the GM food issue in place (Table 13.3).

---

[28] For more on the need for a casuistry for business, see (Calkins 2001, pp. 237–259).

Table 13.3 A Preliminary Taxonomy of Cases Relevant to the GM Food Issue

Agent	Casuistry			Virtues[a]
Proponent	*Case*	*Story*	*Strength*	*Virtue/Vice*
Monsanto	Story of Sweet Potatoes	Better nutrition via gene enhanced vegetable	Strongly positive (paradigm)	Generosity
Merck & Co.	Free ivermectin	Knowledge distribution within developing countries		
		Coordinated and free distribution of drug in remote tropical areas to fight river blindness	Strongly positive (paradigm)	Magnificence
Johnson & Johnson	Tylenol tainting	Recall of contaminated product due to tampering	Strongly positive (paradigm)	Courage
N.E. Borlaug	Green revolution	Higher food yields through modern technology	Strongly positive (paradigm)	Prudence
Ag-biotech industry & USDA	Doubly green revolution	Using GM crops to keep up with growing starving populations	Moderately/weakly positive	Prudence
Opponent	*Case*	*Story*	*Strength*	*Virtue/Vice*
Greens	Butterfly people	Endangered species threatened due to GM varieties	Strongly/moderately negative	Gluttony
Folklorists	Frankenstein	Science gone awry	Moderately/weakly negative	Imprudence
Naturalists	Silent Spring	DDT and disruption of natural processes	Moderately/weakly negative	Imprudence

[a] Virtues and vices per Aristotle, *Nicomachean Ethics*, trans. Martin Ostwald (Englewood Cliffs: Prentice Hall, Inc., 1962), III 115b–119b, IV 1120a–1125b, VI 1140a–1145a

As can be seen in this table, cases can be graded from strong to weak and delineated as positive (praiseworthy) and negative (cautionary). Cases can also relate directly or indirectly to the healthcare and pharmaceutical industries: Merck and Co.'s decision to freely distribute ivermectin to combat river blindness in less developed countries and Johnson & Johnson's decision to pull tainted product off the shelves during the Tylenol Crisis to name two prominent examples.[29] Some cases can also be regarded as benchmark cases, illustrating how industries that impact public health have acted responsibly in the past when faced with uncertainty. They can show, too, how people within corporate settings exercised what most people would regard as virtues.

What the table reveals, too, is that not all paradigmatic cases are positive. Cases can also recount unambiguous instances of wrongdoing and show the dark side of business practices. These negative paradigms can act as cautionary tales and be as helpful to managers as the positive cases that inspire people to act appropriately.

What is important to observe in all of this is that both positive and negative paradigm cases can advance moral discussions about GM foods and that for an approach to be considered casuistic, both sorts of cases must be used *together* and in an ordered manner. Moreover, to accommodate virtue ethics, cases must highlight the positive or negative moral traits of those involved in the case. Character-revealing cases, in other words, need to be used in an orderly and sequential manner to be helpful to the moral deliberations about GM foods.

Limping Toward Resolution

The GM foods debate continues to make headlines. In a 2013 Wall Street Journal interview, Monsanto's Chief Executive, Hugh Grant, summarized the ongoing challenges his company faces by highlighting the Company's successful initiative to defeat California's ballot initiative Proposition 37 that would have required companies to label all foods containing genetically modified products.

What is clear from the interview is that GM food proponents have not changed their tactics and that they and their opponents are still locked in the same cat-and-mouse game of one-upmanship as in the past (Berry 2013). Robert Paarlberg echoes these sentiments in citing the erosion of food availability to the world's poorest and hungriest due to the long-term campaign waged against GM food producers (Paarlberg 2013).

Despite these sentiments, the U.S. Supreme Court ruled in May 2013 in favor of Monsanto in a dispute involving an Indiana farmer who challenged the Company's

---

[29] For the Merck & Co. river blindness case, see (Reporter, 1987, p. 78). (Hanson and Weiss 1991). (Donaldson and Werhane 1999, pp. 148–153). (Cavanagh 1998, pp. 235–236).

For the Johnson & Johnson Tylenol case, see (Buchholz 1989, pp. 212–232; Cavanagh 1998, pp. 237–238; De George 1999, pp. 3–5).

intellectual property, holding that patent exhaustion does not permit a farmer to reproduce patented seeds through planting and harvesting without the patent holder's permission (Supreme Court of the United States, Argued February 19 2013—Decided May 13 2013).

Not long before the Court's decision, UK-based PG Economics Limited (a specialist provider of advisory and consultancy services to agriculture and other natural resource-based industries) published the results of its latest annual assessment of the global value of crop biotechnology. The report established that the commercialization of GM crops during the period 1996–2011 proceeded at a rapid rate with "very significant net economic benefits at the farm level amounting to $ 19.8 billion in 2011 and $ 98.2 billion for the 16 year period (in nominal terms)" (Brookes and Barfoot 2013). Most important, the "majority (51.2 %) of these gains went to farmers in developing countries" (Brookes and Barfoot 2013).

In other words, the greatest beneficiaries of GM technology during the time of greatest opposition to it were the people in the poorer regions of the world.

In the end, it seems that GM food production has benefited its producers as well as those in the field. Because of it, food is now available in places where it was not previously and at more affordable prices than it was in the past. Even so, the drumbeat of politicized opposition to GM foods continues.

What to do? One suggestion put forward by the Roman Catholic Pontifical Academy of Life is to give a "prudent yes" to the genetic engineering of plants and animals, but subject environmental risks such as those associated with GM crops to evaluation on a case-by-case basis. Bishop Elio Sgreccia, vice president of the Academy, expresses this sentiment, saying:

> We are increasingly encouraged that the advantages of genetic engineering of plants and animals are greater than the risks. The risks should be carefully followed through openness, analysis, and controls, but without a sense of alarm.[30]

Such a moderate, reflective, and practically wise case-base approach seems to be a good option. It is not a sweeping compromise of ideologies. Rather, it is a virtue-imbued casuistic approach that addresses the various complexities of the GM food dispute. It allows that cases about the positive aspects of technology such as those related to agronomist and 1970 Nobel Peace Prizewinner Norman Borlaug be considered alongside the prevalent negatives ones of hardcore GMO opponents. With the insistence on this sort of more balanced case use, GM food proponents can be shown to be as concerned about the 800 million people who are undernourished and 180 million kids who are underweight as opponents seem to be (Conway 2000).

To paint GM food proponents as ne'er do wells unconcerned with anything but profit or, conversely, to depict GM food opponents as nothing more than tree hugging ideologues, might satisfy a perverse sense of abstract purity but cannot justify the waste and uncertainty related to the current standoff.

What is clear is that there is a need to resolve the current stalemate—and virtue-imbued casuistry just might be the right way to do it.

---

[30] Elio Sgreccia quoted in (Thavis 1999).

Chapter 14
Cases Can Caution: Polio Eradication, Risk Exposure, and the Smallpox Case as Precedence

> *...no man dared to count his children as his own until they had had the disease.*
>
> —*Comte de la Condamine*
> *18th century mathematician and scientist*
> *referring to smallpox (Shors, 2011, 130)*

With its emphasis on precedence, comparisons by analogy, moderation, and prudence in deliberations, virtue-imbued casuistry can be valuable at critical junctures in strategic planning. At times, its holistic and moderating capacities can help key decision makers avoid disastrous missteps. In such circumstances, virtue-imbued casuistry can provide cases that caution users and help them bring about more prudent strategic decisions.

In the following, we will see how these notions are now playing out in the move to eradicate poliomyelitis ("polio"). We will see here by means of comparison, how today's effort is similar to the drive to get rid of smallpox years ago and how the eradication of a major disease is not simply a matter of applying money and technical resources to a problem. It also demands an understanding of the history of fighting diseases, knowledge about the problems associated with keeping, destroying, and monitoring stocks, and shrewdness in terms of the vicious agents and imprudent yet powerful authorities who can undermine a widely regarded positive effort.

Goal: Eradicating Polio

To begin, the effort to eradicate polio came to widespread attention in early 2013 when Michael Bloomberg agreed to donate a substantial amount of money to aid the Bill and Melinda Gates Foundation's effort to eradicate polio by 2018—a lofty goal that would both rid the world of a scourge and purposefully drive a part of nature to extinction (Bill and Melinda Gates Foundation 2013; Bloomberg 2013; McKay 2013; Rotary International 2013).

While the donation and goals of the Foundation were roundly applauded, the announcement concentrated on the monetary and public health aspects of the initiative

M. Calkins, *Developing a Virtue-Imbued Casuistry for Business Ethics,* Issues in Business Ethics 42, DOI 10.1007/978-94-017-8724-6_14, © Springer Netherlands 2014

but largely overlooked some of the complex ancillary issues associated with the eradication of a deadly disease.

One aspect that went mostly unnoticed was the competing interests of the stakeholders attracted to the issue by the large sums of money involved. Another had to do with the locus of authority in coordinating a major public health initiative. For one, Bloomberg and Gates as private citizens spearheaded the move, but it was not clear initially who would coordinate the drive in terms of its widespread health considerations.

While these issues will likely be addressed in time, they exist within a cluster of other issues having to do with the monitoring and control of disease stocks and the oversight of operations. Concerns such as the proper role and degree of influence of independent and government-sponsored health programs, the locus of decisions made locally with international consequences, the degree of transparency in the progress of the venture, and the checks and balances to ensure that overseers do their jobs will need to be addressed fully as well. Most pressing (and frightening) of all, the responsibility for vigilance against malevolent agents attracted to the destructive potential of the disease and its widespread elimination will have to be established—and, most important, enforced.

That these concerns are raised here is indicative that the issues are not being overlooked. Moreover, there is plenty of precedence to guide the current initiative. Other diseases have been similarly targeted in the past and other programs are already quietly in process.[1]

One strongly correlative disease that was mostly exterminated recently is smallpox, a disease thought to have killed more people than all other infectious diseases combined (Medline Plus 2013). It is therefore a good basis of comparison as the drive to eradicate polio gets under way.

Smallpox: A Cautionary Tale

Smallpox, an infectious illness caused by the *variola major* virus, is a flu-like disease with symptoms that include high fever, fatigue, headache, and backache followed by a rash with flat red sores. Although deadly, it was stopped by worldwide immunization three decades ago.[2] That initiative was so successful that routine smallpox vaccinations were discontinued in 1972 and today only the military and other high-risk groups receive smallpox vaccinations (Medline Plus 2013).

Although smallpox has been almost completely eradicated, it reemerged as a pressing issue when it was linked to bioterrorism after the anthrax scare following the September 11th, 2001 terrorist attacks in America. It then became apparent that the nearly extinct disease was important to national security and that there were a number of competing stakeholder interests involved in the issue.

---

[1] For some of the diseases slated for destruction, see (Ridley 2013).

[2] My thanks to Eric Pinsoneault for research assistance on this the history of smallpox.

Killing a Deadly Disease

To understand the complexity of the developments involving smallpox, we need to consider its background as a disease and the reasons for it being targeted for extinction.

One of the most deadly diseases to plague humanity, smallpox is considered so lethal and infectious that the U.S. Center For Disease Control and Prevention lists it as a category A (most severe) agent. An easily disseminated disease, smallpox operates by means of a "replicating agent" or live organism that can be spread from person to person (Anderson and Bokor 2012, p. 522). It is also exceptionally deadly, having a case-fatality rate of 30 % or more among unvaccinated persons with the absence of specific therapy (Henderson et al. 1999). Not surprisingly, smallpox has a high mortality rate, an ability to cause public panic and disruption, and requires that healthcare providers take special precautions when in contact with those infected.

Although hazardous, smallpox is controllable. Once scientists understood its mechanisms in the mid-twentieth century, they established protocols to thwart the disease's effectiveness and put into place a campaign to inoculate the public against it.

Efforts began locally in America with stations set up throughout communities where people lined up to take sugar cubes laced with smallpox vaccine. Then, in 1967, a global campaign under the auspices of the World Health Organization (WHO) was set up to take the initiative worldwide.

The results of these efforts were impressive. By 1972 incidents were so rare that routine smallpox vaccinations were discontinued. By 1977 naturally acquired varieties of smallpox were wiped out and by 1979 the global eradication of smallpox was certified.[3]

Shortly thereafter, the WHO recommended the continued surveillance of monkeypox in West and Central Africa and that stocks and the use of the *variola* virus in laboratories be subject to supervision to insure against the return of the disease. The Organization also recommended the maintenance of international reserves of freeze-dried vaccine under its control and certain other measures to ensure that laboratory and epidemiological expertise in human poxvirus infections did not dissipate (Global Commission for the Certification of Smallpox Eradication 1980, p. 11).

Overall, the eradication of smallpox was met with satisfaction, but extermination also meant that inoculations were no longer necessary. As a result, today few people younger than 27 years old have been vaccinated against the disease and many are now completely unfamiliar with its destructive past.[4]

---

[3] The U.S. Center for Disease Control and Prevention claims that the last naturally acquired case of smallpox occurred in Somalia in 1977 (Centers for Disease Control and Prevention 2002, p. 2).

[4] Prior to 1972, a smallpox vaccination was recommended for all U.S. children at 1 year of age and most states required evidence of vaccination for school entry. Vaccination was required as well for military recruits and tourists visiting certain countries. In contrast, the 1998 U.S. Census shows that approximately 114 million persons age 29 years or younger have not been vaccinated against smallpox (Henderson et al. 1999).

Systematic Destruction

On many levels, the near eradication of smallpox is a success story. Vaccines were distributed effectively worldwide such that the last case of smallpox was reported in 1977. In 1979 the WHO not only certified the demise of smallpox, but also recommended that remaining *variola* virus stocks be consolidated and held at no more than four collaborating facilities (Global Commission for the Certification of Smallpox Eradication 1980, p. 13). Other groups holding reserves were asked to destroy their stocks or transfer them to WHO collecting centers (Global Commission for the Certification of Smallpox Eradication 1980, p. 13).

In 1990 the WHO went on to establish an Ad Hoc Committee on Orthopoxvirus Infections to assess the progress and current activities of the post-eradication program from 1986 onward and, more specifically, to review the previous recommendation that all remaining stocks of live *variola* virus be destroyed.

The Committee returned with a decision that, pending the consensus of members, the remaining stocks be destroyed by December 31, 1993 and that until that time, existing stocks be sent for holding to two WHO collaborating centers—high-security laboratories in the United States and the Soviet Union (now the Russian Federation). These were located respectively at the Centers for Disease Control and Prevention in Atlanta and the State Research Centre of Virology and Biotechnology VECTOR in Koltsovo (Siberia).[5]

The destruction of all remaining stocks did not take place, however, once the scientific community expressed its public health and research concerns and certain members refused to sign on to advance the recommendation.

Undeterred, the Committee held a second meeting in September 1994 followed by a third in January 1999. In fact, Committee meetings concerning the destruction of the virus stocks continued through 2007 and all ended with the same lack of consensus about a willingness to destroy existing reserves (World Health Organization Fifty-fifth World Health Assembly 2002; World Health Organization Fifty-second World Health Assembly 1999, p. 1–2; World Health Organization Sixtieth World Health Assembly 2007; World Health Organization Sixtieth World Health Assembly Executive Board 2007).

While the exact nature of the Committee's discussions is not known, in effect the WHO had turned over the smallpox destruction issue to a committee that then spent nearly a decade talking about the issue without actually resolving it.

Gone But Not Forgotten

Meanwhile, by 1980 reports began to emerge about the Soviet Union's research program to produce the smallpox virus in large quantities for adaptation for use in

---

[5] (World Health Organization 2010, p. 5). Civil unrest in Moscow in 1994 resulted in Russian stockpiles being moved from Moscow to Siberia (Tucker 2011, p. 57).

weapons. As Jonathan Tucker observed, the program remained hidden until 1999 when reports by Kanatjan Alibekov (also known as Ken Alibek, a former deputy director of the Soviet Union's civilian bioweapons program) revealed that the Soviets had grown their industrial capability to produce tons of smallpox virus for use in bombs and intercontinental ballistic missiles. Even more alarming, over a span of about twenty years the Soviets were well on their way to producing more virulent and contagious recombinant strains of the disease for eventual military purposes (Tucker 2011, p. 56).

While these developments were troubling enough, the worldwide threat that the Soviet actions posed was aggravated by the fall of the Soviet Union and the subsequent decline of financial support for laboratories in Russia. Now, with little funding and oversight and no real effective authority to stop a potentially lucrative sale of expertise and equipment to anyone with sufficient funds, smallpox stores could be more easily stolen or purchased (Alibek and Handelman 1999; Henderson et al. 1999).

An Effective Bioweapon

With the September 11, 2001 attacks and the subsequent use of anthrax poisonings to terrorize the American population, the threat of the use of deadly diseases as bioweapons became front-page news.[6]

By 2003, fear of smallpox as a bioweapon had grown to such an extent that it was widely believed that smallpox' dissemination on large populations was both immediate and pressing. The claims of Hazem Ali (a virologist in the Iraqi biological weapons program), whose interest was the closely related camelpox, only strengthened the widespread perception that Saddam Hussein intended to weaponize smallpox and use it against his enemies. That perception along with the notion that Hussein had large stores of so-called "weapons of mass destruction" that he would be willing to use to wreak widespread havoc became central in debates on whether or not to enter into war in Iraq. Only after the war began did a group of researchers with the American Central Intelligence Agency (CIA) known as "Team Pox" determine that no stockpiles of the virus or weapons of mass destruction existed.[7]

The fear that smallpox could be used as a bioweapon was not unfounded, since the disease had been used effectively to fearsome ends numerous times in the past.

---

[6] As an aside, the anthrax scare of 2001 illustrates how self-interested and wealthy individuals can exert influence should a need for a vaccine arise and people cause a run on Cipro, an antibiotic used to treat patients exposed to the inhaled form of anthrax (Terhune 2002).

[7] (Tucker 2011, p. 59). Not long after the Team's announcement, many of the politicians who had publically voiced their concerns about weapons of mass destruction in 1998–2003 and voted for the Iraq War tried to obscure their involvement by calling the War "Bush's War."

In fact, there had been long-term and widespread agreement about the dangers posed by Saddam Hussein's regime prior to the war's start in 2003. On November 15, 1998, for example, Bill Clinton called for a new government in Iraq in explaining his signing of the "Iraq Liberation Act of 1998." For more on this era, see (105th Congress 1997–1998, 1998; Clinton, Bill Clinton 1998 Iraq Liberation Act 1998; Knott 2013).

During the French and Indian Wars of the eighteenth century, for example, British soldiers distributed blankets that had been used by smallpox patients to North American Indians, killing more than 50% of the affected tribes (Henderson et al. 1999). Smallpox had been used as well in the American Revolution and both the Allies and the Axis experimented with its application during WWII (Alibek and Handelman 1999).

Playing Catch-Up

Fearful of a pandemic and recognizing the vulnerability of a general population not inoculated against the disease, the various centers for disease control scrambled to secure vaccines against smallpox and other deadly pathogens.

In America, the Center for Disease Control (CDC) was confirmed in January 2002 as the lead agency for upgrading national public health capabilities for responding to biological terrorism. It then quickly acted to update and extend a response plan developed in the 1970s that had been used successfully to control smallpox outbreaks decades ago.

Earlier approaches relied mostly on containment since the most frequent mode of transmission of smallpox is via direct deposit of infective droplets onto the nasal, oral, or pharyngeal mucosal membranes, or the alveoli of the lungs from close face-to-face contact with an infectious individual (Centers for Disease Control and Prevention 2002, p. 1). The CDC's revived document entitled, *Smallpox Response Plan & Guidelines*, reinvigorated many of these older approaches and added more nuanced operational aspects to deal with a contemporary smallpox emergency (Centers for Disease Control and Prevention 2004, p. 3).

The establishment of workable plans was, in some ways, the easy part of what was clearly a catch-up process. The hard part was what to do with quarantined individuals and the acquisition of sufficient vaccines to inoculate the public.

As late as March 2002 (6 months after the terrorist attacks) the United States had only 15 million doses of smallpox vaccine (Engel 2002). This meant that had a smallpox outbreak occurred in tandem with or shortly after the September 11th attacks, the American government would have been hard pressed to respond adequately to mass illness and death.

Recognizing this vulnerability, the CDC attempted to quickly procure sufficient stores of smallpox vaccine by amending its existing contracts for the replacement of out-of-date smallpox vaccines and awarding the British company Acambis PLC's US subsidiary, Acambis Inc., two new contracts to supply the American government with a total of 209 million doses of smallpox vaccine.[8]

---

[8] In September 2000, Acambis was awarded its first contract by the CDC to develop and manufacture a stockpile of smallpox vaccine. The first contract was valued at $ 343 million and requires Acambis to maintain the stockpile over the 20-year life of the contract through the continued replacement of out-of-date doses. This first contract was recently amended to bring forward production of 54 million doses of vaccine in 2002 and to accelerate the clinical development plan relating

While impressive, the 209 million doses still left America vulnerable because the contract was for future deliveries and it would take time to actually produce sufficient quantities of the vaccine. In addition, the strategy left the government vulnerable to foreign concerns since it was relying on an overseas business enterprise to supply an ingredient essential to national security.[9]

In late March 2002 in a rather lucky turn of events, the American government's position was strengthened considerably with the "discovery" of 90 million doses of smallpox vaccine in the freezers of a French pharmaceutical company (later reported to be Aventis Company's Aventis Pasteur unit) (Terhune 2002). This trove proved to be so big that it could be used to inoculate the American population should a bioterrorist attack occur (Engel 2002).

At present, the CDC allegedly has an effective plan and sufficient *variola* virus stocks in place. If an incident were to occur now, it would not only isolate individuals with smallpox in an "identify and contain" strategy, but also vaccinate and monitor all those in contact with infected persons.

Rather than reinstituting the mass vaccinations of the past, it would identify particular priority groups for treatment to allow the Center to accommodate both intentional and naturally occurring mutations of the disease and to enable the CDC to allocate personnel optimally (Centers for Disease Control and Prevention 2004, p. 3).

Lessons From a Near-Miss

While the world's population is now more protected from a smallpox outbreak than it was a decade or two ago, the chain of events from the 1980s to the present illustrates the vulnerability of society when it becomes complacent to the effects of deadly diseases, inured to the reality of malevolence, and unprepared to deal with the competing stakeholder interests at work should vaccines become scarce.

The smallpox case also calls into question the wisdom of giving the WHO (a specialized agency of the United Nations) authority to assert its judgments as if they were binding international policies. It reveals how this agency was structurally unable to achieve widespread consensus and, more alarming, how unelected WHO representatives were attempting to make policies that would impinge on individual national security decisions and thereby effectively undermine the traditional central protective role of sovereign governments.

Second, the "discovery" of massive holdings of *variola* virus stock after the WHO pronouncements reveals just how seriously certain member representatives

---

to the vaccine being developed under that contract. The second contract is to produce 155 million doses of smallpox vaccine within the next 12 months (from 28 November 2001). The value of this new, fixed-price contract is $ 428 million (Acambis PLC 2001).

[9] Although Acambis has a strategic alliance with Deerfield, Illinois' Baxter Healthcare Corporation that will ultimately result in Baxter owning 20 % of Acambis, today Baxter's shareholding in Acambis is only 12.6 % (Reporter 2001).

take the WHO's recommendations—that is, not seriously at all. The assumptions that all members are equally committed to decisions and that all approach so-called binding resolutions in the same way are unwarranted.

Third, the handling of smallpox at a critical juncture in the past suggests that governments and the WHO were either unaware or unconcerned with the depth of malevolence in the world. This aspect is perhaps most troubling of all because the history of bioweaponry is so rich and longstanding and these two institutions have been particularly charged with protecting the public against health-based harms.

Not unlike international arms control and the American "war on drugs," the smallpox case illustrates how compliance by the virtuous and cheating by the wicked works to the advantage of the malevolent.

That the institution charged with national security (government) and the institution charged with securing public health (WHO) were so unprepared to deal with dangerously aggressive agents attests, at a minimum, to the ineptness of the management of the two institutions. Had Hussein actually stored and unleashed smallpox-laden weapons on civilian populations, the resulting deaths would not have just called into question this management, but would have threatened the viability and ongoing legitimacy of the institutions themselves.

Polio Eradication in Perspective

All of these lessons related to the handling of smallpox are relevant to the current initiative to eradicate polio. While polio and smallpox are not the same disease, both are viral, infectious diseases spread from person to person. Thus, the lessons gained from dealing with smallpox are helpful to preparing for polio's eventual eradication.

First, the smallpox case illustrates the importance of case use in deliberations about other deadly diseases. The vulnerabilities and various stakeholder interests that arose about what to do with smallpox stores and how to handle the threat of bioterrorism are instructional for how to deal with polio. The smallpox case is therefore a helpful deliberative tool in long term planning for polio's demise.

Second, the smallpox case underscores the complexity of overlapping interests. At its core, the smallpox case underscores the complexity of the issue of whether or not a disease should be extinguished completely. Had WHO members reached consensus, *variola* virus stocks might have been destroyed—at least by people of good will if not by malcontents and the vicious. A similar question about extinguishing polio completely will surely arise and should be factored into plans now rather than later.

Third, the smallpox case highlights the importance of delineating clear lines of authority when dealing with deadly diseases.

The WHO is a supranational organization but the general public does not elect its members nor are its members' interests always aligned with those of particular nation states. WHO decisions in the smallpox case, had they been effective, would have intruded upon governments' primary traditional role of protecting the citizenry.

In like manner, governments' willingness to hand over their responsibilities for securing public health to supranational organizations as it did in large measure to the WHO is questionable and should be central to discussions about the handling and eventual fate of polio reserves.

Fourth, the loci of initiatives in the smallpox case versus the emerging polio case bear consideration. Unlike smallpox, the initiative to eradicate polio is being undertaken by the private sector, with Gates and Bloomberg leveraging their considerable wealth and business acumen to advance good public ends. While their philanthropy is to be lauded, the substantial investiture by a narrow group of individuals raises concerns about the lines of authority and responsibility in such decision-making. In addition, it raises practical concerns about the fate of polio stocks, the location of reserves, the transparency of monitoring, and so forth. These, too, should be determined at the outset rather than as an afterthought.

Fifth, the smallpox case illustrates the need for prudence in policymaking and strategy regarding polio. As we saw, malevolent agents exist despite the rules established by agencies and the good intentions of peaceful people. Turning a blind eye to evildoers will not make them go away and overreaction is rarely helpful. Instead, a deliberative balance—a golden mean of practical wisdom to advance good ends while containing malefactors—is essential to shrewd and cautious planning. This became evident in the chain of events associated with smallpox and it will surely be a critical factor in dealing with polio.

In the end, the smallpox eradication program and its aftermath highlight the importance of case use, prudence, and balancing various competing stakeholder interests when managing risk exposure on a grand scale. Oddly, the actual eradication of the disease is in some ways the easy part of the process. The more difficult part is balancing competing stakeholder interests while striving to advance good ends and thwarting wrongdoers. Virtue-imbued casuistry can go a long way toward helping to balance these interests while offering needed caution to deliberations.

Chapter 15
Risk Exposure: Using Cases in Strategies Involving an Aging Medication

> *It is better by noble boldness to run the risk of being subject to half the evils we anticipate than to remain in cowardly listlessness for fear of what might happen. (Herodotus 1890).*
> —Herodotus

In the previous chapters we saw how virtue-imbued casuistry can help users resolve disputes, balance competing interests, and use cautionary cases to derive more prudent strategies.

In this chapter, we will see how virtue-imbued casuistry can help users sidestep the unforeseen liabilities associated with shifting moral and social norms when assessing risk exposure.

Using the example of an established drug with known side effects, the following reviews the processes managers typically use to determine whether or not to continue to promote an aging drug. It shows how managers are fairly good at balancing obvious risks, but sometimes fail to recognize the risks associated with shifting moral or social norms.

To remedy this oversight, the following suggests the prudent use of cases along with the usual numbers-based processes of analysis in risk management.

Risk Exposure in an Environment of Experimentation

The search for a breast cancer cure has been a long-sought goal of the health-care industry, yet breast cancer remains the third leading cause of mortality in America among neoplastic diseases, surpassed only by lung and colon malignancies. Well over 200,000 people (mostly women) in the United States alone are newly

---

The quote here is a summary of the following: It is better to have good courage about everything and to suffer half the evils which threaten, than to have fear beforehand about everything and not to suffer any evil at all: and if, while contendingagainst everything which is said, thou omit to declare the course which is safe, thou dost incur in these matters the reproach of failure equally with him who says the opposite to this. This then, I say, is evenly balanced: but how should one who is but man know the course which is safe? I think, in no way. To those then who choose to act, for the most part gain is wont to come; but to those who reckon for everything andshrink back, it is not much wont to come.

M. Calkins, *Developing a Virtue-Imbued Casuistry for Business Ethics,* Issues in Business Ethics 42, DOI 10.1007/978-94-017-8724-6_15, © Springer Netherlands 2014

diagnosed with breast cancer each year (Bankhead 2008; Chen and Colditz 2008; Radiological Society of North America 2008).

One therapy involving the drug tamoxifen (or raloxifene) has been approved as a preventative against the development of breast cancer later in life. It is typically prescribed for select individuals and has been a longstanding and significant profit generator for its producers. Even so, it is not without problems. It is an aging medication that has been superseded by other therapies. It can also sometimes produce side effects. As a result, it poses vexing problems for its producers in regard to the shifting social acceptance of risk and raises questions about whether or not its makers should continue to produce and market the drug aggressively.

On the one hand, the answer to the dilemma about going forward with the drug is simple. Since there is no cure for breast cancer and experimentation with various therapies continues, tamoxifen's producers should continue to promote the drug aggressively. The drug already meets safety standards, generates significant profits for its producers, and is part of a protocol where cancer is treated by means of a variety of probability-based approaches. The highly publicized preventative double mastectomy of 37-year-old Angelina Joie, for example, was based on the statistical likelihood that she might contract cancer later in life.[1] Tamoxifen should therefore be marketed aggressively because it plays a role as one of the many options available to cancer patients as they search for therapies and weigh their various risks.

On the other hand, tamoxifen's producers might be wise to either discontinue the drug's production or stop promoting it aggressively. Alternative therapies exist and tamoxifen is an aging drug with side effects. The risks of continuing to produce and market a drug with known side effects could expose its producers to potentially costly liabilities at some point. Prudence would therefore dictate that the drug be discontinued or gradually removed from the market.

Given these options, what should tamoxifen's producers do? Should they continue to produce and market the drug or stop both in light of the possibility of the drug's potential to expose the company to harm?

To answer these questions, it is necessary to first understand the nature of the drug and current breast cancer therapies.

Background: Tamoxifen Therapy

Today, several treatments and preventatives therapies are available to doctors and patients. These range from mammalian target of rapamycin (mTOR) inhibitors and insulin-like growth factor type 1 receptor (IGF-R1) inhibitors to the steroidal anti-estrogen TAS-108 (Bankhead 2008).

---

[1] In April 2013, American celebrity and actress Angelina Jolie had a preventative double mastectomy based on an 87% risk of breast cancer and a family history of the disease. She reports that now her chances of developing breast cancer have dropped to under 5% (Jolie 2013).

While this array of therapies is impressive, the road to such variety has neither been smooth nor without risk. Before most of today's drug protocols came on the scene, doctors and patients relied on tamoxifen citrate—aka tamoxifen (brand names: Nolvadex®, Istubal, Valodex, Nolvadex D®, Emblon®, Fentamox®, Soltamox®, Tamofen®, etc.)—as both a first-line treatment for post-menopausal early-stage cancer patients and a cancer preventative treatment (BioPortfolio Limited 2009).

Taken orally in pill form, tamoxifen interferes with the activity of estrogen (a female hormone). It has been used for nearly 30 years to treat patients with advanced breast cancer and, more recently, to treat those with early stage breast cancers (Susan G. Komen Breast Cancer Foundation 2002).

The way the drug works is complicated and not fully understood, but as one of a class of designer estrogen drugs called selective estrogen receptor modulators (SERMs), tamoxifen's main function is to reduce or stop the action of estrogen (CancerBACUP).

In 1998, medical researchers found that taking tamoxifen for 5 years significantly reduced both breast cancer recurrence (42%) and mortality (22%) for women (Susan G. Komen Breast Cancer Foundation 2002). Further tests showed tamoxifen to reduce cancer recurrences by 40–50% in post-menopausal women and about 30–50% in pre-menopausal women (Breastcancer.org 2007; Peshkin et al. 2007). Studies revealed, too, that tamoxifen provided more benefits to post-menopausal than to pre-menopausal women (Sellman 1998). Among a list of desired benefits was the reduction of contralateral breast cancer tumors and relapses of around 30% (Grilli 2006).

A Therapy with Risks

Despite such positive results, doctors in continental Europe, Asia, South America, and Australasia who were asked about the prescription of adjuvant tamoxifen for breast cancer typically indicated they would use tamoxifen in older women with disease, but only half (54%) said they would do so in cases involving younger diseased women (Davies et al. 1998; Litsas 2008; Regan et al. 2008; Schilder et al. 2009).

The chief reason for doctors' reluctance to prescribe tamoxifen for younger women is its tendency to produce unwanted patient side effects (AstraZeneca Pharmaceuticals LP 2001). Another compelling reason for its non-use is skepticism about the drug's efficacy.[2]

---

[2] Online sources typically appeal to the claim that, "In 1992 the Lancet published a review of a number of studies in which a total of 30,000 breast cancer patients were randomly assigned either to take tamoxifen or not. The average patient in this collaborative study was followed up for between five and six years. Of the patients taking tamoxifen, 74.4 per cent survived, as compared with 70.9 per cent in the non-tamoxifen group—a less than impressive improvement than was declared at the time the drug passed the clinical trials." In addition, they point to claims that "Despite tamoxifen's proven ability to reduce breast cancer recurrence in post-menopausal women, major

Doctors who continued to prescribe tamoxifen considered the drug's side effects to be mild and not severe enough to discontinue patients' use of the drug (AstraZeneca Pharmaceuticals LP 2001; Sirisabya et al. 2008). Proponents maintained that the drug's benefits outweighed the risks associated with it (Susan G. Komen Breast Cancer Foundation 2002). Some went further to claim that tamoxifen had certain positive side benefits (Overmyer 2008).

Even so, cancer specialists in 1998 were skeptical of tamoxifen's safety and became fearful that its side effects were not harmless. Their particular concern was the drug's potential to increase the risk of uterine cancer—a concern precipitated by a widely publicized study of the drug funded by the National Cancer Institute (Reporter 1998).

Doctors then began to turn away from tamoxifen, prescribing other drugs and therapies as breast cancer preventatives instead. Others continued to use the drug in the hope that an improved version that offset the drug's side effects might be on the horizon, producing the same positive results without the current potential side effects.

The controversy over tamoxifen took a turn on April 20, 1998 (less than three weeks after the announcement of tamoxifen's problematic side-effects) with the publication of reports containing the results of tests of raloxifene (Evista®), a similar selective estrogen receptor modulator (SERM) produced by Eli Lilly and Company that lacked tamoxifen's side effects. Tests showed that raloxifene, a drug commonly used to prevent and treat osteoporosis in postmenopausal women, worked as well as tamoxifen in reducing breast cancer risk for postmenopausal women at increased risk of the disease (National Cancer Institute 2006).

The problem, however, was that the trials of Evista as a breast cancer preventative went back only 2 years and scientists and health officials were unconvinced of the drug's long-term effectiveness as a breast cancer preventative. The announcement of the application of Evista/raloxifene as a breast cancer preventative was therefore greeted with the same mix of hope and suspicion that tamoxifen had received (Burton 1998). Nevertheless, at the mention of Evista's clinical trials, investors drove up the price of Lilly's shares by $ 5.125 to $ 68.375 (Reporter 1998).

Subsequent studies concerned with the cancer prevention efficacy of tamoxifen and raloxifene were intense, with some tests stopped before their deadlines because the tests revealed positive effects of breast cancer. Others validated longstanding worries about the drug's side effects such as the development of liver cancer and liver disease, lung cancer, uterine (endometrial) cancer, and side effects such as eye damage, or blood clots. Certain psychological pathologies (including loss of libido and mania) were also noted (Perez et al. 2003; Yildiz 2008).

Longstanding and Profitable

In 2006, a large international trial of postmenopausal women surgically treated for early-stage, hormone responsive breast cancer, found letrozole (Femara®) did better

---

studies have shown that tamoxifen reduces death from breast cancer only marginally. The majority of women who take tamoxifen live no longer than women who do not take it" (Sellman 1998).

to prevent a recurrence of disease (especially distant metastases) than tamoxifen.[3] As a result, doctors began to turn away from tamoxifen, prescribing it mainly for those with breast cancers sensitive to the hormone estrogen.[4] These included:

- Women older than 60 years.
- Postmenopausal women between age 35 and 59 with an increased risk of breast cancer of at least 1.66 (as determined by the Gail model, which estimates probability of getting breast cancer based on several factors).
- Postmenopausal women age 35 or older with a history of lobular carcinoma *in situ* (LCIS).

Tamoxifen's user population is now much reduced but remains significantly large. Premenopausal women (those with generally higher estrogen levels) at high risk of developing breast cancer prefer tamoxifen despite there being no data about the safety of the drug for the group and the current recommendation based on use of the drug on women with breast cancer being just 5 years. Because this demographic is increasing, the number of likely tamoxfen users should grow in the immediate future as well.

The preferences of certain populations combined with tamoxifen's long life have made the drug a significant profit generator for its manufacturers. Until 2003 its initial producer had exclusive control of it. In 1992 alone, the drug generated $ 265 million in revenue in America for the company. By 1995, worldwide sales of one brand of tamoxifen, Nolvadex, reached $ 400 million and by 2001, global sales of tamoxifen were $ 1.024 billion (BioPortfolio Limited 2009).

Most variants of the drug have also been profitable such that at the mention of the clinical trials in 1998 of the tamoxifen alternative raloxifene, producer Eli Lilly's shares jumped by $ 5.125 to $ 68.375 (Reporter 1998). Profits rose for tamoxifen and related drugs so much that by October 2008 manufacturers' shares were traded at $ 33.10 per share and Evista, along with five other products (Humalog, Gemzar, Cialis, Alimta, and Humulin) each contributed more than $ 1 billion in revenues to their producers (Eli Lilly and Company 2009).

In sum, the status of tamoxifen today is that it is an approved drug with a niche market and a proven ability to generate profit. It has an appeal to those who cannot take other drugs or who have used it for a long time and are comfortable with it. At the same time, it has the potential to produce side effects that can pose significant risks to some of its users. Because it is now a mature drug, tamoxifen's original producer no longer has exclusive control over it and other therapies now compete against it. As a result, tamoxifen's producers must weigh the benefits and costs associated with marketing a drug more aggressively to maintain its profit stream.

---

[3] (Breast International Group (BIG) 1–98 Collaborative Group et al. 2005; Taras et al. 2000; Young 2007). A large international trial of postmenopausal women surgically treated for early-stage, hormone responsive breast cancer found that letrozole (Femara®) did better to prevent a recurrence of disease (especially distant metastases) than the commonly prescribed tamoxifen (Nolvadex®) (Coates et al. 2007).

[4] It should be mentioned that some bodybuilders use tamoxifen illicitly to thwart the gynecomastia (bitch tits) that results from overusing androgenic anabolic steroids.

Assessing the Risk Exposure of an Aging Drug

Tamoxifen is an approved drug that can be sold legitimately, but its possible side effects could expose its producers to financial and reputational risks should society's norms related to the acceptability of the risks of its side effects shift.

Such change is not unprecedented. What was once accepted as a normal risk—think of driving a car without a seat belt or riding a bicycle without a helmet—has changed in the past. Lawsuits and settlements have been exorbitant at times and companies are now wary that they can find themselves in deep financial trouble and cast as villains should norms change without their knowledge. Should this happen with tamoxifen, producers could find their reputations dulled and their money maker to be a financial liability, not an asset.

What should managers do? Should they continue to sell the drug and if so, how aggressively should they do so?

Step One: Weighing Losses Against Profits

The first step to answering these questions is to assess the impact of risk on the drug's profits. Doing so is fairly straightforward and common business practice. Consider how it is done:

Say a company that produces an aging drug has 100,000 patients and nets $ 20,000 per patient from the drug over a lifetime.[5] Since the drug is mature, research and development costs are no longer an issue and the drug's significant costs are now mostly related to production (negligible) and sales. Together, this means that the company could make $ 2 billion on the drug ($100,000 \times \$ 20,000 = \$ 2$ billion) over its expected lifetime.

At $ 2 billion, the drug is a good moneymaker and it's the manufacturer' managers cannot simply dismiss it, even if they have moral qualms about marketing a drug with known side effects. The fact that the drug is a legitimate product with $ 2 billion in potential sales means that those with qualms will be replaced with those who do not and the marketing process will continue without disruption.

Even so, the drug does produce certain side effects that could become costly to the company should society's sentiments change. The company cannot simply dismiss these potentialities because they could expose the company to significant losses should they occur. The company will therefore need to determine its level of risk exposure by identifying, quantifying, and modeling each risk factor. The PricewaterhouseCoopers practical guide to uncertainty and risk analysis is a good example of how this is done (Rodger and Petch 1999).

In assessing risks, should managers find that 1 % of the people using the drug have harmful side effects that cost the company $ 500,000 each, then 1,000 patients (100,000 patients $\times$ .01 = 1,000 patients) will be involved and the company will have

---

[5] My thanks to Mark Sioma for assistance in framing the profit/risk example here.

to pay out $ 500 million in settlements ($1,000 \times \$ 500,000 = \$ 5$ million). This will diminish profits such that now the company will net $ 1.5 billion instead of $ 2 billion.

If, however, managers market the drug as aggressively as possible and double their sales, they will make $ 4 billion for the company. In doing so and at the same failure rate, they will also incur $ 1 billion of costs. While these cost increases are certainly significant, through the managers' actions profits have doubled (gone from $ 1.5 billion to $ 3 billion). Thus, from a financial perspective, managers *should* sell the drug as aggressively as possible.

Step Two: Recognizing that Something is Missing

At first blush, it seems that managers should go ahead with an aggressive campaign to market the aging drug. Step One has provided straightforward and accurate indicators that doing so will increase profits significantly.

Unfortunately, Step One does not capture all of the variables associated with risk exposure. It only captures those that are identified, delimited, quantified and entered into the first step process. While this is necessary for effective risk planning, Step One is insufficient because it is limited and can miss risks that exist outside the parameters of preselected variables.

Step One is mathematically precise, but cannot account for unanticipated or "unforeseen risks" that can be surprising and harmful. Worse, its very sophistication can obscure the fact that one or more variables might be missing. In this way, it can mislead because its accuracy and detail lull users into thinking they have considered all the contingencies of an issue when they have not. A whole wide range of risk factors might be lurking in the shadows only to pounce on the unsuspecting company later without warning.

Unforeseen risks can be dangerous to businesses, but they need not be in all cases. Unexpected risks can vary in terms of their source and content and be relatively benign. At other times, they can be devastating to the financial stability of a business. That is the main problem with unforeseen risks—they are the uncertainties that reside in a lacuna or blind spot outside the sphere of normal business practice.[6] They can vary widely and go unnoticed.

In general, unforeseen risks are unanticipated because they contain unique elements of serendipity, obscurity, and breadth that are outside the normal range of business activities. Businesses recognize some of these liabilities. They attempt to grapple with risk's serendipity, for example, by using modeling and scenario-based techniques. We will consider these in greater detail in subsequent chapters of this book.

Businesses do less well with risk's aspects of obscurity and breadth, however, because these attributes are often associated with shifting social or moral norms

---

[6] For more on ethical blind spots, see (Moberg 2006).

rooted in highly subjective ideals and values that are difficult to encapsulate and express. This subjectivity makes them easy to dismiss by some and overlook by others. Worse, even when risks are recognized they can be difficult to incorporate into or alongside numbers-based models. Because the attributes are qualities, they are difficult to quantify and because they are sometimes values-based and tied to shifting populations and opinions, they can be hard to comprehend fully and incorporate into analytic strategic processes.

Unforeseen risks grounded in shifting assumptions about risk can lead companies into unexpected trouble. The McDonald's hot coffee lawsuit is a good example of a company hit with an unforeseen liability based on a shifting acceptance of risk. There, the company, despite repeated warnings, assumed its customers wanted piping hot coffee but found that that norm had subtly changed when a customer took the company to court for selling a dangerous product.[7] People (or at least the courts) decided that they were no longer willing to accept the risks related to hot coffee in a take-away cup. The social norm had shifted to a new and less forgiving understanding of the assumptions of risk when buying hot coffee.

The same sort of shift can occur with moral or ethical norms where the general understanding of a risk related to the abridgment or compliance with an ethical standard can change with little or no notice.

As in the hot coffee case, managers need to be mindful of society's shifting sentiments about business' social responsibilities, standard of truthfulness, transparency, customer mindfulness, and so forth. Some or all of these sentiments can change because of an unexpected incident and threaten a business' reputation and financial stability.

In light of these potential threats, managers need to adapt their approaches to strategy. They need to recognize that their numbers-based approaches have limits and that their current risk management practices are vulnerable to missing non-quantifiable yet essential risk elements.

Step Three: Augmenting With Cases

One way to uncover the foreseen risks mentioned above is to familiarize oneself with the lessons conveyed through cases because through cases, risks that would otherwise go unnoticed can become obvious.

Cases, as we saw in earlier chapters, are simply events or happenings in which there is a "confluence of persons and actions in a time and a place" (Jonsen 1995, p. 241). They are helpful in risk analysis because they contain lessons from the past that can be illustrative of an imminent threat. While it is true that, as Mark Twain observed, "History doesn't repeat itself—at best it sometimes rhymes," it is also true that cases can provide cautionary lessons from the past that can help stimulate

---

[7] See (Bernalillo County 1994). For commentary on the case, see (Cain 2007; Ramseyer and Rasmusen 2010).

awareness and advance an understanding of the liabilities possibly embedded in a present situation.[8]

Moreover, cases can be helpful because cases' narrative qualities can capture the complexity of human and other interactions that can sometimes be overlooked in more spare approaches. The fullness of stories, in other words, can highlight particular details that can either be relevant to the issue at hand or become important as a consequence of some proposed action.

Finally and perhaps most important, cases can be helpful in risk assessment because cases have an ability to stir the imagination in compelling ways. While they remain grounded in the concrete, cases can encourage the user to abstract certain features, reflect upon them, and then make relevant and meaningful connections between the story and the present circumstance. The outcome of this process can then be expressed in ways that are inspiring, cautionary, and more powerful than statistics alone. In this way, not only is risk management more nuanced and enhanced, but also managers become more proactive than they otherwise might be.

Despite these positive contributions to risk management, cases need to be used judiciously to be effective. Current situations are rarely analogous to the past and risk managers need to be careful when identifying the pertinent elements of the situation at hand and the relevant aspects of the cases they intend to use for cases to be helpful.

Managers also need to be able to reflect well to be able to draw out and differentiate the various relevant elements of cases and situations. They need to be able to bridge similarities, draw distinctive differences, and weigh similarities and differences in terms of their relevance to the situation at hand.

Finally, managers need to be able to make shrewd and insightful judgments based on their findings. They need to exercise prudence and, as we saw earlier, this trait is only learned and practiced over an extensive period of time.

In fact, not just prudence, but all of the skills mentioned so far are honed through practice. Their habituation is important because they need to be invoked quickly and rather naturally at opportune times. This means that effective case use relies on managers having two important ancillary characteristics: a good memory and astuteness.

Managers need to have good memories to be able to recall relevant situations and cases of the past. These abilities are possibly the most important elements to effective strategizing and the main reason that seasoned veterans are important to organizations.

Managers also need to be astute to be able to direct their organizations away from unnecessary risks. Astuteness, not unlike prudence, is sharpened with practice until it is habituated. In general those who are regarded as astute tend to be seasoned veterans of the firm who have proven their ability to make wise decisions under different circumstances.

---

[8] It should be noted that there is disagreement over whether true cases must be based *solely* on firsthand experience.

Although it is certainly true that not all senior members of firms are shrewd let alone exceptionally smart or insightful, older and more experienced members of firms tend to be those who have contributed well to the decision making processes of the past. Their historical knowledge, familiarity with past cases, prescience, and proven wise decisions of the past are therefore valuable to the risk management and strategic planning processes of companies.

Problems and Opportunities With Case Use in Business

While case use in business has many advantages, managers do not always have the ability to draw on cases, mainly because they have no effective business casuistry at their disposal. Other significant impediments to effective case use tend to flow from this central deficiency.

Impediments to Case Use in Business

Although there are a number of good search mechanisms to locate cases and today's case warehouses have extensive caches of business-related cases, cases can be rather disparate, not ordered well, and inaccessible.

This stated, it should be noted that locating helpful *law* cases pertinent to business is easy. LexisNexis and Westlaw are two computer-assisted legal research services by which managers can find business-related law cases in which judgments have already been rendered. These cases can be helpful to managers because they are timely and settled, which means they are contemporary and reliably directive.

Law cases can be helpful, too, because they reveal the back and forth of criticisms leading to particular judgments. This enables the user to prepare for the sorts of opposing points he or she might face when taking a similar stance in the present situation.

Nevertheless, law cases can miss critical components of risk exposure. For one, not all legal cases end in clear judgments nor are all elements of legal cases fully disclosed. Sometimes judgments end in confidential settlements and the details of settlements can be, by law, withheld and undisclosed. The McDonald's hot coffee case is a good example of a case in which such a settlement was reached. That settlement's confidentiality meant that important elements of the case remain hidden to others and along with them, one or more potential risk.

In addition, law cases are primarily concerned with compliance or the abridgment of law and are not necessarily bellwethers of social or moral change. This is an important distinction for risk management for at least two reasons. For one, unforeseen risks can simply be related to shifting social or moral customs and not related to a violation of the law.

For another, law, morality, and social customs are separate albeit sometimes overlapping realms. As the disputes over abortion, euthanasia, the death penalty, and gay marriage attest, not everyone agrees with the morality of legal rulings and the social acceptance of customs can change over time.

Second, cases outside of law designated as "business cases" by their authors or case providers can often be difficult to locate. This difficulty has many causes but stems mostly from the inadequate naming, coding, and ordering of cases within case repositories.

Typically, business cases can be located by a search for the name of a company (General Electric, General Motors, Johnson & Johnson, etc.), the products or issues related to a business (R20 light bulbs, hybrid autos, Tylenol, etc.), or some abstract quality related to business operations (sustainability, crony capitalism, corporate responsibility, etc.).

For a case search to be effective, cases must first be named and coded accurately. Key word associations must also be precise; otherwise the cases will remain hidden, undiscoverable, isolated, and dissociated from other relevant cases.

Case isolation can be particularly troublesome for case use because cases are used most effectively in combination. Isolation puts the weight of an argument on a single case rather than a cluster of cases and this can be a problem in situations with a high degree of ambiguity. When pluralism and society's shifting ethical norms are an issue, for example, agreement about the specific tenets of morality can be difficult to settle on and multiple cases can strengthen the defense of a position better than recourse to a single and isolated case.

Third, some aspects of cases are hard to delimit, quantify, and weigh. As we saw in Steps One and Two above, all numbers-based frameworks (statistical analysis, model-based scenario planning, and so forth) depend on quantifiable variables and some aspects of cases are vague. As narratives, cases contain features that can remain as outliers because they cannot be incorporated into numbers-based frameworks. The risks they caution against can therefore also remain largely marginalized, unseen, and become a potential liability to a business. While the problem of overreliance on numbers based approaches will be explored in greater depth in the next chapter, it is important to mention here that it impacts case use significantly.

Fourth, even if cases could be more accurately identified, coded, and collated, the databases themselves are not very accessible to managers. This is due, in part, to marketing decisions that focus efforts on educators and not business managers.

In a rather odd twist, case purveyors seem to be missing an important business-education link in pushing case use with business educators but not with the students who go on to become managers. Today, as a result of these marketing decisions, even those managers who might want to use cases for business planning purposes find cases largely unavailable to them.

Lacking ongoing exposure to cases after graduation, business managers gradually lose an affinity for case use and cases eventually drop out of business strategic planning. This erosion of case use leads in turn to the inevitable narrowing of business strategy to numbers crunching and a greater exposure of businesses to unforeseen risks.

Overcoming the Impediments to Case Use in Business

To offset these problems and to enable managers to locate and apply cases in ways that will allow them to uncover unforeseen risks, managers will need access to a reliable business casuistry. To bring this about, it will be necessary to do the things recommended above, that is, to accurately identify, code, and collate cases and then set these cases in an ordered arrangement according to each case's ability to convey certainty along some predetermined criteria.

Once a case taxonomy has been established, cases must then be made more accessible if business people are to use them. At present, cases are readily available for education purposes, but not for use in business practice.

That cases are used so heavily in education but not very much in practice is curious. It suggests an odd chasm between the two and that educators and practitioners might value cases differently. It also suggests that there is no market for case sales outside of education. Whatever the reason, most managers leave case use behind once they complete their formal education and along with it, leave behind certain skills of interpretation and discernment that can be helpful to uncovering unforeseen risks.

If cases are to be used in business settings, they must be made available to the managers who will use them. Managers, in turn, must be able to trust the reliability of the taxonomy of cases at their disposal and then employ cases in their deliberations. We will cover these issues presently.

Criticisms of Using Ethics as a Tool of Risk Management

Before going on, it should be recognized that not everyone agrees with all of the points made here.[9] In particular, some object to the suggestion that tamoxifen production is to be allowed to go on at all and some criticize the way ethics is used here in risk management.

In regard to the first objection, critics maintain that a company manufacturing an aging drug should stop marketing the pharmaceutical altogether when it has been established that another drug is more effective and/or has fewer side effects.

While this criticism has an initial intuitive appeal, it neglects not only that the drug has passed safety standards and been a significant profit generator for its producers, but that it is one of many therapies that doctors can offer patients.

In this last regard, the critics fail to appreciate the ongoing experimental nature of breast cancer treatment and the frustration that patients and doctors experience in trying to find suitable therapies for particular patients. They fail to account, too, for the fact that sometimes people choose one drug over another—even one with known side effects—because that drug's debilitating side effects are not as bad as

---

[9] My thanks to Society for Business Ethics 2013 Conference reviewer #1 for his or her helpful insights about some of the features of this chapter.

those of other drugs. They disregard as well patient and doctor autonomy and presume that the company should make decisions for users. Finally, they manifest a subtle insensitivity to patients and doctors by overlooking patient drug sensitivity and the trauma of patients as they experiment to find one tolerable drug among many that might stem a dreaded disease.

The second objection to the process outlined here centers on the way ethics is used as a tool in the business decision-making processes. According to this criticism, ethics is portrayed as strictly instrumental—nothing more than a tool—to control risk factors that could threaten a business. In the critics' view, ethics is more deserving than this and should be thought of as valuable in itself. Businesses should simply do the right thing and not regard ethics as just another element to lower risk exposure.

Again, this criticism has an initial appeal but fails on inspection. For one, the objection exalts ethics as something isolated and lofty. While ethics certainly has critical and judgmental qualities that allow it to "rise above" the mundane, it is fundamentally about doing the right thing in real world contexts. It is embedded in actions and not something that stands aloof in some netherworld.

In addition, the criticism is essentially an absolutist deontological objection. The weaknesses of this approach are numerous, have been mentioned in earlier sections of this book, and make the approach untenable for situations that are vague and multifaceted.

Doing the right thing in the context of an aging drug therefore cannot be adequately resolved by means of the application of a vague universal, norm, but rather, by balancing the harms, benefits, social norms, and so forth of each of these embedded aspects of the decision.

Virtue ethics and casuistry capture these aspects of ethics well in that both attempt to make practically wise decisions in the here and now of everyday business decisions.

Going Forward

To recapitulate, in Step One we saw why there is a preference for numbers-based approaches in business strategizing. In Step Two we saw the reasons for attempting to account for the unforeseen risks that can undermine a business. In Step Three we saw how augmenting current practices with case use can benefit companies that need to understand and contain risk exposures that are vague and tied to social and moral norms. Finally, in the last two sections we saw both the impediments to case use and the ways to overcome these obstacles in the practical contexts of business.

What is next and how can the suggestions here be accomplished?

First, managers need to recognize that they might have blind spots in relation to shifting social or moral norms. This acknowledgment is the biggest step for managers to make because it establishes a cautionary mindset in the strategic process. With the recognition of the possibility of unforeseen risks, managers can then proceed to consider the potential outcomes associated with omitting one or more important risk factor in their assessments.

Second, managers must find ways to broaden their perspectives so that potentially damaging moral and social lacunae can be addressed. This is where cases come into play because through cases individuals are encouraged to reflect and consider alternatives (become more prescient,). The narrative basis of cases aids this reflection by stimulating the imagination of users while also cautioning them. It also facilitates the development of new insights and provides direction to users as they attempt to settle on more well-rounded trajectories for business strategy.

Third, managers need to find better ways to access cases. At present, managers have access to law cases, but need better access to the applied ethics and social issues in management cases that are contained in business case repositories. Academicians typically use these cases for andragogical purposes but cases need to be made available to business managers to be truly effective.

As we saw, cases are now mostly used in education for practical reasons. They are written (and purchased) with classroom use in mind and are typically purchased with their educational value in mind by central agencies (academic departments or the library purchasing offices) within institutions.

While this arrangement gives the case provider a consistent revenue stream, provides schools a way to reduce certain materials costs, and gives students lower rates on the cases used in class, it is essentially a dead end process. Students become familiar with instruments that will be inaccessible to them after graduation. They are exposed to cases and a method of using cases that they will never see again because cases will be, for the most part, unavailable to them.

Ultimately, educators need to ask themselves why they use cases in business education without providing the context of case use and why they teach case related skills that their graduates will not be able to put into practice later in life.

Similarly, case providers need to ask themselves why they do not provide better access to products that could be of practical value to business managers. Although there might be good market-based reasons for these discrepancies, the dearth of cases in business practice is lamentable. Without cases, virtue-imbued casuistry cannot get off the ground in business settings.

Fourth and finally, managers must find effective ways to grapple with the unsavory elements of moral and cultural relativism. Cases can be helpful in this regard because their narrative qualities that facilitate better understanding of the nuances of complex situations as well as the different ways people understand the world and interpret circumstances. Such understanding is important because many moral and social lacunae are tied to shifting norms and these, in turn, are tied to demographic changes. The capacity to "read the signs of the times" through narrative-based cases is important for managers as they develop strategies for their companies.

In the end, many of the discrepancies and recommendations mentioned here can be addressed easily, others not so readily. Naming, coding, establishing a case taxonomy, and providing easier access to cases should not prove to be too difficult. Recovering case analytical practices that have gone dormant among active managers should also be achievable, albeit with more resolve.

What is less easy to accomplish is a change in the prevailing perspectives about ethics and case use. If ethics is to be utilized well, it will need to be incorporated deeply and alongside other factors of business practice. It cannot be set outside of everyday activity as some unreachable halo. So, too, if cases are to be used effectively in business practice, then educators and case providers will need to adopt different approaches to cases use and distribution. They will need to reach out to managers as clients and customers.

Until such time, both ethics and case use will be difficult to implement and an effective virtue-imbued casuistry will be hard to establish for business practice.

Chapter 16
Risk Management: Capturing the Right Situation with Prudent Case Use in Scenario-based Modeling

I'm tempted to stop acting randomly. (Adams 2012)
—Dilbert by Scott Adams

The last chapter about whether or not to promote tamoxifen aggressively suggests that accounting for shifting norms is a concern for business strategists, particularly those charged with monitoring risk exposure.

In this chapter, we will see how managers can accommodate risk better by means of a combination of model-based scenario planning and wise case use. We will set aside the tamoxifen issue here and instead concentrate on a fictional case about a company with a critical risk factor.

At the outset it should be mentioned that the use of a hypothetical case diverges from one of the central tenets of the business case method that holds that cases should be accurate recollections of real events. Even so, a hypothetical "mini-case" such as the one presented below provides a naïve decision heuristic for the purpose of illustrating a complex business problem.

The simplicity of the case is based on the assumption that most readers of a text such as this one will be unfamiliar with statistics-driven planning and the deterministic and stochastic modeling often employed there. While some might object to the case's simplicity ("would any reasonably sized organization be this naïve in their planning and decision making processes?"), one need only read the account of the WHO's handling of smallpox in a prior chapter for a real-life example of how organizations can engage naïve planning.[1]

A simple scenario such as the one here is meant to summarize the context and the methods employed in risk management today, illustrate the notions of moral lacunae highlighted already, and argue for the need for prudence and cases in risk management and strategic planning.

Most important, the simple hypothetical case here is meant to spur on others to develop robust cases involving real organizations in real situations.

Dilbert in response to the boss' suggestion that they schedule a scenario-based roundtable discussion about their enterprise project management using the company's infrastructure survey tool to architect a risk-based tiering system.

---

[1] My thanks to Academy of Management 2013 Conference reviewer #3 for his or her helpful insights about this chapter.

M. Calkins, *Developing a Virtue-Imbued Casuistry for Business Ethics,* Issues in Business Ethics 42, DOI 10.1007/978-94-017-8724-6_16, © Springer Netherlands 2014

Coming Full Circle: Cases→Models→Cases

Surprise is the manager's enemy. If something bad happens and the manager has accounted for it, he or she has done his or her job well. But, if s/he has planned and modeled like crazy and finds out later that his or her strategies missed something, s/he is in deep trouble. Avoiding surprises by being on top of the relevant risks, knowing the nature of the moral violations that a business faces, and capturing the right scenarios are central to good planning.

At present, managers rely heavily on analytical tools in risk planning. This orientation has come at a price. On the one hand, it has helped managers bolster their recommendations with numbers, but on the other hand it has left them and their businesses vulnerable to unforeseen forces, including moral violations. Let me explain.

Sliding Toward Numbers

Over the last few decades, businesses have moved to ever-greater reliance on analysis using statistical modeling. As computer use and modeling techniques have become more sophisticated and widespread, business executives have realized verifiable benefits in grounding their plans in computer generated statistics. They therefore sought out number crunchers, the "Calculator Dundees" of graduate business school programs, and increasingly recruited actuaries—experts who use mathematics to quantify contingent outcomes and evaluate the probability of events that pose a risk to businesses.

Today, actuaries are in such demand that they have a near 0 % unemployment rate, making them some of the most sought-after people on the job market (Censky 2012; Weber 2012). They are so valuable to business because they can accomplish "deep" statistical analysis of the risk factors affecting business operations. They can also determine the likelihood of the success or failure of particular plans and policies.

Fixated on limiting their risk exposures and adamant about avoiding the uncertainties that might increase costs, businesses now attempt to construct management teams to have actuaries work alongside strategists to build and use models derived from mathematical analyses.[2]

Companies such as PricewaterhouseCoopers, for example, employ protocols that delineate the various "phases" of risk analysis, breaking it down to identify, isolate, quantify, model and present each aspect of risk exposure (Rodger and Petch 1999). This parsing does not come cheaply as companies have to hire ancillary people to run Monte Carlo simulations and handle pricey add-in software packages such as Crystal Ball.

Even so, risk sensitive companies are increasingly committed to these sorts of analytical approaches. In short, numbers now rule.

---

[2] My thanks to Mark Sioma for insights regarding the use of actuaries in strategic planning in large businesses.

What has been Helpful and What is Missing

As part of many of today's standard analytic processes, analysts construct models that are then used in scenario planning. Scenario planning—a form of forecasting that conjures up hypothetical situations based on the probabilities generated from analysis—enables managers to frame the potential risks that might harm their businesses. In it, scenarios are derived from two sorts of models: deterministic and stochastic.

In most cases, analysts produce deterministic models, but in businesses prone to high risk, they often produce stochastic models that are more complex but able to be "tweaked" to accommodate the informational flux related to economic downtrends, government interventions, natural catastrophes, and so forth. All of these models can then be used to forge plans and policies to keep the company within its acceptable risk exposure limits.

While statistical modeling has many benefits related to variable interaction and the efficiency of operations, its detail and accuracy can lull managers into false complacency. A variation on "garbage in-garbage out," it can manipulate input variables well, but cannot account for unforeseen factors. As a result, the models produced by such analysis can miss important elements that expose the business to risk beyond the business' tolerance.

That strategists miss key elements of the process and fail to account for critical factors because they simply do not see them is troubling. Moberg attributes these lapses to "ethical blind spots" located in common perceptual frames. These, he argues, undermine moral agency. He then offers self-improvement regimens to offset them (Moberg 2006). George Gotsis and Zoe Kortezi focus differently on organizational politics and then explore the interaction of ethics and political behavior in business (Gotsis and Kortezi 2010).

While both of these approaches are helpful to understanding the reasons for critical lacunae in business, they are broad and conceptual and therefore rather difficult for managers to implement in everyday practice.

To remedy this problem, the following suggests the use of cases alongside statistical analysis and modeling in specific strategic planning contexts. In does so by presenting a case about a hypothetical company called Home Health Corporation—a fictional company that faces a specific risk.

Case: Home Health Corporation[3]

Home Health Corporation is a health care provider in Shivers City with a mission to provide high quality home health and end of life (a.k.a palliative) care at prices that are affordable by the city's low-income residents.

---

[3] I am grateful to Eric Pinsoneault for the research and charts related to this case.

Background: Home Health Corporation

As a company, Home Health Corporation has always tried to create a positive work environment for its employees. Its wages and policies were considered fair and it enjoyed a reputation as one of the area's better employers since its founding. At present, it employs a total of 30 people with 20 skilled medical professionals and 10 people on its administrative staff and management and executive teams, including Bob Myers (CEO), Ralph Trabue (CFO), and Margaret Fritz (VP of Human Resources).

Recently, Myers and Trabue met to review the ways the firm compensates its skilled medical staff. They had recently become aware of murmurs of employee discontent and wanted to stem any problems. Because they trusted Fritz' business acumen, the two executives invited her to attend and discuss the various options the company has to keep its costs low while increasing employee satisfaction.

The Big Question: To Pay or Not to Pay for Overtime

For years Home Health Corp.'s skilled medical employees were paid a fixed annual salary and expected to work a 40 hour week with overtime without additional compensation. Recently, however, employees began to balk at the policy. The economy had soured, some of the employees' spouses had lost jobs, and many were finding it harder to make ends meet.

While there had been no disruption of operations, Myers and Trabue were aware of growing employee discontent and wanted to explore whether or not the company should begin to offer additional compensation to medical employees for overtime work. The issue was not entirely clear and could result in substantial additional costs should it be handled poorly.

Myers pointed out the risks to the company in his opening comments, asserting that any new policy to compensate employees for overtime would inevitably increase the cost of the company's operations. These costs, he went on, would have to be passed on as higher prices to customers, thereby adversely affecting many of Home Health Corp.'s low-income clients.

Trabue agreed with Myers but then offered that paying employees for overtime might actually lower the firm's overall costs. The current overtime policy, he maintained, undermines employee morale and encourages employees to think about leaving the company. This not only increases turnover costs, but also leads to additional costs related to recruiting and training new personnel. The combination of high turnover, recruitment, and training, he argued, would dwarf the additional costs related to overtime alone and result in even higher prices to low-income customers.

In a quandary, the two executives decided that they could either (1) continue to require salaried medical employees to work more than 40 hour a week without paying them for overtime or (2) continue to require salaried medical employees to work more than 40 hour a week but pay them additional compensation for work beyond 40 hour a week.

Table 16.1 Annual Turnover Given the Average Number of Overtime Hours Worked Annually (Average)

Average number of overtime hours worked per year	Average number of medical personnel who leave per year
None	2
10 h per week	5
20 h per week	9
30 h per week	12

To get a better sense of how they should proceed, they asked Fritz to research the options and prepare an executive report as soon as possible.

The Deterministic Approach

Having a clear task before her, Fritz ferreted out the data on the number of overtime hours worked as well as the turnover rates of the salaried medical employees over the past 25 years. In doing so, she found that the average number of annual overtime hours that skilled medical staff worked varied significantly over 25 years. In several years, employees worked an average of 70 hour a week (for a total of 31,200 hour of overtime annually) while in other years employees worked no overtime at all.

Fritz also noticed that the turnover among employees seemed to fluctuate based on the number of overtime hours they worked in a given year. She therefore separated the data into two categories based on the average number of overtime hours worked and the average level of staff turnover and constructed Table 16.1.

Next, Fritz began to inspect the company's payroll records. There she found that the firm now has a total of 20 skilled medical employees who are paid on average $ 15 an hour based on their annual salaries. Should the company decide to pay these people 10 hour of overtime a week annually, she reasoned, the cost to the company would be $ 156,000 per year (20 employees × 10 hours a week × 52 weeks × $ 15 an hour = $ 156,000 per year in overtime).

Because the figure for overtime seemed high, Fritz decided to compare straight overtime costs against the costs for recruitment and training. Perhaps, she thought, it would be less costly to let disgruntled employees quit and hire and train new people.

Fritz dug a bit more through the personnel files and found that the hiring and training costs to replace a skilled medical employee who left the company amounted to $ 40,000 on average. While helpful, she knew that this figure told only part of the story because the costs to the company could vary wildly based on the number of people who left the company in any given year. Fritz knew, too, that she had to first estimate the turnover rate of employees before she could go ahead with comparisons.

In inspecting the data further, Fritz found that the average level of turnover that occurred when medical personnel work no overtime is 2. She then assumed that any turnover above 2 would be associated directly with the number of overtime hours

Table 16.2 Cost of Paying Employees for Overtime Versus not Paying Employees for Overtime

Average number of overtime hours worked per year	Cost associated with paying employees for overtime hours worked	Cost associated with employee turnover resulting from unpaid overtime hours
None	$ 0	$ 0
10 h per week	$ 156,000	$ 120,000
20 h per week	$ 312,000	$ 280,000
30 h per week	$ 468,000	$ 400,000

that employees worked. Next, she calculated the cost of turnover as a result of unpaid overtime based on an average of 10 hour of overtime a week and found that the cost to the company was $ 120,000:

- 5 employees − 2 employees = 3 employees
- 3 employees @ $ 40,000 per employee = $ 120,000 per year

Fritz then constructed Table 16.2.

Then, she plotted her findings on the graph Table 16.3.

Fritz concluded at this point that paying Home Health Corp.'s medical employees for overtime would be more expensive than incurring the costs associated with employee turnover related to unpaid overtime.

Confident in her assessment, she forwarded her findings to Myers and Trabue and scheduled a meeting to strategize further.

The Upset of a New Competitor

When Fritz arrived at the strategy meeting, she noticed that Myers and Trabue appeared concerned. It quickly became apparent why—a major national health care provider had just announced plans to open an operation in the city and everyone knew that this would affect the labor market for skilled medical personnel. Trabue as CFO was especially concerned because, depending on the overtime policies and salaries offered by the new health care provider, the presence of a new competitor would drive up the cost of compensation, increase staff turnover, and threaten the profitability of the company.

Fritz took the news with alarm because she realized that the new information added a dimension of uncertainty that was not accounted for in her model. After asking for more time to refine her estimates, she dug for more information but found that her company had no historical data on the affect of a new competitor on wages and turnover. She then decided to look outside of the organization for information.

One of her professional contacts directed her to a number of cases about the effect of competition and labor prices on small and mid-sized businesses. Reading

Table 16.3 Graphs—Cost of Paying Employees for Overtime Versus not Paying Employees for Overtime

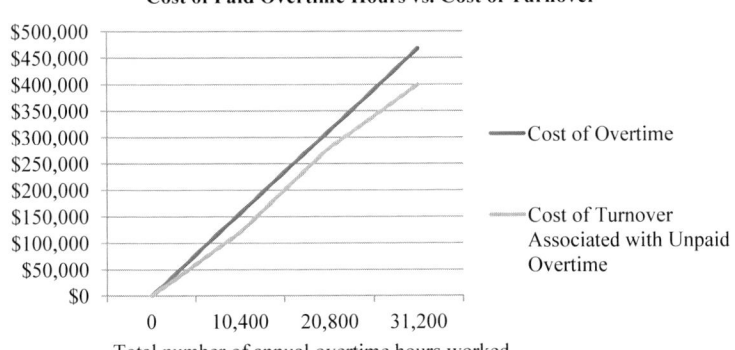

through them, she found that although they were not always directly related to her small company's context, some of them were helpful in highlighting important operational facts about the health care industry that she had not previously considered. These included the fact that:

- In most regional health care markets, the entry of a new competitor typically drives up the wages of skilled healthcare professionals by 2–10%.
- In most regional health care markets, the entry of a new competitor increases the cost of recruiting and training a new healthcare professional by 3–25%.
- There is no information about whether or not the amount of unpaid overtime hours that employees are willing to work changes as new competitors enter the market.

The Stochastic Approach

Despite the vagueness of some of her findings, Fritz realized that Home Health Corp.'s medical employees would likely have more options and bargaining power should a new employer enter the company's market. Employees would also be less willing to work overtime without additional pay. In fact, her findings indicated that the number of employees who would quit as a result of unpaid overtime would increase by 0–2 employees once the new competitor entered the market.

Fritz realized, too, that the new information she gleaned from cases would upset her prior assumptions and the accuracy of the deterministic models that she had constructed. She knew that she would have to redo her models to make them more nuanced, better able to cover a wider range of possibilities, and more appropriate for scenario planning.

Having previously worked for a large insurance firm, Fritz knew about the powerful computer generated modeling programs that helped managers develop more

Table 16.4 Annual Turnover Given the Average Number of Overtime Hours Worked Annually (Range)

Average number of overtime hours worked per year	Average number of medical personnel who leave per year
None	2–4
10 h per week	5–7
20 h per week	9–11
30 h per week	12–14

accurate scenarios. While she did not have access to the same computer programs, she knew enough about them to develop a simpler version that might guide her choices. Accordingly, she developed a stochastic model to accommodate certain random variables and to give a wider range of possibilities than her earlier deterministic models. She also modified her previous assumptions in light of the following new information gleaned from cases involving other companies (Table 16.4):

- That with a new competitor, the average cost per hour of overtime for a healthcare worker will be between $ 15.30 and 16.50.
- That with a new competitor, the average cost to recruit and train a new healthcare worker will be between $ 41,200 and 50,000.
- That with a new competitor, the likelihood that healthcare workers will leave as a result of working unpaid hours of overtime increases.

In combination, the new information above and Fritz' new modeling method enabled her to construct Table 16.4 that illustrates the number of skilled medical employees who will likely quit Home Health Corp. in relation to the number of overtime hours they are required to work.

By randomly assigning values to the variables in the Table and calculating the various costs associated with paying healthcare personnel for overtime hours, Fritz' new stochastic model could now accommodate many more possible outcomes that might occur should a new competitor enter the Corporation's market.

Fritz decided to test the model by letting the computer generate a random hourly wage of $ 16.20 per hour, random costs of $ 46,000 associated with recruitment and training and using random variables and turnover rates (see Table 16.5):

She was then able to forge a different set of general costs for employee overtime. She assumed that personnel worked an average of 10 hour of overtime per week annually to derive the following equation:

20 employees × 10 hours a week × 52 weeks × $ 16.20 an hour = $ 168,480 per year

Next, she determined the annual cost of turnover in a year in which healthcare professionals work an average of 10 hour of overtime a week:

- 6 employees − 3 employees = 3 employees
- 3 employees × $ 46,000 = $ 138,000

Table 16.5 Annual Turnover Given the Average Number of Overtime Hours Worked Annually (Random)

Average number of overtime hours worked per year	Average number of medical personnel who leave per year
None	3
10 h per week	6
20 h per week	10
30 h per week	14

Table 16.6 Cost of Paying Employees for Overtime Versus Cost of not Paying Employees for Overtime

Average number of overtime hours worked annually	Cost associated with paying employees for overtime hours worked	Cost associated with employee turnover resulting from unpaid overtime hours
10 h per week	$ 168,480	$ 138,000
	$ 171,600	$ 180,800
	$ 160,680	$ 148,800
	$ 166,920	$ 230,000
	$ 163,800	$ 226,000
20 h per week	$ 336,960	$ 322,000
	$ 343,200	$ 361,600
	$ 321,360	$ 347,200
	$ 333,840	$ 368,000
	$ 327,600	$ 361,600
30 h per week	$ 505,440	$ 506,000
	$ 514,800	$ 497,200
	$ 482,040	$ 496,000
	$ 500,760	$ 460,000
	$ 491,400	$ 452,000

She then ran a total of five scenarios. The results can be seen in Table 16.6.

Fritz then plotted the results on a graph in Table 16.7.

At the end of the statistical run, Fritz noticed that her assessment changed when she took into account the case-based information about the effects of new competition in regional markets for health care services.

Through her stochastic modeling, selective use of cases, and wise application of certain assumptions, Fritz had confirmed that demand for health professionals would be higher in her regional market and that it would be more cost effective to pay employees for overtime hours insofar as healthcare employees work an average of 10 or 20 hour of overtime a week. At the same time, however, she determined that it would still be more cost effective to not pay employees for overtime hours if employees work an average of 30 hour of overtime a week. In short, through incorporating the information she derived from cases and adopting a more sophisticated modeling technique, Fritz derived a more comprehensive understanding of the financial risks that her company now faced.

Table 16.7 Graphs—Cost of Paying Employees for Overtime Versus Cost of not Paying Employees for Overtime

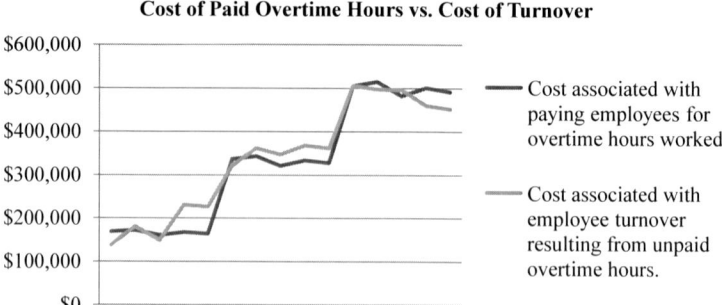

Armed with these more nuanced findings, Fritz called Myers and Trabue for another meeting to discuss paying for employee overtime[4].

Strategy and Modeling

The Home Health Corp. case highlights the different modeling methods used in strategizing as well as the link between input assumptions and the effectiveness and distinctiveness of various analytical methods. It also shows how cases can be important and why wisdom is crucial to selecting the right elements in cases for effective modeling and strategic planning.

In the following, we will explore the details of the processes highlighted above, that is, the nature of strategy, the two main modeling methods used in risk assessment, and the importance of cases and wisdom in selecting measurement variables.

Strategy as a Guiding Process

To begin, strategy is often focused on data analysis, but at its core strategy is not an analytical process. Although it often benefits from methods such as the deterministic and stochastic modeling, it is fundamentally an interpretive process dependent upon wise individuals.

As described by Jeremy Kourdi, strategy is "the plans, choices and decisions used to guide a company to greater profitability and success."[5] It is a planning and guiding process that explains the underpinnings of the present, the advantages of

---

[4] I would like to thank David Thibeault for his fine research assistance in regard to strategy and stochastic modeling.

[5] (Kourdi 2009, p. 3). For other good descriptions of business strategy, see (Campbell et al. 2002, pp. 14–15; Freeman and Boeker 1984, pp. 73–86; Kaplan and Norton 2004; Mintzberg, 1987,

actions of the past, and the likelihood of future outcomes, trends, and events associated with a decision.

In business, effective strategizing requires individuals to have broad financial and economic backgrounds, specific quantitative skills, and access to and facility with specialized technical tools. In particular, good strategy depends on strategists having a broad understanding of economic theory and trends, a historical sense of markets, experience with a wide range of business situations, an ability to interpret financial documents, up-to-date information on government and political maneuverings, and an ability to use and troubleshoot the sophisticated computer programs that produce models. In short, strategists need to be history buffs, economic geeks, quant jocks, political junkies, and computer nerds—able to read the signs of the times broadly and in terms of their organizations.

Managers involved in strategic planning also need to be familiar (if not facile themselves) with computer software instruments and, in some high risk and uncertainty prone businesses such as financial investment and insurance, software specific to their industry or business that helps individuals identify, measure, monitor, direct, and control risk. In banking, for example, industry-specific software helps strategists track and assess capital adequacy. In insurance, software programs help strategists determine risk tolerance as well as the degree (or rate) of risk exposure. In both industries, specialized computer software programs assist strategists to demarcate, monitor, and control price decisions, authority distribution, reporting, and communication. Information is then used to manipulate variables to produce models that are interpreted as scenarios and used as a basis of discussion in strategizing.

Strategists also need to be familiar with at least two general sorts of modeling processes: descriptive and stochastic modeling. For most business strategizing, descriptive modeling suffices, but as in the case above, at certain times the more intricate stochastic modeling process is preferred.[6]

Descriptive Modeling: A Two-dimensional Snapshot

Descriptive modeling (also known as deterministic modeling) is the most common sort and is called *descriptive* because the models it produces illustrate or describe

---

pp. 11–24, 1994, pp. 23; Parthasarthy 2007, pp. 5–13; Porter 1980, p. 4, pp. 34–38; Quinn 1980, pp. 7–9; Williamson et al. 2004, p. 145).

[6] Herbert Maisel et al describe the difference between descriptive and stochastic modeling as follows: "A system may be regarded either as deterministic or stochastic, depending upon the casual relationship between input and output. The output of a deterministic system can be predicted completely if the input at the initial state of the system are known. That is, for a particular state of the system, a given input always leads to the same output. However a stochastic system in a given state may respond to a given input with any one among a range or distribution of outputs. For a stochastic system—given the input and the state of the system—it is possible to predict only the range within which the output will fall and the frequency with which various particular outputs will be obtained over many repetitions of the observation." (Maisel and Gnugnoli 1972, pp. 13–14).

one aspect of a business' activity. It is also *deterministic* because the models reflect the predetermined relationship of the variables assigned to the model.

In descriptive/deterministic modeling one variable is framed in terms of its relationship to one or more other variables. In this way, the relationship of the variables is predetermined and the outcome is static. The models are helpful in capturing the relational association of elements as roadmaps do, that is, they provide an image of the relationships of variables that can help establish a trajectory from point A to point B in a set linear way.

Descriptive models capture movement in the way a snapshot does. They convey the idea of movement without having dynamism of their own. The relationship of variables is caught and frozen and then used in analysis. They are two-dimensional and static in that the relationship of variables does not change from that established at the outset. Change is simply simulated through modification of the data, not the modification of the variables' relationships.

Descriptive models are good at depicting causal arrangements, organizational structures, networks, and other features related to a firm, industry, or system in which the firm is embedded. They paint a picture of the firm at a particular point in time and are suggestive of trajectories.

Profit and loss statements are good examples of descriptive models. Essentially static in representation, they show what has happened in the past to profits as assets gained value or liabilities increased/decreased. They are prognostic only insofar as the business continues on course and the relationship of variables (not to be confused with the amounts) do not change. In P and L statements as in all descriptive models, the variable relationships are predetermined.

Descriptive/deterministic models are helpful to business as a tool to frame important causal relationships. They are not so helpful, however, in capturing the dynamism of many business situations because their two-dimensional representations can overly simplify complex business realities. Put another way, they are good at capturing particular aspects of business for narrow scrutiny, but their stasis and rigidity can blind managers to the business' breadth, complexity, nuance, and fluidity.

Stochastic Modeling: A Three-dimensional Hologram

As we saw in the case above, deterministic models can produce accurate depictions of what happens when variables track in a predetermined way, but they cannot accommodate randomness. For this, stochastic modeling is useful.

Stochastic modeling (derivative of the Greek *stochazesthai* to aim at or guess at) is a process based on at least one random variable so as to capture the uncertainty and probability associated with a situation. Jayanta Sarma Kakoty describes stochastic modeling as follows:

> The meaning of stochastic is directly related to random variable. A stochastic model is a simulation model for estimating probability distribution of potential outcomes by using the random variation in one or more inputs over time. The random variation is nothing but the

fluctuations of observed historical data by using time series techniques. Distributions of potential outcomes are based on generating large number of data (i.e., simulations) which reflect the random variation in the inputs. A mathematical model consists of an objective function (a mathematical expression which is to be maximized or minimized) and the constraints or restrictions. Business decision making is always affected by some environmental factors which are controllable or uncontrollable. Controllable inputs are generally specified. If the uncontrollable inputs are uncertain and subject to variation, the model is referred to as stochastic or probabilistic model.[7]

When represented, stochastic models sometimes appear conical or parabolic in shape—three-dimensional and fluid as opposed to two-dimensional and map-like, as descriptive models tend to be. Although the stochastic chart in the case above was flat, had it been on a computer screen rather than paper, it would have appeared as a hologram and the shape within the parameters could have been changed with a cursor. Each new shape could then be framed as a scenario and thereby tell a story about what might happen should variables act in the manner depicted.

Because of their ability to capture randomness and change, stochastic models are more complex but better suited to representing highly changeable and risky situations. Consequently they are favored in banking and finance. A number of researchers, (Aït-Sahalia and Kimmel 2007; Barakat and Terry 2010) for example, have shown how they are used in risk management while others (Lin 2006; Ortega and Escudero 2010; Robinson 2001) have shown their broad use in finance and insurance contexts. In specific applications, some (Amendola et al. 2000; Ermoliev et al. 2008; Giebel and Rainer 2011; Marhavilas and Koulouriotis 2011; Regnier 2008; Schmidt and Simmons 2004; Wüthrich and Merz 2008) have detailed aspects of their use in the insurance industry's catastrophic risk assessments. Similarly, (Albrecher et al. 2009; Barnhill Jr. and Maxwell 2002; Grundke 2004; McLeish 2005; Natcheva-Acar et al. 2009) have illustrated their use within certain applications within banking and finance.

In general business practice, stochastic modeling facilitates continuous strategy or portfolio rebalancing by showing how each variable influences one or more other variables and how the entire mix of variables can fluctuate as random variables change over time. This helps to advance an understanding of certain features of markets, economies, governments, and events as well as the fluidity of the business environment.

Such knowledge can, of course, be a powerful planning tool as it can highlight the ongoing changes that businesses face as well as how widely diverse inputs, often sourced in deeply embedded complex interrelationships, can impact a business' future. It can also reveal the synergies of variables as they modify, moderate, or intensify as they come into contact with each other, leaving high-risk businesses vulnerable to serendipitous catastrophe.

---

[7] (Kakoty 2011, p. 29). Kakoty goes on to explain: "A stochastic model is used for simulating the evolution of finite populations. It consists of stochastic algorithm which controls the generation of each individual according to the life cycle model. The life cycle consists of production of outputs by randomly picking origin(s)" (Kakoty 2011, p. 30).

At the same time, however, stochastic models are limited by the same set up problems of deterministic models. Despite their ability to capture randomness, they are limited by the nature of the variables within the construct. In other words, they can capture randomness within a broad range, but not the randomness of life. They are sophisticated and expensive to produce, but limited to the variables set down at the outset. In short, they cannot capture elements outside the parameters of the model any more than deterministic models can. Overreliance on them therefore enhances the likelihood that the user will miss key elements not contained in them and be blindsided by outside events.

Strategic Prescience

While the parameters of modeling are a concern, a greater problem with overreliance on models is the tendency to assume that the past will be repeated. In reality, it is rarely replicated intact. History must be interpreted to be useful and, as we will see next, the thrust of strategy is not to dwell on past judgments but to use aspects of the past and elements of the present to plan for the future.

Strategy in business' purpose is generally to "guide (the) company to greater profitability and success" (Kourdi 2009, p. 3). This means that the thrust of strategy there is forward and not backward. It is future directed and so depends upon the prescience or forethought of strategists.

While the topic of prescience is all but untreated by scholars, it is crucial to effective strategic business management.

Prescience is an active thought process where one considers what might happen in the future. As a mental exercise, it uncovers the underlying aspects of what is at hand through an initial exercise of imagination. It rests on imagination or the formation of an image because, as Aristotle explains in *De Anima*, "the soul never thinks without an image" and "the faculty of thinking… thinks the forms in the images."[8]

Prescience is an act of partially removing oneself from the immediate hubbub to reflect upon the present situation and its potential. It is an act of discernment where one ferrets out the essence of a situation (its form), the various aspects of the situation, and the relationships of the parts to the whole.

In the context of business strategy, prescience is key to scenario-based planning because that sort of planning relies on flexible long-term thinking. Accordingly, it requires strategists to be able to apply strong contemplative and deliberative skills to practical situations. This means that strategists must be able to think non-linearly and draw out the causal relationships between factors so as to spot the underlying issue of a situation, assess its implications now and in the future, and then plan in a way that protects and serves the best interests of the client.

---

[8] Again, as Aristotle explains in full: "To the thinking soul images serve as if they were contents of perception (and when it asserts or denies them to be good or bad it avoids or pursues them). That is why the soul never thinks without an image" (Aristotle 1928). For more, see (Lowe 1983).

The Importance of Prudence in Case Selection

Good strategy and effective scenario-based analysis demand that managers be shrewd, insightful, have a good memory, and be capable of bridging (or drawing distinctive differences among) experiences. In short, strategists must be practically wise and able to reflect, discern, and make good choices.

Prudent Elders as Key to Effective Strategy

As we saw in the virtue sections of this book, the capacity to discern wisely is a key component of virtue ethics. Prudence or *phronēsis*—the characteristic habit of deliberating well about what is good and advantageous for oneself in practical affairs—is also a key component of strategic planning.

Typically, prudence is exercised by people with good historical retention, those who have experience and can bring that experience as well as cases of success and failure in the past at appropriate times. These prudent figures, often veterans of the company, are able to quickly discern the crux of an issue and frame it in terms of past experiences. They are also able to interpret sophisticated stochastic models in terms of what they convey and omit in terms of other similar scenarios.

The input of veterans, prudent elders or "older wise guys," is perhaps the most critical component of even the most sophisticated statistics and model driven forms of strategic business planning today.

The Importance of Business Cases in Strategizing

While the input of practical wisdom is important, wise people need something on which to build their arguments. Cases are therefore helpful content sources. As we saw in Ms. Fritz' situation in the case above, access to relevant cases is an important element of effective strategic planning.

Why is this so, that is, what do cases bring to bear on decision making?

As we saw in the casuistry sections in the earlier part of this book, cases capture the complex human interactions at work in a given situation by distilling and synthesizing the seemingly disparate components that comprise an event into a compelling narrative that acts as both an action-drama and a fable. These qualities make them accessible and convincing because they distill complex motives and reasons to an easy to understand format. Their ability to convey a story enables them to stir the imagination yet remain focused on particular concrete problems. This makes cases helpful in moderating the narrow analytical modeling processes of strategic planning.

In the Home Health Corp. case, we can see how models capture and manipulate data effectively but often leave out important information crucial to effective strategizing. The prudent use of cases can therefore overcome this limit and enable strategists like Ms. Fritz to make better judgments and recommendations.

Complications Inhibiting Case Use in Business

The Home Health Corp. case illustrates many of the impediments to case integration explored in prior chapters. As we can saw here, although the introduction of cases in strategic planning seems simple and straightforward, several practical issues can hamper their implementation.

First, the Home Health Corp. case revealed the practical difficulties of case implementation in strategizing. Ms. Fritz had to go searching for appropriate cases because cases were difficult to locate and a good case taxonomy was not available.

Not unlike the situation of the aging drug in the prior chapter, relevant cases were not readily apparent. Cases were not labeled effectively and as a result cases were isolated and disconnected.

While it is true that cases are not hidden, sometimes labeled well, and that many large case providers identify and categorize cases adequately, cases are often not apparent or very accessible to users. Cases are typically named according to broad concepts, narrow academic disciplines, or specific products or issues. They are, as examples, justice, human rights, or sustainability cases. Alternatively, they are marketing cases, accounting cases, or medical products cases. Sometimes they are cases about specific products or issues such as R20 light bulbs, windmills, Prius cars, and so forth.

As a result, cases are pigeonholed in ways that leave them unreachable by those not already familiar with them. In the Home Health Corp. case, Ms. Fritz had to use personal contacts and her own sleuthing skills to locate relevant cases because there was no accessible taxonomy of cases.

Second, the Home Health Corp. case revealed the difficulty of assigning variables to aspects of cases so they can be incorporated into statistical analysis and modeling.

As we saw, risk management today is based on scenarios derived by means of statistics and deterministic and stochastic modeling. The inability to assign quantifiers to important aspects of cases therefore makes cases nearly impossible to integrate into today's modeling processes.

Just as it is difficult to quantify a quality, so it is hard to isolate and weigh aspects of cases for eventual inclusion in statistics-driven models. While this problem will likely never be adequately resolved, unless there is some attempt to delimit case features, cases will remain marginalized from strategic processes.

Third, the Home Health Corp. case illustrated the value of short, simple, and hypothetical mini cases to strategy. Although it was not a typical business case of the sort described in the business case method in previous chapters of this book, it served to introduce terms that are unfamiliar to most readers. The challenge now is to develop more sophisticated cases that capture the full complexity of real business strategy decisions for deeper analysis.

Fourth and finally, the Home Health Corp. case highlighted the importance of prudence in strategic planning. Ms. Fritz repeatedly exercised practical wisdom in determining when and how to use both models and cases in planning. Her ability to reflect, discern, and compare the current situation to other similar ones of the past enabled her to locate previously unforeseen risks that contributed to discussions about Home Health Corp.'s risk exposure.

Chapter 17
Going Forward: Developing a Workable Virtue-imbued Casuistry for Business

The End
This is the end
Beautiful friend
This is the end
My only friend, the end
Of our elaborate plans, the end
Of everything that stands, the end
No safety or surprise, the end

—The Doors, written by Jim Morrison

The approach taken in *Developing a Virtue-imbued Casuistry for Business Ethics* has been unconventional but also charted new ground in moral theory and business practice.

What has Been Done

Part 1 attempted to revive interest in casuistry by explaining its long and varied history and by comparing it to other moral methods. The value of narrative-based cases in decision-making was established here and was applied in the examples in the last part of the book.

Part 2 explained virtue ethics, in particular the virtue theory of Aristotle and its adaptation by those who followed him. Prudence, the *phronimos-protégé* relationship, moral prescience, and other moral laden concepts were highlighted and drawn upon in later application sections of the book.

Part 3 brought the first two parts of the book together to show that the concepts there not only overlap, but also dovetail in a way that creates a synergy when used in combination. This section also compared and contrasted casuistry to the business case method. In both of these ways, the book not only bridged methods but also broke new ground in theory.

Part 4 applied virtue-imbued casuistry to select areas of business. The first chapter of the section showed how the method can be employed in disputes over genetically modified food products to break stalemates borne of ideological entrenchments. It

M. Calkins, *Developing a Virtue-Imbued Casuistry for Business Ethics,* Issues in Business Ethics 42, DOI 10.1007/978-94-017-8724-6_17, © Springer Netherlands 2014

also illustrated the importance of remaining in concrete cases while maintaining the aspirational qualities of *telos*/virtue-based perspectives when problem solving.

The second chapter of Part 4 considered two initiatives involving deadly diseases (polio and smallpox) to show how a case about a past circumstance can inform and caution in a present one. This chapter also underscored the complexity of overlapping stakeholder interests, the importance of delineating clear lines of authority, the need for vigilance against malevolence, and the value of steadfast prudence in policymaking.

The final two chapters of Part 4 illustrated the ways virtue-imbued casuistry can aid in risk management through drawing attention to the unforeseen moral hazards that can ruin a business.

The chapter on an approved but aging drug showed how managers need to be aware of their potential blind spots in regard to shifting moral and social norms and work to moderate their inclination to rely too heavily on statistics-driven modeling techniques.

The chapter that followed the drug-based chapter expanded on the specific processes of today's risk management to show how different sorts of statistics-based models are constructed and used. The idea of doing so, as in prior chapters, is to show how current practices can be augmented significantly with virtue-imbued casuistry.

What Remains to be Done

While *Developing a Virtue-imbued Casuistry for Business Ethics* has delved into a number of theoretical and practical fine points, much more work remains to be done. It is, as the title indicates, a process in development.

First, ethicists will need to develop a workable business casuistry. They will need to develop cases, explain the moral content of cases, and make judgments in the cases. Unlike typical business cases, the cases in casuistry are settled and so ethicists will have to take a stand and make judgments in cases. They will then have to name and weigh cases according to some set of moral criteria. To do so, they will have to work with case providers to identify, code, and collate cases effectively.

Second, law cases need to be augmented with business cases for greater effectiveness in business application. As we saw, law cases can be helpful to business managers because they are timely, settled, reliably directive, and able to convey the back and forth of criticisms leading to particular judgments. Computer-assisted legal research services such as LexisNexis and Westlaw are also especially useful to managers. Even so, law cases have limited use in business management and managers need cases specific to business. Developing a business case cache similar to that of law and then bringing the two together in a more integrated and accessible way would aid case use in business management a great deal.

Third, case providers need to provide business managers with better access to relevant cases. As we have seen, case purveyors are missing an important business-education link in pushing case use in business education but failing to keep up with business school graduates who go on to become managers. Today, even those managers who might want relevant cases for business planning purposes find cases largely unavailable. Until cases are made both available and readily accessible to managers, cases will not be used and virtue-imbued casuistry will not be employed satisfactorily in business practice.

Fourth, business managers need to be aware of their moral lacunae. As we saw, blind spots in regard to shifting social and moral norms can only be uncovered by means of discernment and reflection. Although such traits are not always of obvious value to firms, perspicacity with an eye on the objectives of the firm is essential to containing the business' risk exposure. Thus, businesses and managers alike will benefit from the greater exercise of moral prescience, prudence, and case use within firms.

Fifth, managers and businesses need to acknowledge and support various formal and informal mentoring (*phronimos-protégé*) relationships within firms. While these relationships are mainly friendship-based, they can benefit organizations by helping to infuse them with needed prudence and thereby limit unnecessary risk exposure to the firm.

Sixth, business ethicists, risk managers, and case providers need to work together to develop sophisticated cases that capture the full complexity of real business strategy decisions for deeper analysis. The Home Health Corp. case at the end of the book shows how a short, simple, and hypothetical mini case can highlight the value of prudence, foresight, and case use to risk management and strategy as a whole. The next step will be to develop more robust business cases along these lines for use in both academia and business practice.

In the end, *Developing a Virtue-imbued Casuistry for Business Ethics* addressed Cromwell's "use it or lose it" observation about moral entropy by exploring new ways of doing business ethics in specific contexts. The next step is for managers to figure out how to apply some of the ideas about morality here within the contexts of their day-to-day business practices.

Appendix

Table 30: List of Quotes

- **Overview**:

"Let us endeavour, then, to think well;
this is the principle of morality."[1]
–Blaise Pascal

"He who stops being better
stops being good."
–Oliver Cromwell

- **Chapter 1**: Casuistry's Features and History

"Writing intellectual history
is like trying to nail jelly to the wall."
–attributed to William Hesseltine

- **Chapter 2**: Casuistry versus Ethical Pluralism with Applied Principles

"You always admire
what you really don't understand."
–Blaise Pascal

- **Chapter 3**: Normativity and Analogy in Casuistry

"It is the weight, not numbers of experiments that is to be regarded."[2]
–Isaac Newton

- **Chapter 4**: The Role of Principles in Casuistry

"The pure and simple truth is rarely pure and never simple."[3]
–Oscar Wilde

---

[1] (Pascal 1958, p. 347).

[2] (Povinelli 2012, p. xvi).

[3] (Wilde 2005, p. 12). The full quote is: "Algernon. The truth is rarely pure and never simple. Modern life would be very tedious if it were either, and modern literature a complete impossibility!".

M. Calkins, *Developing a Virtue-Imbued Casuistry for Business Ethics,* Issues in Business
Ethics 42, DOI 10.1007/978-94-017-8724-6, © Springer Netherlands 2014

- **Chapter 5**: Reflective Equilibrium and Casuistry
  "People are usually more convinced by reasons
  they discovered themselves
  than by those found by others."
  –attributed to *Blaise Pascal*

- **Chapter 6**: Criticisms of Casuistry
  "A bad carpenter quarrels with his tools"
  (Japanese: こうぼうふでをえらばず, Koukou fude o erabazu)
  –Japanese proverb

- **Chapter 7**: Casuistry's Revival
  "History doesn't repeat itself—
  at best it sometimes rhymes."
  –attributed to *Mark Twain*

- **Chapter 8**: Aristotle's Virtue Ethics
  "Different men seek after happiness
  in different ways
  and by different means,
  and so make for themselves
  different modes of life."[4]
  –Aristotle

- **Chapter 9**: Other Virtue Theories and Applications to Business
  "Ability will enable a man to get to the top,
  but character will keep him from falling."
  –Chinese Proverb

- **Chapter 10**: Virtue Ethics' Value
  "Watch your thoughts for they become words.
  Watch your words for they become actions.
  Watch your actions for they become habits.
  Watch your habits, for they become your character.
  And watch your character, for it becomes your destiny.
  What we think we become."
  –Margaret Thatcher (played by Meryl Streep) in "The Iron Lady"[5]

- **Chapter 11**: Establishing Virtue-imbued Casuistry: A Synergy of Methods
  "Synergy: A Code Word Lazy People Use
  When They Want You to Do All the Work."[6]
  –Demotivator by Despair, Inc.

- **Chapter 12**: Casuistry and the Business Case Method
  "Coming together is a beginning;
  keeping together is progress;
  working together is success."
  –attributed to Henry Ford

---

[4] (Aristotle 2009a, per p. 73

[5] (Lloyd 2011).

[6] (Despair 2012).

- **Chapter 13**: Breaking Stalemates: Using the Method to Upset the Genetically Modified Foods Impasse

  "Up till now I always thought bickering
  was just something children did and they outgrew it.
  Of course, there's sometimes a reason to have a 'real' quarrel,
  but the verbal exchanges that take place here
  are just plain bickering."
  –Anne Frank (Frank, 2010, 42)

- **Chapter 14**: Cases Can Caution: Smallpox, Polio, and Managing Risk Exposure

  "...no man dared to count his children as his own until they had
  had the disease."
  –Comte de la Condamine
  18th century mathematician and scientist referring to smallpox
  (Shors 2011, p. 130)

- **Chapter 15**: Managing the Risks of an Aging Medication: The Case for Cases

  "It is better by noble boldness to run the risk of being subject to half the evils we anticipate than
  to remain in cowardly listlessness for fear of what might happen."[7]
  –Herodotus

- **Chapter 16**: Capturing the Right Scenarios with Prudent Case Use in Modeling

  "I'm tempted to stop acting randomly."
  (Dilbert in response to the boss' suggestion that they schedule a scenario-based roundtable
  discussion about their enterprise project management using the company's infrastructure survey
  tool to architect a risk-based tiering system.) (Adams 2012)
  –Scott Adams

- **Chapter 17**: What's Next

  The End
  This is the end
  Beautiful friend
  This is the end
  My only friend, the end
  Of our elaborate plans, the end
  Of everything that stands, the end
  No safety or surprise, the end
  –The Doors, written by Jim Morrison

---

[7] (Herodotus 1890). The quote here is a summary of the following: "It is better to have good courage about everything and to suffer half the evils which threaten, than to have fear beforehand about everything and not to suffer any evil at all: and if, while contending against everything which is said, thou omit to declare the course which is safe, thou dost incur in these matters the reproach of failure equally with him who says the opposite to this. This then, I say, is evenly balanced: but how should one who is but man know the course which is safe? I think, in no way. To those then who choose to act, for the most part gain is wont to come; but to those who reckon for everything and shrink back, it is not much wont to come."

References

105th Congress 1997–1998. 1998. Iraq Liberation Act of 1998. H.R.4655.ENR. City of Washington.

Abbas, Hassan. *Ulema versus Ijtihad: Understanding the nature of the crisis in the Muslim world.* The Fletcher School—Tufts University, 2004. http://209.85.141.104/search?q=cache:bstpW97P-CgJ:fletcher.tufts.edu/al_nakhlah/archives/fall2004/abbas.pdf+%22closing+of+the+gates+of+Ijtihad%22&hl=en&ct=clnk&cd=2&gl=us&client=firefox-a. Accessed 18 July 2008.

Abell, Derek. 1997. What makes a good case? *ECCHO: The newsletter of the European case clearing house.* Autumn/Fall 4–7.

Acambis, PLC. 2001. *Acambis wins second smallpox vaccine contract* (28 November 2001). http://www.acambis.com/cfm/index.cfm?cvar=3news2&news_id=141506463. Accessed 7 May 2002.

Adams, Scott. 2012. *Dilbert 2013 day-to-day calendar: I'd like to thank all of you for your utter apathy.* Riverside: Andrews McMeel Publishing.

Aï t-Sahalia, Yacine, and Robert Kimmel. 2007. Maximum likelihood estimation of stochastic volatility models. *Journal of Financial Economics* 83: 413–452.

Albrecher, Hansjorg, Wolfgang J. Runggaldier, and Walter Schachermayer, eds. 2009. *Advanced financial modelling.* Radon Series on Computational and Applied Mathematics. Berlin: Walter De Gruyter.

Alibek, Ken, and Stephen Handelman. 1999. *Biohazard: The chilling true story of the largest covert biological weapons program in the world—told from inside by the man who ran it.* New York: Random House.

Alzola, Miguel. April 2012. The possibility of virtue. *Business Ethics Quarterly* 22 (2): 377–404.

Amendola, A., Y. Ermoliev, T. Y. Ermolieva, V. Gitis, G. Koff, and J. Linnerooth-Bayer. May 2000. A systems approach to modeling catastrophic risk and insurability. *Natural Hazards* 21:2–3.

American Dietetic Association. 1998. *Food biotechnology: Safe, nutritious, healthful, abundant, and tasty food, hot topics.* The American Dietetic Association. Fact Sheet.

Andersen, Bjorn, Manuel Fradinho, Paul Lefrere, and Veli-Pekka Niitamo. 2009. The coming revolution in competence development: Using serious games to improve cross-cultural skills online communities and social computing. In ed. A. Ozok and Panayiotis Zaphiris, 5621 vol, 413–422. Berlin: Springer.

Anderson, Peter D., and Gyula Bokor. October 2012. Bioterrorism: Pathogens as weapons. *Journal of Pharmacy Practice* 25 (5): 521–529.

Anslow, Mark. 2008. *10 reasons why gm won't feed the world.* Ecologist. http://www.theecologist.org/PAGES/archive_detail.asp?content_id=1185. Accessed 15 May 2009.

Aquinas, Saint Thomas. 1984. Treatise on the virtues. Notre Dame: University of Notre Dame.

Aquinas, Thomas. 2012. *The Summa Theologica.* Kevin Knight. http://www.newadvent.org/summa/1081.htm. Accessed 23 June 2012.

Aramo-Immonen, Heli, Hannu Jaakkola, and Harri Keto. 2011. Multicultural software development: The productivity perspective. IGI Global.

Aristotle. 1928. De Anima (On the Soul). In *The works of Aristotle translated into english,* ed. W. D. Ross and J. A. Smith, Book III, part 7. Oxford: Clarendon Press.

Aristotle. 1962. *Nicomachean ethics.* Trans. Martin Ostwald. Englewood Cliffs: Prentice Hall.

Aristotle. 1995. *The politics.* Trans. Ernest Barker. New York: Oxford University Press.

Aristotle. 2009a.*The politics.* Trans. Benjamin Jowett, 350 B.C.E. http://classics.mit.edu/Aristotle/politics.7.seven.html.

Aristotle. 2009b. *Rhetoric.* Trans. W. Rhys Roberts, 350 B.C.E. http://classics.mit.edu/Aristotle/rhetoric.1.i.html. Accessed 1 June 2012.

Arjoon, Surendra. 2000. Virtue theory as a dynamic theory of business. *Journal of Business Ethics* 28 (2): 159–178.

Arras, John D. July/August 1990. Common law morality. *Hastings Center Report* 20 (4):35–37.

Arras, John D. February 1991. Getting down to cases: The revival of casuistry in bioethics. *The Journal of Medicine and Philosophy* 16 (1): 29–51.

Arras, John D. Fall 1994. Principles and particularity: The roles of cases in bioethics. *Indiana Law Journal* 69:983–1014.

Arras, John D., ed. 2010. *A case approach.* In *A companion to bioethics,* eds. Helga Kuhse and Peter Singer, 2nd ed. Oxford: Wiley-Blackwell.

AstraZeneca Pharmaceuticals LP. 2001. *NOLVADEX® (tamoxifen citrate).* AstraZeneca Pharmaceuticals LP. http://www.usa.zeneca.com/products/ta_page.asp?ta=1-17. Accessed 4 May 2002.

Audi, Robert. April 2012. Virtue ethics as a resource in business. *Business Ethics Quarterly* 22 (2): 273–291.

Awaya, Allen, Hunter McEwan, Deborah Heyler, Sandy Linsky, Donna Lum, and Pamela Wakukawa. 2008. Mentoring as a journey. *Teaching and Teacher Education* 19 (1): 45–56.

Baltzly, Dirk. 4 October 2010. *Stoicism.* Stanford encyclopedia of philosophy. http://plato.stanford.edu/entries/stoicism/. Accessed 29 June 2012.

Bankhead, Charles. 23 January 2008. *New therapies vie for role in breast cancer.* MedPage Today, LLC. http://www.medpagetoday.com/HematologyOncology/BreastCancer/12581. Accessed 8 April 2009.

Barakat, Mounther and Rory Terry. December 2010. A re-evaluation of event-study methodology a re-evaluation of event-study methodology. *Journal of International Finance and Economics* 10(4): 13–28.

Barboza, David. 12 November 1999a. Biotech companies take on critics of gene-altered food. *The New York Times,* A1 and A18.

Barboza, David. 20 December 1999b. Monsanto and pharmacia to join, creating a pharmaceutical giant. *The New York Times* A1, A22.

Barnes, Louis B., C. Roland Christensen, and Abby J. Hansen. 1994. *Teaching and the case method: Texts, cases, and readings.* 3rd ed. Boston: Harvard Business School.

Barnhill Jr., Theodore M., and William F. Maxwell. March 2002. Modeling correlated market and credit risk in fixed income portfolios. *Journal of Banking & Finance* 26 (2–3): 347–374.

Beabout, Gregory R. April 2012. Management as a domain-relative practice that requires and develops practical wisdom. *Business Ethics Quarterly* 22 (2): 405–432.

Beadle, Ronald, and Kelvin Knight. April 2012. Virtue and meaningful work. *Business Ethics Quarterly* 22 (2): 433–450.

Beauchamp, Tom L., ed. 1998. *Case studies in business, society, and ethics.* 4th ed. Upper Saddle River: Prentice-Hall.

Bedau, Hugo Adam. 1997. *Making mortal choices: Three exercises in moral casuistry.* New York: Oxford University.

Bentham, Jeremy. 1781. *An introduction to the principles of morals and legislation.* http://www.utilitarianism.org/jeremy-bentham/index.html—one. Accessed 14 Jan 2008.

Bernalillo County, N. M. 1994. Dist. Ct. Liebeck v. McDonald's Restaurants, PTS, Inc., No. D-202 CV-93-02419, 1995 WL 360309.

Berns, Laurence. September 1994. Aristotle and Adam Smith on justice: Cooperation between ancients and moderns? *Review of Metaphysics* 48 (1): 71–90.

Berry, Christopher J. 1992. Adam Smith and the virtues of commerce. In *Virtue: NOMOS XXXIV*, ed. John W. Chapman and William A. Galston, 69–88. New York: New York University.

Berry, Ian. 30 January 2013. Monsanto: Battered, bruised, and still growing. *The Wall Street Journal* B5.

Bill & Melinda Gates Foundation. 2013. *Who We Are—Foundation Fact Sheet*. http://www.gatesfoundation.org/Who-We-Are/General-Information/Foundation-Factsheet. Accessed 22 March 2013.

BioPortfolio Limited. 2009. *Cancer: The generic impact*. http://www.bioportfolio.com/news/datamonitor_16.htm. Accessed 30 March 2009.

BioValidity. 2000. *BioValidity assists food industry clients with regulatory research needs in wake of FDA letter to industry regarding supplements*. BioValidity. http://www.biovalidity.com/. Accessed 4 May 2002.

Blackler, Frank. November 1995. Knowledge, knowledge work and organizations: An overview and interpretation. *Organizational Studies* 16 (6): 1021–1046.

Blake, David C. January-February 1992. The hospital ethics committee health care's moral conscience or white elephant? *Hastings Center Report* 22 (1): 6–11.

Block, John R. 24 December 2012. A reality check for organic food dreamers. *The Wall Street Journal* A11.

Bloomberg, Michael, and Bill Gates. 28 February 2013. Our plan to eradicate polio. *The Wall Street Journal* A13.

Boatright, John R. October 1999. Does business ethics rest on a mistake? *Business Ethics Quarterly* 9:583–591.

Boeyink, David E. 1992. Casuistry: A case-based method for journalists. *Journal of Mass Media Ethics* 7 (2): 107–120.

Bok, Sissela. Summer 1980. Whistleblowing and professional responsibility. *New York University Education Quarterly* 11 (4): 2–10.

Bolton, Sue. 24 March 2008. *MAdGE Marches against GM food*. Green Left Weekly. http://www.greenleft.org.au/2008/752/38890. Accessed 13 May 2009.

Bowie, Norman. July-August 1991. New directions in corporate social responsibility—moral pluralism and reciprocity. *Business Horizons* 34 (4): 56–65.

Bowie, Norman E. January 2000. Business ethics, philosophy, and the next 25 years. *Business Ethics Quarterly* 10:7–20.

Breast International Group (BIG) 1-98 Collaborative Group, B. Thürlimann, A. Keshaviah, A. S. Coates, H. Mouridsen, L. Mauriac, J. F. Forbes, R. Paridaens, M. Castiglione-Gertsch, R. D. Gelber, M. Rabaglio, I. Smith, A. Wardley, K. N. Price, and A. Goldhirsch. 29 December 2005. A comparison of letrozole and tamoxifen in postmenopausal women with early breast cancer. *New England Journal of Medicine* 353 (26): 2747–2757.

Breastcancer.org. 20 April 2007. *Benefits of tamoxifen*. http://www.breastcancer.org/treatment/hormonal/benefits/tamoxifen.jsp. Accessed 21 January 2009.

Brinkmann, Johannes, and Knut J. Ims. 2004. A conflict case approach to business ethics. *Journal of Business Ethics* 53:123–136.

Broadie, Sarah. 1991. *Ethics with Aristotle*. New York: Oxford University.

Brody, Baruch A. 1989. A historical introduction to Jewish casuistry on suicide and euthanasia. In *Suicide and euthanasia: Historical and contemporary themes*, ed. Baruch A. Brody, 39–76. Dordrecht: Kluwer Academic Publishers.

Brookes, Graham, and Peter Barfoot. 2013. The global income and production effects of genetically modified (GM) crops 1996–2011. *Landes Bioscience* 4 (1): 74–83.

Brookhiser, Richard. 1996. A man on horseback. *The Atlantic Monthly* (January): 50–64.

Bruner, Robert F., and Katarina Paddack. 1996. Case writing project overview: The transformation of allied signal. In *Casewriting workshop handout*, ed. William Rotch. Charlottesville: Unpublished.

Buchholz, Rogene A. 1989. *Fundamental concepts and problems in business ethics*. Englewood Cliffs: Prentice-Hall.

Burnyeat, M. F. 1980. Aristotle on learning to be good. In *Essays on Aristotle's ethics*, ed. Amélie Oksenberg Rorty, 69–92. Berkeley: University of California.

Buroker, Jill Vance. January 1992. Cartesian method and the problem of reduction. *Analytic Philosophy* 33 (1): 9–11.

Burton, Thomas M. 20 April 1998. New drugs give cause for hope in fight against breast cancer. *The Wall Street Journal* A1:1.

Cain, Kevin G. Fall 2007. The McDonald's coffee lawsuit. *Journal of Consumer & Commercial Law* 14–19.

Calkins, Martin. April 2001. Casuistry and the business case method. *Business Ethics Quarterly* 11 (2): 237–259.

Calkins, Martin. July 2002. How casuistry and virtue ethics might break the ideological stalemate troubling agricultural biotechnology. *Business Ethics Quarterly* 12 (3): 305–330.

Calkins, Martin. 2007. Casuistry and the business case method. In *Religious perspectives on business ethics: An anthology*, ed. Thomas O'Brien and Scott Paeth, 149–170. Lanham: Rowman & Littlefield Publishers.

Calkins, Martin J., and Patricia H. Werhane. March 1998. Adam Smith, Aristotle, and the virtues of commerce. *The Journal of Value Inquiry* 32 (1): 43–60.

Callahan, Elletta Sangrey, Terry Morehead Dworkin, and David Lewis. 2004. Whistleblowing: Australian, U.K., and U.S. approaches to disclosure in the public interest. *Virginia Journal of International Law* 44 (3): 879–912.

Campbell, David, Bill Houston, and George Stonehouse. 2002. *Business strategy*. Woburn: Butterworth-Heinemann.

Campbell, William F. May 1967. Adam Smith's theory of justice, prudence, and beneficence. *The American Economic Review* 57 (2): 571–577.

CancerBACUP. December 2001. *The CancerBACUP Factsheet*. CancerBACUP. http://www.cancerbacup.org.uk/info/tamoxifen.htm. Accessed 29 April 2002.

Carr, Mark F. 2002. The narrow conception of temperance. In *Passionate deliberation: Emotion, temperance, and the care ethic in clinical moral deliberation*, 47–59. Boston: Kluwer Academic Publishers.

Cavanagh, Gerald F. 1998. *American business values with international perspectives*. 4th ed. Upper Saddle River: Prentice-Hall.

Cavanagh, Gerald F., and Mark R. Bandsuch. 2002. Virtue as a benchmark for spirituality in business. *Journal of Business Ethics* 38 (1–2): 109–117.

Cavanagh, Gerald F., Dennis J. Moberg, and Manuel Velasquez. July 1995. Making business ethics practical. *Business Ethics Quarterly* 5 (3): 399–418.

Censky, Annalyn. 23 May 2012. *4 Degrees with 0 % unemployment*. CNN Money. http://money.cnn.com/galleries/2012/news/economy/1205/gallery.high-demand-jobs/index.html. Accessed 13 January 2013.

Centers for Disease Control and Prevention. 29 January 2002. *Interim smallpox response plan & guidelines*. Department of Health and Human Services Centers for Disease Control and Prevention. http://www.bt.cdc.gov/DocumentsApp/Smallpox/RPG/index.asp. Accessed 6 May 2002.

Centers for Disease Control and Prevention. 2004. *Smallpox response plan and guidelines (Version 3.0)*. Department of Health and Human Services Centers for Disease Control and Prevention. Last update 6 February 2007. http://www.bt.cdc.gov/agent/smallpox/response-plan/index.asp-toc. Accessed 1 March 2013.

Chen, Wendy Y., and Graham A. Colditz. 12 February 2008. *Tamoxifen and raloxifene for the prevention of breast cancer*. UpToDate, Inc. http://www.uptodate.com/patients/content/topic.do?topicKey=~3RkRGSmwhqwH. Accessed 21 January 2009.

Chertow, Mark, Janet Lenz, and Rodney P. Plourde. January 1993. Whistle blowing and professional responsibility. *Journal of Professional Issues in Engineering Education and Practice* 119 (1): 27–30.

Ciulla, Joanne B. 1994. Casuistry and the case for business ethics. In *Business as a humanity*, ed. Thomas J. Donaldson and R. Edward Freeman, 167–183. New York: Oxford University.

Clinton, Bill. 1998a. *Bill Clinton 1998 Iraq Liberation Act*. Last update 12 September 2007. http://www.youtube.com/watch?v=457jp8VGhEE. Accessed 19 March 2013.

Clinton, Bill. 26 January 1998b. *Response to the Lewinsky allegations (January 26, 1998)*. Rector and visitors of the University of Virginia. http://millercenter.org/scripps/archive/speeches/detail/3930. Accessed 18 April 2012.

Coates, A. S., A. Keshaviah, B. Thürlimann, H. Mouridsen, L. Mauriac, J. F. Forbes, R. Paridaens, M. Castiglione-Gertsch, R. D. Gelber, M. Colleoni, I. Láng, L. Del Mastro, I. Smith, J. Chirgwin, J. M. Nogaret, T. Pienkowski, A. Wardley, E. H. Jakobsen, K. N. Price, and A. Goldhirsch. 10 February 2007. Five years of letrozole compared with tamoxifen as initial adjuvant therapy for postmenopausal women with endocrine-responsive early breast cancer: update of study BIG 1-98. *Journal of Clinical Oncology* 25 (5): 486–492.

Coleman, Janet. 1994. MacIntyre and Aquinas. In *After MacIntyre: critical perspectives on the work of Alasdair MacIntyre*, ed. John Horton and Susan Mendus, 65–90.Oxford: Polity Press.

Coleman, Kari Gwen. July 2007. Casuistry and computer ethics. *Metaphilosophy* 38 (4): 471–488.

Collins, Denis. 1987. Aristotle and business. *Journal of Business Ethics* 6 (7): 567–582.

Conly, Sarah. 1988. Flourishing and the failure of the ethics of virtue. In *Midwest studies in philosophy 13: Ethical theory: Character and virtue*, ed. Peter A. French and others, 83–96. Notre Dame: University of Notre Dame.

Conway, Gordon. 2000. *Eliminating global hunger: USDA millennium lecture*. Television Trust for the Environment (TVE's Life). Streaming video. http://www.oneworld.net/tve/life/archive/life26main.html. Accessed 3 July 2001.

Copeland, Melvin T. 1954. The genesis of the case method in business instruction. In *The case method at the Harvard Business School: Papers by present and past members of the faculty and staff*, ed. Malcolm P. McNair, 25–33. New York: McGraw-Hill Book Company.

Cordero, Ronald A. 1988. Aristotle and fair deals. *Journal of Business Ethics* 7 (9): 681–690.

Council for Biotechnology Information. 2001. *Plant biotechnology: A new agricultural tool emerges as the world sets to vanquish chronic hunger*. http://www.whybiotech.com/. Accessed 4 May 2002.

Council of the European Communities. 1990. *Council directive of 23 April 1990 on the deliberate release into the environment of genetically modified organisms (90/220/EEC)*. Belgian Biosafety Server. http://biosafety.ihe.be/GB/Dir.Eur.GB/Del.Rel./90.220/TC.html. Accessed 23 June 2001.

Csikszentmihalyi, Mihaly. 1991. *Flow: The psychology of optimal experience*. New York: HarperCollins Publishers.

Daniels, Norman. May 1979. Wide reflective equilibrium and theory acceptance in ethics. *The Journal of Philosophy* LXXVI:256–282.

Daniels, Norman. 1980. On some methods of ethics and linguistics. *Philosophical Studies* 37 (1): 21–36.

Dasgupta, Siddhartha, and Ankit Kesharwani. October 2010. Whistleblowing: A survey of literature. *UP Journal of Corporate Governance*, 9 (4): 57–70.

Davies, Christina, Paul McGale, and others. 16 May 1998. Variation in use of adjuvant tamoxifen. *Lancet* 351 (9114): 1487, 1482 p.

Davis, Michael. Winter 1989. Avoiding the tragedy of whistle blowing. *Business & Professional Ethics Journal* 8 (4): 3–19.

Davis, Michael. December 1997. Developing and using cases to teach practical ethics. *Teaching Philosophy* 20:353–385.

Davis, Richard B. Fall 1995. The principlism debate: A critical overview. *Journal of Medical Philosophy* 20 (1): 85–105.

De George, Richard T. 1993. Ethical responsibilities of engineers in large organizations: The pinto case. In *Ethical theory and business,* ed. Tom L. Beauchamp and Norman E. Bowie, 130–137. Englewood Cliffs: Prentice-Hall.

De George, Richard T. 1999. *Business ethics*. 5th ed. Upper Saddle River: Prentice Hall.

DeGregori, Thomas R. 2001a. *Agriculture and modern technology: A defense*. Ames: Iowa State University.

DeGregori, Thomas R. 2001b. *Genetically modified nonsense*. Institute of Economic Affairs (IEA). http://www.iea.org.uk/record.php?type=article&ID=20. Accessed 4 May 2002.

DeMarco, Joseph P. July 1991. The abuse of casuistry. *Southwest Philosophy Review* 7:17–30.

Deogun, Nikhil, and Robert Langreth. 21 December 1999. Investors are wary of Pharmacia Merger. *The Wall Street Journal* A3 and A6.

Deogun, Nikhil, Robert Langreth, and Thomas M. Burton. 20 December 1999. Pharmacia & Upjohn, Monsanto boards approve $ 27 Billion Merger of equals. *The Wall Street Journal* A3 and A4.

DePaul, Michael R. January 1986. Reflective equilibrium and foundationalism. *American Philosophical Quarterly* 23:59–69.

Derrett, J. Duncan M. January 1974. Review of books: Introduction to the Jewish law of the second commonwealth, Part 1. *Journal of the Royal Asiatic Society (New Series)* 106 (1): 53–54.

Despair, Inc. Demotivators. Austin: Despair, Inc., 2012.

Dewing, Arthur Stone. 1954. An introduction to the use of cases. In *The case method at the Harvard Business School: Papers by present and past members of the faculty and staff*, ed. Malcolm P. McNair, 1–5. New York: McGraw-Hill Book Company.

Dierksmeier, Claus, and Michael Pirson. 2009. Oikonomia Versus chrematistike: Learning from Aristotle about the future orientation of business management. *Journal of Business Ethics* 88 (3): 417–430.

Dierksmeier, Claus, and Anthony Celano. April 2012. Thomas aquinas on justice as a global virtue in business. *Business Ethics Quarterly* 22 (2): 247–272.

Donahue, James A. 1990. The use of virtue and character in applied ethics. *Horizons* 17:228–243.

Donaldson, Thomas, and Patricia H. Werhane, eds. *Ethical issues in business: A philosophical approach*. 6th ed. Upper Saddle River: Prentice-Hall.

Donham, Wallace B. 1954. The case method in college teaching of social science. In *The case method at the Harvard Business School: Papers by present and past members of the faculty and staff*, ed. Malcolm P. McNair, 244–255. New York: McGraw-Hill Book Company.

Donnelly, William J. June 1994. From principles to principals: The new direction in medical ethics. *Theoretical Medicine* 15:141–148.

Dowie, Mark. September/October 1977. Pinto madness. *Mother Jones*.

Drucker, Peter F. Spring 1981. What is business ethics? *National Affairs* 63:18–36.

Drucker, Peter F. 1993. *Post-capitalist society*. New York: HarperBusiness.

Duska, Ronald F. 1993. Aristotle: A pre-modern post-modern? Implications for business ethics. *Business Ethics Quarterly* 3 (3): 227–249.

Easterbrook, Gregg. 1997. Forgotten benefactor of humanity. *The Atlantic Monthly* January: 75–82.

Editor. January/February 1998. Environmentally correct since 1506. *Environment* 40 (1): 23.

Editor. 15 February 2000. Friends of Al? *The Wall Street Journal* A26.

Eli Lilly and Company. 27 February 2009. *Investor relations: Annual report and 10-K*. Eli Lilly and Company. http://investor.lilly.com/financials.cfm. Accessed 30 March 2009.

Engel, Matthew. 29 March 2002. Discovery of 90 m Smallpox doses eases fear of attack. *The Guardian* 15.

Ermoliev, Y. M., T. Y. Ermolieva, G. J. MacDonald, and V. I. Norkin. January 2008. Stochastic optimization of insurance portfolios for managing exposure to catastrophic risks. *Annals of Operations Research* 99 January: (1–4).

Fairclough, Gordon. 25 June 2001. Technology (A Special Report)—What's ahead for…Tobacco. *The Wall Street Journal* R15.

Falk, Ze'ev Wilhelm. 1972. *Introduction to Jewish law of the second commonwealth (Arbeiten zur Geschichte des Antiken Judentums und des Urchristentums Band XI)*. Leiden: E. J. Brill.

Fialka, John J. 17 January 2000. EPA gets stricter on altered corn to aid butterflies. *The Wall Street Journal* B12.

Fitzgibbons, Athol. 1995. *Adam Smith's system of liberty, wealth, and virtue: The moral and political foundations of the wealth of nations*. Oxford: Clarendon Press.

Foot, Philippa. 1978. *Virtues and vices and other essays in moral philosophy*. Berkeley: University of California.

Frank, Anne. 2010. *The diary of a young girl*. Trans. Susan Massotty and Francine Prose, (ed. Otto H. Frank and Mirjam Pressler). New York: Knopf Doubleday Publishing Group.

Freeman, John, and Warren Boeker. 1984. The ecological analysis of business strategy. *California Management Review* 26 (3): 73–86.

Friedman, Milton. The social responsibility of business is to increase its profits. *The New York Times Magazine* september 13, 1970: 122–126.

Fumento, Michael. 14 January 2000. Why europe fears biotech foods. *The Wall Street Journal* A14.

Gaunt, Peter. 2004. *Oliver Cromwell (British Library Historic Lives)*. New York: New York University.

Geirland, John. September 1996. Go with the flow. *Wired*. http://www.wired.com/wired/archive/4.09/czik_pr.html.

Gibson, Paul S. 2008. Developing practical management wisdom. *Journal of Management Development* 27 (5): 528–536.

Giebel, Stefan, and Martin Rainer. May 2011. Stochastic processes adapted by neural networks with application to climate, energy, and finance. *Applied Mathematics and Computation* 218 (may): 1003100.

Global Commission for the Certification of Smallpox Eradication. 1980. *The global eradication of smallpox*. Geneva: World Health Organization.

Goleman, Daniel. 1995. *Emotional intelligence*. New York: Bantam Books.

Gotsis, George N., and Zoe Kortezi. 2010. Ethical considerations in organizational politics: Expanding the perspective. *Journal of Business Ethics* 93 (4): 497–517.

Gragg, Charles I. 1954. Because wisdom can't be told. In *The case method at the Harvard Business School: Papers by present and past members of the faculty and staff*, ed. Malcolm P. McNair. New York: McGraw-Hill Book Company 6–14.

Greenberg, David, and Mary Graham. 2000. *Improving communication about new food technologies*. Issues in Science and Technology Online. http://www.nap.edu/issues/16.4/greenberg.htm. Accessed 4 May 2002.

Grilli, Sandro. 2006. Tamoxifen (TAM): The dispute goes on. *Annali dell'istituto superiore di sanità* 42 (2): 170–173.

Grosholz, Emily. 1991. *Cartesian method and the problem of reduction*. New York: Clarendon Press.

Grundke, Peter. Winter/Spring. 2004. Integrating interest rate risk in credit portfolio models. *The Journal of Risk Finance*.

Hanley, Ryan Patrick. 2006. Adam Smith, Aristotle, and virtue ethics. In *New voices on Adam Smith: Volume 82 of Routledge studies in the history of economics*, ed. Leonidas Montes and Eric Schliesser, 2. Florence: Routledge Taylor & Francis Group.

Hanson, K. O., and S. Weiss. 1991. *Merck & Co., Inc.: Addressing third-world needs*. Cambridge: Harvard Business School Publishing No. 9-991-021 to 024.

Hariman, Robert. 2003 *Prudence: Classical virtue, postmodern practice*. University Park: Pennsylvania State University Press.

Harris, Howard. June 1999. Courage as a management virtue. *Business & Professional Ethics Journal* 18 (3/4): 27–46.

Harrison, Peter. January 2011. Adam Smith and the history of the invisible hand. *Journal of the History of Ideas* 72 (1): 29–49.

Hartman, Edwin M. 1996. *Organizational ethics and the good life*. The ruffin series in business ethics. New York: Oxford University Press.

Hauerwas, Stanley. October 1983. Casuistry as a narrative art. *Interpretation: A Journal of Bible and Theology* 37:377–388.

Hayek, Friedrich A. 1945. *The road to serfdom in cartoons*. Ludwig von Mises Institute; originally published in Look Magazine. http://www.mises.org/books/TRTS/. Accessed 24 July 2012.

Hayek, Friedrich A. 1978. *Law, legislation and liberty, Volume 2: The mirage of social justice*. Chicago: University of Chicago

Hayek, Friedrich A. von. 2007. *The road to serfdom (text and documents–the definitive edition)*. II vol (ed. Bruce Caldwell). Chicago: University of Chicago.

Heilbroner, Robert L. ed. 1987. *The essential Adam Smith*. New York: W. W. Norton and Company.

Henderson, Donald A., Thomas V. Inglesby, John G. Bartlett, and others. 9 June 1999. Smallpox as a biological weapon. *Journal of American Medical Association (JAMA)* 281 (22): 2127–2137.

Herodotus, tr. G. C. Macaulay. 1890. *The history of herodotus book 7: Polymnia [50]*. http://www. sacred-texts.com/cla/hh/hh7050.htm. Accessed 2 February 2013.

Hindo, Brian. 23 June 2008. Monsanto on the mend. *Businessweek* 32.

Hirsi Ali, Ayaan. 18–19 May 2013. Swearing in the enemy. *The Wall Street Journal* C1.

Ho, Mae-Wan, Joe Cummins, and Peter Saunders. 2007. GM food nightmare unfolding in the regulatory sham. *Microbial Ecology in Health and Disease* 19 (2): 66–77.

Hobbes, Thomas. 1988. *The leviathan*. Buffalo: Prometheus Books.

Hobbes, Thomas. 2012. *The leviathan*. Athenaeum library of philosophy. http://evans- experientialism.freewebspace.com/hobbes06.htm. Accessed 29 June 2012.

Hoffman, W. Michael. 1995. The ford pinto. In *Business ethics: Readings and cases in corporate morality*, ed. W. Michael Hoffman and Robert E. Frederick, 552–559. New York: McGraw Hill.

Holmgren, Margaret. March 1989. The Wide and Narrow of Reflective Equilibrium. *Canadian Journal of Philosophy* 19 (1): 43–60.

Hosmer, LaRue Tone, and Christian Kiewitz. January 2005. Organizational justice: A behavioral science concept with critical implications for business ethics and stakeholder theory. *Business Ethics Quarterly* 15 (1): 67–91.

Huber, Peter. 20 December 1999. Ecological eugenics. *The Wall Street Journal* A26.

Human Genome Program. 5 November 2008. *Genetically modified foods and organisms*. U.S. Department of Energy Office of Science, Office of Biological and Environmental Research. http://www.ornl.gov/sci/techresources/Human_Genome/elsi/gmfood.shtml. Accessed 13 May 2009.

Hume, David. 1983. *An enquiry concerning the principles of morals* (ed. J. B. Schneewind). Indianapolis: Hackett Publishing Company.

Hunter, Kathryn Montgomery. April 1989. A science of individuals: Medicine and casuistry. *Journal of Medicine and Philosophy* 14:193–212.

International Food Information Council Foundation (IFIC). *Benefits of biotechnology—just around the corner, food biotechnology*. International Food Information Council Foundation (IFIC). Fact Sheet.

International Food Information Council Foundation (IFIC). 1999. *Food biotechnology: Health & harvest for our times*. International Food Information Council Foundation (IFIC). Pamphlet.

Jackall, Robert. Winter 1987. Bureaucracy and moral casuistry: A sociological perspective. *Quarterly Review* 63–71.

Jenkins, Jr., Holman W. 17 November 1999. Fun facts to know and tell about biotechnology. *The Wall Street Journal* A23.

Jensen, Kipton E. 2009. Shadow of virtue: On a painful if not principled compromise inherent in business ethics. *Journal of Business Ethics* 89 (1): 99–107.

Johansen, Baber. 1995. Casuistry: Between legal concept and social praxis. *Islamic Law and Society* 2 (2): 135–156.

Johnson, Mark. 1993. *Moral imagination: Implications of cognitive science for ethics*. Chicago: University of Chicago press.

Johnson & Johnson. 2012a. *Johnson & Johnson 2011 Annual Report*. Johnson & Johnson. http://www.investor.jnj.com/2011annualreport/index.html. Accessed 5 June 2012.

Johnson & Johnson. 2012b. *Our credo values*. Johnson & Johnson. http://www.jnj.com/connect/about-jnj/jnj-credo/. Accessed 5 June 2012.

Jolie, Angelina. 14 May 2013. *My medical choice*. The New York Times. http://www.nytimes.com/2013/05/14/opinion/my-medical-choice.html?smid=tw-share&_r=2&. Accessed 9 June 2013.

Jonsen, Albert R. 1986a. Casuistry. In *The Westminster dictionary of christian ethics*, ed. James F. Childress and John Macquarrie, 78–80. Philadelphia: The Westminster Press.

Jonsen, Albert R. 1986b. Casuistry and clinical ethics. *Theoretical Medicine* 7:65–74.

Jonsen, Albert R. 1987. Casuistry. In *The encyclopedia of religion*, ed. Mircea Eliade, 3, 112–114. New York: Macmillan Publishing Company.

Jonsen, Albert R. December 1991. Casuistry as methodology in clinical ethics. *Theoretical Medicine* 12:295–307.

Jonsen, Albert R. Fall 1993. Platonic insults: Casuistical. *Common Knowledge* 2:48–66.

Jonsen, Albert R. 1995. Casuistry: An alternative or complement to principles? *Kennedy Institute of Ethics Journal* 5:237–251.

Jonsen, Albert R., and Stephen Toulmin. 1988. *The abuse of casuistry: A history of moral reasoning*. Berkeley: University of California.

Kakoty, Jayanta Sarma. 2011. Stochastic modeling of some managerial aspects of production planning. *The IUP Journal of Operations Management* X (1): 29–42.

Kant, Immanuel. 1785. *Fundamental principles of the metaphysics of morals*. Trans. Thomas Kingsmill Abbott. http://philosophy.eserver.org/kant/metaphys-of-morals.txt. Accessed 14 August 2012.

Kant, Immanuel. 1964. *Groundwork of the metaphysic of morals*. Trans. H.J. Paton. New York: Harper & Row Publishers.

Kant, Immanuel. 1990. *Foundations of the metaphysics of morals*. New York: Macmillan Publishing Company.

Kaplan, Robert S., and David P. Norton. 2004. *Strategy maps: Converting intangible assets into tangible outcomes*. Boston: Harvard Business School Press.

Kaplan, Tamara. 2005. *Case study: The tylenol crisis: How effective public relations saved Johnson & Johnson*. http://www.grif.com.au/Tylenol-Poisonings.79.0.html. Accessed 5 June 2012.

Keenan, James F. 1993. The casuistry of John Major: Nominalist professor of Paris (1506–1531). *Annual Meeting of the Society of Christian Ethics* (8–10 January): 205–221.

Keenan, S. J., James. March 1996. The return to casuistry. *Theological Studies* 57:123–139.

Keenan, James F., S. J. and Thomas A. Shannon. 1995. William Perkins (1558–1602) and the birth of british casuistry. In *The Context of casuistry*, ed. James F. Keenan, S. J and Thomas A. Shannon, 105–130. Washington, D.C.: Georgetown University.

Keenan, James F., S. J. and Thomas A. Shannon, eds. 1995. *The context of casuistry*. Washington, D.C.: Georgetown University Press.

Keenan, James F., S. J. and Thomas A. Shannon. 1996. William Perkins (1558–1602) and the birth of british casuistry. *Virtues for Ordinary Christians*. Kansas City: Sheed & Ward.

Keenan, James F., S. J. and Thomas A. Shannon. 2010. William Perkins (1558–1602) and the birth of british casuistry. *A history of catholic moral theology in the twentieth century: From confessing sins to liberating consciences*. New York: Continuum International Publishing Group.

Kekes, John. April 1991. Moral Imagination, Freedom, and the Humanities. *American Philosophical Quarterly* 28:101–111.

Kendall, David E., Nicole K. Seligman, Emmet T. Flood, Max Stier, Alicia L. Marti, Gregory B. Craig, Charles F.C. Ruff, Cheryl D. Mills, and Lanny A. Breuer. 8 December 1998. *Submission by counsel for president Clinton to the committee on the judiciary of the United States house of representatives*. JURIST: The Law Professors' Network. http://jurist.law.pitt.edu/whiteh.htm. Accessed 19 April 2012.

Khare, R. S. 1999. *Perspectives on islamic law, justice, and society*. Lanham: Rowman & Littlefield.

Kilman, Scott. 19 November 1999a. FDA signals tighter biofood oversight as pressure from opponents increases. *The Wall Street Journal* A8.

Kilman, Scott. 15 December 1999b. Monsanto is sued over genetically altered crops. *The Wall Street Journal* A3 and A6.

Kilman, Scott. 19 November 1999c. Once quick converts, farmers begin to lose faith in biotech crops. *The Wall Street Journal* A1 and A8.

Kilman, Scott. 4 April 2000. Biotech ad campaign attempts to shape U.S. attitudes toward modified crops. *The Wall Street Journal* B6.

Kilman, Scott, and Scott Burton. 21 December 1999. Monsanto Boss's vision of 'Life Sciences' firm now confronts reality. *The Wall Street Journal* A1 and A10.

Kitay, Jim and Christopher Wright. November 2007. From prophets to profits: The occupational rhetoric of management consultants. *Human Relations* 60 (11): 1613–1640.

Kline, William. January 2012. Hume's theory of business ethics revisited. *Journal of Business Ethics* 105 (2): 163–174.

Klinefelter, Donald S. Spring 1990. How is applied philosophy to be applied? *Journal of Social Philosophy* 21:16–26.

Knott, Stephen. 16–17 March 2013. When everyone agreed about Iraq. *The Wall Street Journal* A13.

Koehn, Daryl. July 1992. Toward an ethic of exchange. *Business Ethics Quarterly* 2 (3): 341–355.

Koehn, Daryl. July 1995. A role for virtue ethics in the analysis of business practice. *Business Ethics Quarterly* 5 (3): 533–539.

Kopelman, Loretta M. March 1994. Case method and casuistry: The problem of bias. *Theoretical Medicine* 15:21–37.

Kopfensteiner, Thomas R. 1995. Science, metaphor, and moral casuistry. In *The context of casuistry*, ed. James F. Keenan, S. J. and Thomas A. Shannon, 207–220. Washington, D.C.: Georgetown University.

Kourdi, Jeremy. 2009. *Business strategy: A guide to taking your business forward*. London: Profile Books.

Kuczewski, Mark G. June 1994. Casuistry and Its Communitarian Critics. *Kennedy Institute of Ethics Journal* 4:99–116.

Kuczewski, Mark G. 1997. *Fragmentation and consensus: Communitarian and casuist bioethics*. Washington, D.C.: Georgetown University.

Kuhn, Thomas S. 1970. *The structure of scientific revolutions*. 2nd ed. Chicago: The University of Chicago.

Lacayo, Richard, and Amanda Ripley. 30 December 2002. Persons of the year. *Time Magazine*.

Lagnado, Lucette. 14 December 1999. For those fighting biotech crops, santa came early this year. *The Wall Street Journal* A1 and A8.

Lamb, Robert Boyden. October–December 1974. Adam Smith's system: Sympathy not self-interest. *Journal of the History of Ideas* 35 (4): 671–682.

Larmore, Charles. 1992. The limits of Aristotelian ethics. In *Virtue*: Nomos XXIV, ed. John W. Chapman and William A. Galston, 185–196. New York: New York University.

Larsen, Ralph S. 2007. *Best practices: Making the hard decisions*. Ethix. Last update 2012. http://ethix.org/2007/06/01/making-the-hard-decisions. Accessed 5 June 2012.

Lee, Matthew T., and M. David Ermann. February 1999. Pinto madness as a flawed landmark narrative: An organizational and network analysis. *Social Problems* 46 (1): 30–47.

Leenders, Michael R., and James A. Erskine. 1978. *Case research: The case writing process*. 2nd ed. London (Canada): The University of Western Ontario: Research and Publications Division of the School of Business Administration.

Lewis, Richard D. 1999. *Cross culture: The lewis model*. Richard Lewis Communications. Last update 2000. http://www.google.com/url?sa=t&rct=j&q=linearactivemultiactivereactive&source=web&cd=1&ved=0CCIQFjAA&url=http%3A%2F%2Ffaculty.fuqua.duke.edu%2Fciber%2Fice%2FCross%20Culture%20The%20Lewis%20Model.pdf&ei=8eF0T5jhLYWx0AGc3OGYDQ&usg=AFQjCNGdYeJc6KXb39fSG21VS-vZUXv8jg&cad=rja. Accessed 29 March 2012.

Lewis, Richard D. 2003. *When cultures collide: Managing successfully across cultures*. 2nd ed. Yarmouth: Nicholas Brealey Publishing.

Lin, X. Sheldon. 2006. *Introductory Stochastic analysis for finance and insurance*. Hoboken: Wiley.

Lipin, Steven, Anita Raghavan, and Stephen D. Moore. 2 December 1999. AstraZeneca and Novartis near a deal. *The Wall Street Journal* A3.

Litsas, Georgia. July 2008. Sequential therapy with tamoxifen and aromatase inhibitors in early-stage postmenopausal breast cancer: A review of the evidence. *Oncology Nursing Forum* 35 (4): 714–721.

Lloyd, Phyllida. 2011. *The iron lady*. Film. US: The Weinstein Company.

Lowe, Malcolm F. 1983. Aristotle on kinds of thinking. *Phronesis* 28 (1): 17–30.

Lundberg, Craig C. 1993. Case method. In *Mastering management education: Innovations in teaching effectiveness*, ed. Charles M. Vance, 45–52. Newbury Park: Sage Publications.

Lundberg, George D., John P. Peters, and the Committee of 430 Physicians. 2002. *Yale Journal of Biology and Medicine* 75 (1): 23–27.

Lynch, Ceclia. 2005. Public spheres transnationalized: Comparisons within and beyond Muslim majority societies. In *Religion, social practice, and contested hegemonies: Reconstructing the public sphere in Muslim majority societies*, ed. Armando Salvatore and Mark LeVine, 239–243. New York: Palgrave Macmillan.

MacIntyre, Alasdair. 1984. *After virtue: A study in moral theory*. 2nd ed. Notre Dame: University of Notre Dame.

MacIntyre, Alasdair. October 1990. Review of the abuse of casuistry: A history of moral reasoning. *Journal of the History of Philosophy* 28 (4): 634–635.

Macpherson-Smith, Malcolm. 1994. Anchor and course for the modern ship of casuistry. *Cambridge Quarterly of Healthcare Ethics* 3:391–402.

Maguire, Stephen. 1997. Business ethics: A compromise between politics and virtue. *Journal of Business Ethics* 16 (12/13): 1411–1418.

Maisel, Herbert, and Giuliano Gnugnoli. 1972. *Simulation of discrete stochastic systems*. Chicago: Science Research Associates.

Marhavilas, P. K., and D. E. Koulouriotis. March 2012. Developing a new alternative risk assessment framework in the work sites by including a stochastic and a deterministic process: A case study for the greek public electric power provider. *Safety Science*. 50 (3): 448–462.

May, William F. 1995. The virtues of the business leader. In *On moral business: classical and contemporary resources for ethics in economic life*, ed. Max L. Stackhouse, Dennis P. McCann, Shirley J. Roels, and Preston N. Williams, 692–700. Grand Rapids: William B. Eerdmans Publishing Company.

McCloskey, Donald. Spring 1994. Bourgeois virtue. *American Scholar* 63:177–191.

McKay, Betsy. 28 February 2013. Anti-polio campaign gets big cash infusion. *The Wall Street Journal* A6.

McLaren, B. M. July-August 2006. Computational models of ethical reasoning: Challenges, initial steps, and future directions. *Intelligent Systems, IEEE* 21 (4): 29–37.

McLeish, Don L. 2005. *Monte Carlo simulation and finance*. Hoboken: Wiley.

McMahon, Thomas F. 1986. Creed, cult, code and business ethics. *Journal of Business Ethics* 5 (6): 453–463.

Medline Plus. 1 March 2013. *Smallpox*. U.S. National Library of Medicine. http://www.nlm.nih.gov/medlineplus/smallpox.html. Accessed 26 March 2013.

Meikle, Scott. 1996. Aristotle on business. *The Classical Quarterly* 46 (1): 138–151.

Meilaender, Gilbert C. 1984. *The theory and practice of virtue*. Notre Dame: University of Notre Dame.

Melé, Domènec. 2010. Practical wisdom in managerial decision making. *Journal of Management Development* 29 (7/8): 637–645.

Miceli, M. P., and J. P. Near. 1992. *Blowing the whistle*. New York: Lexington Books.

Mill, John Stuart. 1979. *Utilitarianism* (ed. George Sher). Indianapolis: Hackett Publishing.

Miller, Richard B. Fall 1994. Narrative and casuistry: A response to John Arras. *Indiana Law Journal* 69:1015–1019.

Miller, Richard B. 1995. Moral sources, ordinary life, and truth-telling in Jeremy Taylor's casuistry. In *The context of casuistry*, ed. James F. Keenan, S. J and Thomas A. Shannon, 131–157. Washington, D.C.: Georgetown University.

Miller, Richard B. 1996. *Casuistry and modern ethics: A poetics of practical reasoning*. Chicago: The University of Chicago.

Mintz, Steven M. 1996. Aristotelian virtue and business ethics education. *Journal of Business Ethics* 15 (8): 827–838.

Mintzberg, Henry. 1987. The Strategy Concept I: Five P's for Strategy. *California Management Review* 30 (1): 11–24.

Mintzberg, Henry. 1994. *The rise and fall of strategic planning: Reconceiving roles for planning, plans, planners.* New York: The Free Press.

Moberg, Dennis. April 1999. The big five and organizational virtue. *Business Ethics Quarterly* 9 (2): 245–272.

Moberg, Dennis. 2002. Immoral imagination and revenge in organizations. *Journal of Business Ethics* 38 (1–2): 19–31.

Moberg, Dennis. October 2003. Managers as judges in employee disputes: An occasion for moral imagination. *Business Ethics Quarterly* 13 (4): 453–477.

Moberg, Dennis. 2008. Mentoring and practical wisdom: Are mentors wiser or just more politically skilled? *Journal of Business Ethics* 83 (4): 835–843.

Moberg, Dennis, and Martin Calkins, S. J. October 2001. Reflection in business ethics: insights from St. Ignatius' Spiritual Exercises. *Journal of Business Ethics* 33:257–270.

Moberg, Dennis J. 2006. Ethics blindspots in organizations: How systematic errors in person perception undermine moral agency. *Organizational Studies* 27 (3): 413–428.

Moberg, Dennis J. 2007. Practical wisdom and business ethics presidential address to the society for business ethics Atlanta, August 2006. *Business Ethics Quarterly* 17 (3): 535–561.

Moberg, Dennis J. 2008. Mentoring for protégé character development. *Mentoring & Tutoring: Partnership in Learning* 16 (1): 91–103.

Moberg, Dennis J., and Mark A. Seabright. October 2000. The development of moral imagination. *Business Ethics Quarterly* 10:845–884.

Moberg, Dennis, and Edward J. Romar. 2003. *Case study: WorldCom.* Markkula Center for Applied Ethics. http://www.scu.edu/ethics/dialogue/candc/cases/worldcom.html. Accessed 30 May 2009.

Monsanto. 2001. *A story of sweetpotatoes.* Monsanto Company. http://www.monsanto.com/monsanto/biotechnology/background_information/00sept27_swpotatoes.html. Accessed 28 June 2001.

Monsanto Company. 2009a. *Increasing farm prosperity with innovation.* http://www.monsanto.com/responsibility/our_pledge/prosperous_economy/farm_income.asp Accessed 13 May 2009.

Monsanto Company. 2009b. *Sustainable agriculture.* Monsanto Company. http://www.monsanto.com/responsibility/sustainable-ag/default.asp. Accessed 14 May 2009.

Monsanto Company. 2013. *Agent orange: Background on Monsanto's involvement.* Monsanto Company. http://www.monsanto.com/newsviews/Pages/agent-orange-background-monsanto-involvement.aspx. Accessed 31 January 2013.

Moore, Geoff. October 2005a. Corporate character: Modern virtue ethics and the virtuous corporation. *Business Ethics Quarterly* 15 (4): 659–685.

Moore, Geoff. April 2005b. Humanizing business: A modern virtue ethics approach. *Business Ethics Quarterly* 15 (2): 237–255.

Moore, Geoff. April 2012. The virtue of governance, the governance of virtue. *Business Ethics Quarterly* 22 (2): 293–318.

Moore, Geoff, and Ron Beadle. March 2006. In search of organizational virtue in business: Agents, goods, practices, Institutions and Environments. *Organization Studies* 27 (3): 369–389.

Morris, Thomas V. 1997. *If Aristotle ran general motors: The new soul of business.* New York: Henry Holt and Company.

Morse, John. 1999. The missing link between virtue theory and business ethics. *Journal of Applied Philosophy* 16 (1): 47–58.

Morse, John, and Suzanne Morse. Spring 2002. Teaching temperance to the 'Cookie Monster': Ethical challenges to data mining and direct marketing. *Business & Society Review* 107 (1): 76–98.

Mueller, Gustav E. June 1958. The Hegel legend of thesis-antithesis-synthesis. *Journal of the History of Ideas* 19 (3): 411–414.

Murphy, Patrick E. June 1958. Character and virtue ethics in international marketing: An agenda for managers, researchers and educators. *Business Ethics Quarterly* 18 (1): 107–124.

Natcheva-Acar, Kalina, Sarp Kaya Acar, and Martin Krekel. Spring 2009. Modeling credit spreads with the cheyette model and its application to credit default swaptions. *The Journal of Credit Risk* 5 (1): 47–71.

National Agricultural Library. 5 April 2001. *Biotechnology Information Resource (BIC)*. US Department of Agriculture (ARS). http://www.nalusda.gov/bic/. Accessed 5 May 2002.

National Cancer Institute. 21 June 2006. *Results of the study of tamoxifen and raloxifene (STAR) released: Osteoporosis drug raloxifene shown to be as effective as tamoxifen in preventing invasive breast cancer*. http://www.cancer.gov/newscenter/pressreleases/STARresultsApr172006. Accessed 30 March 2009.

Naughton, Michael J., and Jeffrey R. Cornwall. January 2006. The virtue of courage in entrepreneurship: Engaging the catholic social tradition and the life-cycle of the Business. *Business Ethics Quarterly* 16 (1): 69–93.

Near, J. P., and M. P. Miceli. 1985. Organizational dissidence: The case of whistle-blowing. *Journal of Business Ethics* 4:1–16.

Near, Janet P., and Marcia P. Miceli. October 1996. Whistle-blowing: Myth and reality. *Journal of Management* 22 (3): 507.

Nielsen, Kai. Spring 1982. Grounding rights and a method of reflective equilibrium. *Inquiry* 25:277–306.

Nielsen, Kai. 1997. Reflective equilibrium. In *The Blackwell encyclopedic dictionary of business ethics*, ed. Patricia H. Werhane and R. Edward Freeman, 546–549. Malden: Blackwell Publishers.

Nussbaum, Martha C. 1990. *Love's knowledge: Essays on philosophy and literature*. New York: Oxford University Press.

O'Malley, John W. 1993. *The first Jesuits*. Cambridge: Harvard University.

Office of the Independent Counsel. 9 September 1998. Volume III: Document Supplement, Part A: William J. Clinton Statements. In *H. Doc. 105–311, SuDoc Class Number Y 1.1/7:105-311/ PT.1-2: Appendices to the referral to the United States House of representatives pursuant to title 28, United States Code, Section 595(c)* U.S. Government Printing Office.

Oral Tradition. 2013. *The story of goldilocks and the three bears*. DLTK. http://www.dltk-teach.com/rhymes/goldilocks_story.htm. Accessed 1 June 2013.

Orland-Barak, Lily. 2010. *Learning to mentor-as-praxis: Toward a conceptual framework*. 4 vol. Professional Learning and Development in Schools and Higher Education. New York: Springer Science + Business Media.

Ortega, Eva-María, and Laureano F. Escudero. 2010. On expected utility for financial insurance portfolios with stochastic dependencies. *European Journal of Operational Research* 200 (1): 181–186.

Overmyer, Mac. 1 November 2008. Tamoxifen eases ADT-related gynecomastia, pain. *Urology Times* 36 (14): 8–9.

Paarlberg, Robert. 15 April 2013. The world needs genetically modified foods. *The Wall Street Journal* A15.

Painter, Richard W. January 1995. Toward a market for lawyer disclosure services: In search of optimal whistle blowing rules. *George Washington Law Review* 63 (2): 221–296.

Parthasarthy, Raghavan. 2007. *Fundamentals of strategic management*. Boston: Houghton Mifflin Company.

Pascal, Blaise. 1656. *The provincial letters—Letter IX*. http://oregonstate.edu/instruct/phl302/texts/pascal/letters-b.html—LETTER%20IX. Accessed 6 March 2013.

Pascal, Blaise. 1941a. Letter XIV: To the reverend fathers, The Jesuits (23 October 1656). In *The Provincial Letters*, 515 and 520. New York: The Modern Library.

Pascal, Blaise. 1941b. Letter XIV: To the reverend fathers, The Jesuits, October 23, 1656. In *The Provincial Letters*, 522–523. New York: The Modern Library.

Pascal, Blaise. 1958. Section VI: The philosophers. In *Pascal's Pensées*. New York: E. P. Dutton & Co.

Pascal, Blaise. 1999a. *The Provincial letters—Fragment of a letter XIX addressed to father Annat*. Bill Uzgalis. http://www.orst.edu/instruct/phl302/texts/pascal/letters-c.html. Accessed 9 May 2002.

Pascal, Blaise. 1999b. *The provincial letters—Letter II January 29, 1656*. Bill Uzgalis, 1999. http://www.orst.edu/instruct/phl302/texts/pascal/letters-a.html—LETTERII. Accessed 9 May 2002.

Pascal, Blaise. 1999c. *The provincial letters—Letter XIV*. Bill Uzgalis. http://www.orst.edu/instruct/phl302/texts/pascal/letters-c.html. Accessed 5 May 2002.

Pascal, Blaise. 1999d. *The provincial letters—Letter XV: To the reverend fathers, The Jesuits, November 25, 1656*. Bill Uzgalis. http://www.orst.edu/instruct/phl302/texts/pascal/letters-c.html. Accessed 5 May 2002.

Perez, Edith, David Gandara, Martin Edelman, Robert O'Donnell, Ignacio Lauder, and Michael DeGregorio. February 2003. Phase I trial of high-dose tamoxifen in combination with cisplatin in patients with lung cancer and other advanced malignancies. *Cancer Investigation* 21 (1): 1–7.

Peshkin, Beth, Karen Lisa Smith, and Claudine Isaacs. 2007. Management of women at increased risk for hereditary breast cancer. *Breast Disease* 27 (1): 51–67.

Pfizer Inc. 2013. *2003: Pfizer and Pharmacia Merger*. Pfizer Inc. http://www.pfizer.com/about/history/pfizer_pharmacia.jsp. Accessed 14 May 2013.

Phillips, Robert A. and Joshua D. Margolis. October 1999. Toward an ethics of organizations. *Business Ethics Quarterly* 9:619–638.

Pincoffs, Edmund. 1983. Quandary ethics. In *Revisions*, ed. Stanley Hauerwas and Alasdair MacIntyre, 92–112. Notre Dame: University of Notre Dame.

Pollack, Andrew. 30 January 2000. 130 nations agree on safety rules for biotech food. *The New York Times* A1 and A6.

Pollack, Andrew. 22 October 2008. Drought resistance is the goal, but methods differ. *The New York Times* B1.

Porter, Michael E. 1980. *Competitive strategy: Techniques for analyzing industries and competitors*. New York: Free Press.

Porter, Jean. 1990. *The recovery of virtue: The relevance of aquinas for Christians*. Louisville: Westminster/John Knox Press.

Povinelli, Daniel J. 2012. *World without weight: Perspectives on an alien mind*. New York: Oxford University.

Quinn, James Brian. 1980. *Strategies for change: Logical incrementalism*. Homewood: Richard D. Irwin.

Radin, Tara J., and Martin Calkins. March 2004. International approaches to whistle blowing. In *International Association of Business and Society*. Jackson Hole, Wyoming.

Radiological Society of North America, Inc. 7 August 2008. *Breast cancer*. American College of Radiology and the Radiological Society of North America. http://www.radiologyinfo.org/en/info.cfm?pg=breastcancer. Accessed 8 April 2009.

Raloff, Janet. 1 July 2000. *The case for DDT*. Science News. http://www.findarticles.com/cf_0/m1200/1_158/63692741/p1/article.jhtml. Accessed 18 May 2002.

Ramseyer, J. Mark, and Eric B. Rasmusen. November 2010. *Comparative litigation rates*. Harvard John M. Olin Center for Law, Economics, and Business. http://www.law.harvard.edu/programs/olin_center/papers/pdf/Ramseyer_681.pdf. Accessed 6 March 2013.

Rawls, John. 1955. Two concepts of rules. *Philosophical Review* 64:3–33.

Rawls, John. 1958. Justice as fairness. *Philosophical Review* 67:164–195.

Rawls, John. 1971. *A theory of justice*. Cambridge: The Belknap Press of Harvard University Press.

Rawls, John. 1980. Kantian constructivism in moral theory. *Journal of Philosophy* 77 (9): 515–572.

Rawls, John. Summer 1985. Justice as fairness: Political not metaphysical. *Philosophy & Public Affairs* 14:223–251.

Rawls, John. 1993. *Political liberalism*. New York: Columbia University.

Raz, Joseph. Spring 1982. The claims of reflective equilibrium. *Inquiry* 25:307–330.

Regan, M. M., O. Pagani, B. Walley, R. Torrisi, E. A. Perez, P. Francis, G. F. Fleming, K. N. Price, B. Thürlimann, R. Maibach, M. Castiglione-Gertsch, A. S. Coates, A. Goldhirsch, and R. D. Gelber. July 2008. Premenopausal endocrine-responsive early breast cancer: Who receives chemotherapy? *Annals of Oncology* 19 (7): 1231–1241.

Regnier, Eva. January 2008. Public evacuation decisions and hurricane track uncertainty. *Management Science* 54 (1): 16–28.

Reisler, Mark and others. 1994. *Academic support handbook 1994–1995*. Charlottesville: Colgate Darden Graduate School of Business Administration.

Reporter. 2 November 1987. Miracle worker. *Time* 78.

Reporter. 8 July 1996. Germany gets in a lather about altering beer genes. *The Wall Street Journal—Eastern Edition* A5.

Reporter. 20 April 1998. What's news. *The Wall Street Journal* A1:2.

Reporter. 6 and 7 April 1998. What's News. *The Wall Street Journal* A1:3.

Reporter. 21 December 1999. Novartis wins court ruling in Europe on plant patents. *The Wall Street Journal* A10.

Reporter. 28 November 2001. Acambis wins second smallpox vaccine contract. *PR Newswire*.

Rickaby, John. 1999. *Cardinal virtues, The catholic encyclopedia, Volume III*. New Advent. http://www.newadvent.org/cathen/03343a.htm. Accessed 1 June 2002.

Ridley, Matt. 9–10 February 2013. When species extermination is a good thing. *The Wall Street Journal* C4.

Riggio, Ronald E., Weichun Zhu, Christopher Reina, and James A. Maroosis. December 2010. Virtue-based measurement of ethical leadership: The leadership virtues questionnaire. *Consulting Psychology Journal: Practice and Research* 62 (4): 235–250.

Robinson, Peter M. April 2001. The memory of stochastic volatility models. *Journal of Econometrics* 101 (2): 195–218.

Rodger, Chris, and Jason Petch. 1999. *Uncertainty & risk analysis: A practical guide from business dynamics*. PricewaterhouseCoopers, MCS.

Romar, Edward, and Martin Calkins. 2008. WorldCom update. In *Business ethics: Decision making for personal integrity and social responsibility*, ed. Laura Hartman and Joseph DesJardins, 464–467. Burr Ridge: McGraw-Hill.

Ross, W. D. 1960. *Aristotle: A complete exposition of his works and thought*. New York: Meridian Books.

Rotary International. 2013. *The rotary foundation*. http://www.rotary.org/en/AboutUs/TheRotary-Foundation/Pages/ridefault.aspx. Accessed 22 March 2013.

Rotch, William. 1992. *Casewriting*. Charlottesville: University of Virginia Darden School Foundation, No. UVA-G–0364.

Rotch, William. 20 May 1996. Casewriting workshop handout. Charlottesville: Unpublished.

Sadler-Smith, Eugene. April 2012. Before virtue: Biology, brain, behavior, and the moral sense. *Business Ethics Quarterly* 22 (2): 351–375.

Sandel, Michael. 15 February 2011. *Justice: What's the right thing to do? Episode 07: A lesson in lying* 2011. http://www.youtube.com/watch?v=KqzW0eHzDSQ. Accessed 14 August 2012.

Saunders, Trevor. 1998. Theophrastus in the tradition of Greek casuistry. In *Theophrastus: Reappraising the Sources*, ed. J. M. Van Ophuijsen and M. Van Raalte, 81–96. New Brunswick: Transaction Publishers.

Schacht, Joseph. 1964. *An introduction to islamic law*. Oxford: Oxford University.

Schelling, Thomas C. May 1984. Self-command in practice, in policy, and in a theory of rational choice. *The American Economic Review* 74 (2): 1–11.

Schilder, Christina M., Petronella Eggens, Caroline Seynaeve, Sabine Linn, Willem Boogerd, Chad M. Gundy, Louk Beex, Frits Van Dam, and Sanne B. Schagen. January 2009. Neuropsychological functioning in postmenopausal breast cancer patients treated with tamoxifen or exemestane after ac-chemotherapy: Cross-sectional findings from the neuropsychological TEAM-side study. *Acta Oncologica* 48 (1): 76–85.

Schmidt, J. P., and Martin Simmons. 2004. Catastrophe modeling: The regulator's perspective. *Risk Management* 51 (8): 46

Schumpeter, Joseph. 1954. *History of economic analysis*, (ed. Elizabeth Boddy Schumpeter). New York: Oxford University.

Schwartz, Barry, and Kenneth Sharpe. 2006. Practical wisdom: Aristotle meets positive psychology. *Journal of Happiness Studies* 7 (3): 377–395.

Schwartz, Barry, and Kenneth Sharpe. 2010. *Practical wisdom: The right way to do the right thing*. New York: Riverhead Books.

Seabright, Mark A., and Marshall Schminke. 2002. Immoral imagination and revenge in organizations. *Journal of Business Ethics* 38 (1–2): 19–31.

Sellman, Sherrill. 1998. *Tamoxifen: A major medical mistake?* Nexus Magazine, Volume 5, #4 (June–July 1998) excerpted by Natural Health and Longevity Resource Center. http://www.all-natural.com/tamox.html. Accessed 21 January 2009.

Shanahan, Kevin J., and Michael R. Hyman. 2003. The development of a virtue ethics scale. *Journal of Business Ethics* 42 (2): 197–208.

Shelley, Mary Wollstonecraft. 1831. *Frankenstein*. London: Henry Colburn and Richard Bentley Publishers.

Sher, George. 1992. Knowing about virtue: In *Virtue*; NOMOS XXXIV, ed. John W. Chapman and William A. Galston, 91–116. New York: New York University Press.

Shors, Teri. 2011. *Understanding viruses*. Burlington: Jones & Bartlett Learning.

Sirisabya, N., Y. Li, A. Jaishuen, H. G. Zheng, D. M. Gershenson, and J. J. Kavanagh. July 2008. Tamoxifen is Safe and Effective in Gynecological Cancer Patients with Renal Dysfunction. *International Journal of Gynecological Cancer* 18 (4): 648–651.

Sison, Alejo José G., and Joan Fontrodona. April 2012a. The common good of the firm in the Aristotelian-Thomistic tradition. *Business Ethics Quarterly* 22 (2): 211–246.

Sison, Alejo José G., Edwin M. Hartman, and Joan Fontrodona. April 2012b. Guest editors' introduction: Reviving tradition: Virtue and the common good in business and management. *Business Ethics Quarterly* 22, (2): 207–210.

Smith, Adam. 1976a. *The theory of moral sentiments*, (ed. A. L. Macfie and D. D. Raphael). Oxford: Oxford University

Smith, Adam. 1976b. *The wealth of nations*, (ed. R. H. Campbell and A. S. Skinner). London: Oxford University.

Smith, Adam. 1978. *Lectures on jurisprudence (A) and (B)*, (ed. R. L. Meek, D. D. Raphael and P. G. Stein). Oxford: Oxford University Press.

Smith, Adam. 1982. *Lectures on jurisprudence*, (ed. R. L. Meek, D. D. Raphael and P. G. Stein). Indianapolis: Liberty Classics.

Smith, Wendy K. 1989. *James Burke: A career in American business (B)*. Cambridge: Harvard Business School. case, no. 9-390-030.

Snyder, Leonard. Autumn 1983. An anniversary review and critique: The tylenol crisis. *Public Relations Review* 9 (3): 24–34.

Solomon, David. 1988. Internal objections to virtue ethics. In *Midwest studies in philosophy 13: Ethical theory: Character and virtue*, ed. Peter A. French and others, 428–441. Notre Dame: University of Notre Dame.

Solomon, Robert C. July 1992a. Corporate roles, personal virtues: An Aristotelian approach to business ethics. *Business Ethics Quarterly* 2:317–340.

Solomon, Robert C. 1992b *Ethics and excellence: Cooperation and integrity in business* the ruffin series in business ethics. New York: Oxford University.

Solomon, Robert C. 1994. Business and the humanities: An Aristotelian approach to business ethics. In *Business as a humanity*, ed. Thomas J. Donaldson and R. Edward Freeman, 45–75. New York: Oxford University.

Solomon, Robert C. January 2003. Victims of circumstances? A defense of virtue ethics in business. *Business Ethics Quarterly* 13 (1): 43–62.

Sophocles. 2000. *Antigone*. The Internet Classics Archive. http://classics.mit.edu/Sophocles/antigone.html. Accessed 29 June 2012.

Sousa, Célio Alberto Alves, and Paul H. J. Hendriks. November 2007. Connecting knowledge to management: The case of academic research. *Human Relations* 15 (6): 811–830.

Spence, Jonathan D. 1984. *The memory palace of Matteo Ricci*. New York: Viking Penguin.

Stackhouse, Max L., Dennis P. McCann, Shirley J. Roels, and Preston N. Williams, eds. 1995. *On moral business: Classical and contemporary resources for ethics in economic life*. Grand Rapids: William B. Eerdmans Publishing Company.

Statman, Daniel, ed. 1997. *Virtue ethics: A Critical reader*. Washington, D.C.: Georgetown University.

Stecklow, Steve. 30 November 1999. How a U.S. gadfly and a green activist started a food fight. *The Wall Street Journal* A1 and A10.

Stewart, John Alexander. 1892. *Notes on the Nicomachean ethics of Aristotle—Volume 1*. Oxford: Clarendon Press.

Stone, Christopher D. June 1982. Corporate vices and corporate virtues: Do public/private distinctions matter? *University of Pennsylvania Law Review* 130: 1441–1509.

Striker, Gisela. 1992. Stoicism. In *Encyclopedia of ethics*, ed. Lawrence C. Becker and Charlotte B. Becker, II, 1208–1213. New York: Garland Publishing.

Sunstein, Cass R. January 1993. Commentary on analogical reasoning. *Harvard Law Review* 106:741–791.

Supreme Court of the United States. 2013. Bowman v Monsanto Co. et al.; Certiorari to the United States Court of Appeals for the Federal Circuit. 11–796, Argued February 19 2013—Decided May 13 2013.

Susan G. Komen Breast Cancer Foundation. 2002. *Tamoxifen as a treatment for breast cancer*. http://www.breastcancerinfo.com/bhealth/html/tamoxifen.asp. Accessed 18 May 2002.

Tallmon, James M. February 1994. How Jonsen really views casuistry: A note on the abuse of father Wildes. *The Journal of Medicine and Philosophy* 19:103–113.

Taras, T. L., G. T. Wurz, G. R. Linares, and M. W. DeGregorio. 2000. Clinical pharmacokinetics of toremifene. *Clinical Pharmacokinetics* 39 (5): 327–334.

Taylor, Jeremy. 1831. *Holy living and dying; with prayers: Containing the complete duty of a Christian*. Philadelphia: Thomas Wardle.

Temple, James. 17 April 2009. The future of food: The no-kill carnivore. *Wired*.

Terhune, Chad. 9 May 2002. Smallpox vaccine: Who gets it is the subject of current debate. *The Wall Street Journal* D6.

Thavis, John. 22 October 1999. Vatican experts ok plant, animal genetic engineering. *St. Louis Review*.

Thomasma, David C. June 1994. Clinical ethics as medical hermeneutics. *Theoretical Medicine* 15:93–111.

Tierney, Nathan L. 1994. *Imagination and ethical ideals: Prospects for a unified philosophical and psychological understanding*. New York: SUNY Press.

Time.com. 2007. *Tylenol's miracle comeback*. Time Inc. http://www.time.com/time/magazine/article/0,9171,952212-1,00.html. Accessed 4 May 2007.

Tomlinson, Tom. March 1994. Casuistry in medical ethics: Rehabilitated, or repeat offender? *Theoretical Medicine* 15:5–20.

Treasurer, Bil. June 2009. Courage goes to work. *Leadership Excellence* 26 (6): 14.

Treasurer, Bil. January 2011. Leading with courage. *HR Professional* 28 (1): 50.

Treviño, Linda Klebe, and Gary R. Weaver. October 2001. Organizational justice and ethics program follow-through influences on employees' harmful and helpful behavior. *Business Ethics Quarterly* 11 (4): 651–671.

Tucker, Jonathan B. October 2001. Breaking the deadlock over destruction of the smallpox virus stocks. *Biosecurity and Bioterrorism: Biodefense Strategy, Practice, and Science* 9 (1): 55–67.

US Food and Drug Administration. January-February 2000. *Methods for genetically engineering a plant*. FDA consumer magazine. http://www.fda.gov/fdac/features/2000/biochart.html. Accessed 23 June 2001.

van der Burg, Wibren, and Theo van Willigenburg, eds. 1998. *Reflective equilibrium: Essays in honour of Robert Heeger*. Dordrecht: Kluwer Academic Publishers.

Vance, Charles M. ed. 1993. *Mastering management education: Innovations in teaching effectiveness.* Newbury Park: Sage Publications Inc.

Vanderschraaf, Peter. January 1999. Hume's game-theoretic business ethics. *Business Ethics Quarterly* 9 (1): 47–67.

Velasquez, Manuel G. 1994. Some lessons and nonlessons of casuist history. In *Business as a humanity*, ed. Thomas J. Donaldson and R. Edward Freeman, 184–195. New York: Oxford University

Velasquez, Manuel G. 1998. *Business ethics: Concepts and cases.* 4th ed. Upper Saddle River: Prentice-Hall.

Velasquez, Manuel, and F. Neil Brady. March 1997. Natural law and business ethics. *Business Ethics Quarterly* 7:83–107.

Velasquez, Manuel, Gerald F. Cavanagh, and Dennis J. Moberg 1983. Organizational statesmanship and dirty politics: Ethical guidelines for the organizational politician. *Organizational Dynamics* (Fall): 65–80.

Vidaver-Cohen, Deborah. October 1997. Moral imagination in organizational problem-solving: An institutional perspective. *Business Ethics Quarterly* 7:1–26.

Viner, Jacob. April 1927. Adam Smith and laissez faire. *Journal of Political Economy* 35 (2): 198–232.

Waitman, Andrew. 2008. Power, prescience, and the paradox of patterns. *National Capital Scan* 3 (10): 7.

Warner, Melanie. 17 April 2009. The future of food: Frankenfood to GMourmet. *Wired.*

Weber, Lauren. 10 April 2012. *Best and worst jobs of 2012. The Wall Street Journal.* http://online.wsj.com/article/SB10001424052702304587704577335703058909284.html. Accessed 13 January 2013.

Wells, Thomas, and Johan Graafland. April 2012. Adam Smith's bourgeois virtues in competition. *Business Ethics Quarterly* 22 (2): 319–350.

Wenley, R. M. 1911. Casuistry. In *Encyclopaedia of religion and ethics*, ed. James Hastings, 3 vol, 239–247. New York: Charles Scribner's Sons.

Werhane, Patricia H. 1998. The rashomon effect. In *Perspectives in business ethics*, ed. Laura Pincus and Edwin M. Hartman, 189–197. Chicago: McGraw Hill.

Werhane, Patricia H. 1999. *Moral imagination and management decision making.* The Ruffin Series in Business Ethics. New York: Oxford University.

Werhane, Patricia H. 2002. Moral imagination and systems thinking. *Journal of Business Ethics* 38 (1–2): 33–42.

Whetstone, J. Thomas. 2001. How virtue fits within business ethics. *Journal of Business Ethics* 33 (2): 101–114.

Wight, Jonathan B. 2001. *Saving Adam Smith: A tale of wealth, transformation, and virtue.* New York: Pearson Education.

Wight, Jonathan B. Summer 2007. The treatment of Smith's invisible hand. *Journal of Economic Education* 38 (3): 341–358.

Wilde, Oscar. 2005. *The importance of being earnest: And other plays.* New York: Random House Publishing Group.

Wildes, Kevin Wm. 1993. The priesthood of bioethics and the return of casuistry. *The Journal of Medicine and Philosophy* 18:33–49.

Wildes, Kevin Wm. February 1994. Respondeo: Method and content in casuistry. *The Journal of Medicine and Philosophy* 19:115–119.

Williams, Susan H. Fall 1994. Bioethics and epistemology: A response to professor arras. *Indiana Law Journal* 69:1021–1026.

Williamson, David, Peter Cooke, Wyn Jenkins, and Keith Michael Moreton. 2004. *Strategic management and business analysis.* Burlington: Butterworth-Heinemann.

World Health Organization. 2010. *Scientific review of variola virus research, 1999–2010.* Geneva: World Health Organization.

World Health Organization Fifty-second World Health Assembly. 1999. *Smallpox eradication: Destruction of variola virus stocks, A52/5.* Geneva: World Health Organization.

World Health Organization Fifty-fifth World Health Assembly. 2002. *Smallpox eradication: Destruction of variola virus stocks, WHA55.15*. Geneva: World Health Organization.

World Health Organization Sixtieth World Health Assembly. 2007. *Smallpox eradication: Destruction of variola virus stocks, A60/9*. Geneva: World Health Organization.

World Health Organization Sixtieth World Health Assembly Executive Board. 2007. *Smallpox eradication: Destruction of Variola Virus Stocks, EB120.R8*. Geneva: World Health Organization.

Wüthrich, Mario V., and Michael Merz. 2008. *Stochastic claims reserving methods in insurance*. Hoboken: Wiley.

Yildiz, Aysegül. May 2008. Novel treatment for mania. *Brown University Psychopharmacology Update* 19 (5): 5.

Young, Donna. 1 September 2007. Raloxifene examined for breast cancer prevention. *American Journal of Health-System Pharmacy* 64 (17): 1774–1776.

Name Index

Subject Index

Business Index

M. Calkins, *Developing a Virtue-Imbued Casuistry for Business Ethics,* Issues in Business   281
Ethics 42, DOI 10.1007/978-94-017-8724-6, © Springer Netherlands 2014

Printed by Books on Demand, Germany